Anonymus

Report from the Select Comittee on Parliamentary Reporting

Anonymus

Report from the Select Comittee on Parliamentary Reporting

ISBN/EAN: 9783742832634

Manufactured in Europe, USA, Canada, Australia, Japa

Cover: Foto ©Suzi / pixelio.de

Manufactured and distributed by brebook publishing software
(www.brebook.com)

Anonymus

Report from the Select Comittee on Parliamentary Reporting

R E P O R T

FROM THE

SELECT COMMITTEE

ON

PARLIAMENTARY REPORTING;

TOGETHER WITH THE

PROCEEDINGS OF THE COMMITTEE,

MINUTES OF EVIDENCE,

AND APPENDIX.

Ordered, by The House of Commons, to be Printed,
31 July 1878.

Ordered,—[*Tuesday, 28th May 1878*]:—THAT a Select Committee be appointed to consider the question of Parliamentary Reporting.

Select Committee nominated—[*Monday, 17th June 1878*]—of—

Mr. William Henry Smith.	Mr. Dunbar.
Mr. William Edward Forster.	Mr. Hall.
Viscount Crichton.	Mr. Mitchell Henry.
Dr. Lyon Playfair.	Sir Henry Wolff.
Sir Alexander Gordon.	Mr. Barclay.
Mr. Walter.	Mr. Mills.
Lord Francis Hervey.	

Ordered, THAT the Committee have power to send for Persons, Papers, and Records.

THAT Five be the Quorum of the Committee.

Ordered—[*Thursday, 20th June 1878*]:—THAT the Committee do consist of Seventeen Members.

THAT Sir Henry Holland, Mr. Hutchinson, Mr. Cowen, and Major Arbuthnot be added to the Committee.

R E P O R T.

THE SELECT COMMITTEE appointed to consider the question of PAR-
LIAMENTARY REPORTING;——HAVE come to the following RESOLUTION,
which they have agreed to Report to the House:—

THAT your Committee, having regard to the late period of the Session, are
of opinion that it would not be desirable to conclude their inquiry this year,
and they recommend the re-appointment of the Committee at the commencement of the next Session.

31 *July* 1878.

PROCEEDINGS OF THE COMMITTEE.

Monday, 24th June 1878.

MEMBERS PRESENT:

Mr. Walter.
Mr. Mills.
Mr. William Henry Smith.
Mr. Mitchell Henry.
Mr. Cowen.
Major Arbuthnot.

Lord Francis Hervey.
Sir Alexander Gordon.
Dr. Lyon Playfair.
Mr. Dunbar.
Mr. Hutchinson.
Mr. Barclay.

Mr. WILLIAM HENRY SMITH was called to the Chair.

The Committee deliberated.

{Adjourned till Friday next, at Twelve o'clock.

Friday, 28th June 1878.

MEMBERS PRESENT:

Mr. WILLIAM HENRY SMITH in the Chair.

Lord Francis Hervey.
Mr. Dunbar.
Sir Henry Holland.
Mr. Cowen.
Mr. Mitchell Henry.
Mr. Mills.
Mr. Hall.

Mr. Walter.
Sir Alexander Gordon.
Mr. Hutchinson.
Mr. William Edward Forster.
Sir Henry Wolff.
Mr. Barclay.
Viscount Crichton.

Mr. R. A. Gosset, Serjeant at Arms, and Mr. Thomas Crane Hayward were severally examined.

{Adjourned till Monday next, at Twelve o'clock.

Monday, 1st July 1878.

MEMBERS PRESENT:

Mr. WILLIAM HENRY SMITH in the Chair.

Major Arbuthnot.
Mr. Dunbar.
Mr. Hutchinson.
Sir Alexander Gordon.
Mr. Walter.
Sir Henry Holland.
Mr. William Edward Forster.

Mr. Cowen.
Mr. Mitchell Henry.
Dr. Lyon Playfair.
Mr. Mills.
Sir Henry Wolff.
Mr. Barclay.

Mr. Charles Raw and Mr. John Lewell were severally examined.

{Adjourned till Friday next, at Twelve o'clock.

Friday, 5th July 1878.

MEMBERS PRESENT:

Mr. WILLIAM HENRY SMITH in the Chair.

Mr. Dunbar.	Sir Henry Holland.
Major Arbuthnot.	Mr. Mitchell Henry.
Mr. Hutchinson.	Mr. Barclay.
Sir Alexander Gordon.	Dr. Lyon Playfair.
Mr. Walter.	Mr. Hall.
Sir Henry Wolff.	Mr. William Edward Forster.
Mr. Mills.	Viscount Crichton.
Mr. Cowen.	Lord Francis Hervey.

Mr. *Edward Lloyd*, Mr. *William Saunders*, and Mr. *Charles Alfred Cooper* were severally examined.

[Adjourned till Monday next, at Twelve o'clock.

Monday, 8th July 1878.

MEMBERS PRESENT:

Mr. William Edward Forster.	Sir Henry Holland.
Mr. Hall.	Mr. Mitchell Henry.
Major Arbuthnot.	Mr. Dunbar.
Mr. Hutchinson.	Viscount Crichton.
Sir Alexander Gordon.	Sir Henry Wolff.
Mr. Walter.	Dr. Lyon Playfair.
Mr. Mills.	

In the absence of the Chairman, Mr. WILLIAM EDWARD FORSTER took the Chair.

Mr. *Speaker* and Mr. *William Henry Gurney Salter* were severally examined.

[Adjourned till Friday next, at Twelve o'clock.

Friday, 12th July 1878.

MEMBERS PRESENT:

Mr. WILLIAM HENRY SMITH in the Chair.

Major Arbuthnot.	Mr. Walter.
Mr. Hutchinson.	Mr. Mills.
Sir Alexander Gordon.	Lord Francis Hervey.
Sir Henry Holland.	Dr. Lyon Playfair.
Mr. Mitchell Henry.	Mr. William Edward Forster.
Mr. Dunbar.	Viscount Crichton.

The Viscount *Barnley* (attending by permission of the House of Lords), Sir *John Rose*, Mr. *T. Wemyss Reid*, and Mr. *John Jaffray*, were severally examined.

[Adjourned till Monday next, at One o'clock.

Monday, 15th July 1878.

Mr. WILLIAM HENRY SMITH in the Chair.

Major Arbuthnot.
Mr. Hutchinson.
Sir Alexander Gordon.
Mr. Walter.
Mr. Mills.
Mr. Cowen.

Mr Mitchell Henry.
Mr. Dunbar.
Dr. Lyon Playfair.
Mr. William Edward Forster.
Mr. Barclay.
Lord Francis Hervey.

Mr. *Thomas Senior Toward*, and Mr. *Edmund Dwyer Gray* (a Member of the House), were severally examined.

[Adjourned till Friday next, at half-past Two o'clock.

Friday, 19th July 1878.

MEMBERS PRESENT:

Mr. WILLIAM HENRY SMITH in the Chair.

Mr. Walter.
Sir Alexander Gordon.
Sir Henry Holland.
Mr. Hutchinson.
Major Arbuthnot.
Mr. Cowen.
Mr. Mitchell Henry.

Mr. Dunbar.
Sir Henry Wolff.
Mr. Mills.
Mr. Hall.
Viscount Crichton.
Lord Francis Hervey.

Mr. *John Taylor* and Mr. *Henry Dunphy* were severally examined.

Mr. *Thomas Curson Hansard* was further examined.

[Adjourned till Wednesday, 31st July, at Three o'clock.

Wednesday, 31st July 1878.

MEMBERS PRESENT:

Mr. WILLIAM HENRY SMITH in the Chair.

Sir Henry Holland.
Major Arbuthnot.
Mr. Dunbar.
Mr. Walter.
Lord Francis Hervey.
Sir Alexander Gordon.

Viscount Crichton.
Mr. Mitchell Henry.
Mr. Barclay.
Mr. Hall.
Mr. Mills.

Motion made, and Question proposed, " That your Committee, having regard to the late period of the Session, are of opinion that it would not be desirable to conclude their inquiry this year, and they recommend the re-appointment of the Committee at the commencement of the next Session "—(Mr. *Walter*):—

Amendment proposed, to leave out from the word " That " to the end of the Question, in order to add the words, " The Committee do now consider their Report "—(Lord *Francis Hervey*),—instead thereof.

Question,

Question, " That the words proposed to be left out stand part of the Question,"—put, and agreed to.

Main Question put:—

Resolved, " That your Committee, having regard to the late period of the Session, are of opinion that it would not be desirable to conclude the inquiry this year, and they recommend the re-appointment of the Committee at the commencement of the next Session."

Ordered, To report the above Resolution, together with the Minutes of Evidence, and an Appendix.

MINUTES OF EVIDENCE.

·

MEMBERS PRESENT:

Mr. Barclay.
Mr. Cowen.
Viscount Crichton.
Mr. Dunbar.
Mr. William Edward Forster.
Sir Alexander Gordon.
Mr. Hall.
Mr. Mitchell Henry.

Lord Francis Hervey.
Sir Henry T. Holland.
Mr. Hutchinson.
Mr. Mills.
Mr. William Henry Smith.
Mr. Walter.
Sir Henry Drummond Wolff.

THE RIGHT HONOURABLE WILLIAM HENRY SMITH, IN THE CHAIR.

Mr. *Ralph Allen Gossed*, Serjeant at Arms ; Examined.

1. *Chairman.*] IT is not necessary to ask you if you are the Serjeant at Arms of the House of Commons?—I am.

2. You are acquainted with the arrangements which are made for Parliamentary Reporting?—Yes, they were made under my control.

3. Is this plan which you have just handed to me a plan showing the accommodation provided for the reporters?—It is a plan of the whole accommodation that the reporters have at present, and the way in which the seats are appropriated.

4. And you put this plan in for the information of the Committee?—Yes.

5. Are the Committee to understand that this is the whole of the space which is available for the purposes of reporting in the House of Commons?—Yes.

6. So that your power of giving accommodation, or the power of the Speaker, who acts in the matter, is limited entirely to the space which is here provided?—It does not extend beyond that.

7. The Committee understand that you have no authority whatever to give accommodation in any other part of the House than that which is appropriated in this way in the Gallery to the reporters?—Certainly I have not.

8. Will you state in what way you make use of the accommodation that has been provided. Perhaps you will state, first of all, to the Committee the number of seats which exist on this plan before us?—The number of front seats in the Gallery is 19; those are the only seats that they can report from properly. There are 15 seats appropriated to the London daily press, 3 to the Press Association, and 1 to Mr. Hansard.

9. With regard to the Press Association, will you be so good as to tell the Committee what they are?—There are three companies that provide the provincial papers and the Irish and Scotch papers with certain reports of the debates.

10. So that a provincial newspaper must make its arrangements with one of these three companies in order to obtain a report?—Yes.

11. Has any individual, not being a newspaper proprietor, or a member of a Press Association, at any time access to the Gallery?—No, certainly not.

Mr. R. A. Gossed.

28 June 1878.

12. So that the qualification for a seat in one of these boxes of the Gallery is being a representative of the newspapers?—Yes, I give the orders for the Gallery on the application of the editors of the different daily papers at the beginning of the Session.

13. Has the accommodation been found to be sufficient to meet the demands made upon you from time to time?—Yes, just sufficient.

14. No more than sufficient?—No more than sufficient.

15. Are there any newspapers which have been excluded in consequence of want of accommodation at any time?—There was a new newspaper started last year, called the "Daily Chronicle," to which I am obliged to give the place of the "Echo" after six o'clock in the evening.

16. And with regard to the evening papers, do I rightly understand that you exercise a discretion in giving their boxes or places to morning papers after a certain hour?—Yes, after six o'clock, after the time when the last edition of the evening paper has been published.

17. You have mentioned that Mr. Hansard has a box in the Gallery; will you state to the Committee under what circumstances Mr. Hansard occupies that box or seat?—I received an order from the Speaker; the Speaker stated that the Government had made an arrangement with Mr. Hansard, and that I was to find him a place in the Gallery for reporting.

18. I understand you to say that no complaints have been made to you by either London or provincial papers of an insufficiency of accommodation?—I have received one complaint from the "Globe" about having taken their place after six o'clock; that is the only complaint I have had.

19. Mr. Mills.] It appears from this plan which you have put in, that the seat in the Reporters' Gallery, which is allotted to the "Globe," is the one which is also allotted to Hansard's reporter; are we to understand that it is allotted to Hansard's reporter after six?—That is the arrangement; the seat allotted to the "Globe" newspaper is occupied by Mr. Hansard's reporter after six o'clock.

20. And it appears from this plan that in the case of, I think, six London daily papers, there are seats given to the reporters, and also to those who write the summaries?—Yes.

21. Has it been the practice, so long as your official experience goes, to give seats to the reporters, and to those who write the summaries?—On the occupation of this building by the House of Commons in 1852, the "Times," the "Standard," the "Morning Post," the "Globe," and the "Daily News," had those seats in the Gallery; the "Times" three, and the other papers two; and the "Daily Telegraph" in 1858, and the "Daily Chronicle" last year.

22. At present the "Times" has one seat, one seat for the reporter, and another for the writer of the summary?—The "Times" has three; Mr. Ross has a seat.

23. And the other papers have two?—Two.

24. In answering the Chairman, I think you mentioned that there were three associations which provided reports for the Provincial Press, those are the "Central Press," the "Press Association" and the "Central News"?—Yes.

25. How long has that been in existence, so far as your experience goes?—That has been in existence for about six or eight years.

26. All three?—No, two of them; I think one of them is more recent.

27. Which is the last that has come into existence?—The "Sun and Central Press."

28. As a matter of structural arrangement, would there be any possibility of providing more seats than there are at present in the Reporters' Gallery?—It would be impossible to enlarge the Reporters' Gallery without taking away from the side galleries, in which there is scarcely room for Members on a crowded night.

29. Mr. Hutchinson.] You have not told us what seats there are besides those front seats?—There is a row of back seats, but I am informed by the reporters that it is quite impossible to report from them. They are occupied now by the reliefs, and a few weekly papers, and the leader writers of the daily papers.

30. Then there are these 19 seats, from which alone you say a proper report can be taken, and those are distributed in this way; there are 15 belonging to the London daily papers, three belonging to the various associations which report for the Provincial Press, and one to Hansard?—Yes.

31. And from your statement the "Times" has three seats; that is to say, exactly the same proportion as the whole of the associations representing the Provincial Press?—Yes.

32. And you have not had any complaints respecting that distribution from the Provincial Press?—No; I have had applications from the Provincial Press for places in the Gallery.

33. But not any complaint?—No, not any complaint.

34. Lord *Francis Hervey.*] You said that Mr. Hansard's reporter has a seat after six o'clock?—Yes.

35. Do I rightly understand that he is not entitled to a seat until six o'clock?—He does not require it before that time.

36. But a good deal of business goes on before six, does there not?—I think Mr. Hansard is going to give evidence, and he will inform you on that subject better than I can.

37. Sir *Henry Drummond Wolff.*] Some of the representatives of the papers are allowed in other parts of the House besides the Gallery, are they not?—Not in the House itself.

38. In the Lobby?—Yes, in the Lobby, but not in the House.

39. And do they get that access to the Lobby from the fact of having seats in the Gallery?—No, they get it by my order.

40. Mr. *Mitchell Henry.*] Are you aware how often the reporters are changed in reporting a debate?—The "Times'" reporters are changed every quarter of an hour, and I think some of the other morning papers every quarter of an hour, and the others every half hour.

41. Mr. Hansard having only one seat, is at liberty to change his reporter if he pleases?—Certainly; he has four of his own reporters, one reporting at a time, and several others that he employs from the newspapers.

42. Have you any official knowledge of the number of reporters employed by the different papers which have seats in the Gallery?—Certainly I have; I have a return here which shows it.

43. Can you give us that return?—The Central News employs 7 reporters, the Press Association 10, the "Globe" 6, Hansard 4, the "Morning Post" 11, the "Standard" 17, the "Morning Advertiser" 16, the "Daily Telegraph" 12, the "Times" 16, the "Daily News" 10, the "Pall Mall Gazette" 2, the "Daily Chronicle" 7, the "Echo" 2, the "Sun and Central Press" 3, and Reuter's Agency 1; the last named occupies a back seat.

44. Do we rightly understand that the whole of this number of reporters are employed during any full day's sitting of the House?—I cannot answer that question; I think the answer to that would come from the newspapers themselves; only a certain number are admitted in the Gallery at a time.

44ᵃ. But you do not know whether this means that taking the number 17, for instance, that number are employed daily on the reporting?—Yes, every day.

45. What is the date of that return?—It is made out for this Session.

46. Are you aware whether there has been of late years, within the last four or five years, a change in the number of reporters employed upon the newspapers?—No, I think not; certainly not; they have generally had the same number; there might have been one or two less or more upon different papers.

47. Could you obtain for the Committee a return of the number of reporters employed by these different newspapers during the past six years, commencing with six years ago?—No, I could not. This is a return (*producing it*); there has been no variation since my time.

48. Do you not remember that some years ago, when there were complaints as to the shortness of the reports in some of the newspapers, there were statements made that the number of reporters had been greatly diminished?—No, I am not aware of that.

49. Would it not be possible to ascertain whether any change has taken place during the past six years in the number of reporters employed by the different daily journals?—I can only state what has been the case for the last three years; and I am quite sure there has been no change during that time.

50. It is precisely for the time previous to that that I want the information?—I have only held the office three years, and I can only speak for my own time of office.

51. It was the previous Serjeant at Arms then who held the office at that time?—Yes.

0.121. A 2 52. *Chairman.*]

Mr. *R. A. Grant.*

13 June 1878.

Mr. R. A. Gosset.

21 June 1878.

52. *Chairman.*] I think I understand you to say that you give out tickets to the newspapers?—Yes.

53. Which are supposed to represent the number of reporters employed by the newspapers?—Yes.

54. You have no knowledge whether the newspapers themselves make use of the whole of those tickets?—No, I have not the slightest knowledge as to that; I give them as they are asked for.

55. So that any return which contained the number of tickets issued would not necessarily imply that so many reporters are employed by the newspapers themselves?—Quite so.

56. Mr. *Mitchell Henry.*] Have not the provincial papers frequently made application to be admitted into the Gallery?—Not lately; I have had verbal applications from members, but not any official application from any newspaper, except from the editor of the "Scotsman," two years ago.

57. Did the "Scotsman" newspaper propose to make a special arrangement for reporting?—No; they asked for a place in the Gallery.

58. Although you do not know it officially, yet are you aware that some years ago there was a considerable stir amongst the provincial papers, in the time of your predecessor, desiring to get accommodation in the Gallery?—No, I am not aware of it.

59. Is it a rule made by the Speaker, that no newspaper, except a London newspaper, shall have access to the Gallery?—That has been the rule ever since we have occupied this building, because there are 134 daily provincial newspapers in England, Scotland, and Ireland, and they would all be entitled to the same privilege if one were admitted.

60. With regard to the Lobby of the House; is is under your charge?—Yes.

61. What are the regulations for the admission of reporters there?—They apply to me, and I always grant leave for one from each paper to be admitted to the Lobby.

62. But that is not restricted to the London Press?—No, certainly not; that applies to the Provincial Press as well.

63. On application you will, in your discretion, give admission to the Lobby to anybody connected with the newspapers who applies as a reporter?—Provided he brings a letter from the editor of his paper.

64. Have there not been considerable changes in the way of admitting strangers to the Lobby of the House within the last few years?—No, not within the last few years. Strangers were all admitted some years ago, and it was found so inconvenient to Members that an order was given that no stranger was to be admitted except he had an order from me, and his name was on the list.

65. Mr. *Cowen.*] I think you may say that all the space available for reporting is now occupied?—Quite.

66. The London newspaper daily press has not increased during the last 30 years; but there are the same number now as there were 30 years ago; in the event of their increasing, there would be no means available for them to have reporters in the Gallery?—There are five papers which have been discontinued in the last few years; the "Morning Chronicle," the "Morning Herald," the "Sun," the "Star," and the "Hour," have been discontinued; but then we have the Press Associations in their place. All the space in the House available for the reporters is fully occupied.

67. Then 30 years ago there were six daily morning political papers published in London, and there are now seven, or, since the "Morning Chronicle" has gone, six; therefore there has been no increase in the number of daily papers published in London in 30 years; and the number of evening papers is the same also. What I wish to know is this; in the event of an increase in the number of the London papers taking place, is there any means, with the present construction of the Gallery, to afford them accommodation?—No, I could not provide for such an increase in the front seats of the Gallery.

68. During the same time that there has been no increase of daily papers in London, there have been established in the provinces something like 140 daily papers; I believe that is the number?—There are 92 daily provincial papers in in England, 2 in Wales, 21 in Scotland, and 19 in Ireland; making 134.

69. Then

Mr. R. A. Gaunt.

28 June 1878.

69. Then these 134 are represented by three Press Associations?—Yes.

70. And you say that you have had no representation made from the Provincial Press in recent years asking for admission to the Gallery?—No, not for the last few years certainly.

71. As far as you know, they are content with the reports they get from these three associations?—I cannot answer that question.

72. As far as you know?—As far as I know, they are.

73. Does it come within your knowledge that some of the reporters who represent the London papers represent at the same time provincial papers, and thus supply the want complained of?—That may be the case, but I cannot state in evidence that they do.

74. Is it the fact that some few years ago an intimation was put in the Gallery that the London newspaper reporters were not to accept retainers from provincial newspapers?—I am not aware of that.

75. That they were to confine their services exclusively to the London papers?—That, again, is beyond my knowledge.

76. During your holding of the office such an intimation has not been put up?—No, certainly not.

77. Therefore any reporter on the London Press can, if he is so inclined, and make arrangements, undertake to supply reports to any provincial paper with which he chooses to come into an engagement?—Such a matter is not within my jurisdiction, but is at the discretion of the reporters.

78. And during your holding of this office there has been no such restriction as I have mentioned?—Not officially made.

79. And you do not know that during the late Speaker's time and the late Serjeant's time such a restriction was made?—I am quite sure it was not made in the late Serjeant's time.

80. An intimation made by the Serjeant, I mean?—I must answer again that no such intimation was made to the reporters by the late Serjeant.

81. The back seats in the Gallery are occupied by leader writers?—By leader writers, and by a few weekly papers the evening before publication for one day in the week, and by the reliefs for the reporters in the front seats of the Gallery.

82. Has any complaint come to you that the presence of leader writers is a source of inconvenience and annoyance to the ordinary reporters?—No, I have heard no complaints.

83. Supposing that these leader writers were removed, would there be additional space for reporters?—They could not report in the back seats, so I am informed by the reporters; the constant passing to and fro for the relief would prevent their making an accurate report.

84. As to the accommodation provided for the reporters to write out their reports, has there been any complaint of that as to the ventilation or general convenience?—No, I have had no complaint.

85. The room in which they write out their reports is beneath the Ladies' Gallery, I think?—Yes; and No. 18 Committee Room is, also, placed at the service of the reporters.

86. They have that room at certain times, but there is still a room beneath the Ladies' Gallery where the telegraphing goes on?—That is the case; and the plan I have put in shows the Committee exactly how that space is appropriated.

87. The telegraphing takes place underneath the Ladies' Gallery, but the reporters write out in a Committee Room in this passage?—Yes.

88. How many newspapers have telegraphic communication?—I cannot tell; that is not in my province.

89. There has been no restriction imposed by the House in that respect?—No.

90. Therefore any newspaper that chose might bring the telegraph to the House?—I should think so, provided the sanction of the Postmaster General and the First Commissioner of Works is obtained.

91. The fact is that, as you think, the 134, or, as I think, 140 daily papers are represented by three Press Associations?—Yes.

92. And by three seats; and the six or seven London newspapers are represented by 18 seats?—Yes.

93. Mr. *Forster*.] With regard to these Press Associations, I will take them just in their order; take first, the "Press Association;" when was that first

Mr. R. A. Gover.
16 June 1878.

allotted a place in the Gallery?—About six or eight years ago, I am informed.

94. And that has how many seats?—One.

95. Then the Central News came in, when?—More than six years ago; I cannot exactly say the number of years.

96. Did the Central News come in at the same time as the Central Press Association?—It was in 1870, I believe, that the Central Press came in.

97. The Central Press came in at the same time as the Press Association, and the Central News came somewhat later; is that so?—Yes.

98. Before these associations came in, how were the provincial newspapers represented?—By the Electric and Magnetic Telegraph Company.

99. And had they the same number of seats as three present associations?—That company had one seat, and employed two or three reporters.

100. Can you at all tell the Committee how the different provincial newspapers are divided amongst these three associations?—No; I have no return from them.

101. You were not in your present office at the time that any of them were admitted?—No.

102. In what way do you imagine that the Irish papers get their reports at this time?—From the London daily papers, and the Press Associations too.

103. Do you mean by that that they copy their reports from the London papers after they are printed, or that they have arrangements with the reporters of the London papers?—I believe they have arrangements with the London reporters, but I really cannot answer the question.

104. You said something about the London weekly newspapers having seats in the Reporters' Gallery?—For one day; the day before they are published.

105. How many weekly newspapers have that?—Six seats at the back of the Gallery are used for that purpose.

106. Chairman.] I think you wish the Committee to understand that the seats behind the front seats are occupied by the reporters who are waiting as reliefs?—Yes.

107. And by the leader writers of the London daily papers?—Yes.

108. And by some of the weekly papers the night before publication?—Yes, for one day in the week.

109. But that the seats are not occupied by any provincial newspaper at all?—None whatever.

110. Have you any knowledge of the reporters as reporters?—No.

111. You simply issue these tickets to them?—On the application of the editors of the newspapers which employ them.

112. You have no control over the reporters in any shape or way?—Except to keep order in the Gallery.

113. But you would exercise that control through the editor of the newspaper, if it were necessary?—Yes, that would be my course.

114. So that so far as the Serjeant at Arms is concerned, it is open to the proprietor or editor of any one of these newspapers to make any arrangement he may think fit with regard to the reports which he obtains through their seats in the Gallery?—Yes, certainly.

115. You do not follow those reports at all?—No, I have no control over the reports.

116. Will you state to the Committee when the arrangement was first made for the introduction of Mr. Hansard into the Gallery?—This year, at the beginning of the Session.

117. Prior to the beginning of this Session Mr. Hansard had no reporter at all in the Gallery?—No, none at all.

118. Mr. Walter.] Do you happen to know to what extent, if any, the accommodation for reporters in the present House of Commons exceeds that in the old House?—I think it is about the same, as far as I can remember.

119. Sir Henry Drummond Wolff.] Do you know whether the reporters hear well up in the Gallery?—No; you will get that evidence from the reporters themselves.

120. You have not had any complaints from them?—No, I have not.

121. Lord

121. Lord *Francis Hervey*.] Are the reporters allowed in the Members' Gallery?—No, not in any other part of the House.

Mr. R. A. Gossett.

23 June 1878.

122. Mr. *Hutchinson*.] Is there any difference in point of quality in the seats in the front row; are some better than others?—In the centre seats they hear better, I think, than in the others.

123. Will you tell us whether these three seats that are distributed among the representatives of the Provincial Press are in the most eligible part?—They are on each side of the Gallery (*pointing to the Plan*).

124. So that it comes to this, that the whole amount of accommodation at present provided for the representatives of the Provincial Press is three seats in the worst part of the Gallery?—Yes, but they can hear perfectly.

125. Mr. *Mitchell Henry*.] Does the circumstance, that the Provincial Press occupies what has been called the worst part of the Gallery, arise from the fact that the London Press was previously in possession?—Most certainly.

126. And must be dispossessed unless the accommodation was enlarged?—That is the case; most of the London papers have occupied their seats since 1852; and the "Daily Telegraph" came in in 1858, as I have already stated, and the "Daily Chronicle" in 1877.

127. Mr. *Cowen*.] There are three Press Associations?—Yes.

128. They have three seats at the sides of the Gallery, where, necessarily, the reporters hear worst?—Yes.

129. Now, in the event of another Press Association being established, or any other society for reporting and for admission to the Gallery, with a view to improve or extend the reports, there would be no accommodation provided for them?—Except in the back seats, until a vacancy occurred through some paper being discontinued, for instance.

130. The present arrangement practically gives these three Press Associations a monopoly of supplying Parliamentary reports to the 140 provincial newspapers?—Well, I suppose it does.

131. Mr. *Forster*.] Supposing that the Irish newspapers were to wish to have a special report for Ireland, that again could not be obtained, could it?—No, certainly not.

132. Nor for the Scotch?—Nor for the Scotch.

133. And supposing there was any fresh London newspaper started, what would happen then?—They must wait until the first vacancy occurs; I could not give them a place at the moment.

134. Would you answer this question: we will suppose that the provinces, either Ireland or Scotland, or any part of Great Britain, were to wish for a fresh seat, and also a fresh London newspaper were to be started, which would get the preference, do you imagine?—The London newspaper, if it were a London daily paper.

135. *Chairman*.] But is it not open to any one to make arrangements with the possessor of an existing seat in the Gallery for a report?—Certainly.

136. So that either a country newspaper or a new London paper would have the occupants of the existing seats in the Gallery, to whom they could go in competition with each other and obtain a report?—I believe it is frequently done.

137. You have no certain knowledge of the fact?—I have no official knowledge of the fact.

138. But you believe that the occupants of these seats in the Gallery do furnish special reports whenever required?—I have no official knowledge of it, but I believe they do.

139. Sir *Henry Drummond Wolff*.] May I ask on what principle it would be that the new London paper should have a preference over the country paper?—Because all country papers are excluded at this moment, and if you admit one you must admit all the 134.

140. Sir *Henry T. Holland*.] But I understood you to say that a London paper would have the preference over a central association?—I did not say that.

141. The question of the Right honourable Member for Bradford proceeded upon the assumption that a new central association was started at the same time as a new London paper, and you said that the new London paper would have the preference; supposing that a new central association was started, and that at the same time a new London paper was started, are we to understand

that the London paper would have the preference?—A London daily paper; but I could provide for neither the one nor the other at present, because the Gallery is quite full.

142. But I am assuming, of course, that there is a vacancy, and that at the same time there are two applications for the vacancy, one from a central association and another from a new London paper; which would have the preference?—I think this consideration would weigh very much with me, what number of papers the new Press Association would represent.

143. Mr. Gann.] You go under the assumption, I think, that the London daily Press has the first claim; that they are to be served first, and that after them the Provincial Press, either through the Press Associations or otherwise, can be served; but the first condition is the London Press?—That has been the established regulation regarding the Reporters' Gallery.

144. Mr. Mills.] I think you said that you did not know precisely the dates at which the Central Press Association and the Central News had been admitted into the Gallery?—I think, in 1870.

145. But I mean with reference to all those three; can you give us the dates?—It was when the Government bought the telegraphs.

146. I thought you said they were admitted at different dates; I do not know whether you can put in any Paper about that?—No, I cannot; I think they were all admitted in 1870.

147. Sir Henry Drummond Wolff.] The "Daily Chronicle" has only recently had access to the Gallery?—Only recently, that is to say, in 1877, and I can only give them a place after six o'clock.

148. May I ask what vacancy did they get; how was the vacancy made for the "Daily Chronicle"?—The vacancy was created by the discontinuance of the "Hour" newspaper.

149. Mr. Mitchell Henry.] Am I correct in supposing that the Central Press and the Press Association were admitted to the Gallery, not because they represented newspapers, but because they enabled provincial newspapers to obtain through their agency telegraphic reports?—I am not certain of that.

150. They are not newspapers in any way?—No.

151. Then are we to understand that the reason why the London Press has a preference in the Gallery is because the Gallery cannot, in its present condition, afford accommodation to the provincial papers, represented each by a separate staff of reporters?—It would be quite impossible to admit the Provincial Press in the present state of the Gallery.

152. Is it the fact that in the desire to supply that accommodation, seats were given to the Telegraphic Association which supplied the Provincial Press?—Yes.

153. Mr. Walter.] In fact, I understand that these arrangements were made at a time when the Provincial Daily Press had scarcely any existence, and when no need of undertaking reports for their accommodation existed; is not that so?—They were formed when the telegraph company was done away with; the telegraph company did it to a certain degree, and then these companies were formed.

154. These arrangements were made originally in the old House, and subsequently continued in the new House, at a time when the Provincial Daily Press had hardly any existence?—Yes.

155. Not that you excluded them, but there was no necessity for it at that time?—Just so.

156. Sir Henry Drummond Wolff.] You said just now, in answer to the honourable Member for Midhurst, that the decision between a new Press Association and a London paper would be determined by the consideration of the number of papers that the new association represented; may I ask, are the present Press Associations admitted as the representatives of certain papers, or as associations whose reports circulate, more or less, throughout the country?—As the representatives of provincial, and Irish, and Scotch papers.

157. Are they admitted on the application of these Irish and Scotch papers, or on their own?—They sent me a return of the names of the papers that they represent, and then they were allowed to occupy a seat in the Gallery.

Mr. *Thomas Curson Hansard*, called in; and Examined.

Mr.
T. C. Hansard.

28 June 1878.

158. *Chairman.*] ARE you the Proprietor of Hansard's Parliamentary Debates?—I am.

159. Will you state to the Committee the relation of Hansard to the House of Commons from the year 1803 to 1870?—The relation of my father and myself to the House of Commons from the period when Hansard's Debates were first undertaken, has been entirely of a private character; in fact, it can scarcely be said that there have been relations at all; I have had no official recognition whatever until this year.

160. Will you state to the Committee, then, how you obtained the reports which appeared in Hansard's Debates?—Hansard's Debates were commenced by my father in 1803, ten years before I was born, and therefore I can give you no precise information as to the nature of the compilation until about 1830 or 1832, when, on my father's death, I, still a young man, became the proprietor and manager of the work. I can only tell you that before that time the work was compiled by gentlemen of some literary importance, from every source which was at that time available; newspapers, pamphlets, manuscripts, and other very miscellaneous sources; but, I believe, never from reports in the Reporters' Gallery.

161. When you say, never from reports in the Reporters' Gallery, I suppose you mean to say, never by the employment of reporters by Mr. Hansard himself in the Reporters' Gallery?—That is my meaning.

162. So that up to 1870 you availed yourself simply of the reports which appeared in the daily newspapers, and such other means as were at your disposal, to get a good report?—That is so; such other means as were at my disposal, other than reports from the Reporters' Gallery.

163. That you state to be the fact from 1830 up to what date?—I should say up to the end of last year, with the exception of special occasions when special reports were called for, or asked for, when special arrangements were made, and they were reported at my expense.

164. When you speak of special arrangements and special reports asked for, by whom were they asked for?—By associations or individuals interested in particular subjects then before Parliament.

165. It was necessary that a previous application should be made to you for a report, which you then obtained?—Yes.

166. From special reporters in the Gallery?—Yes.

167. What other means had you for ensuring the accuracy of the report which appeared under your name?—In the first instance, a staff of collators and revisers employed and paid by me. The reports so collated having been got into type, the proofs of the speeches were sent to almost every individual speaker, in slips, with a request that the proof slips should be returned at a proper time.

168. As a matter of fact, were those slips usually corrected by Members of the House of Commons?—In prodigious numbers. I have here a book (*producing it*) which has been kept at the office of Hansard. It is a register, day by day, of the subjects of debate, of the speakers, of the date when the proofs were sent out, when they were requested to be returned, and when they were returned—which last column, of course, tells whether they were returned or not. From these books I have had some papers drawn up in a statistical form, which I think will give you some very surprising information, if I may be allowed to hand them in (*handing in the same*).

169. This is a book in which the name of the speaker is entered in the first instance, then the subject, then the date when the copy is sent out to the speaker, and the date on which it is returned?—Yes.

170. So that in every case in which the date is entered of the return of the speech that is a proof that it has been returned to you?—Yes; and I may add that as to a very large number of those which have not been returned, I am informed that the speakers do not return them, because they are satisfied.

171. Then you employed collators, who took the reports they found in the daily newspapers, and with their assistance these speeches were set up in type?—Yes.

172. And the proofs were sent to the speakers, who were requested to correct them, and within a given number of days to return them to you?—Yes.

173. And in the great majority of cases you say that those proofs were returned?—Yes. There is an abstract at the end of each of those papers which I have handed in to you which will give you the exact number; a tabular summary.

174. Will you read one of those abstracts, and explain it?—In the year 1869, in the House of Lords, there were 12 speeches, of which the copy was sent; 799 proofs of speeches were sent out, and 455 were returned corrected. In 1870, eight speeches were sent.

175. Will you explain what that "eight speeches sent" means?—That the Peer sent me the report of his own speech. 722 speeches were sent to Peers, and 363 were returned corrected. In 1871, 17 speeches were sent by Peers who spoke; 788 speeches were sent out, and 391 were returned corrected. In the House of Commons, in 1869, 98 speeches were sent to me, 2,673 speeches were sent out, and 1,890 were returned corrected. In 1870, 105 speeches were sent to me, 3,116 speeches were sent out for revision, and 1,720 were returned corrected. In 1871, 226 speeches were sent to me, 3,599 speeches were sent out, and 1,895 were returned corrected.

176. Will you give similar figures for the Session of 1877?—These returns having been drawn up hastily—I have not got the number of speeches that were sent to me in that year.

177. Then will you take the last year that you have?—In 1875, in the House of Lords, 19 speeches were sent to me; 829 speeches were sent for revision, and 369 were returned revised. In the House of Commons 140 speeches were sent to me, 4,268 speeches were sent for revision, and 2,363 were returned revised.

178. Are you able to give the Committee any information as to discussions in Parliament which took place in 1875 and 1877 on reporting, and the steps which were then taken?—Yes; on the 30th April 1875, Mr. Mitchell Henry gave notice of a Motion respecting an inquiry into the reporting of debates, which is to be found in this volume of Hansard (*handing it to the Chairman*), and that (*handing it in*) is the Notice. On the 4th of May 1875, the Marquess of Hartington moved a Resolution regarding the exclusion of strangers. Mr. Mitchell Henry moved an Amendment to that Resolution, to the effect that a Select Committee be appointed to consider Parliamentary Reporting. After debate, Mr. Sullivan called attention to strangers being present, and they were ordered to withdraw. The result was that the debate was adjourned. On the 31st of May the debate was resumed. After long debate the Amendment was withdrawn, and the original Resolution was agreed to; and the Hansard which contains those debates has been handed in.

179. What are the existing arrangements under which you now occupy a seat in the Gallery?—Do you wish to know the origin of the present arrangement?

180. You have stated to the Committee what your system was up to the commencement of this year; I want you now to state to the Committee wherein the arrangements of this year differ from those of previous years?—Having undertaken with the Chancellor of the Exchequer, to report more fully the four points of the debates in Parliament which are very imperfectly given by the newspapers—that is to say, of the discussions on Private Bills "by Order," discussions in Committee of Supply, discussions in Committee on Public Bills, and debates after midnight, I undertook for the sum of 2,000 *l.* to have special reports of those four points, and generally to improve the reports of debates in other respects. It was obvious that those special reports would very greatly increase the expense of the printing and paper; and I undertook that in consideration of another 1,000 *l.* I would print and deliver the whole debates of the Session without increasing the ordinary subscription beyond the usual price of five guineas.

181. Have you any memorandum or record of that understanding on which you have acted?—Yes, I have here my own memorandum of the interviews that I had with the Chancellor of the Exchequer upon that subject; they are of considerable length.

182. Have

182. Have any letters passed between you and the Chancellor of the Exchequer, recording the arrangement?—Yes.

183. Will you read the letters?—This is the principal letter; it is written by Mr. H. S. Northcote, the Chancellor of the Exchequer's Private Secretary: "19th December 1877. Sir,—With reference to the correspondence which has passed between the Chancellor of the Exchequer and yourself as to the best means to be adopted for effecting an improvement in the present system of reporting the Debates and Proceedings of the Houses of Parliament, I am desired by Sir Stafford Northcote to inform you that he is prepared to give a trial to the scheme you have already discussed with him. He will sanction the introduction of a Supplementary Estimate, to be submitted to Parliament at the commencement of next Session, providing for the payment to yourself of a sum at the rate of 3,000 l. per annum for the unexpired period of the current financial year; and he will be ready to propose a vote for the full sum of 3,000 l. In the estimates for the year 1878-9. If the experience of the first two months of next Session shall justify his doing so. Sir Stafford understands that you are willing, on the terms specified, to guarantee to report more fully.—(1) Discussions on Private Bills ' by Order '; (2) Discussions on Committee of Supply; (3) Bills in Committee; (4) late Debates; and, generally speaking, to make your Parliamentary Record as full and accurate a publication as possible. This arrangement will not disturb that for the purchase of a certain number of copies of the Debates for public use; and, on the other hand, it is not to affect the price charged for the work. I am, Sir, your obedient servant, H. S. Northcote." My letter, in reply to that, was as follows: "27th December 1877, 4, Paper Buildings, Temple, E.C. Sir,—I have received, with great satisfaction, your communication (through Mr. H. S. Northcote), in which, after referring to the correspondence (conversations) which have passed between you and myself, ' as to the best means to be adopted for effecting an improvement in the present system of reporting the Debates and Proceedings in the House of Parliament,' you state the conditions on which you are prepared to give a trial to the scheme I have already discussed with you. The terms specified in your letter are perfectly satisfactory; and I, on my part, guarantee to report more fully—(1) Discussions on Private Bills ' by Order '; (2) Discussions in Committee of Supply; (3) Bills in Committee; (4) late Debates; and generally speaking, to make my Parliamentary Record as full and accurate a publication as possible; but I have to point out that the words ' and, generally speaking, to make my Parliamentary Record as full and accurate a publication as possible,' are to be interpreted by the passage in Mr. H. S. Northcote's letter above cited, and by the words ' guarantee to report more fully' the points therein specified, and are not to be construed as meaning ' full and verbatim reports.' I have the honour to be, Sir, your faithful servant, Thomas C. Hansard."

184. Has there been any other communication, any other letter from the Chancellor of the Exchequer to you, or from you to the Chancellor of the Exchequer since?—Not respecting the arrangement: those two letters contain the arrangement.

185. Are you able to say whether the Supplementary Estimate was taken or not?—That Supplementary Estimate was not taken. In lieu of a Supplementary Estimate, the Chancellor of the Exchequer put down in the Second Class of the Civil Service Supplementary Estimate, a sum of 100 l., "payment to be made before the 31st of March 1878 in respect of a Grant in aid of the publication and preparation of Hansard's Parliamentary Debates, at the rate of 3,000 l. for the Session or Sessions of each year, commencing with the Session of 1878. 100 l."; and to that is added this memorandum: "The nominal sum of 100 l. has been provided amongst the Supplementary Estimates for 1877-78, solely in order that the general question of the policy of the Grant in Aid may be discussed as early in the Session as possible, and may be brought in the most convenient shape before the House of Commons; but any payment that may be made in respect of the present Vote of 100 l. will be abated from the payments to be made from the Grant of 3,000 l. included in the Stationery Office Estimate for 1878-79, so that the whole sum paid to Mr. Hansard for the Session or Sessions of 1878 shall not exceed 3,000 l."

186. Has the Vote been taken in the Stationery Estimate for 3,000 l. ?—Yes, in the Stationery Estimate for 1878-79; not a Supplementary Estimate.

187. Is the Committee to understand that you still maintain your staff of collators for dealing with the reports which are provided by the newspapers, and that in addition to that staff you have reporters who now report more fully on the four subjects that you have stated, Private Bills "by Order," Committees of Supply, Committees on Bills, and Debates after Midnight?—Who report absolutely fully—not verbatim, but absolutely fully—excepting in some of those extremely protracted debates which have been attended with constant divisions for adjournment, and on the Question that the Speaker leave the Chair, when my reporters sit through it and take such reports as appear to be essential for covering the history of it. You asked me just now whether I still maintain my corps of revisers; I do, but I have increased them considerably, so that that part of the debates in Parliament which is not included in the four points under-goes a very much more careful revision than it did before.

188. Will you explain to the Committee in what way these gentlemen, these collators, are able to exercise an accurate revision of the reports; I have not understood from you that they have seats in the gallery; how do they qualify themselves to collate so as to produce a perfectly accurate representation of the speeches which have been delivered in Parliament?—In the case of those which have not been taken by my staff of reporters, they have no means, except their own literary ability, in collating and selecting from the newspaper reports and other sources not derived from my staff of reporters.

189. Then the speeches which are not reported by your own reporters undergo a species of editing, so to speak; is that so?—More than that; it is literary work; it is collation. But those speeches which are reported by my own staff are passed into the revising room, and they undergo also a collation and revision where there are other sources of information.

190. So that it might happen that you put into a Member's mouth what he ought to have said, rather than what he said?—That would not be a very great evil.

191. Are you able to tell the Committee the extent to which the speeches are corrected when they are returned by Members; have you any sort of data or statistics on that point?—No; even if I had thought you would have asked me that question, I do not think I could have produced the returned proofs; the communications between myself and the Members are confidential; that is, I should not choose to do it except under pressure.

192. Is it the fact that Members express satisfaction with the attention given to them by your editors in dealing with their speeches?—All but universal satisfaction. When you bear in mind that the proofs of speeches are sent out by thousands it is impossible but when there should be a number of gentlemen who are dissatisfied; and many of them, I am bound to say, are, as regards the collated speeches, justly dissatisfied. In many instances no amount of collation from any existing authorities will produce an adequate report of what has been said; no man is more dissatisfied on that point than I am myself.

193. But is it the fact that the reports become more lengthy under the careful revision of the Members themselves?—I could not answer that in a universal negative; but I may be permitted to say that it is one of the great sources of pride that I have felt in being entrusted with my present position, that the Members, almost as a rule, are so just and considerate that it may be viewed as a matter of great gratification, not to myself only, but to those generally who are interested in the debates of the House of Commons.

194. There are some speeches which occur in Hansard with an asterisk affixed to them; what does that mean?—Those are speeches which are sent to me, and which I carefully examine myself. If I find that it has every appearance of being a bona fide report of the speech delivered, although it may evidently not be a verbal report—still if I am satisfied that it is a bona fide report, I accept it; but I put the asterisk to it to signify that I publish it on the authority of the Member with my own ratification of it.

195. Then the asterisk signifies a report of a speech sent to you by the Member himself, and not a report collated from the newspapers or furnished by your own reporters?—That is so.

196. The asterisk, then, distinguishes those speeches of which you spoke just now, when giving the figures, the two hundred and odd speeches sent by Members of the House of Commons to you, and some twenty and odd speeches sent

Mr.
r. G. Hansard.
18 June 1878.

sent by Members of the House of Lords to you?—Not quite; many of them I know to be genuine reports taken by shorthand writers, or compiled from their own memoranda; and in cases where I am perfectly satisfied that I am fully justified in putting those reports before the world on my own authority, I put no mark on them; in that case the speech is taken on my authority, without any intervention of the authority of the Member himself.

107. Will you now state the four classes of speeches prepared by Hansard? —Those taken by my own staff of reporters; those which are the result of collation and revised by the Members; those which, as I have just explained, are marked by an asterisk; and those which I accept and do not mark by an asterisk.

198. Then as regards those which are marked by an asterisk, you say in effect, "I have no reason to doubt that this is an accurate report, but I am not responsible for it"?—That is so.

199. Have you on any occasion received remonstrances from Members who object to your reports, or object to refusals on your part to make corrections which they have sent in; that is to say, who, having sent corrections to you, complain that you have not accepted those corrections and introduced them into your report?—As to the first, I have occasional remonstrances, and since I have had a special staff of reporters those special reports appear to give so much satisfaction that the other part which is not specially reported has become a subject of remark, and so this Session I have had more complaints than I have ever had before. As to your second question, there have been a few occasions on which I have had that objection, that I have refused to accept the corrections made; I should not be justified, I think, in naming them, except the one particular instance which was the subject of a debate in the House of Commons, and which is very well known; it is rather a painful subject, and I would rather leave it as it stands in the report in Hansard if you wish to inquire into it.

200. But, as a rule, you do accept Members' corrections?—As a rule, I have not the slightest cause to complain; there are exceptional cases (they are not numerous) in which, having received a report which I think not fairly corrected, I take no further notice of it; that is to say, I do not use the corrections.

201. Mr. *Forster*.] With regard to that return of the number of speeches that were sent out and the number that were sent back corrected, I suppose a very large number of the speeches sent out are very short speeches indeed?— My manager of the publishing department informs me that those small speeches are not taken into account in that return.

202. At present we will suppose that a Member makes six or seven remarks in Committee; you would consider that in the return as one speech, I suppose?—Yes. Perhaps it is a detail that you will not care for, but where, in Committee, a considerable number of Members take a share in the discussion of an item, and one Member, as often happens, speaks four or five times, the whole of that debate is sent to each Member, but he is only allowed to touch his own speech.

203. Now we will take an evening in which there are many questions to Ministers; are you in the habit of reporting the questions put by different Members?—Yes.

204. Do you count a question as one of the speeches which you would include in that return?—They are sent to the Ministers to whom the questions are put and his answers are counted.

205. But not the questions?—No; the questions, in fact, are taken verbatim from the Notices.

206. I understood you to say that your reporter obtained his seat in the Gallery in order to report those four different kinds of debate which you have mentioned?—Yes.

207. But in a debate of general interest which is not in Committee your reporter is still there; what does he do during that time?—The four gentlemen that I have engaged are waiting for their turns; waiting to be called on.

208. Your reporter does not make one of his opportunity for assisting the collators afterwards in preparing a better report of those debates?—No.

209. Could you give the Committee a little idea in detail of how the collation

Mr.
T. C. Howard

18 June 1878.

is managed. Take a debate of interest and a speech of considerable length; would the collator take the newspaper which appears to give the longest report, or would he take several newspapers and compare them together?—You take the newspaper which appears to give the best report and collate it with every other newspaper, and the best reports from other parts of the country, in cases where good reports are sent to provincial newspapers.

210. We know, as a matter of fact, that constituents are supposed to take rather more interest in their Members' speeches than a great many other parts of the country, and that consequently a Member's speech is rather better reported in the local newspaper of his own borough than it would be in other provincial papers, and sometimes at greater length than in the London papers. I suppose that paper is taken, is it not?—That paper is taken. I am not sure that I can give you accurate particulars of it, but we know that one of the Press Associations (I am not certain that I am at liberty to hand this paper in, which I have to my hand, as it is marked " Private ") ;— It is a list of the newspapers and of the individual Members who are to be specially reported by their staff. Their special reports go down to their local newspapers, and are used there, and are in many cases, or, I may say, in most cases, sent by the Member to me.

211. Sir Henry Drummond Wolff.] Daily papers, do you mean?—All kinds of papers. This which I hold in my hand is the list, and you will see that it is very numerous; it contains the papers and the individual Members who are to be reported for the papers.

212. With regard to the time at which speeches are sent to Members, can you give any information about that; how long after the speech has been delivered is it sent to the Member for correction?—The speeches of the 20th of June of this year are now before the Members for correction.

213. Pray do not suppose that I am in the slightest degree complaining against the way in which you have conducted your reporting, but I think it is true, is it not, that in the latter part of the Session they are sent quicker this year to Members than they were before?—This Session has been entirely different from any other; the alteration which has been made in consequence of the arrangement with the Chancellor of the Exchequer has been wonderfully effectual in every point; I venture to say so, though I am not now under examination on that point.

214. One advantage that you have been able to give Members, from having a larger staff, is, that as the Session has gone on you have not been obliged, as you were before, to lengthen the time between the delivery of the speech, and sending it for correction?—I have shortened it very much.

215. I suppose another result of that is, that your weekly publication comes out quicker, does it not?—Yes; we are now printing the 4th of June.

216. What is the time that you now give to Members for revision; how long a time?—Four to six days.

217. Is there any alteration there from what there was last year?—No.

218. I suppose that another result will be that Members will receive the last of your publications a much shorter time after the end of the Session than they have done in previous years?—I hope as the 20th of June is to the 28th of June, so the 12th of August will be to the 25th of August.

219. So that we are not so likely to have our speeches come upon us in our autumn holiday, as we were?—I hope you will be relieved from that.

220. Could you give us any information as to how the reports of other Legislative Assemblies are conducted?—Yes, I can give you considerable information on that point. If you wish to go into that subject now, I am able to give you a great deal of information concerning it.

221. For instance, have you made it your business to see how the reporting is conducted in Paris?—Yes.

222. And what is the principle upon which their reports are made?—My information, which I have noted down, is taken from the Parliamentary Report as to France.

223. Have you any information obtained from personal knowledge with regard to the reporting in foreign countries besides what is given in this Parliamentary Return which is already before the Committee?—I have additional information with regard to the United States.

224. Is that with regard to the publication of the " Congressional Globe "?—

The

The "Congressional Globe" has ceased to exist. The "Congressional Globe" was a private undertaking, being a contract with the United States Government for the two years of the Congress. It was published in two kinds; the "Daily Globe," of which this is a copy (*producing a copy*), was brought out daily; the details of the "Congressional Record" are curious and not agreeable; but this "Daily Globe" was afterwards made up into the "Congressional Globe," and published in this form (*producing a copy*). The American people were dissatisfied with the nature of the "Congressional Globe," and directions were issued for tenders, but in the meanwhile it was managed and published, the reporting, the printing, and the distribution of it, by the Government Printing Office, and there it remains. The "Congressional Globe" is discontinued altogether, and the "Congressional Record" takes its place.

225. But at one time the "Congressional Globe" was published as a private speculation, was it not?—It was published by contract, and in that sense as a speculation.

226. That is to say that the publisher obtained some pecuniary assistance from the Government, but also relied upon his sale?—There is a great deal said in words, but I doubt the fact: I doubt there being any sale at all.

227. Did that appear the next morning?—It bears the date of the next morning, but the first edition is the one, I believe, which is the true date, and the "Record" although it purports to be of the same date, is really a later publication. They call this (*producing it*) the book edition.

228. Was there any other matter published together with the reports of the speeches?—They appear to have filled up any blank pages with some curious information; the addresses of Members, railway times, public exhibitions, museums, and places of amusement.

229. And you do not imagine that there was any great demand for that publication among the reading public?—I do not believe there was any.

230. Can you give us your opinion as to how far it would answer in this country to have published every morning a very full report of speeches and nothing else; do you think that that would sell?—No. You have not asked me the question, but I may perhaps say that the distribution of the "Congressional Record" is gratis, they print and distribute 18,000 copies.

231. And the "Globe" was bought, was it?—The "Globe" was bought for a small subscription, five dollars, I think, for the Session.

232. I do not imagine that that is a speculation which you would at all like to engage in, to undertake to publish every morning a verbatim report of speeches?—Not as a speculation, certainly.

233. Have you ever had such a speculation proposed to you, or heard of anybody who is at all likely to undertake it?—No.

234. I suppose, in your opinion, it would require a very considerable subvention from the Government to make it answer?—Very large.

235. Do you think that even if there was that subvention from the Government, or even if it was done gratis, there would be many persons who would take it in?—I presume it would be distributed to public men and to centres of political life; and in the libraries, and those institutions, I have no doubt that it would be readily welcomed, and on great occasions very highly appreciated.

236. Have you ever considered, with your experience, what effect such a report might have upon the reports that at present appear in the London newspapers?—Yes.

237. What is your opinion as regards that?—It becomes rather a delicate question, because it would infer an opinion regarding the conduct or value of other undertakings, but generally I may say that my opinion is that a standard report of debates would act as a considerable moral stimulus to the newspapers in general for the improvement of their reports.

238. You do not think that another result might be likely to happen, namely, that the newspapers which at present report most fully would be less inclined to go on reporting fully with the knowledge that their readers might get the report somewhere else?—That is impossible for me to say; I cannot tell what view newspaper proprietors might take of their own interests.

239. I think there is no other country in which there has been anything like a report published similar to the "Congressional Globe," is there?—There has been in France for a very long while an official publication of their debates;

I believe

I believe as early as the First French Revolution the "Moniteur" published a very wonderful collection of their debates, and that is continued to this day in the "Journal Officiel."

240. But there is nothing like so good a report as the report in the "Congressional Globe"?—No.

241. Mr. Cowen.] I think you say that the publication of Hansard's Debates by your father commenced in 1803?—In 1806; the Parliamentary History in 1803. The Parliamentary History is a collection of all antecedent records of the debates, such as were known up to that time, and is continued up to 1803; and Hansard's Parliamentary Debates, which is the contemporary record of the debates, commenced in 1806, and has been continued from that time to the present; and I should ask leave to hand this in (*handing in a paper*).

242. Then from 1806 to 1877, the speculation was entirely a private one, and you received no assistance or help whatever from the Government, or from Parliament, towards the publication?—None from Parliament. I have a series of papers of correspondence commencing in 1835; do you wish me to go into the history of the applications that I have made to the Government? They are interesting; but it is a question whether the Committee desire to go into these details.

243. The point I wish to bring out is, that from 1806 till 1877, the publication was an entirely private speculation, and all you received from the Government during that period, either by you or your father, was the purchase of a certain number of copies of your publication?—Not quite so. Up to 1835, we received no specific subscription from the Government; each public offices as required the Debates subscribed individually; but in 1835, in consequence of a Memorial of Peers and Members to Lord Aberdeen, the Prime Minister, the then Chancellor of the Exchequer, Sir Cornewall Lewis, brought the matter before the Treasury, and I was ordered to discontinue supplying the public offices individually, and in lieu of that, the Stationery Office was directed to subscribe for 100 copies at the price at which they were supplied to private Members. Three years subsequently to that, namely, in 1858, Mr. Disraeli being Chancellor of the Exchequer, that number was increased to 120; and, if you please, I will hand in the directions that I had from the Comptroller of the Stationery Office, for the distribution of those 120 copies. I am now told that there are 124 copies taken.

244. Then, until recently, all the Government or Parliament has done towards the publication of these Parliamentary Debates of yours has been subscribing for 120 or 124 copies?—That is all the assistance that I have ever had from the Government; but there is a great deduction to be made from that, because, whereas formerly the subscription for the year was fixed according to the quantity, and was seldom less than eight guineas, and sometimes was nine guineas, and in one or two instances, ten guineas, it was an implied condition with the Chancellor of the Exchequer, that the subscription should be a fixed sum of five guineas, in lieu of these other sums; and the consequence of this assistance given to me by the Government by the purchase of copies, accompanied by the reduction of the subscription, and the discontinuance of individual copies, was, that I obtained a pecuniary gain of 40 l.

245. By reducing the price, although they did take the 120 copies, the amount of help that the Government gave to you in that way was practically 40 l. a year?—Yes; it was of great value, but not in a pecuniary sense.

246. Then during the whole of these 70 years, I think, the reports that have appeared have been got exclusively from newspaper reports, either provincial or London newspapers; up till the beginning of this year you had no representative in the Gallery whatever?—That is so.

247. You say that you have had no complaint generally from Members as to the way in which their speeches are reported?—Very much the reverse; the approbation that I receive is most gratifying to me, with exceptions.

248. Are we to understand that to-day the Members are satisfied with the reports that appear in your publication, that is to say, considering the circumstances under which it is published?—I have no doubt that that is so, considering the circumstances under which it is published.

249. It is not an absolute approval of the reports which appear, but it is an approval of your work, considering the difficulties under which it is engaged in?—That unquestionably is so; it cannot be put too emphatically.

Mr.
T. C. Howard.
——
26 June 1876.

those two columns an independent Member may introduce a Bill, and his remarks may be reduced into 90 or 80 lines containing the statement of the objects of the Bill, while the answer of the Minister who opposes it may occupy the best part of a column?—Yes.

262. So that you have no statement in favour of the Bill, but you have the Ministerial reply to it in full?—It operates both ways. If the Minister introduces a Bill the report is a full one, while, perhaps, the answer to it, however conclusive, is insufficiently reported; and, vice versa, a Ministerial reply upon a private speech, introducing a Bill, would be given at great length, or usually is given at great length.

263. You spoke of having an official report, and I gather your opinion to be that an official report published alone would not sell?—Yes.

264. You have that opinion upon the experience of America?—I think that neither the United States nor France, where a system of the greatest distribution prevails, will give you an example, because in those countries they do not try to sell; you cannot tell whether they would sell, or otherwise.

265. Is it not the fact that in America every Member of Congress receives 90 or 30 copies of his paper, and that every public institution also receives a number, and that that of itself destroys the circulation?—Every Member of the Senate receives two copies for his own use, one at his private house, and one laid upon his desk in the Senate House; and he has 12 copies for distribution as well. Every Member of the House of Representatives has two copies also for his own use, and he has 24 copies for distribution. I am not certain how the transmission is managed; it has varied a great deal, but I believe it to be that the Members are now supplied with a sufficient number of a peculiar official stamp for the transmission of national documents—national Dime Books.

266. The fact is that in America a Member gets a dozen of those papers, and can on certain conditions get two dozen?—The Members of the House of Representatives get two dozen.

267. And these publications are not only given free, but are distributed free?—They are practically distributed free.

268. Therefore that upsets the question of sale altogether; you could not have a sale under such circumstances?—Quite so; they distribute in that way to public offices and others that you may suppose entitled, 13,000 copies, and that effectually puts an end to any chance of a sale.

269. Then in France the distribution is on a limited scale, but still there is a sale for the Official Journal; I think you will find that Official Journal circulates as an ordinary newspaper; the "Moniteur" is a private speculation, but the Official Journal is the journal of the Government?—On looking at my papers I do not seem to have taken that point.

270. You do not know, therefore, as a fact, that the Official Journal which contains the report of the proceedings in the French Assembly is published as a newspaper, and that it has a fair circulation, a paying circulation?—I believe it is not circulated as a distinct publication; it is a part; the reports may be official, and they are inserted in the official part of the "Journal Officiel."

271. The "Moniteur" is an entirely private speculation?—I find this in the Blue Book: "The full reports appear in the unofficial part of the 'Journal Officiel,' of the morning after the sitting, signed by the Director of the Stenographic Service"; but whether that "Journal Officiel" is sold as a newspaper, or distributed in any other way, I do not know.

272. In France there are four reports, a verbatim report, a condensed report, a less condensed report, and a summary; and these four reports are distributed amongst the French papers for sale. Does it occur to you that it would be practicable to publish an official report in this country after the model of the French?—I think if I may be permitted an opinion on the subject, that would be a very ruinous and destructive proceeding. I do not think that you have quite stated the system correctly. The first report is the compte-rendu in extenso; that is a full verbatim report, and it appears in the "Journal Officiel" the next morning. A distinct staff apparently, though under the same direction, draws up that same evening a compte-rendu analytique, and that is distributed gratis to the French newspapers; it must not exceed two and a-half columns, and the French newspapers must insert that analysis without alteration. That is further distilled

tilled into a *compte-rendu analytique sommaire*, and that must not exceed one column; but that summary the newspaper that asks for it must use as it stands. There is a fourth, which is not a publication and is never printed—which is in fact our Votes and Journals.

273. The object of the French Government in publishing these reports was, that the reports that appear in the Journals, whether long or short, shall be impartial, and a fair reproduction of the discussion that takes place; that was the object?—That may be their intention, but I am afraid that their impartiality is altogether on the side of the Government which draws it up. It was that which induced me to say, at the commencement of your questions on this subject, that I thought the plan would not succeed in this country.

274. Your belief is, that you would not find a sufficient number of people to purchase a paper containing the reports of the speeches of Members of Parliament?—Not a paper confined exclusively to the reports of the debates; you would not find persons who would purchase them.

275. In France, with their official report, they also publish the Government advertisements; would it be possible, do you think, to add to the publication of the reports of Parliament the advertisements that appear in the "Gazette;" the "Gazette" is a source of revenue to the Government, to the extent of some 30,000 *l.* a year; if that were added to the publication of an official report, would that be likely, in your judgment, to have a sale?—I think the effect would be to smother the Parliamentary Report; nobody would purchase the Government advertisements for the sake of reading them; and those who were interested in them, and would purchase this paper for the sake of the Government advertisements, certainly would not trouble themselves to read the reports of the debates; that is my opinion.

276. Your opinion, I suppose, is, that the reports of speeches in Parliament are not a saleable commodity for newspapers, and therefore they are not published?—It is not a saleable commodity by itself to be remunerative as a speculation; that is my opinion.

277. Sir *Henry T. Holland.*] You said that the time allowed to Members for revision varies from four to six days; what regulates that variation of time, the length of the speech, or the period of the Session?—The exigencies of the printing office.

278. With regard to the Wednesday reports, have you found that larger additions are made to your reports of Wednesday's speeches by Members who are revising such speeches?—No; but the reports of the Wednesday's debates in "Hansard" are not altogether open to the charge of deficiency, because I have many other sources from which Wednesday's debates are very largely extended in "Hansard," and I do not think that, as regards the length of the report of Wednesday's debates, we are open to much condemnation. But it is a blot upon the whole system.

279. But when you speak of its being a blot, you are rather referring to the reports as they appear in the daily papers, are you not?—And in "Hansard" too, only in a less degree.

280. I suppose as regards your reports in "Hansard," that there is no difficulty, you having all the other reports to compile from?—The Wednesday's discussions being for the most part on questions introduced by private Members, or on subjects in which societies are interested, there are a very great number of special reports that I am able to make use of; and we have at this moment an instance of that in the fact that the debate on the Women's Disabilities Removal has been reported by me at my own expense (I have received some consideration for it), and I believe there is nothing omitted.

281. With reference to the United States, I gather that the "Congressional Record" is subsidised by the Government?—It is entirely managed and printed by the Government.

282. And the Members now receive that gratis?—Yes.

283. It is the case, is it not, that they used to have to purchase a number of the "Congressional Globe"; a certain number of copies was assigned to each Member, but he had to purchase them, had he not?—No, I think not.

284. Are you speaking of that from your own knowledge?—I have read the matter up very much, and I have not made a note to that effect.

285. "By a Resolution of the Senate of the 7th August 1846, each Member of the Senate was authorised to subscribe for 12 copies of the debates of Con-

Mr.
T. C. Hansard.
28 June 1878.

grets as published in the 'Congressional Globe.'"—They pass a great many resolutions, and do not act up to them; I do not see any direction for purchase there.

286. The word subscription generally implies a payment; however, you do not know anything more than appears in this Parliamentary Return?—I have never had that subject mooted.

287. With respect to the system in the colonies, can you add any information to the Return which was made in 1874, to Parliament?—Yes, I can give you some information upon that point. This (*pointing to a Paper*), with regard to the Dominion of Canada, is an entire addition.

288. Can you state shortly now, whether an official paper, containing the debates is subsidised by the Government of the Dominion?—The "Dominion Hansard" is a Government publication, and is under the management of a Select Standing Committee.

289. It appears from the extract from the Journals which you hand in, that arrangements have been made that after daily distribution of the printed sheets, 24 hours will be allowed the Members to make corrections of verbal errors in their speeches before the edition for binding is struck off?—Yes.

290. Have you got any further information as regards the great Australasian colonies?—I can give you no further information with regard to the Colony of Victoria than appears in the Blue Book. With regard to Queensland, Brisbane, the report are got out by the next morning, and members are allowed to correct their speeches; copies are sold at three half-pence each. In New Zealand the publication of debates is a private speculation, and I have a newspaper scrap soliciting the payment of the subscriptions to the "New Zealand Hansard."

291. Do you mean that in New Zealand there is no sum paid by the Government?—None; at least I have looked into the Appropriation Act for the colony, and there is no sum for that purpose.

292. Has there been any alteration in New South Wales?—I know nothing more than what may be in that Blue Book.

293. With regard to New Zealand, the reporters there are paid by salaries; are those salaries not paid by the Government; there is one chief reporter at 500 l. a-year, and five reporters at 250 l. a-year; are not those reporters paid by the Government?—I think not.

294. Can you suggest to us any improvement with respect to the existing arrangement which has been sanctioned by the Chancellor of the Exchequer?—So far as the existing arrangement is concerned, and especially as to the four points, I cannot suggest any improvement. I am not satisfied with the method in which the effect is produced, but the result I believe to be unexceptionable—that is to say those four points are reported as perfectly as reports can be.

295. May I ask you what you mean by not being satisfied with the manner in which the effect is produced?—My arrangements are very excellent and effectual for the purpose of reporting a part of the debates of the House, but are not effectual for reporting the debates generally.

296. Have you any suggestion to make as to any mode by which the existing arrangements might be improved?—I should like an improvement for Wednesday—at a greater expense of course; but as to the rest of the debates not included in these four points, I have great difficulty in seeing any half-way-house between letting matters stand as they are (which, as regards those parts of the debates I think eminently unsatisfactory), and having full reports provided and paid for.

297. Full and official reports?—I do not say official; that is a matter for consideration; there is a distinction in principle between official reports and full reports.

298. But have you thought over the matter sufficiently to say whether in your own judgment you think that the reports should be official?—I have thought over it a great deal; it is a complete subject; if you are prepared to go into it I would go into it, but it is a very large subject and would require much consideration. It is a thing too large to come in incidentally, I think, if I may be permitted to say so; I am quite prepared to go into it whenever you please.

299. I should like to have your judgment upon it?—In my opinion official reports have for some time become a public necessity. I think that the Imperial Parliament, which is the mother of Parliaments, is behind all the other Legislatures in Europe, and almost in the world, in not having an official record of its spoken proceedings, of the argumentative and deliberative part of legislation.

300. Probably

Mr.
T. C. Hansard.
26 June 1878.

300. Probably you would not think it necessary to interfere in any way with any private reports of the proceedings in Parliament, but you would allow those to go on concurrently with the official report which you desire to see as an official report?—I would not interfere with any report. But allow me to say that this touches upon a subject which is of very great importance to me, because my fortune and position is entirely involved in "Hansard's Parliamentary Debates," and I have a great moral claim to consideration in any changes that may take place. In giving you frankly my opinion upon this subject, I am bound to say that I reserve all equities. I say so, because I do not assert any exclusive right, nor have I any rights that I could maintain, either at law or in equity.

301. Mr. *Mitchell Henry*.] You were asked a question as to whether your collation of the reports of Members' speeches, and your editing of them, amounted to your putting into the mouth of Members what they ought to have said, rather than what they did say; does your manipulation of speeches amount to anything of that kind?—No; what we find that is good, and that is well sustained, the collators retain; in fact, it would require very great ability to supply arguments to individual Members.

302. To the extent, then, to which you answered that question in the affirmative, did you mean that you do for their speeches that which the newspapers profess to do, put them into good English grammar?—We do that.

303. Is that what you meant by the answer you gave?—I meant to exclude the inference of that suggestion, that material is put into a speech by revisers which is not found to be supported by authority.

304. It was not my suggestion; I asked the question in reference to an answer of yours which had been given to that question in three words. Do you in your great experience find, or have you found, that Members generally attempt unfairly to revise their speeches?—Decidedly not.

305. If an attempt were made which in your opinion was unfair to alter a speech, should you permit it?—No.

306. Do you consider that you have a kind of moral responsibility to the House of Commons to deal with speeches in the manner that you have described, and not to permit unfair alterations?—I consider that I have a moral duty to exercise that power.

307. You have on some occasions had difficulties with particular Members on that very point, I believe?—I have.

308. I will not ask you anything further upon that. Do you ever receive from Members reports of their speeches taken especially for themselves by reporters in the gallery?—Yes.

309. As a general rule, I presume those reports are longer than would be obtained in other ways?—Much longer.

310. And do you publish them then without question?—If I know that they are specially reported, I know that they are true, and I use them.

311. Have you found that there is a general desire for verbatim reporting, or for full and accurate reporting?—I think that while some enthusiasts go to verbatim reporting, the general opinion is for full and accurate reporting; the public do not require verbatim reports.

312. Then the official reports to which you refer would not be verbatim reports, but full and accurate reports?—They would be full and accurate, but they would not be verbatim in this respect, that certain duplications, and small matters which, as any gentleman in the House of Commons knows perfectly well, are not necessary to the argument or sense to be recorded, would be omitted; otherwise they should be verbatim.

313. Now at the time when "Hansard" first appeared, in 1806, I believe, can you tell us what arrangement existed for newspaper reporting?—I was not born then.

314. Am I correct in supposing that it was not until after that date that very full and accurate reports were given in any of the newspapers?—My first recollection of newspaper reporting, I think, must be taken to be of the great debates, first upon the Reform Bill, but more particularly what are generally called the great Protection debates.

315. The "Morning Chronicle," I think, was one of the earliest of the papers which obtained celebrity on account of its report?—It was one of the earliest and one of the best.

316. That

Mr.
T. C. Hansard
26 June 1878.

316. That was considerably later, if I am not mistaken, than 1606?—I do not know the date; I can only speak with reference to the debates of Sir Robert Peel's Administration, about 1844. The great debates which took place upon the great reforms of commerce and the corn laws; the great Protection debates, in fact.

317. Then is it the inference from what you state, that the fact of "Hansard" being quoted in the House of Commons as almost an official publication arises from the fact, that it was almost the only publication which gave reports of the proceedings in the House of Commons on which Members could rely?—I think so; the authority of "Hansard" is not, and never has been in any sense official or authoritative; it has rested always upon the confidence placed in the character of those who conduct it.

318. My question is, whether the quoting of "Hansard," which is the ordinary mode of referring to past Proceedings in Parliament, arises from the fact that "Hansard" was really the best report which was obtainable in the early part of the century?—There was a period of four or five years in which a publication called the "Mirror of Parliament," was superior to "Hansard," but for the remainder of its existence it fell away and is worthless except for certain speeches. But for some four or five years the reports of the "Mirror of Parliament" were much longer, and I believe more extensively corrected than "Hansard."

319. Is it within your knowledge that until the last few years it was considered rather irregular in Parliament to quote reports from newspapers?—Yes.

320. But that the reports which were quoted were quoted from "Hansard," whether by Ministers, or by other persons speaking with authority; they referred to the report which appeared in "Hansard"?—Yes.

321. It is the case that in late years that rule appears to have been somewhat relaxed, and we have reports of speeches quoted from certain newspapers by name?—I believe it is so; but whether it is lawful or not, I cannot say.

322. You attach very great value to the copyright of "Hansard"?—Undoubtedly.

323. Do you think that you have a moral and equitable claim to be considered in this matter, although not actually officially recognised by the House of Commons as their Reporter, yet as really and virtually their Reporter since the commencement of this century?—I think I have the greatest moral claim for consideration in any arrangements that may be made.

324. Can you tell us in what countries "Hansard" has been adopted for the name of the Parliamentary official reports?—When Prussia first had a Constitutional representation there was a record of their debates, called "Das Preussisches Hansard," and since that time some of our colonies have established authorised reports of their debates without adopting that name. The "Queensland Hansard," the "Victorian Hansard," the "Dominion Hansard," the "New Zealand Hansard," are examples, and I believe there are others; and even when the title of the publication is not specifically "Hansard," the name is dropped, and "Hansard" is used to represent it; at least so I am informed. These are matters that interest my vanity, but are not important, perhaps.

325. Of course this is a great honour done to "Hansard;" have any of these assemblies made you any official acknowledgment of the adoption of this title; I do not mean pecuniary acknowledgment?—No; they have invaded the copyright of my name without asking my leave.

326. Referring to the book that you have put in in reference to speeches sent out for correction, and the period when returned, I see against some of them the word "cancelled" written?—It was not intended that those books should be criticised, except for the numbers; I did not intend that the name of any individual Member should be spotted. With permission, I would rather not go into some of those details.

327. I will ask my question in a different way: if you have taken reports through your own reporter, and are persuaded that the reports are accurate, do you ever cancel those reports?—Not my own report; I have refused one request of that sort to-day.

328. You have refused to do it?—Yes; and I have refused one to-day.

329. Do Members occasionally ask you to cancel a report for "Hansard" of
                                                      a speech

a speech which you know was delivered in the House?—I am asked to cancel reports of speeches made in the House which are the result of collation: and if the report sent to me is obviously fairly within the rule of correct reports, I would not hesitate to cancel my own.

330. To substitute a more correct report?—If I was satisfied that it was a more correct report I would not hesitate to substitute the one for the other.

331. But the term " cancelled " does not amount to the term " suppressed "? —No.

332. You never suppress a report?—No.

333. Do I rightly understand that you occasionally substitute in your publication a better report than that which you have in your own hands?—If I am satisfied that it is a better report sent to me *in bond fide*.

334. But you never suppress a report?—Never.

335. Mr. *Dunbar*.] When you send a report to a Member, and he does not return it, what do you do?—I use the type as it stands.

336. What per-centage of Members generally correct their reports?—If you mean what per-centage of all the Members of the House correct their reports, I cannot tell what per-centage of the 658 Members speak.

337. I mean what per-centage of those who had taken any part in the debates?—Those tables that I have handed in will tell you that directly; they tell you to the last figure; it is from one-half to two-thirds who return their speeches corrected.

338. If you were to report the whole proceedings in as full a manner as you do now on the four points, what staff do you suppose you would require?—I apprehend that there must be a staff of 10 to 18 shorthand writers, perhaps, or more.

339. If you gave official reports of all the proceedings you would have largely to increase the quantity of the reports?—Yes.

340. What do you sell the reports at now, five guineas?—Yes.

341. If there were full reports, what could you sell them at?—I could only go by the rule of three; if four volumes cost five guineas, so many volumes will cost so much.

342. Sir *Henry Holland*.] You might keep down the price to five guineas if the Government gave you a larger subvention?—If the Government increases its subvention proportionately, then the price to an individual Member need not be more than five guineas.

343. Mr. *Hall*.] I understand that your reporters have nothing to do with an ordinary debate now?—No; except after twelve o'clock.

344. And then they come in?—Yes.

345. What have your collators to do with the reports which your reporters take in Committee; have they anything to do with that, or is the work quite distinct?—No; the manuscripts of the shorthand writers are handed in to the manager of the reporting staff; they are put into consecutive order by him, and by him are passed to the printing and publishing office, or rather into the revisers' hands; they are then taken in hand by the revisers, and are read carefully, and passages verified if required: and where there are collateral reports they go through precisely the same collation as if there was no manuscript at all.

346. But what are they verified by?—I mean that they verify extracts, quotations from previous volumes of " Hansard "—everything which a conscientious reviser would do at his desk.

347. I notice in looking over " Hansard " that the general run of speeches are given in the third person, but some in the first; is that always the doing of the Member who corrects the speeches, or is there a difference made to certain Members by you?—There is no difference made to certain Members as such; no Member is entitled to ask or press me to report either in the first person or in the third; it depends upon the reporter.

348. And it is not always the result of the Member's own correction?—Never.

349. He does not transfer from the third to the first person?—Almost never.

350. There are many speeches that appear in your publication and occur in a debate which in the newspapers are given in the third person, but in yours in the first?—When they are derived from a source where the speech is given in the first person.

351. What source would that be?—The special reports for country news-papers

Mr.
T. C. Hansard.
15 June 1878.

papers and other sources in which the original is in the first person. But more frequently the report in the first person is the speech of some very important Member or Minister whose speech it is desirable to take at full length, and then it is more easy to take it in the first person than in the third.

352. Can you give me the date of the "Mirror of Parliament"?—I do not recollect it.

353. Do you know whether there are any copies extant; they are not obtainable now. I suppose?—Scarcely.

354. Sir *Henry T. Holland*.] Was not the date 1633?—The "Mirror of Parliament" was commenced in 1828, and was continued in foolscap folio to 1837; in 8vo. from 1837 to 1841.

355. Mr. *Hall*.] Why are the Wednesday's debates in the London papers less reported than those on other days; what is the reason of that?—I think that is a question I cannot answer; that is within the breast of the newspaper proprietor.

356. But you know no reason?—I know none.

357. But as a fact, your collators have greater difficulty, have they, in putting Wednesday's speeches into type, than other speeches on other evenings?—Yes; we cannot make anything of them unless there is some special report.

358. I suppose reporters practically have a certain space given them by their editors into which they must get the report of the night's or the day's debate; is that so?—I believe that is so; but that is information which I am not in a condition to afford; I never had anything to do with that.

359. The expense of collating against reporting is very considerably less, I suppose?—Much less.

360. Mr. *Barclay*.] I wish to ask you this; supposing the House of Commons sits to 12 o'clock at night, within what time could a verbatim report of the speeches up to 12 o'clock be delivered in type; how soon could the speeches be delivered in type?—That is a matter of organisation and money.

361. But within reasonable limits, it could be practically carried out?—With organisation and money they might be printed the next day.

362. Do you mean in 12 hours or 24 hours?—I conceive that it is possible, if desirable, that a debate up to 12 o'clock at night might be laid upon the Table at the meeting of the House the next day at 4 o'clock; but it would be a very tremendous task, and everything approaching to revision must be abandoned; there must be no interruption from the reporters' pen to the laying of the print upon the table.

363. The newspapers occasionally have a speech made at 12 o'clock at night, in type the next morning; a verbatim report, do they not?—The performances of the best London journals in that respect are most admirable; but I cannot answer the question specifically.

364. You do not know about the arrangements of the London newspapers for giving verbatim reports of the speeches, when they so desire, up to midnight?—I do not.

365. You are in favour of having an official report of the proceedings of the House?—I think it a necessity.

366. Do you mean by that a verbatim report of the speeches of Members?—Yes.

367. With such a report, to what extent would you allow corrections to be made?—Do you mean an immediate report?

368. I mean a report that you call an official report; I want to know a little more about the character of the official report that you recommend?—Whenever the Committee think it right, I would put a scheme before them for an official or a full non-official report. The time that must be allowed for revision must depend upon the rapidity with which Parliament desires to have the report produced.

369. The point which I wish to have your opinion about is this; you recommend an official report of the proceedings of the House including a verbatim report of the speeches by Members, and that report I understand from what you say you are going to send to Members for revision before final approval and printing; to what extent do you contemplate in this scheme to allow Members to re-touch their speeches in proof?—Very little more than trimming

trimming the grammar and language, and occasional elision of redundancy; but I should not propose to allow correction of substance.

370. Under the present system of the reports in "Hansard" where a Member happens to express in a single sentence something which he afterwards very much desires he had not said, do you allow such Member to suppress that sentence in the proof which you send him for correction?—No, I exercise a moral judgment in the matter; but when you ask me if I allow a Member to strike out a sentence, and whether it is to be omitted as a matter of course, I certainly would not allow that.

371. Does it ever appear in "Hansard" that we have references by Members who have spoken subsequently to one sentence of a speech which has been delivered by a previous speaker, but which does not appear in the report of that Member's speech in "Hansard?"—That frequently happens; it must necessarily happen in all condensed reports; the Member who hears the whole speech may have specially noticed a sentence which the reporter may have thought unimportant, and omitted to take; and therefore a subsequent speaker may reply upon that statement notwithstanding that it will not appear in the report afterwards published.

372. Are you able to say that a hiatus does not arise in consequence of the speaker not having excised that sentence from the report when sent to him by you?—I have never discovered such a thing.

373. In the official report to which you refer do you contemplate allowing such a proceeding?—No.

374. Mr. *Hutchinson*.] You receive a subsidy of 2,000*l.* a year from the Government?—No; there is a vote for this one year of 3,000*l.*

375. Will you tell us how many copies you sell of "Hansard's Debates," and at what price: If you do not like to answer the question, do not answer it?—I do not think I ought to answer that at present: I do not wish to conceal it ultimately; but it is evident that it must have a great effect on the personal question.

376. Now, you say that you have a staff of reporters; how many in number?—My staff consists of four.

377. You say that you have a staff of four reporters, and that they report for you in a manner which you have described as absolutely fully?—I have a staff of four reporters.

378. Who report, as you say, absolutely fully; the question I wish to ask is whether they report for you alone?—Those four report for me alone.

379. You tell us that you have reason to believe that honourable Members are satisfied with the reports in "Hansard," and you gave us a list of 4,268 speeches sent out and 2,363 returned, which leaves a margin of 1,905 unreturned; do you suppose that the 1,905 who did not return their speeches did not return them because they were satisfied with them?—I have been told by a considerable number of Members that when they do not return their speeches, it is because they are satisfied with the report.

380. And you accept that as the explanation, when a speech is not returned, that it is satisfactory?—I am pleased to take it so; it is no business of mine.

381. Now let me ask you this question; how do you distribute the work between your four reporters on the one hand, and your collators and compilers on the other; do you put the four reporters on one set of Members, and leave the other set of speeches to the compilers and collators?—I must ask you to allow me to interpose a piece of information which is of great importance. The four reporters who are my staff are assisted very largely, almost *ad libitum*, by reporters who are called in from the Gallery as occasion may require. The number of gentlemen who are willing to assist my staff in that way is very considerable; and I have what is considered a perfect report of a whole day's proceedings which were reported by 14 gentlemen in 16 turns (*handing it in*).

382. That is not my question; my question is, how you distribute the work between the gentlemen who report and the gentlemen who collate and compile; is there a division of labour by which the speeches of certain gentlemen in the House are to be reported, and the speeches of certain gentlemen are to be collated and compiled?—Certainly not; the report taken for me in the House is confined,

Mr.
F. C. Howard.
22 June 1878.

confined, not to the persons, but to the classes that I have undertaken to report, namely, the Private Bills by Order, the Discussions in Committee of Supply, the Discussions in Committee on Public Bills, and the Post Midnight Debates; but as to who speaks in them is no concern of the reporters; every gentleman who speaks during debates on those four points is reported, and reported in full.

383. Then upon the Wednesdays, when the reports are confessedly inadequate, the proceedings not generally coming within the limits of the four points which you have mentioned, your staff of four reporters are not concerned; they are not engaged on the Wednesday?—They are not employed. Those are the directions (handing some papers to the Chairman) to the chief of my staff as to the business of each day that falls within his province—those which are underlined with red ink; and if you will turn over a few of those and see the amount of business put down for him on each day, I think you will see that there is quite enough work cut out.

384. Sir Alexander Gordon.] I understood you to say that your reporter comes into the Gallery at six o'clock?—We are entitled to our seat at six o'clock; but if there is business for him he must be there before.

385. Then does not your business include the questions that are put to Ministers?—We desire them from the proper sources; they are not reported by my staff.

386. What do you call the " proper sources " for the answers of Ministers?—The answers of Ministers are cut and dried, and generally there is no difference.

387. I ask you what are the proper sources for recording the answers which Ministers give to questions?—They are taken from the daily London papers.

388. Is it not within your experience that if you take, say, four London newspapers, they will give four different reports of an answer?—No, I think not.

389. And if I were to tell you that only last week I was met in the lobby by some one who showed me four different reports of an answer, and asked me which was correct, what should you say to that?—I cannot say.

390. Then the business for which you are paid does not include the answers of Ministers?—No.

391. But are not the answers given by Ministers sometimes of a very important character?—Most important.

392. May I ask your opinion whether answers of Ministers ought not to be reported as correctly and authoritatively as any other proceedings?—I have already said that I think you should have official reports. I conceive with regard to the answers of Ministers, that is is of the greatest possible importance that the answers of Ministers should be reported with the uttermost exactitude.

393. Then in this copy of one of your books, in which the answers are very elaborately put, you have obtained them from the London newspapers?—The answers of Ministers published in " Hansard " may be, almost without exception, relied upon as being the answers given.

394. Then I must go back again and ask what authority you trust to for that?—They are included among the 5,000 speeches that are sent out for revision; I do not think I can go closer than that.

395. Is this form in my hand the form in which you propose to issue "Hansard" in future?—No; it is one of the schemes that I have drawn up; that happens to be a convenient form; it contains on each page exactly two pages of "Hansard," and it is a day taken throughout by my reporters, excepting the questions and answers.

396. I understood you to say that you have given a verbatim report of the debate upon Women's Disabilities?—Yes.

397. Was that because you thought it was so important?—No; I was asked by those who do think it important to report it specially, and I paid for it, and I shall be repaid a portion.

398. By those who asked you to have it reported?—Yes; rather more than half the actual money it cost me.

399. That will form part of your volume of Reports?—Yes.

400. Therefore

400. Therefore that debate upon Women's Rights would be more accurately reported than some of the other debates which we have had?—Certainly.

401. Does not that open the door to the political bias of the editor influencing the record which Parliament has of a debate?—No; as long as the report is accurate I do not see that any exception can be taken to it on the ground that other reports are not so accurate.

402. You do not profess to report all debates verbatim, and if you select one debate to be reported verbatim, it gives greater prominence to that debate than any other not so reported?—It does.

403. May I ask (do not answer this if you would rather not), do Members ever ask to be reported verbatim?—Yes; not very frequently, but it is so sometimes.

404. I believe persons, Members of Parliament even, cannot purchase "Hansard" in individual volumes?—No.

405. One condition you expect is, that the subscription shall be continuous?—For the Session.

406. Now, is it not the case that old copies of "Hansard," complete sets of "Hansard," are very much sought after by persons when they establish libraries and institutions?—No doubt.

407. And in the Colonies they are sought after?—Very much.

408. You know what the Congress pay for the publication of their reports?—Yes.

409. Will you state what it is?—As far as I can make out, it costs 50,000 l. a-year.

410. So the American Congress think it worth while to pay 56,000 l. a-year to have their proceedings correctly reported?—Yes, and they have them badly done.

411. Do you know what they pay in France?—I do not; it is not in the Blue Book, but I have asked the Foreign Office to obtain that information for me: when I receive the answer I will, if you wish it, hand it in; and also the Prussian payment.

412. I understood you to say that Parliament pays you 1,000 l. upon the condition that the subscription to "Hansard" does not exceed 5 l. 5 s.?—Yes.

413. Do I understand you also correctly that this 1,000 l. of public money goes to assist certain Members in buying a private work; let me illustrate that; if I undertake to pay 5 l. 5 s. for my "Hansard," I get a work which is worth more than 5 l. 5 s., and the public pay the difference; is not that so?—Yes, that is the arithmetic of it.

414. Do not those Members of Parliament who pay the 3 l. 5 s. obtain a benefit by public money?—I cannot consent to put it in that way. I think that Members of Parliament are performing public duties, and if they are compelled to pay 5 l. 5 s. for having that which is essential to the perfect performance of their public duties, I do not see why they should be called upon to pay more than 5 l. 5 s. Or (not to conceal my opinion upon the matter), I do not see why they should pay anything at all; I think that these reports are the tools, if I may use the expression, of their trade, and I can no more conceive how a conscientious Member of Parliament can get on without "Hansard," than how he can get on without his Blue Books; and if he has the Blue Books supplied to him for nothing, I do not see how the public can complain that they let him have "Hansard" for 5 l. 5 s.

415. Are you aware of the extent to which "Hansard" is used in the Library by Members of Parliament?—I am it constantly going, and I know that in those public libraries which I frequent it is a perfect nuisance; the tables are covered with it.

416. Is it not the case that Members at present obtain that valuable document, which you say is a tool necessary for their trade, solely in consequence of the liberty they have, or because private Members choose to subscribe to your work?—Yes; some do it because they feel it necessary to their work; and others are, to a certain extent, induced by the conviction that if "Hansard" is not supported it will be dropped, and they do not wish it to be.

417. Your experience of dealing with reporters, as I understand it, is a very recent experience?—Yes, dealing with them to any extent.

418. But are you sufficiently acquainted with their abilities to know whether they could be trusted to report for an official report what is necessary in a

Mr.
T. C. Howard
22 June 1878

speech ?—If you have official reports, they must report those parts of speeches that are unnecessary as well as those that are necessary, and they must also report unnecessary speeches.

419. You do not quite catch my meaning : you stated, I think, that you did not consider verbatim reports necessary, but you considered that reports of an authentic character were necessary ; can you select the reporters to report the part of a speech that is necessary ? —I would not trust them.

420. You would expect them to report verbatim ?—Yes ; there are, however, certain duplications that all speakers indulge in, and I would not have the same words taken twice over consecutively.

421. I understood you in an early part of your evidence to say that the reporter sometimes sat and did nothing, because the business going on was not of a character to require him to report it ?—That is only under my arrangement ; I do not remember having answered this question; I will answer it as a substantive question if you wish.

422. Can you make any suggestion for increasing the facilities for reporting with regard to hearing ; it was stated by the Serjeant at Arms that only the front row of the Gallery was of any value for hearing ?—And only part of that.

423. Could you make any suggestion for increasing the facilities ?—I think the Reporters' Gallery is an institution that I could not deal with, and I should not like to touch it. If you have official reports, or if you choose to have private reports sanctioned by Parliamentary recognition ; if " Hansard," in fact, was continued as a private undertaking, with a Government subvention of a sufficient extent—I should try my uttermost to have a special reporting box or boxes for the reporters, not in the Gallery, but on the floor of the building.

424. You stated, I think, that a report of a speech might be printed, and delivered some time the next day ; could not you, in your department, do what is done by the " Scotsman " newspaper; only the other day a Bill was discussed up to two o'clock in the morning, and at five o'clock that morning the proceedings up to the close of the debate were in type ?—There is very little difference between Edinburgh and London in point of time : but you must bear in mind that these reports upon Scotch subjects are special reports on special occasions, and that what may be done and well done for one day, could not be done five days in the week for 20 weeks consecutively.

425. But if the " Scotsman," as a private undertaking, can publish so rapidly in Edinburgh, matter which takes place in Parliament up to two o'clock that morning, surely if Parliament ultimately have a report for themselves, no practical difficulty would exist ?—It is a question of expense and organisation ; whatever is done in the one case might be done in the other ; there is no doubt of that. You were asking me about the position of the reporters : if you would like to ask me further, I can give you information on the question, if it is of any interest.

426. I mean their position in the House, and the facilities for reporting ?—In the United States the " principals," by whom I understand the primary reporters, those who actually take the shorthand notes, remain on the floor during the whole sitting, taking a verbatim record of the proceedings, and from time to time their shorthand notes are handed to their assistants; the reporters have chairs in the body of the House in front of the clerk's desk. In France, in the Chamber of Deputies at Paris, the reporters' desks are placed at the foot of the stairs leading to the Tribune. I do not know whether the same arrangement obtains at Versailles, but my belief is that their seats are immediately under the Tribune. In Italy the reporters have accommodation in the body of the House ; and so I gather as to the Colonies, they all have seats in the body of the House, and not in the Gallery.

427. If Parliament was to decide upon having a report of its debates on its own authority, and you were asked to undertake the duty, could you suggest what part of the House you would wish your reporters to be in ?—It would require some alteration. My desire is to look upon the Speaker as the centre of sound, and that the reporter should be so placed as to come within the base of the cone ; that is to say, that the sound should be directed to the Speaker and be of necessity not, quite intercepted, but very nearly intercepted

by

by the reporter ; that the reporter, in fact, should hear as well as the Speaker.

428. I understood you to say that the question of reporting was just a mechanical difficulty to be overcome and paid for?—Yes.

429. Do you see any difficulty in delivering to each Member at four o'clock, when the House meets, on any day, a correct report of the speeches of the previous day, not corrected by Members?—Considering that the House meets late, and sits at least till 12 o'clock, though I believe it to be practicable, I doubt very much whether it is desirable.

430. Have you sufficient confidence in the accuracy of your reporters to undertake that those reports should be presentable reports?—If you will pay the best ability you will get the best reports.

431. Then, if Members were allowed the next 24 hours to correct those reports, or say the next 48 hours, would not that be a foundation for a correct record of the debates of Parliament?—Yes; I conceive that a scheme which should allow a certain but sufficient period to a diligent Member to correct his speech in the House might be followed by a publication on the next day, and that publication would be, to all intents and purposes, what Parliament would reasonably desire.

432. In your experience, would it not be a great convenience to Members during an adjourned debate to be able to have the next day some sort of an authentic report of the speeches that had been made?—I have great difficulty about that; if you offer to Members on Tuesday a debate delivered on Monday for the use of the next debate, and if you permit corrections to be afterwards included in the permanent record, you introduce, I conceive, a very great mischief; for a Member, actuated, we will suppose, by the best intentions, may take the first and less perfect report, and keep it, and afterwards might collate the corrected and published report with that original report, and might either taunt the Member with his original expression of opinion, or he might from time to time use that report which he thought most conclusive for his purpose; and I should object to that very much.

433. Could not that difficulty be overcome by adopting the mode which is used in France, of a committee supervising alterations to prevent a Member making corrections which are not the mistake of the reporter?—I should pity the committee, and I do not think it is practicable.

434. In France they do it?—Do they do it? they have got it on paper; but do they do it?

435. Sir Henry Drummond Wolff.] May I ask whether, in the arrangements which have been made for the reporting of debates after 12 o'clock, it means those in the House, or in Committee?—Whether in Committee or in the House.

436. Hitherto sometimes it has appeared in " Hansard," that a Bill has passed a stage without discussion, when really there was a discussion, but the reporters had not waited for it?—Certainly, it has been so. There is a remarkable instance, if you wish to have one, in the Municipal Franchise Bill, which gave the municipal franchise to women; that was passed on the Consideration, as amended, at two o'clock in the morning, after a short and sharp debate, but not any report of the debate appeared in the newspapers; but you will find a short report of it in " Hansard "; it was sent to me by a Member who was interested in the subject; but otherwise, the fact which you mention in your question is quite accurate.

437. As regards collation, I suppose at the present moment speeches are collated from the different newspapers?—The speeches of the general debates.

438. I ask the question because I think I have seen that one newspaper has sometimes chosen to give one argument of a speaker, and another newspaper has given another argument, and then they have been collated and sometimes not put exactly in the order in which they have been made use of?—That is possible.

439. But they are submitted again to the supervision of the reporters who have heard the speech, if I understood you rightly?—To the supervision of the Members only.

440. Did you not say that the reporters assisted the collators?—The reports of the gentlemen in the Gallery are passed into the revising room, and their reports are collated, verified in fact, to see that there is nothing omitted.

D 3 441. I understood

441. I understood you to say that you had great assistance from the gentlemen in the Gallery who assist your collators?—No, I said that the reporters in the Gallery assisted my four reporters.

442. Do the newspapers in America have separate reporting of the debates there?—I think not.

443. Are there any newspaper reporters admitted at Versailles?—Yes.

444. But do they not publish the reports furnished by the official reporters?—Not unless they please. The reports which are furnished by the official reporters are sent, as I understand, to a bureau in Paris, and are delivered to the newspapers that ask for them. With regard to Germany—I cannot answer about the Empire—but in Germany, besides an official report, which appears to be a very imperfect affair, there is a large association, the *Kesner Correspondenz*, which has very considerable reports, which the Blue Book says are wanting in accuracy, as can be proved by comparing them with the official stenographic reports. The "Cologne Gazette" seems to have a very efficient staff, and it is their reports, as I understand, that are used, or were used, in Germany for reference.

445. If it were determined to have a staff of reporters and to have an official report, as has been mentioned by some honourable Members, would it not be feasible for that staff of official reporters to furnish any newspaper that liked with the report on receiving payment which would go, of course, in diminution of the expense?—Yes, it would be possible.

446. I mean as the debate was going on in lieu of the present system adopted by the newspapers?—No, I think not. At least, there might be a great difficulty about it. There is no difficulty while a reporter is translating his notes to his writing many copies at once by the manifold process, but practically, I think it would be found that the scheme would not be acceptable. Official reports must mean necessarily very long reports, and a shorthand writer in writing out his notes cannot write them out in extenso for one, and in a short form for the other.

447. But is it necessary that a shorthand writer should copy out with his own hand, or cannot his notes be copied out by somebody else who understands his shorthand?—There are various ways which can be described by those who understand shorthand, but I do not believe that reports of debates could be taken down in shorthand and be written by another person from that reporter's notes. I conceive that the shorthand of a speech is shorthand shorthanded, and that nobody could really translate those notes except the individual who took them; at least I conceive that there would be great difficulty about it. I admit however, that I am not so perfectly acquainted with these matters as to be able to give you the most accurate information, but I believe that to be the case.

448. You have never known any case in which a debate has been entirely omitted from "Hansard"?—Yes, in early days.

449. I am speaking of a debate being purposely omitted; has there never been any pressure brought to bear upon "Hansard," to omit a debate altogether?—Never. In answer to that question, I might say generally that I am treated, and always have been treated by Members, I may say, as a formidable person—I have never been asked to do what you refer to, and nobody seems to dare to ask me.

450. Mr. *Walter*.] With reference to some answers which you gave me in the early part of the morning, as to the practice which prevailed, both among Members of the House of Commons and among Members of the House of Lords, of sending in reports of their own speeches, and making considerable corrections; you gave us some statistics; has there been any difference, in your experience, between Members of the two Houses in that respect, or do you consider that human nature is pretty much the same in the one House as in the other?—Human nature is much the same among Peers as it is among Commoners; but then, as it happens, Peers are so much more illused that I think they are more eager to send to me important speeches than the Members are in the House of Commons.

451. When I ask whether you have observed any difference, I mean whether you think that the fact of the Members of the House of Commons having constituencies to think about at all affects their conduct in that respect?—No, I think not. I think that when they have sent a special report to their local
                                                                        newspapers

newspapers they have performed the sacrifice to their *amour propre*, and what they tend to me is an afterthought.

452. The main object you think of Members of both Houses is to get the greatest amount of accuracy possible?—Yes.

453. You have told us that prior to the present year you relied entirely on the newspapers and other sources of information that were open to you, and you had no reporters of your own in the House; in fact, you have had no sent in the Gallery until this year?—I have had none before this year.

454. Had you ever applied for a seat for any staff of your own?—No; my applications to the Government for assistance, spread over many years, would have resulted in that, but as they did not result in the application being entertained, I have never asked for seats; and for this reason, that from the nature of the work and the small extent of the sale, it would have been impossible to meet the expense.

455. I was going to ask you that question, whether in a commercial point of view it would have been worth your while or not, without any Government subsidy, to have engaged a staff of reporters to have taken down the debates for you?—It would have been quite impossible.

456. Now is your work printed from stereoplates or from type?—From type.

457. No plates are cast?—No.

458. So that you could not reproduce any particular debate, if there were a demand for it, without recomposing the whole thing?—No.

459. Did it ever occur to you that it might be worth your while to print from plates with that view?—No; you understand that the type must be composed first, and then the plates are cast from a mould taken from the type; and therefore it would be simply doubling or trebling the composition without any possible advantage. Stereotyping is only of value where very large numbers are required, or when the work is very expensive, and when a very few copies are sold in the course of a year so that the expense involved in paper and expenses of that sort would more than counterval the re-setting; stereotyping is not applicable to this at all, though I believe there is something said about it with reference to the " Congressional Record;" but the " Congressional Record " is in everything an example to be avoided.

460. Are you not aware that the cost of employing stereoplate is not at all equal to that of re-composing?—No, not of re-composing, but it is an additional expense to composing.

461. The question has been asked whether it would be possible for any Member who wished to have copies of a particular debate furnished, to obtain them, and you stated that he could not without purchasing the whole complete work; that was my reason for asking the question?—But of course you would be aware that if a Member at some future time wished to have copies of a particular report struck off from stereoplates, that infers that not that debate only, but all debates had been stereotyped.

462. It would not follow that plates should be cast for the whole?—All through. Unless you had some prevision of the debate which would require to be reprinted, you would have to stereotype the whole.

463. I should like to know if you could give the Committee any idea, in a few words, first, of what you think the public really want in the nature of an official report; next, how you think they ought to get that; and thirdly, who is to pay for it. You have stated in general terms that you think the public want an official, that is to say, a verbatim report?—I think the limited public which would take a permanent interest in Parliamentary debates, would require a full and accurate report, nearly verbatim.

464. That being so, how do you propose that they should get it; by what process; what staff of reporters would be necessary to take it, and what would be the size of the publication which such a work would involve, and, lastly, who is to pay for it?—It would require a very large staff of reporters; I conceive that 16 or 18 actual reporters might do it with a staff of superintendents and managers. I do not think it would require more.

465. Supposing such a permanent official report were published in the form of your present work, how many volumes of Hansard would be produced in a year?—Of course the amount would vary with the number of days that the House sits.

Mr.
P. G. Howard.
of June 1878.

Mr.
T. O. Hansard.

13 June 1878.

466. I am supposing four days a week of eight hours a day?—But the House sits five days a week.

467. I am reckoning four; will you take it on that assumption?—My calculations take in the full hours every day, eight hours a day: it is prudent to name the full extent; I believe that the debates of the House of Commons would occupy nine volumes of Hansard.

468. As against how many now?—From four to five of the Lords and Commons; Hansard now runs from four volumes to five full volumes, including the Lords and Commons; and, for the present Session, with this improved reporting, it will certainly occupy six, and I cannot tell what is behind; but I believe a full and accurate report of the debates in the House of Commons might assuredly be contained in nine volumes of Hansard.

469. Have you compared the length of the present publication of Hansard, not in the present year, but up to this year, when the reports were furnished by collation of newspaper reports; have you ever made any comparison between the length of your reports and the fullest reports of the London papers?—I do not think I have.

470. They would probably not greatly exceed in length, would they, the reports of the fullest London papers?—Very much.

471. Have you any idea to what extent?—I do not think I have a clear idea to what extent.

472. But with the exception of particular reports furnished at the expense of societies, reports of debates on questions like the intemperance question and womens' suffrage, and that class, they are furnished exclusively by compilation from reports of the best London papers?—I think my general evidence goes to that.

473. For that reason then should their reports exceed in length the reports in those papers?—My manager informs me that he thinks that the excess of Hansard in past years over the reports of the London journals has been nearly one-half.

474. When you say the London journals, do you mean the average of the London journals, or the reports of the fullest of the London journals?—They vary so; one of the most important journals gives as a general rule very much longer reports than are given in the others.

475. I will take the report of a debate which took place, I think, on the 21st of May on Lord Hartington's Amendment, which occupies in the "Times" nearly 24 columns; do you apprehend that your report would be considerably longer than that?—Yes. As to the leading speeches, No; but the following speeches, I apprehend, will be found to be considerably extended by collation.

476. Have you ascertained that as a matter of fact?—I believe that is a matter of fact; I am informed that it is so.

477. Now, is it your opinion or not that the length of a report ought to depend, to a considerable extent, upon the quality of the speeches?—No; I do not know that any one in the office of Hansard is entitled to judge either of the importance of the Member who makes the speech, or of the importance of the subject to which it refers.

478. Would you apply the same rule to the newspapers, or would you confine it to the official report?—It is universally applicable; I do not think there ought to be any difference.

479. Has it come within your knowledge that it is possible for a Member to make a very long speech and to repeat the same arguments very frequently, so that the Speaker of the House of Commons has called him to order on that account?—I have seen it, and heard it.

480. Do you think that when a man speaks for half-an hour and repeats the same argument repeatedly, and is called to order by the Speaker for such conduct, he should be reported at length, even in the official report?—If I answered that question without reserve, I might say that which Members when they come to read the report of the proceedings of the Committee might not like.

481. It is an important question for us to have your opinion upon?—I think there should be vested in the hands of the director of the reports a power to report in a more concentrated form those debates which take place in the House late at night, after 12 o'clock, which consist for the most part in repetition of arguments.

482. Do you think that if all the speeches in Parliament were reported verbatim,

verbatim, and circulated through the country it would tend to raise the public opinion of the House of Commons, or not?—Yes, I think it would decidedly —Will you allow me to interrupt you there for a moment, and to show you something which bears upon that? You are aware—this is to some extent a crochet of mine—but for the purpose of testing the manner in which my staff were performing their duties, I sat out the debate in Committee upon the Factories and Workshops Bill, and I was so satisfied with the earnestness, the acumen, and the ability with which various points new to me were brought into prominence, that, partly for the sake of showing what I could do, and partly for the sake of bringing the working people into better relations with their employers and the upper class, I printed some thousands of copies of the full debate; they were sent to individual Members; some thousands have been sent all over the manufacturing districts, and, I believe, some to Belgium and elsewhere.—And in answer to your question, I may that, judging from what I have seen and heard this Session, a publication of debates, with, I must say, certain restrictions, would tend very greatly to raise the public opinion of Parliament. And in the same way (and this I did from my personal interest) with regard to these discussions upon the Supplementary Estimates in which my little 100 L was to the front, I sat through those debates, and I consider that the publication of the debates in Supply are very essential indeed to justify the Members to their constituents, and convince them that they are doing their duty as guardians of the public purse. Hitherto, the discussions in Supply have been so very much curtailed that I think the public knew very little about it; and the result of the discussions on the 18th and 19th of March were these two papers (handing in the same), and you will find that they are perfectly full and satisfactory reports.

483. You have selected a debate in which few Members would take part but those who have a very considerable knowledge of the subject?—It was accidental that it happened so; but that which I have just handed in is the result of it.

484. Probably you would apply the same remarks to such debates as that on the Scotch Church, which we had the other night, and to those on the present Contagious (Cattle) Diseases Bill?—If they were fully reported.

485. Would you not consider that there were a great many debates not of that character in which there is a great deal of surplusage?—That is the business of the House, not mine. If they permit it, it is my business to report it.

486. Would you consider that a full report of a debate of that character is equally satisfactory to the House?—I would very willingly sift them, but I do not think it is my province to do so.

487. Have you formed any opinion as to the sources from which the expense of defraying such a publication should be met; I think you have already stated that you think the public would not purchase a report of Parliamentary proceedings unless some other matter were added to it, and therefore I ask from what source do you think the expense should be defrayed? —Not from a private source, certainly. It can but come by a Vote of Supply.

488. Is it your opinion that a public vote of money is desirable, in order to furnish the public at large with a cheap report of Parliamentary proceedings? —It is a matter which is incapable of being measured by money. My conviction is that, in a public sense, it would pay a hundredfold in respect of the benefit that the State would derive from such a publication; but I could conceive no scale of measurement by which to estimate the benefit in money.

489. Have you formed any estimate as to what would be the cost of such a publication?—I must know the scheme adopted before I could give you any sensible answer to that question. All I can say is that I think the cost would be very small when compared with the benefit which, according to my estimation, would accrue from it.

490. You think that the benefit would greatly exceed the cost?—I certainly think so.

491. Mr. Mills.] In the course of your evidence about your plan for Members revising their speeches, you gave us some facts in regard to that—some figures— and I think you said that in 1875 there were as many as 140 speeches sent by

Mr.
T. C. Hansard.

18 June 1878.

Members of the House of Commons themselves to your establishment ?—
Yes.

492. I want to ask you whether, so far as you know, any of those speeches were sent before they were actually made?—No, never; no such thing has ever occurred upon any occasion. If you wish to have any information about it, there are some curious cases. I might state now that one of the provisions made by the Congress of the United States is in respect to providing for the publication of speeches which have not been made.

493. Sir *Henry T. Holland*.] The provision is, is it not, that the speeches which have not been delivered may be printed, but they must not delay the publication of the regular reports?—To the reports of one Session of the Congress there is an Appendix, consisting of 507 pages, of this size (*pointing to a page*), composed entirely of speeches, either retained from publication at the time of delivery or never delivered at all; those are published at the end of the volume.

494. *Chairman*.] You have very strongly recommended an official report of the proceedings of Parliament?—Yes.

495. Have you any information as to the amount of unofficial publication of Parliamentary proceedings in countries where official reports are made?—Do you mean Blue Books?

496. No, I mean newspaper reports which give information to the public of the proceedings in their Parliaments?—I have no knowledge as to that, except that which appears with regard to one or two of the countries about which information is given in the Parliamentary Return before you.

497. Do you know whether in France the reports appearing in newspapers give equal information to the public of the proceedings of their Parliament as compared with the reports which appear in the newspapers in England of the proceedings of the English Parliament?—No, I do not know. I have little knowledge on the subject. I do not know that there is such a report, but it does not follow that it does not exist. My impression however is that it does not exist.

498. Your impression, if I understand you rightly is, that the information which the public derive from the newspapers in France is considerably less than the information which the public in England derive from the newspapers here as to the proceedings in Parliament?—Yes.

499. Have you any knowledge as to what the facts are, so far as the United States is concerned?—No, I have not.

500. Do you know whether the daily papers in New York, or Washington, or Boston, report the proceedings of Congress?—I do not know.

501. In Canada, is that the case?—Not now; it used to be before the "Dominion Hansard" was established, but since that time I believe there is no information conveyed by the newspapers with regard to the proceedings of the Dominion Parliament, except that which is in the form of narratives. There is no reporting of the debates, so far as I know, for the newspapers.

502. Then, so far as you know, prior to the publication of the "Dominion Hansard," for the use of Members of the Canadian Legislature, there was a report of the proceedings of the Dominion Parliament in the newspapers, is that so?—Yes, there was a publication at Ottawa : but before the establishment of the Dominion several of the provinces, New Brunswick and others, had their own publication of the discussions in their Legislative Assemblies, which were very short, and which were included in the newspapers of the day.

503. Then would the facts support this inference, that in those countries in which there is an authorised publication of the deliberations of the Parliament, the newspapers do not report or convey information to the public of the proceedings of the Parliament?—It is a matter of opinion : I cannot tell what the newspaper proprietors might find to be for their interest.

504. I do not want your opinion, I want the fact; I want to know as a matter of fact whether the newspapers do report the proceedings of the Parliament in those countries where there is an official report published, as in the case of the "Journal Officiel," as in the case of the "Congressional Record," as in the case of the "Dominion Hansard," and the "New Zealand Hansard"?—I do not think that I am sufficiently acquainted with the facts to give you reliable information upon that point.

505. You

Mr.
T. C. Hansard.
——
28 June 1878.

505. You have no information to enable you to state whether the newspapers report the proceedings of the Parliament of the country for the information of the public, where there is also an official report published for the use of the Members of the Parliament?—You mean to ask whether, as a fact, the official report extinguishes the private reports; is not that it?

506. I draw no inference, but I want to know whether, in the countries in which there is an official report, there is, side-by-side with that official report, an independent newspaper report, which conveys to the public the most necessary information with regard to the proceedings of the Parliament?—An independent report exists, so far as I know, only in the German Empire.

507. Mr. *Mitchell Henry.*] In regard to this matter, has a change taken place in the general character of newspaper reporting, even in this country, in which there is no official report; have you noticed that, at present, there are sensational reports and sketches of the manner of speaking, and of other incidents of that kind, which are rather taking the place of the old newspaper reports, as we knew them in former days?—I am perfectly aware of that.

508. Therefore, notwithstanding that there is no official report in this country, a change has taken place in the character of ordinary newspaper reports?—Of many newspapers, but not of the best.

509. There are, of course, certain of the London papers which still give as excellent reports as they have always done?—I think so.

Colonel Arbuthnot.
Mr. Barclay.
Mr. Cowen.
Mr. Dunbar.
Mr. William Edward Forster.
Sir Alexander Gordon.
Mr. Mitchell Henry.
Lord Francis Hervey.

Sir Henry T. Holland.
Mr. Hutchinson.
Mr. Mills.
Dr. Lyon Playfair.
Mr. William Henry Smith.
Mr. Walter.
Sir Henry Drummond Wolff.

THE RIGHT HONOURABLE WILLIAM HENRY SMITH, IN THE CHAIR.

Mr. *Charles Ross*, called in; and Examined.

Mr. C. Ross.
1 July 1878.

510. Mr. *Mills.*] I BELIEVE that you write the summary reports for the " Times " in the Reporters' Gallery ?—No; I merely superintend the reporting arrangements; another writes the summary.

511. For what length of time have you done that ?—I cannot call to mind; I think about 25 years in that particular capacity; but I cannot be sure to a year or two.

512. From your opportunities of observing reporting arrangements in the gallery, what should you say with regard to them; do you think that they answer every reasonable purpose that you could require ?—I think so, certainly.

513. From your observations have you any alterations to suggest to the Committee in the present arrangements, and, if so, what alterations would you suggest ?—No. I have none; individual comfort, of course, might be considered more, but perhaps it is not worth speaking of. The accommodation is so extremely good compared to that with which I was acquainted 59 years ago, when I first entered the gallery, that it may be described as luxurious.

514. With reference to the accommodation provided for country newspapers, do you think that there is adequate accommodation in reference to that matter, or do you think that there is any change required in reference to that ?—There is no accommodation for country newspapers; but there is ample opportunity for their obtaining reports through the electric companies.

515. I was aware that there were no spaces allotted to the reporters of country newspapers; will you explain to the Committee what are the arrangements by which, indirectly, country newspapers can obtain information of the proceedings in Parliament ?—They can obtain it through one of the three companies, the names of which the Serjeant at Arms mentioned to the Committee on Friday, and I believe that is done extensively; but I have no practical experience of the matter.

516. With reference to the policy, or otherwise, of Parliament publishing reports of its own debates, have you formed any opinion on that subject ?—Yes; I formed an opinion on that subject a long time ago; I think it was in 1834 that the first proposal of the kind was made, and my attention was recalled to the matter when Mr. Hanbury Tracy moved about three years ago for a Committee.

517. Having formed an opinion upon the subject, perhaps you will tell the Committee what your opinion is ?—I entertain an unfavourable view of that proposal. I do not know whether I am to state the reasons.

518. Will you be good enough to state to the Committee your reasons for entertaining that unfavourable view ?—I think the proposal quite unnecessary. I believe that it would throw much impediment in the way of the transaction

of

Mr. G. Rose,
1 July 1878.

of business. Many debates would be adjourned which no one would think of proposing to adjourn now. In the case of a Member who thought that he could make some observations worthy of the consideration of the House towards the close of the debate when it has been exhausted, under present circumstances it might occur to him that if he rose at a late hour his observations would not attract much attention in the daily papers; but under this proposed regulation he would then move the adjournment of the House, being conscious that his speech would appear ultimately at full length. That is one way in which it would operate unfavourably. It would also, of course, operate unfavourably by multiplying the number of speakers, and by adding to the length of their speeches.

519. Then we understand you to think that a full official report which should be paid for out of the public funds would be, for the reasons you have stated, objectionable?—Yes, for those among others. Another objection is that nobody would read it. Few persons read the debates in the "Times," they are so long; for one who reads a debate in the "Times," I should think there would be 20 who will read the summary. Persons may refer to the report for a particular speech of a particular individual. There is another circumstance which I will refer to. I yesterday hurriedly ran through the Parliamentary list, and it occurred to me as a rough estimate that the number of Members who spoke in the course of the Session would be about 128. About 16 of these, it is admitted on all hands, namely the ex-Ministers and the Ministers for the time being, are quite adequately reported; then deducting them, there would be 112 left; of these 112 I should think there are about 40 Members who will not speak more than six times in the Session, and very briefly; deducting them there would remain 72; then taking away 40 members who speak not more than three times in the Session there would remain only 32 persevering speakers, speakers who address the House very frequently; and it would be to those gentlemen that the proposed publication would be chiefly interesting.

520. Up to what time now do the reporters continue, generally, their work in the gallery?—The "Times" reporters continue later than the others. There was a very full report, as you may recollect, given of the last night of the debate on the Indian troops, Lord Hartington's resolution; Lord Hartington spoke late, and the report was given of the commencement of his speech; then the press was stopped from the necessity of supplying country papers, and it was continued in a later edition an hour or two afterwards, I believe; a complete and very full report of his speech. I think the House did not rise till three o'clock that morning. But in these days of scientific progress means may be found, and I believe that some have been under contemplation by the "Times" for extending the hour up to which reports can be given. This might be done by means, perhaps, of a telephone, perhaps of a machine which the reporter could work here and the type be set up at the other end of the wire in Printing House-square; but of course it would be necessary that the House should furnish a room for the purpose in order that the machines may be placed there.

521. Mr. Walter.] Will you explain a little more fully the nature of the superintendence which you give to the reporting staff?—Yes. I have to see that every gentleman is in his place; that he takes his notes; that he writes them out, which is generally done, I believe, in this and another room; and that then they are despatched to the office. I am not aware that there is any other particular duty which I perform connected with the reporting in the House than that. The next day I read the report, and when I see an error I call the particular reporter's attention to that, and ask him how it occurred, and tell him how I think he might have avoided it, and matters of that kind.

522. The reporters, I believe, occupy entirely the front row of the gallery, do they not?—Yes, the front row, with the exception of myself and the summary writer for the "Times," and I think there is a summary writer for two other papers. The "Times" corps is the largest by about one-third, I should think; our corps is 15, but owing to a temporary derangement this Session it is 14 at present.

523. In the House of Commons?—It is 15 altogether. The reporters go from the House of Commons to the House of Lords when necessary. The Lords generally rising much sooner than the Commons; when the Lords are up, the

the reporters come to the Commons, and then take their turn in the order in which it is set down for the day.

524. By whom are the seats behind the front row occupied?—I have always been puzzled to know; but from what the Serjeant said on Saturday, I find that a good many are occupied by what he calls leader-writers. For instance I think he said that there were 16 or 17 tickets issued for the "Standard." I think there are only 10 reporters, and if that is so, there would be about four or five tickets for leader-writers.

525. For gentlemen, at all events, who are not bonâ fide reporters?—They are not reporters; not connected with reporting. I do not think anybody who sits on the back seat is connected with reporting. With regard to reporters themselves who are waiting to relieve, we will suppose that a reporter who is on duty is about to leave his seat in five minutes, the reporter who is to relieve him in five minutes will get a seat behind, if he can; but recently it has been found somewhat difficult for him to do so, because the seats are occupied by those gentlemen.

526. Are those seats available for reporting, for actually taking notes?—They could be, if a person liked; I have frequently seen reporters taking notes there; there is a little desk which runs along, about a foot in breadth, I suppose, upon which they can place their note-books, and write.

527. It was stated by the Serjeant at Arms the other day that it would be impossible for shorthand notes to be properly taken from those back seats; does that concur with your experience?—I think not. The reporter could not take his notes so well from there, because he could not hear so well.

528. You spoke of the immense improvement in the modern arrangements as compared with those that you recollect in years gone by?—Yes.

529. Are those back seats as good as what the reporters had to put up with at that early period?—Much better; the roof was just about three yards above my head.

530. But I mean for the practical work of hearing and of writing?—Yes; in front there were all the strangers, who, of course, even if in a subdued tone, would talk. Then a Member might be speaking who could not be seen at all, and if you cannot see a man you cannot hear him as well. And the heat was excessive; in fact, it was dreadful in every way; it was almost dark for one thing.

531. I wish to get your opinion upon this question, whether, admitting that the seats behind the reporters' row might be termed second best accommodation, still that accommodation is so bad as to be unavailable for reporting; or is it good enough for a moderately skilled reporter to take his notes from?—Yes, I think it is.

532. Supposing it were thought desirable to have an official verbatim report published in the course of the next day, what addition would be required to the staff in the Reporters' Gallery?—I formed a plan in my own mind upon that subject, as I stated, in 1834, and I have since thought of it; I have mentioned the details frequently to friends, and I think that some of them must have reached Mr. Hansard, from what he mentioned on Friday. It would be necessary to have a considerable staff exclusively for that purpose. I contemplated of course that such a publication would be totally unconnected with any other now in existence, and it would require a considerable staff to do the work properly.

533. Then I gather your opinion to be, that for ministerial speakers, and those who have filled office, as well as for the speakers who seldom speak, the present scale of reporting is sufficient?—Amply.

534. But that an official report would chiefly be for the benefit of a limited number of Members, but Members who speak very frequently?—To the cost of the great body of the House, because I am sure it would subject them to the inconvenience of protracted discussion.

535. I merely wish to keep to the facts; that is your opinion?—Yes.

536. Sir Alexander Gordon.] You said that you thought an official report would tend to protract debates and cause adjournments?—Yes.

537. I should like to know your reason for saying that a little more in detail, because

Mr. C. Ross.
1 July 1878.

because it appears to me that it would be just the other way; a Member who knew that he would not be reported fully, as at present, would ask for an adjournment that he might have an opportunity of speaking the next day, but if he knew that a full report would be published up to any time of the night it would rather tend against adjournment, would it not?—It would, if it was an individual Member. In the case you put, as you will recollect, there will be many Members. After that Member has spoken, another Member on the other side thinks he can controvert all the arguments that he has advanced, and he will have his say, and you cannot stop him.

538. If he knew that his speech would be reported at once is not that an inducement against adjourning?—No, because Members will care very little for this official report; nobody will read it, except that the individual Member may read his own speech; but the public will turn from it with feelings of extreme distaste.

539. Why should the public turn from a speech made late at night if it is worth reading?—It is not the speech itself; it is the length at which the debate will be reported. Few persons read the debate now. The "Times" does it as a point of honour, I suppose, but if I could control it I would give half the quantity; it would be more read, and I dare say the "Times" would save 20,000 l. or 30,000 l. a year; but it is not my business, and I never interfere.

540. I understood you to say that the "Times" proposed to give still fuller reports?—Proportionally fuller, because later. If they give fuller reports I think it will be a mistake. What the public want, in my opinion, is, that the reports should run in the contrary direction: that there should be compression instead of expansion; you want a man's opinions, not his words.

541. I should like to ask, do your reporters condense at the time, or do they condense after they retire from the gallery?—After, generally. A good reporter, in my opinion, should condense at the time; he should take a sufficient note to enable him clearly to understand what the speaker says, and then he should write out a neat account of his opinions; that is my notion of reporting.

542. That is your notion of first-class reporting?—Yes; it is not done sufficiently; it is too much of a mechanical art at present; giving the mere words.

543. Then do you anticipate any difficulty in obtaining men of sufficient acquirements to report the debates in the way which you speak of?—Under the existing system it cannot well be done.

544. Why not?—The great pressure of time has rendered it necessary to shorten the period during which a reporter remains in the gallery.

545. What length of time is that now?—When I first entered the gallery, if the Lords were sitting, we took an hour's turn in each House; a terrible thing. I have had an hour of Canning; of course it was wretchedly done. If the House of Lords was not sitting, we took three-quarters of an hour's turn. When the circulation of the paper increased so greatly as it did about 30 or 40 years ago, then it was necessary to diminish the length of the turn again, and it was made half-an-hour. Then when I entered upon my present office, the pressure became still greater, and I reduced the turns to a quarter of an hour. Now, as regards the report, these short turns are a disadvantage, because a reporter is somewhat more liable to mistake; he cannot carry on the chain of argument, and if there is no vacant place for him to sit in behind before he rushes into the box, and an important speaker be addressing the House, it is quite confusing. The turns now are limited to 15 minutes, but later on, as the hour advances towards midnight, I think after 11, it is 10 minutes; after 12 I think it is five minutes; and I think if it goes beyond 1 it is two-and-a-half minutes. I know it was two-and-a-half minutes ultimately, on the night of Lord Hartington's motion about the Indian troops.

546. Do you mean that the turns are sometimes only two-and-a-half minutes?—The turns which were an hour when I entered, are now at the end of the night two minutes and a-half only.

547. Mr. Hartley.] That is after half-past 12?—After 1, I think; but that is only during an important debate.

Mr. C. Ross.
1 July 1878.

548. Sir *Alexander Gordon.*] Some of the reporters remain in the box much longer than that at a time; some of the reporters remain for two hours, do they not?—No; they may have done so on some of those and nights, when there has been division after division and division after division; but, otherwise, never, I should think, so long as half-an-hour.

549. Do you remember that on one occasion Colonel Stanley made an apology for any mistake he might make in answering a speech that had been delivered late on the previous night by saying that he had not been present, and that he had no proper means of knowing what had been said?—No, I do not remember that; I will take it for granted.

550. If an official report had been issued the following day, say, when the House met, such as has been printed here (*pointing to a Paper*) by Mr. Hansard, of one day's proceedings, would not that have obviated that inconvenience? —It would certainly; he could have seen it, but I do not perceive what advantage that would have been; he was not obliged to answer a speech which he had not heard.

551. A Minister who gets up to answer a speech ought to know what he is going to answer; in this case Colonel Stanley got up to answer a speech of the night before, and he was obliged to say that he had not heard it, and that if he made any error, it must be excused on that ground?—Then I think he should not have answered it.

552. May I ask what steps you take to get correct reports of answers given by Ministers to questions?—I would ask to be allowed to decline answering that question; it involves confidential communications; I never have betrayed one in my life, and I would not begin to do it now.

553. But why should an answer given publicly in the House of Commons be viewed as a confidential communication?—I do not say that the answer delivered in the House is a confidential communication; I am speaking only of communications that I receive.

554. I will put the question again; I allude to the questions put to Ministers when the House meets, and the answers they give in those questions; what means have you of assuring the public that they are correctly reported?— There is no more assurance of that than there is about any other portion of the report; there is no assurance given to the public.

555. Do you, as a matter of course, publish all the questions and answers? —No, but nearly all.

556. That selection rests with yourself, I suppose?—Yes. I might say that that which is omitted is quite unimportant.

557. But the result is, that it depends upon the individual opinion of say, yourself with reference to the "Times," or another person with reference to another paper, whether, or not, the answer of a Minister is reported?—It must always depend upon that; for instance, look at Sir Wilfrid Lawson's speech the other day; it was a very good speech, a humorous speech, and it was given at great length; but if it had been a dull speech, surely the reporter might be allowed to exercise his discretion, and not give it at the same length.

558. But you are going off the subject I am questioning you about, namely, the answers of Ministers, and what security the public has that the answers given are correct answers?—Let us assume for a moment that a Minister might send me an answer; I receive communications from other Members; other Members give me an account of something more than answers; I should hold it a most improper proceeding on my part if I were to state anything of that kind publicly; you must excuse me therefore.

559. But have you not the means of reporting the words made use of by a Minister when he answers a question?—Of course the same means as those of reporting the words made use of by any other Member.

560. It has been stated here that on one or two occasions different versions of the same answers have been reported in different newspapers?—Yes, and I daresay different versions of the same speech will be found reported in different newspapers.

561. If an official report of those answers were given, would not that be a security to the public that they got correct information?—No, it would not be a security any more than the report in a newspaper; they would be done by the same men; there is no security in an official report unless you let the Member

Member look over his speech, and then you have no security that you will not have something quite different from what he said. I know that in the proceedings of a Committee (if you will allow me to state this), a Member, Mr. Warburton, many years ago gave evidence; he answered a question in a single sentence; the paper was sent to him, as I believe it will be sent to me, to correct, as it is called; I think he wrote three of those pages of a blue book for that answer of a single sentence. The matter was brought under the notice of the House; he was a very honourable and a very able man; but he said that he had merely expanded his idea; and what was to be said? I believe there was no censure passed upon him. And so it would be with speeches.

562. Is it your opinion that Members are, as a rule, rather grateful to reporters for sometimes putting their language in a little better order than that in which it was delivered?—Owing to the nature of the manner in which the reports are carried on now that is not done as well as it should be; but in some instances I should think they are very glad to have a report instead of what is called a verbatim report, which is a horrible thing.

463. Mr. *Hutchinson*.] You tell us that the accommodation in the gallery is most luxurious compared with what it was when you entered the gallery?—Yes.

564. A gentleman of your experience will also be quite aware that the standard of accuracy and finish in reporting is very much higher now than it was then?—It is more full, but I do not think it is so elegantly written.

565. You are speaking of condensed reports now?—Yes.

566. But what I mean is that the average standard of Parliamentary reporting is very much higher now in point of fullness, accuracy, and finish than it was then?—I would not allow the finish, but I will the fullness and accuracy.

567. Speaking of the reporter's art?—Yes.

568. Now, bearing that in mind, are you still of the opinion which you expressed at the outset, that the back seats which the Serjeant at Arms said were not places where a report could be properly taken, are sufficient for ordinary purposes of reporting:—I think they would be; I should have no objection to undertake to give a report from there myself. You would not hear as well; I still say that. Of course the reporter can incline his head over the ledge when he is in the front seat; that ledge will intercept the sound before it reaches the back seat.

569. You told us that there were certain disadvantages arising from the shortness of the turns that the reporters take in the box; those disadvantages apply to anybody wishing to take a very full report, do they not?—No, not if he remains; the remark applies to the individuals who have to come in and relieve the others, and as that takes place every quarter of an hour it necessarily breaks the connection; but if an individual remains in the box, we will say during a whole speech, he can take it perfectly.

370. But I understood you to say that this could not be done; that the system would break down?—It could not be done now.

371. Do the disadvantages applying to the frequent reliefs apply in all cases where a full report has to be taken, and where the turn is short?—Yes.

372. Now, bearing that in mind, let me recall to you what you said, that though the provincial press is not directly represented in the gallery, still there are ample opportunities which they have of obtaining reports through the different associations?—Yes.

373. And you are aware that there are three associations, each of which occupies but one seat?—I am not aware of that; but I take it for granted that it is so, as the Serjeant assured.

374. There are three associations to supply the whole of the provincial press?—Yes.

375. Now, considering the system of reliefs, do you still say that under those circumstances there are ample opportunities for supplying the provincial press with what they want?—Yes; it makes no difference at all in that respect, because there is but one seat for the reporters of the "Times;" you know that the reporter who is on duty steps out and another reporter takes his place; so it would be with one of these associations; the gentleman taking the note would step out and another would take his place.

576. Colonel *Arbuthnot*.] I think the "Times" is more favourably situated, both

Mr. C. Ross
1 July 1878

both as regards number of boxes and situation, is it not, than other papers?—
No; we have one more seat, but that has been the case only lately; others
used to have the same number, but gave them up.

577. You have the centre seat?—I do not think that that is as good a place
as one further on. I often find that reporters are prevented from hearing because there is a struggle at the door, which is just behind the centre. If there
should be an important speech, that noise at the door would prevent the reporter from hearing, and he would be very liable to make a mistake; I do not
think that our seat is so advantageous a one as is supposed.

578. I assume that you know sufficiently the acoustic qualities of the House
to know that it is better than the seats at the two ends of the gallery?—No;
I cannot say from experience that it is so.

579. Are you not able to say whether the two seats at each end of the gallery
are less well adapted for hearing than the seats that command the centre of the
House?—It will depend upon circumstances. Let us suppose that the reporter
is on the left hand side of the Speaker. Now, if a Member should speak from
that side and high up from the floor, that is three or four benches from the
floor, the reporter on that side would not bear him as well as if he were in the
centre; but then the reporter on the other side would hear better than any
person in the centre, or anywhere else.

580. Do you know whether it is a fact that the occupants of those end seats
frequently go and occupy places in the seats behind the front bench, which are
described as being told off to leading article writers, in order that they may
hear what is going on?—I do not know that; it may be so; but I think they
would be wrong to do so.

581. Would you kindly tell the Committee, speaking with regard to the
system of reporting as far as the "Times" is concerned, how many reporters
you employ upon a ordinary night in the course of a night?—The same number
always; there is never any deviation; one may be taken off for some particular
event out of doors, but that seldom occurs.

582. Would you kindly state the number and the time taken by each, that
would be necessary to report a speech verbatim as in the case of great speeches?—It
would depend upon the length of the speech; if the speech occupied an hour,
four reporters, each taking a quarter-of-an-hour, might report it.

583. Then, will you kindly say how long it takes to put into longhand a
quarter-of-an-hour's shorthand report; would it take four times the time;
would the reporter write it out in an hour?—Some can write faster than others,
and some take more pains than others, and therefore are a little longer than
others, but I should think a quarter-of an-hour's shorthand, if it were written
verbatim as it is termed, every word that the speaker spoke would take something like an hour and a half or two hours perhaps. But it is long since I
have had to do that work, and I was a slow writer myself; I used to like to
take pains instead of giving verbatim reports.

584. Taking the case of an average speaker, how long would he occupy in
delivering, say, what would amount to three columns of print in the "Times"?—
I think nearly as much as three quarters of a column of this verbatim reporting
might be written for a quarter-of-an-hour's speech; then it would make something near about two-and-a-half columns, would it not.

585. Two-and-a-half columns for an hour's speaking?—For an hour.

586. I am speaking now of the length of duration of time that an ordinary speaker
would be addressing the House to fill three columns of the "Times"?—There,
again, much depends upon the delivery of the speaker; some men are extremely
rapid; others are slow and methodical.

587. I have understood that an average speaker would take about an hour
in delivering matter that would fill three printed columns of the "Times"?—
I think that might be about it; he must be a fast speaker, I think, to do
that.

588. Supposing the debate to be going on after 11 o'clock, say from 11 to
one, and having a view to the time that you are going to press, how long a time
could you leave each reporter in the box?—I explained that if it were an important debate (and I instanced one, that upon Lord Hartington's motion), after
11, the reporter takes 10 minutes, after 12, seven-and-a-half minutes, I think,
and after 12½, five minutes; and then at the conclusion, say after one, we
take two-and-a-half minutes.

- 589. To

589. To come to another matter, you would be very well acquainted with the interior of the House of Commons; can you think of any possible means by which the accommodation for reporters can be improved; I do not mean as to the quality and comfort of it, but the space allotted to them; I mean whether by taking in any side seat or putting up seats at the back, or altering the construction of the part that is now allotted to them?—I do not think so; if there were side seats they would hear much worse than sitting at the back under the existing system, because the side seats then would be thrown further back, and a person speaking from, say a seat behind the Treasury Bench, would not be very well heard by persons up there.

590. I do not wish to confine my question to a particular part; I would include any part of the House; I want to know whether you know of any part of the House which is not otherwise used which could be adapted to the purpose?—No.

591. From your observation of the manner in which the business of the House of Commons has always been conducted for a great many years, what would be your opinion of the introduction of the foreign system of official reports by which the reporter is placed in front of the Chair; from your observation during a long course of years of the manner in which the proceedings of Parliament are carried on, what would be your opinion of the introduction of such a system by which the reporter has a position in front of the Chair; I am speaking now of course of Parliamentary reporting?—Your question refers to the practicability and not to the policy of the step. It is perfectly practicable; as I have said, I formed a plan in my own mind more than 40 years ago, in 1834; but I would be very sorry to see it carried into effect, even if it should do me honour.

592. Would it be detrimental to the interests of the press that there should be an official report, do you think?—No, I think not, but I think it would be very detrimental to Members, because it seems to me that the inevitable consequence would be that the " Times " would no longer feel it a point of honour to give reports at such length when at the public expense they are printed in full; they might curtail their reports. I think, and the consequence would be that, as Members live in public estimation, this official report would be perfectly useless; the public would only know them by what appeared in the newspapers, where they would get less than they have heretofore. Nobody would sit down to read a report three days after, not even in a newspaper.

593. Mr. Barclay.] I understood you to say that in your opinion the " Times " reports the speeches in the House of Commons at the present time at a pecuniary disadvantage to itself?—No doubt of it.

594. If they were going to report them, say at half the length, would they reduce the size of the newspaper, or would they supply matter of more interest? —They would give more interesting matter, and matter that is paid for and kept out by these debates. Matter from various parts of the country is sent up and paid for; then there comes a debate of 12 columns (I have seen 16, I think, this Session, or 18); and that matter from the country is all put on one side; it is all lost. Not only that, there are the advertisements; they must be worth I take it at a rough guess (for I know nothing of these matters of business; I always concern myself with my own duties), at least 20 l. a column; say that upon the average you keep out six columns of advertisements, that is 120 l. a day; and there are five days a week. See how it operates.

595. The public, you think, do not want to see the speeches of Members at any length?—Judging from my own experience I should say not, and I dare-say your own experience would confirm that. If you go into society you will never meet with a person who reads the debates at length; people like to know what the Members have done, and they look to the summary.

596. Then the " Times " is sacrificing itself for the sake of making an official report of the proceedings of Parliament?—I think so; I have thought so for years; I never expressed the opinion till now, publicly, or to any person connected with the paper till the other day, about three days ago; but I have long felt it.

597. Then we may naturally expect that by-and-bye, if such is the case, the reports in the " Times " will become shorter?—I do not know; they would, if I had the power, and I think that the Members would be better served by that

if they had their opinions given. The words are immaterial, except, perhaps, in a few cases; I beg pardon, I am thinking of such men as Canning and Plunket; there it was material; their language was so beautiful.

598. Assuming, as I suppose we may assume, that the "Times" is a mercantile enterprise, it is natural to suppose that they desire to make the most money out of the paper by supplying to the public what they specially want, and, therefore, it is natural to expect, and certainly it is inevitable on such premises, that the reports in the "Times" will gradually become shorter and shorter?—It is an inference that you may draw. I do not say so; I think that the same feeling, whether it is patriotism, or a feeling of honour, which induces them to give the reports at such great length now, would still prevail.

599. I suppose there are a few Members in the House of Commons whose speeches you profess to report verbatim in the "Times"?—No, not verbatim, I hope; I do not think there is anyone who is reported verbatim. You see a speech done at great length, and you are not conscious of any little alteration—improvements in the language, or the construction of a sentence; it should be done, and I trust it is done; that is the reporter's duty.

600. What kind of reporting do you call that?—I call that full reporting; accurate reporting. Verbatim reporting the speaker would think far from accurate.

601. Then instructions with regard to some of the speakers in the House of Commons are for the reporter not to give a verbatim report, but a full report?—Yes, a full report of some particular speeches which possess great interest. Then there is the position of the individual to be taken into account, and his position in connection with the particular question.

602. I was simply wishing to know how you characterise the fullest reports of the speeches of any Members?—A full report. Verbatim reporting has never been known in newspapers.

603. Literally verbatim reporting, you mean?—Yes.

604. When a reporter leaves the box at 10 minutes past 11, having entered it at 11 o'clock, at what time do you expect him to have his extended notes ready for the printer?—As soon as he can get them ready.

605. I daresay he would not be pleased if he did not deliver them till two o'clock, for instance?—It is a matter of importance that he should get them done as soon as he can, but with a short turn, if it is 10 minutes only that he has, he would not take till two o'clock to do it.

606. Should you expect him to have done it by 12?—No, I do not think he could, if he has got what I call a full note; if he came off at 10 minutes past 11 he would have nearly an hour, but if he came off at 10 minutes to 12, then he would have a shorter time; they write off as fast as they can, and the copy is sent off by a messenger every quarter of an hour or half an hour, I believe.

607. And you cannot tell, as I understand you, within what time you expect the reporter to have his full notes extended, because I suppose there is some time within which it is expected that he should have it done?—No; he does it as fast as he can. They differ; some do not write as quickly as others; it is impossible to lay down a fixed rule.

608. Have you the control of the "Times" reporters in the gallery?—Yes.

609. Let us suppose that you are taking a full report of a speech between 11 and 12 o'clock, and that the reporter leaves the box at 12 o'clock, having been in there 10 minutes or 7½ minutes; how soon is it necessary that he should send out the report by special messenger to the "Times" Office, in order that it may appear in the newspaper the next morning?—I can only repeat what I have already stated, that he must write it as soon as he can; then the messenger comes in, takes it from him, and dispatches it to the office.

610. Mr. Dunbar.] Do you exercise any control over the reporters as to the length at which they are to report a speech?—Frequently.

611. Then I suppose you consider yourself responsible for the general character of the reports?—Yes.

612. I believe some years ago there were not so many shorthand writers in the gallery as there are now?—No, they were longhand writers; the shorthand writers were very few; I am speaking of 1820. I have been thinking

over

Mr. G. Rowe.
1 July 1878.

over the matter, and I do not believe that in 1820 there were above four short-hand writers, including myself, on the "Times"; on other papers, probably, fewer still; but they were able men as a rule, chiefly barristers, and they wrote a good style, and took pains; they were indifferent as to the words, but they wrote accurately the substance of the speaker's remarks.

613. I suppose, in those times, a man of that kind would write out a speech quicker than a man who would take it in shorthand?—I do not know about that, but the advantage of that system was that they were not bound to the mere words, and they gave an elegant version, retaining the sense with perfect accuracy.

614. You were asked about a complaint of Colonel Stanley's, that he had no report of a speech made late on the previous night; do you think it would be feasible to have official reporters who would turn out their work so quickly as that the Minister in the morning could see what had been said the night before?—I think it would be possible.

615. Would it require a large staff?—Yes, and many other circumstances would have to be taken into consideration. I do not like to mention my plan, else I have the details; I have done so before, but I should not like to mention them now.

616. If the report were issued in the morning, it would be impossible for any Member to read the proof of his speech?—He could not read the proof; it would cast a shade of suspicion over the report; the official report would then have less chance still of being read, because it would be viewed with great suspicion.

617. Do you think there is any demand on the part of the public for an official report?—Quite the reverse; you would never sell a copy.

618. Mr. *Mitchell Henry.*] I suppose that in these days of telegraphs and rapid communication from all parts of the world, the public generally has not the time to devote to Parliamentary Reports that it had formerly?—No doubt that is so.

619. Do you think that, as far as the public appetite for Parliamentary Reports is concerned, the summary given in some of the leading journals supplies all the Parliamentary Reports which people read?—I believe that the great majority, I think 20 for 1, satisfy themselves with reading the summary; they want to know what side particular men have taken in a particular debate, and they are satisfied with that; if they want more, they would refer to the debate for the speech of a particular Member; I know that from experience—from my own friends; I never met with anybody who read a long debate through.

620. Then, that being the case, can you imagine that a fuller report may be of importance in the direction of our constitutional, commercial, and political history?—I do not see any use that it can be of, and I do not think that it would be applied to any other use than perhaps to rake up at the end of eight or 10 years a particular passage delivered by a Member, and say, "See, you said that 10 years ago, and you say this now; how inconsistent you are." Members of Parliament, when you come practically to statesmanship, know all about it; they have heard the discussions themselves; all the men are trained up by a Parliamentary career; they know all the discussions; they know all the arguments advanced *pro* and *con*; they do not need to go back and wade through that mass of print before they can make up their minds as to the particular course they intend to take.

621. Do you think, then, that in the case of great constitutional questions in past times, for instance, the question of Catholic Emancipation, the question of Parliamentary Reform, and of Free Trade, and questions of a constitutional character which have occurred during this Session, the summary given by the morning papers is all that is necessary for the education of the nation upon those questions?—The education of the nation; I do not know exactly what that means; but I think that the summary is sufficient for those who want to know the parts that individual Members have taken in the debate. Each man has formed his own opinion upon the subject.

622. But cannot you imagine that the arguments used in the debating of a particular question may be of importance hereafter, quite irrespective of the individuals who made use of those arguments?—No, I cannot think that; but I would not confine Parliamentary reporting to the summary; I would have an

Mr. G. Ross
1 July 1878.

enlarged summary; I object to Parliamentary reporting now as being too full, as giving much that might be omitted, and omitted with advantage to the speakers; I would give all the arguments of the speaker and his opinions. You must be aware that a speaker must necessarily go on, speaking, that he cannot stop; he must say the same thing not only twice, but sometimes three or four times; that does not add to the strength of the argument when you come to read it; it may impress it upon the mind of the hearer, and that is the excuse that is made for the iterations of counsel; but when you have it in print to refer to, you do not want all those repetitions.

623. I will put a case to you; during the last Parliament the question of International Arbitration was brought forward by a private Member, and on a division the Government were defeated. In one of the leading newspapers, which is supposed to have a large staff of reporters, the report of that Member's speech who introduced the question, and defeated the Government, was compressed into about a dozen lines; do you think that that was an adequate report for constitutional purposes of a debate of that kind?—I do not remember the circumstance you mention, but I take the fact as you state it. I could not say unless I had heard the speaker, or seen what he had stated. I take it that the arguments which decided the House would not come from this Member as you describe him; I should think they would come from the front opposition bench; from the legal gentlemen there.

624. Now, take questions debated in Committee of Supply, of which very short accounts are given; do you think that if there were a fuller account of the arguments used on particular estimates that might prevent a repetition in future Sessions of the objections to estimates which had been met on former occasions?—Certainly not; the same objections have been urged during the present Session night after night to the same point.

625. I should like to ask you a question with reference to the reporting for the "Times"; do the "Times" reporters, under your directions, take their notes at a certain length according to the importance of the speaker, or of the subject which is under debate?—Generally.

626. When their reports are written out, do they write out the whole of that which they have taken in shorthand?—I cannot tell, because I am not there; they write it out in the room behind the gallery, or, I believe, in this room, and they write according to their judgment; I never see the report until I see it in print.

627. Is it the individual reporter who in point of fact edits, if I may so speak, the speech which he reports?—Yes, he is responsible for that.

628. Does that involve the possession of considerable education, as well as of talent, on the part of the reporter?—It does.

629. Do you then draw a distinction between those who are capable of writing shorthand and those who are capable of really reporting in your sense of that word?—They all write shorthand now; but of course they are not all equally intelligent, not all equally well informed; it is the same with reporters as with any other class of individuals in that respect.

630. But is it not the case that shorthand writing as a mechanical art may be learnt mechanically by any person who can read and write?—Yes.

631. But reporting, whether in shorthand or in longhand, is a totally different thing?—Quite different.

632. That is an intellectual exercise which may be facilitated by writing in a particular way is shorthand?—Yes; and that operates against the suggestion which is now urged of verbatim reporting. You see, when you come to consider, that reporting and verbatim reporting are very different things.

633. Then I may take it that you think the reports now given in the principal London newspapers are adequate for all purposes?—I think so.

634. And that if any change could be effected with advantage it would be in the direction of curtailing them?—I think it should be curtailment by condensation, and not by omission.

635. Then you do not think that the taste of the public is formed by Parliamentary style at present?—No; lately there have sprung up, I am told, monthly publications (I have not seen them) in which Members publish essays; that is another mode in which they can educate the public mind as well as by speaking. I have known Members, not of the present House, or perhaps of the present generation, who have composed essays and delivered them in the House, who would not

not have done so perhaps if these means of bringing their opinions before the public had then existed. I am speaking of a considerable time ago.

636. You were asked a question in reference to reporting the answers which a Minister gives to questions addressed to him in the House; I think I gather that those answers of Ministers are subjected to the same condensation as speeches may be?—No; an answer must necessarily be short; it consists chiefly of facts; it would not be possible without an immense deal of trouble and great delicacy to condense answers; you know that upon the average they are usually six or eight lines.

637. Agreeing with your statement that an answer ought to be short, and to contain matters of fact, is it your experience that the answers of all Ministers are short?—Yes.

638. Do not Ministers differ individually in the length of answers which they give to questions?—No, I think it is the nature of the question which causes some answers to be longer than others.

639. You do not think then that in Ministerial answers of late years there is something involved in the shape of speeches or argument more than was formerly the case?—No, but I think there is a great deal of that involved in the questions sometimes.

640. Sir *Henry T. Holland*.] As I understand, you consider that the present system would be satisfactory if it were altered in one respect, namely, that the speeches should be condensed, and the summaries enlarged?—Yes.

641. Do you mean that the condensed speech should take the place of the present summary?—No, I would not have that, because if you get five or six columns of Parliamentary debates, there are very few that will read them, and what chance is there of people reading 18?

642. Then what you suggest is simply a summary, and no reported speeches?—If I were the proprietor of a paper I would have a staff of excellent reporters, and I would say to them, "Now, unless there is something very remarkable in the language of a speaker, as sometimes there is, merely give his ideas; write it out neatly, and disregard the verbiage altogether."

643. That is looking at the question from a proprietor's point of view, if you were a newspaper proprietor?—No, for the interest of the reader, the public; the reader would like that.

644. Irrespective of the profits of the newspaper, that is what you would do?—Yes, quite; I put that on one side; that is a matter I have nothing to do with.

645. Then what kind of length of summary would meet your views; summaries as long as appear in the present Hansard's Debates?—I have not seen Hansard for years, but I understand that it was done as usual, cut out of the newspaper and sent to the Members. That will be of immense length; a Member will supply what he conceives to be a deficiency, and that will make it of immense length.

646. Your summaries, therefore, would be distinctly shorter than Hansard's?—Yes; I think you will have what is called a full report of a speech which would occupy (as sometimes they do) three columns of the "Times;" it would read much better and be more to the advantage of the speaker, because it would be read, if it were put into a column and a quarter, or a column and a half at the outside, it might be generally read then if he were an eminent man.

647. Now, looking forward, do you think it would be no advantage in the future that there should be a somewhat longer official report of what has passed in Parliament?—I cannot conceive what advantage could arise from it.

648. Perhaps you are not aware how largely Hansard's Debates are now consulted by Members?—I am not.

649. But supposing it to be the case that if a debate comes on upon some international question, or some important question that has been discussed, say 20 years ago in Parliament, Members do make great use of Hansard, would that alter your opinion as to the advantage of having an official report?—No, not at all; because that very thing which you refer to is supplied by the newspapers; that has been sufficient, and will be sufficient always. It would be better, I daresay, for you or other Members, in referring to Hansard, to learn what has passed on the particular subject, to arrive at the knowledge as soon as possible:

possible; when you see six pages of it in print, you say to yourself, "I wish it were not quite so long, and that one might get at the marrow of the thing in about three pages." It is opinions you look to, not all that heap of words in which they are imbedded.

650. But do you consider that it would be sufficient to know that a statesman entertained a certain opinion without knowing what arguments he based it upon?—No; you would have the illustrations and the arguments.

651. Then your summary would necessarily contain more than the mere opinion?—I say that a Member would give the reason for his opinion, or else it is worth nothing; I include that, of course.

652. Then there is another point; I understand that you are against allowing Members to revise their speeches, because you say it would create suspicion?—Yes.

653. Have you any reason to believe that Hansard's Debates are now suspected?—Nobody would pay any attention to what differed materially from that which was in print in the papers.

654. Now, as regards another point, it is a difficulty, we have been told, to report from the back seats, and in that I understand you to agree?—Yes.

655. Assuming more room to be wanted, we must look, then, to the front row. I observe that each paper, or the majority of the papers have, besides the reporter, a summary writer?—Not each paper, I believe; I think there are only two or three that have that, but I do not know.

656. Now, could not the summary writers do their work in the back seats, supposing room were wanted in the front seats?—Certainly they could.

657. Conveniently for themselves and for the work they have to do?—No, not so conveniently.

658. But could the work which they have to do be done conveniently in the back part?—I think it could be done, but not so conveniently.

659. I do not say, "as conveniently;" I say, "conveniently"?—There are degrees of convenience, and I think it could not be done so conveniently.

660. If there are two places, and one is better than the other, it is necessarily more convenient; but I ask whether the work of a summary writer could be done conveniently in the back row; I do not say as conveniently as in the front row, but, assuming that you want room in the front row, could the work of the summary writer be done in the back row?—It could be done.

661. And supposing room were wanted in the front row, do you see any objection to the London papers, with perhaps one or two exceptions, entering into the same kind of arrangement as the provincial papers; that is to say, employing one association to report for them and to furnish them with reports?—I can see no objection, because I am not interested in it at all. If the proprietor of a London paper thinks he can get it done as well and more economically in that way, he will resort to it.

662. But you see no difficulty in the working of the system?—No, I imagine there is none, if they take notes for country papers. They are duplicates; it is done by a style and black paper; they could make a dozen copies, I suppose, as easily as one.

663. And, perhaps, there would be less difficulty now than there used to be, because the reports of speeches are in general much shorter than they used to be in the newspapers generally?—I do not think they are much shorter.

664. Except in two papers, are they not shorter?—They are in the penny papers considerably shorter.

665. And, therefore, the difficulty of entering into any arrangement of that kind would be rather lessened, because the same importance is not attached to the report of Parliamentary speeches?—Yes.

666. Mr. Cowen.] In addition to being a reporter for the "Times," or the director of the reporting staff of the "Times," I think you publish a Parliamentary record of your own?—Yes.

667. How long have you published that record?—I was speaking to Mr. Hansard this morning, and I think he said it was about 20 years.

668. Did you not begin it in 1801?—I think it was about that time.

669. Have you continued it uninterruptedly since that time?—Yes, I continued it at my own cost seriously for a great many years, and at last they gave me a subvention; I said I would give it up, and then the Government found in the public offices that they could not get on without it; they

they had then to search through the "Times," to find out what had been done; and so they gave me a subvention. I have trebled the expense, but I get no more; and I should never have alluded to the subject if you had not asked me the question. I am quite satisfied; I have very little from it; I think the printer's bill last year was 220 l. (the printing is a complicated affair), and there are other expenses which come to about 60 l.; so that out of the 400 l. I had 120 l. for all my labour.

670. Then I understand you to say that you get a subvention from the Government of 400 l. a year for publishing this publication?—Yes.

671. The Government in giving you that subvention did not stipulate as they did with Mr. Hansard for the supplying of a certain number of copies to the Government offices, did they?—Yes, I do supply all the Government offices, and whenever they want more they are supplied.

672. Mr. Hansard guarantees to supply 120 copies of his publication at a given price, namely, five guineas for the set; is there any such engagement with you?—No, I should think that would be somewhere about the number that I supply, but I have a fixed sum.

673. And the 400 l. covers the cost of that supply as well?—It covers everything.

674. What is the price at which the publication is sold?—It is a subscription of 1 l. 10 s.; there are a few subscribers, for I need not say, looking to the general distaste there is for all Parliamentary matter, that although that record is so convenient, as I dare say you yourself will admit, there are very few subscribers.

675. I take it then that the Government get a supply of these to all the offices, and that they give in return to you a subvention of 400 l. a year?—Four hundred pounds.

676. And you have continued that since 1861 with, I think, a year or two's exception?—I think I carried it on unaided for about five years; I then said that I could not do it any more; and then there was a great stir among Members and Peers; and such men as Lord Eversley and Mr. Bouverie, who understand the nature of the work, went to the Government and said, "Well, if you give a subvention to Hansard, surely here is a thing we want to look at every morning almost," and I publish it weekly now for that reason; that is an additional expense; I just make about 120 l.; that is all I get out of the 400 l.

677. There is not a large sale for it, you say?—Certainly not.

678. The demand for it would not be large; it would only be confined to a limited number?—Yes; confined to Parliamentary men of business.

679. Do you think that now the Parliamentary reports are not so much read as they used to be in your early days?—No; there is no time for it. Ever since railways were introduced, which we were told were to save us time, we have never had any, it seems to me; there are so many claims upon one's attention.

680. Your opinion is that the Parliamentary reports are of small value to an ordinary daily paper?—I think so; at such length I rather think they are prejudicial.

681. But you are aware that some of the papers having the largest circulation often give the shortest reports, and that bears out your opinion, I suppose?—I believe that is the case.

682. Do you know that there have been charges made in the House of Commons by Members about the inaccuracy of the reports, and their incompleteness and their unfairness; does your experience warrant such an accusation?—Not as to unfairness; but the others, of course, there must always be some ground for, in particular cases.

683. Newspapers now have to go to press much earlier than they had?—Yes.

684. Does that affect the length of the reports?—Yes, necessarily. I have in past days been writing at the "Times" office at half-past eight in the morning; but now we go to press, I think, at two o'clock; somewhere about that time, or very soon after, with a portion of the publication.

685. Have you any knowledge of the length of time that the House sat after midnight during these last two Sessions?—It has sat during the last two Sessions very frequently after midnight, on account of those prolonged debates in which so many divisions occurred, to a very late hour.

686. According to a report got by Sir Charles Forster the House sat 131½ hours after midnight in 1876, and 153 hours and 45 minutes of midnight last Session. Now supposing we may take it that Members speak from three-and-a-half to four columns an hour, there would have been spoken in these hours, the number of hours that they sat after midnight last year and the year before, about 1,000 columns of the "Times"?—It is dreadful to contemplate, but I suppose it is so; I cannot calculate figures freely.

687. Are you aware then of this, that in the "Times" that 1,000 columns of matter was compressed into 20 columns?—No, I am not aware of that.

688. Would you think that a fair report of the proceedings?—Yes, I have no doubt it was a fair report.

689. Twenty columns of fair report of the 1,000?—Yes.

690. Are you aware that in the discussions after midnight important constitutional changes have been made; we had it in evidence from Mr. Hansard that the change which gave the right of voting to women in municipal elections was made at two or three o'clock in the morning, and that no record whatever of it was in the papers?—I was not aware of that, and I did not hear that evidence of Mr. Hansard; but there would be a record of it in the Votes.

691. No reference was made in the papers even to the fact that a Bill had passed, Mr. Hansard informed us?—I was not aware of that.

692. You are also aware, probably, that a change took place in the mode of registering newspapers during the period of the last Government?—No.

693. You are not aware then that that change which took place in the registering of newspapers was made between two and three o'clock in the morning, and that no record was taken of it by the papers?—No, I was not aware of that.

694. Then your opinion generally would be as to the proceedings that take place after midnight that they are comparatively unimportant, and that although 1,000 columns were spoken in these last two years, 20 columns were an ample record of them?—Yes; if they had been important there would have been more; and with regard to the two instances which you give, I am not aware of them, but I dare say there was good reason for it; some accidental circumstance which I could explain, if I referred to the Votes and to the newspapers.

695. We have it in evidence from Mr. Hansard, and also from Captain Gosset, that the reporters for the London daily press supplement their labours by making special reports for the provincial press?—I dare say they do; in fact, though I have no positive evidence of it, I have no doubt from what I observe that that is the case; that they send reports to the Irish papers, and to the Scotch papers, and to English papers.

696. You have no knowledge of it?—No, I have no knowledge; if such a thing were done by members of my corps I should stop it; I am speaking of other papers, and what I observe of other reporters.

697. Then do I rightly understand you to say that you would stop any reporter on the "Times" reporting for a provincial paper, if you knew it?—Certainly; these gentlemen are engaged to report for the "Times," not to give their services to other papers.

698. But you did not hear, probably, the evidence given on the last day the Committee sat?—I heard some of it.

699. One of the reasons given for the satisfactory state of the gallery was, that the London reporters were permitted, and not only permitted, to report, but did largely report for the provincial press?—Yes, they do; I said I had no doubt of that, although I have no positive evidence of it; it is not my business, you know, to seek for that evidence.

700. Still you know that they do, and you think it is an objectionable practice?—No, if the proprietors do not mind it, I see nothing objectionable in it; and it is evident that the proprietors do not mind it.

701. You do not think that it conflicts with the discharge of their duty to the London newspapers, do you?—I take it for granted that it does not, otherwise they would not do it.

702. The first conditions of good reporting I take to be absolute impartiality and accuracy?—Yes, impartiality and accuracy.

703. Do you not think that one of these conditions, at least, is set aside in the reporting of Parliamentary debates by the political and more or less partisan press?—No, I am sure it is not.

704. Has

704. Has political bias nothing whatever to do with the length of the reports that a paper gives to a Member?—No; I can only speak for the "Times"; of course I do not observe other papers so closely, because I have no reason for doing so. If I saw a report at great length in another paper, I might imagine that the Member had supplied it; I should make no further remark.

705. You do not think that a Liberal paper will report a Liberal Member at greater length than a Conservative, and that a Conservative paper will report a Conservative Member at greater length than a Liberal; is it not within your knowledge that such has been the case?—I daresay it is within my knowledge, but I cannot call a case to mind; but at the same time I must say, that in a Conservative paper I sometimes see a report of the Liberal Members given at greater length than some of the Conservative Members.

706. The point I wish to bring out is this: you do not think that the fact of the agency through which these reports appear being of a political character affects the fairness of the report?—I think not; there may be the political feeling of the reporter himself, but then the editor of the paper would know nothing of that.

707. The editor of the paper never supervises the reports?—No.

708. In making a report of a debate, you have reference solely to the interests of the readers?—Yes.

709. You report what in your judgment the public want?—What we think of most interest.

710. It is what the public want that you are concerned with?—Not that exactly, because I think a great deal, if I were to look at it in that light, should be omitted. If there is a speaker bringing forward a question upon which he is well informed, from his position in life, I should say to the reporter, "This gentleman understands this subject; now give a good account of him, but clear; do not leave out passages, but give a good descriptive account of his argument; let it read flowingly;" that is in substance my general advice.

711. Your object is to present before the readers of the paper such an account as would be acceptable to them; you have no regard whatever to the idea of Parliament possessing your reports as a record of their transactions?—Yes, I say that they are given at too great a length, and I cannot imagine why it is done by the "Times," except there is some feeling of honour and from being long associated with the Legislature, because you will observe that all other papers have found it their interest to abridge the reports greatly.

712. Then I take it that your evidence is this, that you report Ministers and ex-Ministers at length and fully?—Generally.

713. And that the ordinary body of Members of Parliament, about 600 out of the 658, come in for condensed reports, or mere summaries, according to the space that you have at your command?—There are not 100 who ever speak in a Parliament; it is not the 600 who are condensed; they never speak, and therefore they cannot be condensed or dealt with at all.

714. I am speaking broadly of the number; in estimating the amount of space that you give to these, whatever they may be, 30, 40 or 600, just as you like to call them, it is your judgment of the importance of the man that regulates the report?—To some extent.

715. It is not, therefore, a full report of what takes place; but it is the reporter's estimate of the man's influence, ability or character?—It necessarily cannot be a full report, because that would fill the paper.

716. Are you aware that a number of Members of Parliament that have not been in office, that are not in office, and that never expect to be in office, have in many instances complained of the imperfect and unfair manner in which they have been reported?—No, I never heard of such a thing.

717. You never heard a complaint from Mr. Cobden of that kind?—I came across some correspondence with Mr. Cobden the other day, and there was a complaint, but he was entirely wrong, as he was himself satisfied that he was; I showed him that he was, and I have his letters.

718. You never heard of a complaint from Mr. O'Connell?—Yes; and he was unfairly dealt with, but not in the House; it occurred out of doors.

719. Did not Mr. O'Connell move that the reporters be excluded?—I have no doubt he did, and he was very severe in his remarks. I did not know at the time,

Mr. G. Rose.
1 July 1878.

time, but I did know subsequently, that] he was justified in those remarks, although they should not have been applied to a class, when it was owing to the misconduct of an individual, a countryman of his own too.

720. You never heard of Mr. John Stuart Mill making a like complaint?—No.

721. Nor of Mr. Joseph Hume doing so?—Mr. Hume, I dare say, would complain often; but he was a wretched speaker, and I dare say if he was not given as he thought verbatim, although he might appear to more advantage in the newspaper, he would not be satisfied.

722. Your opinion of Mr. Hume was not of a very elevated character, and therefore in giving a report you would condense what he said, I suppose?—No, he was given at immense length, unfortunately.

723. But how was it that he complained, then?—I take it for granted that he complained, if you say so, with reference to some particular occasion; he could not complain generally, or else he would have been a most ungrateful person.

724. Are you not aware that the present Prime Minister made a like complaint at the commencement of his career?—No.

725. You do not recollect a speech in which Lord Beaconsfield declared that it was the greatest credit to be a member of the press?—No.

726. The point I wish to fasten your mind upon is this; I take it that the reports that appear of independent Members, such as Mr. Hume, Mr. O'Connell, Mr. Cobden, and Mr. Mill, and others who are not official or ex-official Members, are necessarily condensed, and condensed according to the estimation of the reporter of their worth?—Mr. Mill was given at great length, and he would have been given at greater length except for an accident.

727. In your opinion, therefore, the "Times" report is as full as the public require, and as much as the Members of Parliament, considering the value of their speeches, deserve?—I do not like to say "deserve." I have the greatest respect for the House and for individual Members; I know many of them, and I should be sorry to use a word which was disrespectful. I think the reports are as long as need be; rather longer than I would like them to be, and I think the way in which they are given is advantageous to the Members of the House.

728. You know the proceedings of Friday last?—Yes.

729. The House of Commons sat five hours, and, according to the ordinary speaking power of a Member, they would have talked about 16 or 18 columns?—Yes.

730. That 16 or 18 columns in Saturday's "Times" is compressed into a column and three-quarters or nearly two columns?—Yes.

731. You think that is quite sufficient?—Was not that in Committee on the Highways Bill?

732. Going into Committee and in Committee?—You will see that the discussion was of a purely technical nature, and it is impossible to give that; it would be repetition over and over again. It is the decision in Committee that people want; a Member moves an amendment to omit so-and-so, and to insert so many words in place of it; what is material is that he states his opinion: "I think this would be beneficial for this reason," and, beyond that, it is quite unnecessary to go; the division is the thing.

733. The entire space in Committee a printer would describe as the length of three sticks; the space taken up by the House going into Committee is a column and a quarter?—That will be a discussion of a more general nature then; but when you get into Committee and go into details, the discussion possesses no interest beyond the moment.

734. From a journalistic point of view, your opinion is that there was a sufficient amount of space given on Friday to the discussion?—I think from every point of view.

735. I am asking you now simply from a journalistic point of view?—Quite sufficient.

736. Does it occur to you that it may be quite sufficient for a newspaper report and for a general report, and yet it may not be sufficient for the House of Commons as a source of reference, or a record of their transactions?—I cannot conceive what use it can be to the House to have a fuller report of such a matter.

737. You

737. You think it would be no use to have a fuller report of a discussion in Committee, in which at least an hour and a half is compressed into six inches of space?—No, you have the Votes, if there is any doubt, which will inform you of the result; the result is the thing.

738. This is a discussion about the Highways Bill: it is interesting to a large section of the public outside, and is it possible for anyone to give a report of proceedings which last over an hour and a half in six inches of space?—I think that the question would be discussed in the preliminary stage before going into Committee; in all probability the point which was discussed in Committee would be discussed then.

739. Now, we will take the report Mr. Hansard gave us of the Factories Bill; this is a Bill; this a full report, according to Mr. Hansard's new arrangement, and it would have made if put into the "Times" something like 60 columns, but you compressed the same report in Committee in the "Times" to about eight or nine; this Bill affects seriously the management of factories and workshops in manufacturing districts; do you think that eight or nine columns, instead of 60, is sufficient to acquaint the people interested in that question with what Parliament is doing so far as their interests are concerned?—Yes, they want to know the result only; it is done; what is the use now of reading all that was said for or against? the thing is settled.

740. Of course, that is your opinion; I am only asking for your practice?—That is my opinion.

741. Mr. Hanbury Tracy cited some facts to which I wish to call your attention; on 21st February 1877, a discussion took place in Parliament which extended to 12 columns; if all the talking had been reported it would have extended to 16, but you gave 12; that was on one day; the next day a discussion took place, the report extended to 30 columns, and you gave three and a half; in your judgment, did the three-and-a-half columns report as accurately and as fairly describe what took place as the 12 columns report did the day before?—I have no doubt it did, but I do not know what the subject was; I take it, from your statement, that the subject was of that nature that the "Times" was fully justified in giving only that amount of report.

742. Is it not the fact that it very often happens when a scene, as it is called in newspaper phraseology, takes place in the House of Commons, you report that with great minuteness?—Yes.

743. But a sober statement of a Member afterwards compressed into a few lines?—That depends upon who the Member is and the matter.

744. Do you never elaborate a little personal encounter and pass over more solid discussions?—Doubtless that is always interesting; that is a matter not only interesting to the Members (you manifest that at the time), but it is interesting to outsiders. Anything of a personal character is sure to attract attention.

745. Mr. Hansard gave it as his evidence, after 40 years' experience, that the reporting of the discussions on Wednesdays, both in the press and in his own publication, was a blot upon the system, and that there is only about one-seventh reported of what takes place on Wednesday; is that your opinion?—No; it does not coincide with Mr. Hansard's; my opinion is that sufficient is given.

746. That one-seventh of what is said on Wednesdays is sufficient?—I would not like to be bound by that figure; it depends upon the matter. Now I referred by accident to what took place on last Wednesday; I think Sir Wilfrid Lawson had two columns; it was readable matter and cleverly done; but if a man will not speak well why should his speech be given at great length? No person is interested in it except himself, perhaps, and his immediate friends.

747. But it is really your judgment of what is interesting?—Yes, exactly.

748. Now, suppose a Member of Parliament speaks for 30 minutes; in an ordinary way that would amount to a column and a-half of the newspaper; but supposing you compress that column and a-half into 30 lines, do you think that it would be possible to give in those 30 lines a fair statement of the Member's opinions?—I do not know who the Member may be. If he is a very able man, full of information and illustration at hand, I do not think that 30 lines, if he spoke for half-an-hour and the subject was interesting, would give a sufficient account.

749. But the reporter goes out of the seat, and you say the terms are a

quarter

Mr. C. Ross.
1 July 1878.

quarter of an hour sometimes, and ultimately come to ten minutes, five minutes, and two or three minutes?—Yes.

750. Now, taking the case of a Member who spoke half-an-hour, two reporters would have to report 30 lines; would it be possible for these two reporters to compress into 15 lines apiece a fair synopsis of what the Member said?—If it was a very able speech I do not think it would, but it all depends upon that. I take it that it was not so in the actual case mentioned.

751. Would it not, in your opinion, be a much fairer thing to the speaker not to report him at all, but simply to give a summary?—He would be very sorry.

752. That is your experience, not mine; I should say that a Member would be better satisfied with a summary of what he says if that is to be compressed into that space rather than report so much curtailed; now, passing to another question, you do not hear well in the gallery?—Yes, pretty well.

753. You say that leader writers come and sit behind you?—I did not know the fact, but I heard the Serjeant say so; I did not know that there were any leader writers that came in; there are none for the "Times."

754. Then do these gentlemen who come and sit behind the reporters engage necessarily in conversation?—They do sometimes.

755. And is not that a source of discomfort to the reporters?—Generally, when there is anything decidedly important going on, silence prevails; they like to hear, themselves, what is going on.

756. Do you not think that it would improve the provincial papers if each of them had simply one box to themselves in the gallery, such as those boxes which are now set aside for the summary writers, and they had liberty to enter when they chose?—It would be physically impossible; it could not be done. If you admit the provincial papers, you must admit all; we will not say anything about weekly papers, but we will say daily papers; then it would be, I believe, somewhere about 150. It is impossible; and you could not say that each-and-such a provincial paper shall come in, because another provincial paper will immediately say, "Why my paper is of much greater importance than that one; I must come in also." You could not draw a line.

757. I understood you to say that you did not profess to report the language of a speaker, except in special instances?—Yes.

758. That it was simply his ideas and his facts that you reported, not the language?—That is what I wish done. It is not sufficiently followed.

759. Then you report the language of some speakers?—Yes, pretty fully.

760. Is that because in your judgment the language is worth retaining?—No, but it saves trouble to the reporter. If he has got a full note, it saves trouble to copy the words.

761. Do you report in the House of Lords as well?—Yes.

762. Is not there a great complaint of the accommodation and the hearing there?—Yes, you do not hear well in the House of Lords.

763. Is it worse in the House of Lords than in the House of Commons?—Yes, much. I attribute that to the fact that in the House of Lords there is a Stranger's Gallery open behind the Reporters' Gallery, and the voice passes over. In the House of Commons there is a partition behind the back seats, and that retains the sound.

764. I take it that your opinion is, that the present arrangement is much better than it used to be, so far as the comfort and the convenience of the reporters are concerned; that the record that appears in the daily papers is, in your judgment, ample, and that any attempt to establish an official system of reporting would be detrimental to the House of Commons, and, I suppose, generally to the country; that is your opinion?—I think so.

765. The fact is, your notion is that the reports which appear in the "Times" are, if not perfect, as nearly perfect as can be?—Yes; only I think they are too full.

766. *Mr. Forster.*] Do you think that the reports in the "Times" now take up a larger proportion of the newspaper than they did 10 or 15 years ago?—No, I do not think, as a rule, that they are so long; I do not think they occupy quite as much space.

767. Do you mean that the whole account of the Parliamentary debates does not occupy as much proportionate space as it did 15 years ago?—I think not quite; that

that is speaking from my general impression; I have not referred at all so as to be able to form an accurate estimate.

768. Do you think there is much difference?—No, I do not think there is much; I think a great deal depends upon the nature of the debate.

769. But take a really important debate?—Then I think it is reported as fully as it used to be.

770. And that the report of such a debate would be as long as it used to be, you think?—Yes.

771. Now, I do not know whether you intended to give the impression which you did give, that Ministers and ex-Ministers generally are more fully reported than others?—As a rule, they are.

772. But that does not apply, does it, to several men who have obtained the attention of the country, and of Parliament; for instance, I suppose Mr. Bright was reported as fully before he went into office as he was afterwards?—I cannot say; but he made better speeches before he was in office. When in office a Member is confined to a particular subject; when he is in opposition he chooses his own subject.

773. I suppose you also report according to the importance of the subject, and the acquaintance that the Member has with it?—Yes.

774. For instance, allusion has been made to last Friday; there was a debate last Thursday, and Mr. Read is reported, perhaps, more fully than other Members?—Yes.

775. I suppose that would not be from the fact that he happened to be in office once, but because he was so well acquainted with the subject?—So well acquainted with the subject, and looked at as the representative of a large class of opinions.

776. If Sir Wilfrid Lawson had been in office, he would not have got a fuller report than he did last Wednesday, I suppose?—No, he could not have made that speech in office. The reason for Mr. Bright's being reported so fully is, that he speaks so very correctly, and his language is so apt.

777. I will not take present Members, but I suppose you report the language of a speaker according to the interest that the public would generally take in that language?—And in the subject.

778. For instance, during the latter part of Mr. Cobden's life, when everybody was very anxious to know the exact words which he used, you would give Mr. Cobden's words as much as you could?—Mr. Cobden was always given very fully.

779. The "Times" upon the whole, taking one day with another, gives a longer report than any other paper, does it not?—Yes, considerably.

780. Have you at all had any opportunity of comparing the report given in the "Times" with that given in the Continental or American newspapers?—Do you mean the report of the same debate?

781. No; comparing the report that is given of a Parliamentary debate in the "Times," and the report given in the "Journal des Débats" of the debates in the Chamber of Deputies; you have never compared them, perhaps?—No.

782. You were connected with the "Times," when interesting debates used to last very much longer than they do now; up to four o'clock in the morning?—Yes, at the earlier period, a long time ago; before the Reform Bill passed.

783. In those very long and interesting debates, were they all reported in the "Times" that appeared the next morning, or were some of them put off to the following day?—Never; they were always reported in the "Times" of the following morning; but there was no reason for keeping them back; there were no railways then.

784. When a debate lasted till four o'clock in the morning, when did the "Times" come out?—I remember that on the second reading of the Reform Bill in the House of Lords, I was writing at the "Times" Office at half-past eight in the morning; the paper would probably be out about 12. There was no post to go out of London till evening.

785. So great was the interest in Parliamentary debates, and in that debate, that the "Times" was aware that its readers would prefer waiting till 12 or one o'clock, in order to get a full report, to its appearing early in the morning?—No, that was the system of business; there was no reason for not waiting for it at, I suppose, they would have waited for a description of a great fire or any other stirring event.

786. I do not know whether you have exactly stated what is the last hour at which

Mr. C. Ross
1 July 1878.

which the "Times" can now receive any Parliamentary report?—No, I cannot speak with certainty, but I think they could take it up to two o'clock. If something which I know has been in contemplation should be perfected, I mean communication by electricity or by a telephone, they could take it much later than that.

787. But taking the present state of things, what do you mean by the statement that they can take a report up to two o'clock: what is the last moment at which that speech can have been spoken?—The last copy has to be sent to the office by that time, the speaking, we will say, may terminate at half-past one; it may go on a little later, but as the reporters have then such short turns, it is not so material; they would take their two minutes or two and a-half minutes and write it out, and then the copy is conveyed by a messenger in a cab to the office.

788. Then, practically, no speech can be reported that is delivered after half-past one?—That is a very late hour; there could not be much then.

789. After what hour cannot a speech be conveniently reported?—I think you cannot be conveniently reported after one.

790. With regard to one particular instance that was mentioned, of the municipal vote being given to women late at night, you do not happen to remember the case, do you?—No; there are so many events of the same kind passing every day, that it is impossible to remember everything.

791. Now you have given us your opinion, and you have expressed it very clearly, that you do not think that an official report would be of much use either to the public or to Members of the House of Commons; but I want to ask you what effect you think an official report would have upon the present reporting in the "Times;" do you think that if there was an official report published a day or two afterwards (and I suppose it could not be published the next morning), it would have any effect whatever upon the present amount of reporting in the "Times"?—I do think so; I can only judge from my own feelings; if I were the proprietor of the "Times," and I found that there was a sort of authorised publication set up, I would say, "I will not give reports as fully as I have done; it is not to my interest, but against my interest, and I will abridge, and by doing so I fear I shall act prejudicially to the interests of Members, but I must now look after my own interests."

792. I think you have stated it as your opinion that no large amount of the public would take in this paper containing an official report, or read it?—I do not think any one would.

793. Then, in so far as the "Times" is now influenced by its desire to supply its readers with what they want, it would not be affected by the appearance of this official report, because its readers would ignore this official report, and pay no attention to it?—Exactly.

794. That would rather show that the report, whether it did good or harm (and you think it would do very little good, or no good at all), would not have any effect upon the circulation of the "Times"?—Not any.

795. Then would not the "Times" go on reporting just the same as it does now?—I confess I cannot understand why the "Times" does give such full reports; I know that they lose a great deal of money, I should think at least 20,000 £ a year, by doing so; but it has come down; it is a traditional custom, if one may apply those words, and they feel it probably, as I said before (and I cannot find any other phrase for it), a point of honour to maintain this reputation for giving full reports.

796. I suppose you have not compared specially upon anything like an important night, the reports in two other newspapers, the "Standard" and the "Morning Post," with that in the "Times"?—I always look at them.

797. Have you not observed that they are not very different in length from the "Times" report?—They are greatly different.

798. The improvement that you would make in reporting would be that you would condense more?—Yes.

799. And omit less?—Omit less; omit unnecessary words, but give a neat, readable account of a man's argument.

800. I suppose from your answers that you would be inclined to assert that there is a disadvantage now in the necessity of shortening a speech, as is being done very often, by an omission which takes out an important bit of argument,

or

or an important fact?—But, of course, that is almost necessarily the case with these short turns.

801. Do you not find that one of the difficulties you have in getting good reports, a difficulty which is inherent in the matter itself, is, that it is easier to report a question of general interest than it is one of special detail?—Yes.

802. And that there is much more danger of a reporter, however able he is, not being fully aware of the proportionate importance of an argument, or of a fact?—Yes.

803. And do you think that that would be better, or worse, guarded against by going on the principle of condensation or of omission?—I think it would be better guarded against.

804. You may say that you think the "Times" loses very largely by its reports; do you think that fewer people take in the "Times" in consequence of the reports?—No, the "Times" must be taken in by those who take it in, but they would be much more satisfied, I think, if the reports were shorter.

805. Then their satisfaction is one thing, the money lost to the "Times" is another?—There can be no doubt about the money loss.

806. But when you speak of a probable loss to the "Times," on account of their reporting the debates so fully, of 30,000 l. a year, is it that you think a great many more people would take in the "Times"?—No, but I think they would save money by having more room for advertisements. I take the advertisements, at a rough estimate, to be 20 l. a column; that is one source.

807. You think that money would be got by putting advertisements in place of speeches?—And money would be saved by using matter which is paid for, which comes up from the country, from all parts, from England, Scotland, Ireland, and abroad, and is cast aside because of the length of the debate.

808. I do not suppose you are at all confident that that matter that was paid for would bring more readers if it was put in?—Yes, nobody reads debates; everybody reads the other.

809. But do you think that this matter which is paid for and comes up would, if inserted in the place of the speeches, gain the "Times" more readers?—That I cannot tell; I think the "Times" has got readers enough.

810. Because, if it did not, there would be no gain to the "Times," would there?—Yes, they would not pay for the matter without using it; there would be something in that.

811. But if the "Times" chooses to pay for matter which it does not use, there is a loss in doing that; but it would not gain anything if it put that matter in and got nothing by it?—There would be no positive gain except in the general character of the paper.

812. Sir *Henry Drummond Wolff*.] I understood you to say some time ago that you thought the necessity of an official report was obviated by the very full reports there are in the "Times"?—Yes.

813. Now, supposing that the "Times" took the view that you take at present, that the reports are too full, and that the proprietors of the "Times" thought it right to abridge them, do not you think that then there would be some ground for having official reports?—No, I do not; I think that the great object which should be kept in view is to give a condensed account of the argument; of the opinions and the reasons for the opinions of the particular speakers; and I think that all enlargement and all tendency that way is a misfortune. Now, there is a very high authority, one of our greatest Speakers, Lord Eversley, and that is the opinion which he expressed to me when he was speaking of my little book of the Debates; and there is another man whose judgment I have the highest admiration of, Sir George Lewis; that was his opinion, also expressed to me. He said that the "Times" report was everything, except that it was too full; he took up a paper and said, "Here is an application from Hansard." Then we talked about that. I need not say anything about that; but he said, "As long as they keep to the 'Times' reports, well, we know what we are about; but when the speeches are supplied, when they are revised, then of course we are at the mercy of each individual." That was his opinion; and he said, "My opinion is that we should go in another direction; and it was that which gave me the hint for my little work.

814. You are in favour of condensation, and many of the newspapers do condense the reports; but what I have observed is this, that according to the ideas

H

ideas of the reporters of the different papers, so they seize rather upon certain arguments of a speaker, and therefore one paper, we will say the "Daily News," has one set of arguments he makes use of, and the "Daily Telegraph" another set; do you not think that in the present day, when in the country, constituents and others look very closely into what their Members do, it would be desirable that a Member should have some authentic record of what he had said, so that he could say that is what I did say, good or bad; whereas now he has not the opportunity of explaining away a misinterpretation or a misapprehension taken from a partial report; I do not mean purposely, but practically partial?—You are now making it a personal question. I think if the Member is so interested in the matter he might send his speech to Hansard; he has that opportunity now, or he might, as I believe some Members do, have it sent by one of the telegraphic agencies to the newspaper in which he wishes it to appear.

815. But then in that case, supposing he did that, his constituents would not read Hansard perhaps, and as you just now said, if a man supplied his own speech to Hansard, he might put into it afterwards some argument which he forgot to make use of, so that it would not be authentic?—Yes, that is so.

816. Whereas an authentic report, taken by official reporters, would prevent his putting anything in that he had not said?—This is a question on which I can only give my opinion; but there are very few Members—according to my rough calculation, there are not above 30 Members who speak very frequently.

817. The honourable Member for Newcastle alluded to the discussion on the Highways Bill; that is a thing in which to many Members, county Members and others, it is of enormous importance that they should not be misinterpreted in their own county as to what they said on a question of that kind?—Doubtless.

818. It turns out that that discussion was very much abbreviated in the "Times"; that might do a considerable injury to a man, because this "Times" report could be read, and people do not call upon him to make explanations, but the country papers would write articles upon him, and he might be denounced by his opponents for having voted in a particular way, without the reasons of his voting having been given?—That is a personal question again; that must apply to the vast majority of the House on any question. Suppose 30 present Members take part in a debate, 400 may vote on it.

819. But then the 380 who did not speak would be able to rest their reason for voting upon some particular speech that was given; "Mr. Read or Mr. Somebody else has said so-and-so, and therefore I voted for this clause;" whereas if the report is so compressed that there are no reasons given, they have no justification for their vote?—But if an elector calls upon a Member to state why he voted, could he not state it then just as easily as saying, "I agreed with Mr. Read;" could he not say, "Mr. Read showed so-and-so."

820. He would do so in canvassing; but I am talking of the interpretation that might be put upon his conduct behind his back without its being challenged, whereas if there was an official report the public would say, "It is evident that a certain number of Members have been influenced by a certain speech"?—I think if any Member felt that it was of importance, he would write to one of his chief supporters in the town or county, and say, "I voted so-and-so, because I was satisfied that, as shown by Mr. So-and-so, the result would be such-and-such."

821. You do not think that the reasons I have now brought forward are sufficient for having an official report?—No; it is the reason that has always been urged, but it is a reason in the interest of individuals, not in the interest of the whole House.

822. *Chairman.*] You must have had from your very great experience complaints made to you from time to time by Members?—Yes.

823. Have they been frequent upon the point which the honourable Member for Christchurch has referred to as to misrepresentation or omission?—No, never as to misrepresentation, and not frequent as to omission; and whenever that is the case there is always an explanation put in at the end of the debate in the "Times."

824. But the requests you have had for the correction of the general impressions conveyed by a report of a speech are rare?—Very.

825. Are they always complied with, or almost always?—They are complied with always, I think.

826. So

826. So that the serious objections on the part of Members to the drift of their observations as conveyed by the "Times," are gauged by the number of letters which have appeared in the newspaper at the end of the report?—Yes.

827. Amounting to, perhaps, one or two in the course of a fortnight, is that the case?—Yes, one in 10 days or a fortnight.

828. Now you, probably, have given great consideration to this question of official reporting, having been in the House for a great many years?—Yes.

829. It has always been present to your mind?—Ever since it was first mooted; I forget the Member by whom it was mooted, but I know Mr. Stanley made a capital speech against it, and I thought of it then, and I have thought of it frequently since; and, never supposing it was likely to come to anything, I have stated some of the details of my plan frequently, but I would rather not do that now.

830. Supposing you were charged with the duty of preparing an official report for the House of Commons, would it be possible in your judgment to prepare such a report without condemnation?—Yes, it would be possible, but it would be most voluminous.

831. Would such a report as would be then prepared be the best representation of the transactions of the House of Commons?—No, I think there would be too much of it. Facts are the important things and the acts of a legislative assembly.

832. If you were changed into a person responsible for the production of such a report, with full authority to do that which you deemed to be best under the circumstances, what sort of a report would you produce?—If a full report were desired, and I undertook it, my own opinion, of course, would be nothing. My ambition has always been faithfully to discharge my duty, and it would be done then. But if my opinion were asked as to the best report, it would be, as I have already described it, a condensed report of the opinions and arguments by which they are supported, of each speaker.

833. Then left to you, with the credit of the House of Commons in your keeping, you would endeavour to present to the country a condensed report rather than a very full or verbatim report?—Yes.

834. Is that report the sort of report which you, in the discharge of your duty, have endeavoured to present?—Yes, but the reports are given more fully than in my opinion is desirable. There is rarely a sentence of an important speech, and sometimes very few words omitted.

835. Are you responsible for the selection of the occasions on which those very full reports are given?—Yes.

836. And are those occasions decided in your mind by the interest which exists out of doors with regard to the subject of debate?—Yes, to a great extent A reporter knows at once instinctively, as it were, whether a debate is important or not.

837. You remarked to the honourable Member for Christchurch just now, that there were only 36 Members who take an active part in the debates of the House?—I made a rough estimate yesterday when looking over the minutes; I stated then early in my evidence; about that was the result; that is deducting the Ministers and the ex-Ministers, and those who speak about six times, and those who speak about three times during the Session.

838. One of the honourable Members who has gone away, has put into my hands the report of the debate upon Mr. Hanbury Tracy's motion last year; he stated that in 1841 there were 231 Members who took a part in the proceedings of the House; in 1851 the number had gone up to 260; in 1861 the number had gone up to 300; in 1871 the number had gone up to 368; and in 1876 the number had increased to 383; is it the fact then that a larger number of Members take part in debates now than used to some time ago?—No; I dare-say that that is strictly accurate; but I daresay that a great many of those were cases in which a Member said a few words, or in which a Member put a question; that would make up the numbers, probably.

839. Mr. Walter.] Is it within your knowledge to what extent the most remarkable speakers within your time have been in the habit of preparing their speeches by writing them out beforehand?—No, I cannot say that to any extent.

840. Then, if not, do you think it desirable that the great speeches of men like

Mr. G. Ross.
1 July 1878.

like Peel, Canning, and the other great speakers whom we all remember, should be preserved fully, and in their own language as much as possible?—On important occasions I think it desirable that such men as those you have mentioned should be fully reported.

841. I mean that we should have publications of the speeches of all the distinguished Parliamentary orators?—Yes.

842. What I want to know is, if there is to be any full and accurate report, almost amounting to a verbatim report, even in an official report, in what way would you contemplate that the speeches of such eminent men should be preserved?—I would treat them in the same way; I would not preserve the mere language.

843. Should you not say that it is important that the mere language of any of Sir Robert Peel's speeches, delivered upon particular occasions, should be preserved?—Only of some, I think.

844. Do you remember Sir Robert Peel's speech in reply to Cobbett in 1833?—Yes.

845. Do you not think that that is a speech of which the language should be preserved as near as possible?—Yes, that is such a speech; there would be exceptions.

846. Would an accurate report of that speech be found in the columns of the "Times" (I have not referred to see); it is in Hansard?—I have no doubt there is a full report in the "Times."

847. Should you not say that any, we will say half-a-dozen of the most eminent Parliamentary speakers in your time could make an accurate collection of their speeches with very little alteration from the reports in the "Times?"—Undoubtedly; there they are.

848. In fact, Hansard has depended upon them?—Of course Hansard has done nothing but cut them out. An eminent statesman, a member of the Cabinet, some years ago asked me to be good enough to look over his speeches as he had not done, and he sent me one and it was printed ready for Hansard; I looked over it and saw that it was from the "Times," and I just made alterations in style, and if there was any particular error I corrected it; and then, in future, to avoid trouble and expense to Hansard, I used to take the newspaper report myself and put it on a sheet of paper and make marginal alterations.

849. Supposing a verbatim official report of the debates to be published, how many columns of Hansard, in your opinion, would they fill?—I should think as many more volumes as are now published, unless Members are in the habit of sending their speeches to Hansard; but I do not think that a great many Members do that; and if they do not do that, I should think that it would require nearly as many volumes more if the debates were all fully reported.

850. But it has been stated by an honourable Member that speeches which would occupy a thousand columns had been condensed into 90 : if that is anything like an accurate representation of the amount reported by the papers from which alone Hansard derives his report, how many would be the volumes of Hansard on such a calculation as that?—It is surprising to contemplate.

851. Would that, in your opinion, give a fair idea of the amount of debate which is lost to the public from the shortness of the reports in the London papers?—I do not think that anything material is lost to the public; it is the interest of the reporter, as well as his duty, to give every point that is material, and I frequently call his attention by touching him, when I see that something is coming.

852. I think you stated that you had a scheme of your own many years ago for obtaining an official report?—Yes.

853. In what way did you propose in that scheme to distribute the reports so provided?—I would rather not enter upon that scheme, if you will excuse me.

854. With reference to the evidence you gave just now as to what would be, or might be, the probable effect of any official system of reporting upon the future length of reports in the columns of the "Times," I understood you to say that you expressed merely your own opinion, and that you are not authorised to convey the ideas of the managers of the paper?—No, the opinions I have advanced are entirely my own.

855. Sir

855. *Sir Alexander Gordon.*] In answer to the honourable Member for Christchurch, you spoke about the ability of a Member to have his speech reported on certain occasions; you said he might send his speech to Hansard; I should like to ask your opinion as to how a Member is to act who rises in debate without any previous intention of speaking; a debate takes a turn on which he is thoroughly conversant with the subject; he rises and makes his speech; how is he to send that to Hansard?—By writing it out.

856. So that you contemplate that a Member is to have the trouble after having made a speech, to write it out in full, and send it to Hansard?—Members take more trouble than that. If a Member is interested in his speech, I think he will do that very readily; in fact, it is done.

857. *Lord Francis Hervey.*] I think you said that the "Times" loses considerably by its Parliamentary reports?—Yes, that is to say, that the "Times" would gain so much if they were shorter.

858. Or if they were altogether omitted?—No; people would like to know what takes place, but it is the facts that they wish to know.

859. I suppose it is the case that the other London daily papers also lose by their Parliamentary reports, in proportion as they are long and full?—No, they sacrifice the Parliamentary reports for the money.

860. But very few of the other papers have advertisements equal in amount to the "Times"?—But do not you see the expense the "Times" must go to in publishing a supplement? All that would be unnecessary, certainly to the same extent, if they could get in six columns more of advertisements each day.

861. You think it desirable, I suppose, in the public interest, that a report, speaking generally, equally full with that of the "Times" of our Parliamentary proceedings, should be published?—I think that it is too full; that is my own opinion.

862. Too full on some points you say, and not full enough on others; they leave out some things, you said, which should be put in, and they do not condense when they should?—I think a report would be more readable, and give everything that even Members desire to know if it were more condensed; but I have stated it so repeatedly that I do not like to say it again.

863. In the absence of anything like an official report, can we expect that the "Times" or any other newspaper, will continue to conduct any large part of their business at a loss?—I do not suppose that any newspaper conducts its business at a loss. The "Times" is a colossal fortune, and therefore they can afford to sacrifice 20,000 *l.*; it is not a question of a loss, but of less gain.

Mr. *John Lovell*, called in; and Examined.

864. *Chairman.*] You are, I think, the Manager of the Press Association?—I am.

865. How long have you occupied that position?—From the time the Association commenced business; I was appointed in August 1869.

866. Under what circumstances was the Press Association started?—It was started in consequence of the transfer of the telegraphs to the Government; prior to that period the Provincial Press was supplied by news collected in London as a centre, by what was called the Intelligence Department of the old telegraph companies; and when their business was transferred to the Government it was found necessary by the provincial papers to make arrangements to carry on, and, indeed, to improve the supply which they had previously obtained from the companies. A series of meetings was consequently held in Manchester and London, which led to the formation of the Press Association.

867. Does your association confine itself to reporting the proceedings in Parliament?—No; we supply foreign news, Stock Exchange news, general news, and news from all parts of the country.

868. So that, in point of fact, you supply the material out of which the newspaper is made?—We supply everything except the news local to the particular paper.

Mr. C. Ross.
1 July 1878.

Mr. J. Lovell.

869. And except the leading articles ?—Yes.

870. There are two other news agencies, are there not, in existence ?—There are.

871. What are they ?—The one is the Central Press, and the other the Central News; but there is an essential difference between those agencies and our association; our association, although in form a limited company, is in reality a co-operative association, and we, that is I and my colleagues who do the work, are really the London staff of the Provincial newspaper proprietors, who are members of the association; so that we are not a trading concern; we are debarred, indeed, by our articles from declaring a dividend; we are simply a co-operative association to supply ourselves with news, being our own consumers, although we supply newspaper proprietors, not members, and also news-rooms and exchanges, with our news. But the other agencies are in the nature rather of trading agencies for supplying news on their own account, and for their own profit.

872. Have you a discretion as to the quantity of Parliamentary news, the extent to which you give the reports, or is that prescribed in any form or shape to you ?—Primarily, I, who am responsible for doing the work, am governed by a committee of newspaper proprietors, who are appointed by the general body year by year. That committee decides generally what it will be necessary to supply ordinarily to the whole constituency of newspapers; but in addition to that each newspaper, gauging its own wants, writes to me, and I make arrangements to supply them with any matter additional to the ordinary report arranged for by the committee at the commencement of the Session: for instance, we have two ordinary reports; one of them averages a column and a half per day during the Session, and we have another shorter report, mostly for small weekly papers, averaging about a third of a column per day, on the day of publication, during the Session; those two summaries meet all wants that are common to the whole body of newspapers; but that does not meet the wants of the larger papers in England; it does not meet the wants of the Scotch papers; it does not meet the wants of the Irish papers; nor does it meet the local wants of some English papers. Therefore we have supplemental reports; for instance, we supplement the column and a half with some five or six columns to the Manchester, Liverpool, Birmingham, and other papers on occasions of great debates. We supplement the ordinary report sent to the Scotch papers; sometimes we have done as much as 17 or 20 columns on the occasion of Scotch debates. In the same manner we supplement the report to the Irish papers to a similar length when there are Irish debates on. And then, above and beyond all that, we receive instructions from each of the papers to report specially for them, the Members representing the localities in which they circulate. In fact, I have a list of Members whom we to report, not a list for publication, but a list of instructions which we print for the use of our reporters in the House (*handing in a copy of the same*).

873. Taking the letter A, Sir Thomas Acland is reported at full length in the "Morning News" whenever he speaks ?—Yes, that is so.

874. So that the "Morning News" of the next morning will have an accurate summary amounting to a column and a half of an ordinary debate ?—Yes.

875. And in substitution for the two or three lines which you would give in ordinary newspapers to Sir Thomas Acland's speech, you would give to the "Morning News" a full and complete report of Sir Thomas Acland's speech ?—Yes, and of any other Member on that list in the same way. I may explain that the list of papers at the head of that sheet is the list to which we supply the long supplemental reports on important occasions. All Ministerial speeches on bringing in Ministerial measures, all speeches of Members bringing in measures of their own, all debates on Bills and administrative questions, are sent, the length being according to our discretion, to all these papers.

876. I see there are newspapers here of different politics; does your report take any political character ?—Not at all; if the paper desires to give any political character to its report, it is done by ordering speeches of Conservative Members or Liberal Members in preference to others; but our ordinary report is colourless, for our association consists both of Conservative and Liberal newspapers, and of papers in the same town. We have, I may say, 179

newspaper

Mr. J. Lowe.
1 July 1878.

newspaper proprietors members of our association. In addition to that we supply 101 newspapers which are not members. In addition to that we supply 99 exchanges and news-rooms, which of course are not members.

877. So that the 200 people or institutions or newspapers, not members, pay you a certain price?—Yes; I may say that they pay 10 per cent. more than the members; we supply members at cost, and the others pay 10 per cent. more, and any profit which remains goes in reduction of the tariff to everybody all round. I may say, too, that that number very nearly exhausts the number of newspapers taking telegraphic news; because although it is true that there are between 130 and 140 daily newspapers in the country, it is not true that there are between 130 and 140 taking telegraphic Parliamentary news; there are not above 70 or 80 doing so.

878. Has there been any increase or decrease in the number of daily newspapers in the country taking Parliamentary news?—There has not been any large increase in the number, but a very large increase in the quantity taken since the telegraphs passed into the hands of the Government; because prior to that period, the provincial newspapers were restricted to the quantity sent them by the telegraph companies, excepting in those cases where the proprietors supplemented the companies' supply, by obtaining reports from gentlemen taking notes in the gallery for London papers; but even that supply was restricted, because the companies had a monopoly in the transmission, and there was not a great deal, in fact, transmitted beyond their own report.

879. I wish to know whether newspapers which formerly received, or have received during the last seven years Parliamentary information, have discontinued taking that Parliamentary information from your association?—No; on the contrary, several take the news now which did not formerly, especially the weekly papers; they could not obtain it formerly.

880. Is there an increased or a decreased interest in Parliamentary news in the country, judging from the demand?—That is a somewhat difficult question to answer; I do not think that there is a greater interest than there was; but I think that a want which was existing before was not properly supplied, and is better supplied now.

881. Have you been called upon to shorten or to increase the length of your reports generally; I suppose some intimation has been given to you?—We have been called upon to increase them in length since we came into existence.

882. Has the number of newspapers taking this full Parliamentary special information, increased or diminished?—It has increased.

883. Is the tendency now to increase?—I should say not; I think we have almost reached the maximum; but that of course is very difficult to say; I should almost think so.

884. Do the other agencies of which you speak supply the same sort of information, information of the same character?—One of them supplies information, I believe, somewhat similar; I do not know what the "Central Press" supplies; but the "Central News" supplies something similar to our Association.

885. Both more condensed and full reports?—I should think so; I do not think to anything like the same extent, but that you will hear from those proprietors themselves better than from me.

886. You heard, I daresay, the evidence given by Mr. Ross; have you any opinion as to the comparative value of verbatim and condensed reports, or full and condensed reports of speeches in Parliament?—Yes, I have an opinion, but I can hardly answer the question negatively or affirmatively without saying perhaps this: The newspapers, I imagine, exist, not for the purpose of doing what is called justice to honourable Members who may make speeches in the House of Commons, but to give the public what it requires (although, of course, in doing that they are bound to see that they do not do an honourable Member an injustice by misrepresenting him), so that, as far as we are concerned, our duty is rather to the public than to the House of Commons. On the other hand, I think it would be most desirable for Members to have something like an accurate historical record of the debates; that is another matter, but I do not think it would be of much use to the newspapers.

887. I understand you to say that an accurate historical account of what transpires in Parliament would, in your opinion, be valuable to Members, and perhaps

perhaps to Parliament and the country, but of very little use to the newspapers? —So I think; and I think it would be useful to Members, because I do not think that the exigencies of press work enable the press to give a proper historical record of Parliamentary proceedings. They supply what is necessary for the public from day to day.

888. Is your supplementary special report, or your full report given in Scotland, of the character described by Mr. Ross, as a full report, or is it a condensed report?—It consists of both; it is in parts a full report; we, for instance, in reporting a debate for a Scotch paper, should exercise precisely the same amount of control over the quantities as Mr. Ross exercises control over the quantities produced by his staff; we should not give each speaker verbatim, nor should we, on the other hand, condense each speaker; we should give what we consider the more important speeches fully; we should give the less important speeches less fully; and what we should consider important would be what we should consider the public would like to read.

889. Sir *Henry Drummond Wolff.*] And some you would not give at all, I suppose?—I do not think that would be the case; it is possible that one of the speeches might take the form of " After a few remarks by Mr. So-and-so," but I do not think that very often happens in what is called a long report.

890. *Chairman.*] The interest of the newspapers and your interest may be taken to represent, to a large extent, the interest which the public feel in these debates; is that so?—I should think so. I imagine that seeing that the success and reputation of a newspaper lies wholly in the amount of favour with which it is received by the public, the action of that knowledge upon the mind of the proprietor would lead him to produce exactly what he thinks the public would like to read, neither more nor less.

891. Are you of opinion that the machinery that at present exists is sufficient to supply the public with all that they require of the proceedings of Parliament?—I believe so, as far as the machinery goes; but I do not think that the accommodation afforded to that part of the machinery which comes more immediately under my purview has room enough to do its work so well as it might do it.

892. That I understand to be another question?—Yes; that is another matter.

893. But I understand you to say that, taking the reporting for the London press, and taking reporting for the country press, the agency which you control, and other agencies of a like character, you are of opinion that the demand of the public for information as to the proceedings of Parliament, is fully met?—I think so.

894. And that is your deliberate opinion?—That is my deliberate opinion.

895. With regard to the question of an official report, I daresay your attention has been called to the Return which was laid before Parliament in 1874 of the proceedings of other countries?—Yes.

896. Supposing that there was an official report of the proceedings in the House of Commons as there is of the French Assembly, a full report, a condensed report, and an analytical report, would those reports be available for the London newspapers, and for the country newspapers, through the agency which you control?—I do not think that the papers would be able to avail themselves of such a report. For one thing, the circumstances are so different in France and in England. For instance, there the whole report supplied to the newspapers in whatever form it is supplied, either long or short, ends at 3.45 p.m., and anything that remains over and above what is printed by that time is kept over till the next day; whereas here, as we know, the House of Commons scarcely yields anything which could be printed by that hour. So that, in any scheme for supplying an official report of the proceedings of this House to the public papers, it is not the printing of it that would have to be taken into consideration, but the sending of it by telegraph; that is to say, the getting it into the hands of the newspapers. Then, again, as to its suitability for the purpose of newspapers, one of two things must happen; either the House must allow the newspapers to have what they like, in which case the House, I presume, would be in very much the same position as the Press Association is now; or the House must give to the newspapers what it likes, and leave the newspapers to do with it as they please, in which case the telegraphs would

would be flooded with so much matter being conveyed to the newspapers that they would not be able to get it in time.

897. That is a question of machinery?—And at that hour of the night it is a very vital question, because the newspapers must go to press at certain hours to meet certain trains, and the telegraphs will only carry so much matter.

898. Have you any acquaintance with the practice of any country in which an official report, take, for instance, Canada, or the United States, do you know whether the newspapers there report as fully, or in any degree at all to be compared with the way in which newspapers report the proceedings of Parliament in this country?—There is scarcely any country, I think, comparable in that respect to this; probably America is more like our own country, and there the newspapers are supplied by an associated press, precisely similar to ours in point of fact. The associated press has its reporters in the House at Washington, and they telegraph their reports to different parts of the Union, making use of the "Congressional Globe," so far as they can avail themselves of it; otherwise filling up their time by giving descriptions of the scenes in the House, and demeanour of the Members, I believe.

899. Colonel *Arbuthnot.*] They sit during the day, do they not?—Yes; I may say that I believe there is no country in which the Legislature does not sit in the daytime, excepting this country.

900. *Chairman.*] Do the New York or Philadelphia papers contain any reports which can at all compare in point of accuracy, and giving a fair general idea of the proceedings of Parliament, with the reports which appear in the London and Provincial newspapers of the proceedings of the British Parliament?—No; so far as my knowledge goes, I do not think there is any country in the world where it would be possible to compile so complete a record as "Hansard," for instance, from the press, except where the report printed is furnished officially.

901. Is there such a thing as a fair report, in America, of the proceedings of Congress, apart from the "Congressional Globe"?—I never saw one. The State interests in America interfere very much with anything like a complete report; the interests of the whole community are not so compact as they are in this country.

902. You stated that the accommodation at the disposal of the Press Association was very insufficient; in what way is it insufficient?—We have, I may say, but one box, and that in the most inconvenient part of the Gallery for us; it is a box which looks not into the House, but into the Members' Gallery, and it is on the Ministerial side; so that one cannot see Ministers when they rise to answer questions, or to make speeches; and we have some difficulty in that position in hearing; but we should be quite content with that which was the box allotted to the old companies, and it would be sufficient for the preparation of our ordinary reports; but the more important part of our work is the supplemental and special reporting, and for the reporters who do that, we have no seat at all beyond liberty to sit with the leader writers and reporters waiting their turn on the back seat of the Gallery. Mr. Ross seems to think that that is a convenient place, and that reporting could be done there; and so far that is true, because we have done it there; but Mr. Ross has not sat there himself, I think, to report, and his staff does not sit there; and probably he has not so keen an appreciation of the difficulties as our reporters have, especially as in our case we have to report many Members who are not ordinarily reported by the London papers, and consequently there is more talking in the gallery while those Members are speaking than there is while the Members who are reported fully for the London papers are speaking; and I am afraid also that there is very frequently more talking in the House when those Members are speaking whom we have to report. In short we have to report proceedings from a back seat amidst the conversation of reporters who have very little to do, amidst the passing backwards and forwards of those reporters, and when the Members of the House themselves are talking; so that, if there is anyone that requires a good place to hear, we require it, and we have no access to the front boxes at all.

903. Are the two other associations in precisely the same position as yourselves?—That I am not quite certain about; I do not know exactly where their seats are.

I   904. Is

Mr. J. Lowell
1 July 1878.

904. Is there a real competition between you, or a mere dividing of the business?—We do not feel any competition, any sense of rivalry about the matter.

905. It is open to any provincial newspaper, I suppose, to obtain by the very best machinery at your disposal a report of any speech in Parliament?—Quite so.

906. Then are you of opinion that you supply the wants of all provincial newspapers, so that there need not be a special representation of provincial newspapers separately in the Gallery of the House of Commons?—Accepting it as impossible to provide accommodation for the reporters of all the provincial papers, I think we furnish everything that can be required, because anything that we are asked for, we are ready to supply.

907. You say there are some 60 newspapers which take your daily reports?—Yes, there are 55 daily newspapers which take our reports, and between 60 and 70 weekly newspapers, and some dozen or two of exchanges.

908. It would obviously be impossible to provide sufficient accommodation in the Gallery for 55 daily newspapers, in addition to the London Press; I suppose that must be admitted to be impossible.—Quite.

909. There would be a difficulty if accommodation were found for one, to the exclusion of another?—Certainly; I do not know which would have the claim. I should think that at least 20 papers would make out what I might call the best claim.

910. A strong claim?—Yes; papers that to a very large extent have something like an imperial circulation, as distinct from being circulated over a small locality.

911. It would be a very difficult thing therefore, even for you, with your experience, to advise the Committee which of those 20 papers should be allowed seats in the Gallery, and which should not?—I should not like to undertake that duty, unless I were going out of the country immediately.

912. Mr. Cross.] In addition to your being manager of the Press Association, I think, before that you had considerable experience as a practical journalist?—That was so, and in the provinces.

913. And your opinion is, that the machinery for supplying provincial papers with the reports is sufficient; the complaint you have is that the accommodation you get is not adequate?—That is so.

914. Supposing you had better accommodation; supposing you could bear better in the Gallery; you believe the machinery which you have, and which other associations have, would be sufficient to supply the Provincial Press with all the reports they require?—Quite so.

915. You think that the provincial papers and the London Press together, now supply reports of Parliamentary proceedings at sufficient length to be of interest to the public?—I think so.

916. But having offered that opinion, is it still your judgment that Parliament should, in addition to the reports in the papers, possess some record of its transactions for historical purposes, or for the purposes of the Members themselves?—Yes. I do not think that the reports published give a sufficiently complete historical account of the proceedings.

917. The fact is, that the newspapers are, in the first place, bent upon selling their issue; that the sale of their issue depends upon the contents, and that they really give as much of Parliamentary news as will afford them a sale; that is your judgment?—Precisely.

918. But while you are of that opinion, you are still of opinion that something should be done towards the preparing of a Parliamentary record?—Yes.

919. And that that is entirely independent of the supply to the newspapers?—Yes.

920. There are two things therefore; the supply of reports to newspapers, and the establishment of a Parliamentary record?—Yes. I believe that both in and out of Parliament there is a large number of persons who require either a full or a tolerably full official report, but that those are not numerous enough to support a paper giving such a report.

921. The Press Association, as you say, is a co-operative association amongst newspapers, and it has upon its lists 172 members, and it supplies 101 newspapers

Mr. J. Landl

1 July 1878.

papers which are not members; in all, therefore, something like 273 newspapers are supplied by the Press Association? - Yes.

922. But there are about 1,700 newspapers in the provinces?—Yes, but very few of them take Parliamentary news; and a great many of those 1,700 are merely issues under different names of some one paper.

923. I wished merely to elicit the fact; there are about 70 or 80 daily papers, however, that publish Parliamentary proceedings?—That is so.

924. Has there not grown up recently in London an addition to the provincial newspaper machinery, in the shape of special wires?—Yes; the special wire system has been largely extended in recent years.

925. There are about 20 special wires, I think?—About that number.

926. The object of the establishment of these special wires is to supplement the work of the Press Association, and the Central News, and other bodies of like character, is it not?—That is so, no doubt.

927. That is, these special wires are established by powerful provincial journals with a view of getting additional or extended or fuller reports of Parliamentary and other proceedings than the Press Association can supply?—That is so, with a very considerable difference, because in the case of the English papers having special wires, for instance, the special wires are used chiefly, I think, to sub-edit the London evening papers, to transmit Stock Exchange reports, and other matters that would be very expensive in telegraphing, but we still supply to the majority of the special wire papers Parliamentary reports for them to transmit over their own wires, or we send such through the public wires, leaving their special wires for them to use in their own way.

928. These are for supplementary information, provided by the Press Association, and there are about 20 of those in existence, you say?—I should think there are 20 now in existence.

929. Three in Glasgow, three in Edinburgh, one in Dundee, two in Manchester, one in Leeds, two in Newcastle, and two in Dublin?—Yes; certain provincial newspapers rent a wire at the Post Office for their own use, from seven at night to three or four o'clock in the morning.

930. You said you would have some difficulty if all those 70 or 80 papers applied for admission to the House of Commons, in saying which ought to be admitted?—Yes.

931. Would it not be fair to say that if a newspaper proprietor chose to be at the expense of establishing an office in London, and having a special wire, that would give him a fair preference?—I do not think so myself; because you see in that case the Serjeant at Arms, granting a seat to such a paper, would be very heavily handicapping that paper's contemporary and competitor, if it could not afford to have a special wire also.

932. I scarcely catch your meaning?—Supposing there are two papers; on the one hand, one that has just started, and, on the other hand, a rich paper which is able to establish a special wire and a special office in London; if Parliament were to grant that paper a seat in the Gallery, because it was rich enough to have an office and a wire of its own in London, it would deal unfairly, I think, inasmuch as it would heavily handicap its competitor, which was not able to have such an office in London.

933. I can see what the point of your argument is; but that applies to everything, does it not?—Only that Parliament does not assist in everything.

934. I merely wished to indicate that that would form a division; I want to know this, supposing the Provincial Press wish to be further represented in the Gallery (I do not think they do, but supposing it was so), is it not reasonable to suppose that a paper that has put itself to the expense of having an office and keeping a staff in London should, at least, have facilities for coming into the House when it would be no injustice to refuse a paper that did not feel disposed to incur that expense?—It would be a very good argument for the papers having special wires to urge, but I do not think that the papers not having special wires would admit the cogency of it.

935. I do not think it is worth while continuing the argument, because I do not think the newspapers possessing special wires have any desire to possess that advantage?—No, I do not think they have.

936. But I think, with your experience as a journalist, you will say there would

Mr. J. Lewis
1 July 1878

would be this advantage, that in the case of a newspaper having representatives in London, they might at present be allowed, when they send them even to the Speaker's Gallery or to the Strangers' Gallery, to take notes, and not be shut up from writing on pieces of paper as they are at the present time?—I think that any reporters that are admitted should be free to have all the conveniences enjoyed by the London papers.

937. But a leader writer does not wish to report; supposing the ordinary representative of a newspaper might hear the proceedings in a debate, and were content to sit and listen and take a note, not making a report, that would answer all the purposes that the provincial papers wished to serve?—I do not know that I quite follow you.

938. I am supposing that the representatives of these provincial newspapers had admission to the Strangers' Gallery or the Speaker's Gallery, and that they were permitted, as they are not now, to take a note, to write a few notes, not to take a report, would not that answer all the purposes required?—I think so; in other words, I think that anyone admitted on behalf of a paper should have the best facilities for doing what the paper requires.

939. You think that if that was accorded to the Provincial Press, that when a representative of theirs did go into those Galleries, he should have liberty to take a note without being disturbed by an official, that would answer all the purposes required?—Yes, I think so.

940. Do you see any objection to the London papers having a Press Association of their own; there is a staff for the "Daily News," for the "Daily Telegraph," for the "Morning Post," for the "Morning Advertiser;" is there any reason why they should not, as Sir Henry Holland suggested, have a Press Association of their own, and have one report?—I see no reason at all why they should not.

941. That was once done, was it not?—Some of the papers coalesced, I believe, but it was for the sake of cheapness; but if there were only room for one staff of reporters in the Gallery, they would be obliged to have an association, as we are.

942. Supposing that these London papers were driven to have a Press Association in the same way as the provincial papers have, would not that create a considerable number of seats in the Gallery?—It would create a great number of seats.

943. I am suggesting that the London papers might have an association of their own; because you have now 15 men employed for the "Morning Advertiser," for instance, and 15 for the "Morning Post," who report at about the same length and the same quality, and one staff might do for both; it was tried but it broke down?—Yes.

944. Do you know the reason?—It was not tried for the purpose of seeing whether such a report could be furnished, but whether it could be done more cheaply, and that, I think, failed.

945. Do you recollect why it failed?—It failed for no reason that the House of Commons could prevent, I think.

946. Sir Henry Holland.] May I ask you is it more important that the "Standard" summary writer, for instance, should be in a better position than the "Standard" reporter, that is, in a more central position in the Gallery; or the "Daily News" summary writer than the "Daily News" reporter?—I do not think so; I think it is more important that the reporter who takes the shorthand report should have a good position.

947. And, therefore, it might be desirable to remove the summary writers to the side, and place the Press Association and the Central Press in a better position for reporting?—One box for reporting is sufficient accommodation in the Gallery, provided that the boxes were re-arranged.

948. Could not the summary writing work be done from the back seats?—I should think so. It is more conveniently done from the front seats, no doubt.

949. I do not mean as conveniently from the back seats as from the front seats; but could it be conveniently done from the back seats?—I may state, as illustrating the practical convenience of it, that on occasions when we can, our reporters will get a summary writer to exchange with them, and will
give

give him their copy, when they come out, to make his summary from.   That
can be done.

950. It is possible therefore to improve the present arrangement, so that the
reporters for the Press Association might be placed more in the body of the
Gallery ?—Yes.

951. Mr. *Mitchell Henry.*] Is there anything now to prevent the London
newspapers combining, if they please, to have one Press Association report ?—
Nothing at all.

952. It is a matter entirely within their own power if they think it a desirable
course ? —Precisely.

953. Then the only thing that the regulations of the Gallery could do to bring
about that result, would be to deprive some of the London newspapers of their
present accommodation, and that would put a pressure upon them to combine to
have one report ?—If they were shut out from the Gallery they would be
obliged to do something of that kind.

954. Did I rightly understand you to suggest that the Provincial Press should
be allowed to have representatives in the Strangers' Gallery who could take
such notes as they pleased of the proceedings ?—No; what I said was that anyone admitted for a paper to do the work of the paper should have the fullest
facilities possible for doing the work which he was admitted to do.

955. The honourable Member for Newcastle in his questions referred not to
the Reporters' Gallery, but to the Strangers' Gallery ?—I understood the
honourable Member for Newcastle to say that it was desirable that provincial
newspapers should send leader writers into the House, and to ask if accommodation for those leader writers were provided in the Speaker's or Strangers'
Gallery, was it not desirable that they should be able to take notes; to which
question I said, yes.   That is what I understood.

956. Then you assume that places are to be found there for an additional
number of newspaper representatives ?—If places are found, it is my opinion that
that liberty should be given to them.

957. Then the effect of that would be, of course, to diminish *pro tanto* the
accommodation for strangers visiting the House of Commons?—Quite so.   I am
not advocating the practice, but I say that if it did obtain it, it should be
effective.

958. May I ask you how many reporters are attached for Parliamentary
purposes to the association which you represent?—We have 10 exclusively
engaged for us, and then we receive assistance from some 6 or 10 others in
the Gallery who are not engaged in reporting for their own
papers.

959. How often do you change your reporters ?—It depends upon the period
of the evening; first they take the half-hour turns; later on they take quarter-
of-an hour turns, and later on five minute turns.

960. Something in the same way as Mr. Ross described in reference to the
" Times " ?—Yes.

961. Does your association supply reports of this kind to private individuals
in the country ?—No, it does not.

962. A private individual, then, would have no means of obtaining from the
Press Association a report either of the daily proceedings in Parliament or of
ordinary occurrences:—If a private individual were to write to ask us for a
special report of any proceedings in Parliament, we should recommend him
where he could get it.

963. Yours is an association entirely connected with newspapers, and not
with the general public?—That is so.

964. Mr. *Dunbar.*] Do you remain on during the sitting of the House till it
rises?—Yes.

965. Does the staff which you have at present, with occasional help, enable
you to supply the newspapers having special reports ?—It does.

966. The back seats on a bench running along the wall !—There is a very
small desk in front, a small table.

967. Is not the passage in front of it very much occupied by men passing to
and fro to the boxes ?—That is so.

968. And it is very difficult for the summary writers to work there !—
It is very difficult for any one to hear there.   I confess that, not being
accustomed

accustomed to the gallery; I cannot hear there myself, although our reporters' who are accustomed to the gallery, can produce reports from there on occasion.

969. Mr. *Barclay*.] Are a great many of the largest provincial papers independent of the Press Association ?—None of them.

970. The "Scotsman," for instance ?—No; the "Scotsman" takes a very large quantity of news from us.

971. I do not see the "Scotsman" in your list ?—Their special reports are taken by other people in the gallery, but they take our ordinary report, and they supplement it by their special wire.

972. You have not got that down in this sheet ?—No; but that is a sheet of special instructions.

973. I do not see in your sheet the "Daily Review and Advertiser," or the "Glasgow Daily Mail" ?—Where the papers have a special wire, the name does not always appear in this list; the agents give orders in the gallery.

974. Am I to understand that those newspapers that I have named occasionally desire to have special reports of Scotch business ?—That is so.

975. Do you supply them all, or do they take other means to have them supplied ?—Sometimes they take other means; sometimes we supply them. I may say generally that the "Scotsman" does its own special work in the gallery, but that it takes our ordinary reports, the column and a half reports that I spoke to you about at the beginning of my evidence.

976. If the "Scotsman" reports occasionally the Scotch business to the extent of eight or 10 columns, how does it obtain those reports ?—From reporters in the gallery; reporters who get in with London papers' tickets.

977. The reporters of certain London newspapers have private arrangements with some of the proprietors of Scotch newspapers to give them special reports of Scotch business, and such other matters as they desire ?—That is so; the "Scotsman" obtains in that way just such reports as we supply to some other Scotch papers.

978. To what hour in the morning do you profess to supply news for the provincial newspapers; reports of proceedings in Parliament, I mean ?—To the close of the House.

979. That morning ?—Any morning; we never cease sending our report until the House is up.

980. If the House sat till four o'clock, for instance ?—If the House sat until seven o'clock we should continue.

981. Your reports would go to the country papers, and they would use them as they pleased ?—Yes, they use them in special editions when too late for the first editions.

982. Can you tell us to what hour you can report for the matter to appear in the morning issues of the Edinburgh and Glasgow newspapers ?—In Edinburgh, up to three or half-past three; in Glasgow, not quite so late.

983. Do you mean that the sitting of the House lasts till three or half-past three ?—Yes, I think in the town edition of the Edinburgh papers you could get news up to that hour.

984. What is the meaning of Members' names being in the list here; is it that they are to be supplied with the fullest report you can give ?—Whenever those Members speak we are to send a full report, a special report, to the paper whose name is attached.

985. Would it be practicable for one reporter to take notes for a quarter of an hour, then retire into the extending room and read off his notes to three or four reporters to write them again ?—To about two, I should think; a great saving of time would be effected by that; I mean that he should dictate to two; it takes him a certain time to dictate, and therefore he would not save any time if he dictated to more.

986. Do you mean that he dictates off his notes again ?—Yes, to the writers.

987. To writers writing them out in full hand ?—No, to writers writing shorthand; a man takes a column, say, and to save time he will read that to two, who take it down in shorthand, and then write it out.

988. But I will suppose that the reporter dictated off his notes to two or three reporters, or four reporters, as many as could hear him, who would write it out slowly in extended hand ?—You mean, to produce four or five copies.

989. Yes ?

989. Yes?—He, himself, would produce four or five copies by writing on manifold paper.

990. Could what I have suggested be done?—Of course it could; he could dictate to as many as could hear him.

991. Could he dictate in such a manner that those who heard him might, if they pleased, produce a full report, or a condensed report, or a summary?—I should not like to trust to the result of their labours if that were done; it is very difficult to write out a condensed speech which you are hearing, that is to say, write and condense at the same time. It is possible, but there are not many men who have the faculty of doing it.

992. A reporter reading from his notes, to read sufficiently slowly for the amanuensis to extend the notes, must be speaking five times, or four times, at least, more slowly than the original speaker?—Yes.

993. Would it be more difficult to condense a speech delivered in that form, than when it was being delivered by the original speaker?—Yes; because you cannot condense till you know what has been said; part of a speech could not possibly be condensed until you had heard it all.

994. Major Arbuthnot.] From what you have just said, you disagree, I understand, with Mr. Ross in supposing that a good reporter can condense a speech as it is being made?—No; I think Mr. Ross meant one thing, and the honourable Member who has been questioning me meant another; I think what Mr. Ross meant was, that the reporter should not overburthen himself with notes, but should take short notes instead of taking a full report; and then his condensation becomes easier for him when he comes to write it out.

995. I understood Mr. Ross to say that there are two courses open to the reporter; one to report in a condensed form as the words were delivered, as the speech was made; and the other course, for him to take the notes into the next room, having taken them in extenso, and condense them?—You see there are two processes; there is the process of taking notes, and the process of transcribing them. If a reporter has to condense a speech he can do it better if he takes what is called a catch note, a note of the important parts of the speech, instead of taking the whole of it.

996. Do these 1,700 newspapers which have been spoken of include weekly's and daily's?—Yes.

997. Do not some of the provincial papers give longer Parliamentary reports than some of the London papers?—On occasion.

998. In the case of those which you supply, do you do it entirely from your own seat in the gallery, or do you obtain the reports from the reporters of other newspapers?—We do it sometimes in the back seats; sometimes, when we can, we borrow a front seat.

999. And is it correct to say, that sometimes your reporters go to the back seats because they think they can hear better there than they can from the seat allotted to you?—I did not understand Mr. Ross to say so, but it is not correct. Our reporters do not go to the back seat because they can hear better there.

1000. Is it not easier sometimes to hear from behind the front bench in the centre of the gallery than it is from the extreme point of the gallery?—I could not answer to that; they are both bad.

1001. Am I right in assuming from your evidence that for the various reasons you have given, it would be impossible to frame an official report and a newspaper report by means of the same machinery?—I think so.

1002. Would they have to be wholly and solely apart one from the other?—I think the newspaper staff could supply a full-length report for the historical record; but I do not think that the staff employed in supplying the historical record would be able to meet the varying and various wants of the different papers of the country.

1003. But is your idea of an historical record that it is to be a verbatim report, or, at any rate, what has been described as a full report?—I think it should be a verbatim report; I do not see any other course.

1004. Leaving out the repetitions?—Yes; of course it should not be slavishly verbatim.

1005. Do you think that if the reports of all the newspapers in the country put together were collated, it would be a verbatim report?—I do not think it is

Mr. J. Last.
1 July 1878.

is possible to collate a perfectly accurate and complete report from all the newspapers.

1006. Sir *Alexander Gordon*.] In this paper put before us by you, I see in some cases put against the Member's name, "not exceeding a quarter of a column"?—That is the order from the newspaper; that is all the space they can afford for that Member.

1007. I understood you to say that there were a large number of persons who would like to have a more full report of the debates, but that the number was not sufficient to pay the expenses of a full report?—I think so. I think the newspapers, libraries, chambers of commerce, and other public bodies, would like to have a complete official report.

1008. I will put into your hands a full report of one day's proceedings of the House of Commons, from four o'clock to two o'clock (*handing the same to the Witness*); if that was issued in time to go by the evening post to the country every day after the sitting of the House, do you think it would be acceptable to a number of people who wish to study the debates in *extenso*?—I have to assume that this is the kind of report which I mean by a complete historical record. If so, then it would. I think that would be quite sufficient.

1009. Mr. *Cowen*.] I wish to ask one question to remove an incorrect impression; this list which you publish, as to the Members that you have to report, is published not at the suggestion of the Members, or the proposal of the Members, but at the proposal and request of the newspapers themselves?—That is so.

1010. The Members know nothing of it?—They are supposed to know nothing about it. Those sheets are not published by us; they are our instructions to our staff in the gallery.

1011. *Chairman*.] Has your attention been directed to the arrangement which Mr. Hansard explained to the Committee?—It has.

1012. Have you seen, practically, the results of that arrangement?—Yes.

1013. Do you consider that it is a satisfactory one so far as it goes?—It fills up, I think, the points in which the reports from the papers are deficient as an historical record.

1014. It supplies the deficiency which is to be found in the reports of the London papers at the present time?—That, I think, is the case.

1015. Are those reports of the daily papers, so far as you know them, a fair account of the proceedings of Parliament, as far as they go?—I think so; meaning by "fair" that they are done without any bias.

1016. And you think that Mr. Hansard's arrangement supplies the deficiency of those reports?—I think he has hit the weak points of those reports in suggesting the four points in which they require strengthening.

1017. Sir *Alexander Gordon*.] Has your association any dealings with Members directly?—None whatever.

Friday, 5th July 1878.

MEMBERS PRESENT:

Colonel Arbuthnot.
Mr. Barclay.
Mr. Cowan.
Viscount Crichton.
Mr. Dunbar.
Mr. William Edward Forster.
Sir Alexander Gordon.
Mr. Hall.
Mr. Mitchell Henry.

Lord Francis Hervey.
Sir Henry T. Holland.
Mr. Hutchinson.
Mr. MP.
Dr. Lyon Playfair.
Mr. William Henry Smith.
Mr. Walter.
Sir Henry Drummond Wolff.

THE RIGHT HONOURABLE WILLIAM HENRY SMITH, IN THE CHAIR.

Mr. *Edward Lloyd*, called in; and Examined.

Mr. E. Lloyd

5 July 1878.

1018. *Chairman.*] WILL you state to the Committee the character in which you appear before us?—I am the proprietor of the " Daily Chronicle."

1019. I think you wrote to the Committee, stating that you desired to give evidence?—Yes.

1020. You stated that the accommodation in the Gallery placed at your disposal, as proprietor of the " Daily Chronicle," was insufficient?—Yes.

1021. Will you state in what way it is insufficient?—What I require is, that I should have accommodation for one gentleman for the whole of the sitting. I find it extremely inconvenient, in fact, impossible, to conduct the journal without that accommodation for the whole of the sitting. At present I have only got it after six o'clock, and I am caused great inconvenience by our being in the back seats, from want of hearing, from twelve to six, or from whatever time the House sits, till six.

1022. Do the Committee rightly understand, that before six o'clock your reporters are excluded from the front seat?—Yes.

1023. They are allowed to be in the back seats of the Gallery, but they are excluded from the front till that hour?—Yes; one seat is wanted by us.

1024. But from six o'clock you occupy one of the front seats in the Gallery?—Yes.

1025. Are you unable to obtain the information necessary for the conduct of your newspaper by the arrangements which are now in existence?—Quite so.

1026. Or is it simply a matter of inconvenience?—No, it is that I am not able to obtain the information necessary.

1027. Mr. *Cowan.*] The " Daily Chronicle," I think, has been in existence about 22 or 23 years as a paper?—Yes.

1028. But it has only reported Parliamentary proceedings within the last 18 months?—Within the last 18 months.

1029. The box that your reporter occupies, up to six o'clock, is occupied by an evening paper?—Yes.

1030. And after the evening paper has done with it, then you come into possession of it?—Yes.

Mr. E. Lloyd.

5 July 1878.

1031. Are the Committee to understand you to wish to have a box for your reporter and a box for a summary writer, as the other daily papers have, or do you only wish for one box?—I wish for two. At the same time, if it is more convenient for the House that the summary writer should sit in the back, we should be, of course, glad to make shift with that.

1032. I believe the "Daily Chronicle" has a considerable circulation?—Yes.

1033. And it is now not a local paper, as it was, but purely a national paper?—Yes.

1034. It was before published in Clerkenwell?—Yes; originally it was a local newspaper.

1035. Sir *Henry T. Holland.*] Is there any reason why the summary writer should not sit in the back seat?—It is not so convenient for him, but, at the same time, there is no absolute reason why he should not sit there.

1036. The summary writing work is not so important as the reporting work? —No.

1037. And, though not so conveniently, it can still be fairly done in the back seat?—Yes; or after six o'clock the summary business, if it was absolutely necessary, might be done there; it is quite impossible to do the other there.

1038. Mr. *Mitchell Henry.*] Have you personally tried the back seat for the purpose of reporting?—Yes.

1039. And in what way is it inconvenient; is it that you are unable to hear or to see?—Both; particularly to hear.

1040. But the summary writing, you think, could be done there, because you do not require to hear so well for that?—Exactly.

1041. I presume that a person employed in writing a summary cannot write that summary until the speech of which he is about to write the summary has been concluded?—No.

1042. Therefore he cannot be listening to the speech which is being made at the time when he is writing the summary; is that so?—Yes.

1043. Is there any reason then why a summary writer should be present at all at the debates?—Yes, I think so.

1044. Is that necessary that he may obtain general impressions from what he hears?—Exactly.

1045. Mr. *Dunbar.*] Are the Committee to understand you to say that the summary writer does not write anything until the debate is over?— He would take his notes, I apprehend, and probably write some of it as it was going on.

1046. Mr. *Barclay.*] I wish to know how much of your paper you are prepared to devote to Parliamentary reports?—We generally average from two to sometimes fifteen columns, according to the requirements, according to the importance of the subject.

1047. Might I ask what is the general rule that you adopt in regard to reporting the speeches of different Members?—We report some subjects verbatim, or pretty nearly so, and others according to the requirements of the subjects.

1048. What is the principle that you adopt in selecting the speakers who are to be reported?—That is left to the discretion of the chief of the corps.

1049. Who is the chief of the corps; is that the summary writer?— Yes.

1050. The summary writer, then, besides writing his summary, has to direct the reporters in the Gallery as to the reporting of the speeches?—Yes.

1051. Then have you any general instructions that you give to your summary writer in regard to the subjects, the discussions on which are to be reported?—No; he reports according to the importance of the subject.

1052. Would your summary writer consider discussion on a Bill dealing with Scotch subjects only to be a matter to be reported in your newspaper?—Decidedly, I should say; not at full length probably, but according to the importance of the subject.

1053. Do you report any of the debates at full length?—Yes.

1054. The whole of the speeches?—I cannot say the whole; the whole when it is an important subject.

1055. There

1055. There was a discussion this morning upon a Scotch Bill which, as I am told, occupied two columns of a Scotch newspaper; how many columns of your newspaper does it occupy?—Only a few lines, not being an interesting subject generally to London readers.

1056. Then that is a case of a Scotch Bill which you do not consider of interest to English readers, or London readers, but the debate on which a Scotch paper has nevertheless reported at the length of nearly two columns?—Yes.

1057. Is the practice similar in regard to Irish subjects?—Yes, the same as to any subjects.

1058. Is there any reason why the London papers which report at similar length to your paper could not combine in order to have a joint report?—I really cannot answer that question.

1059. I asked if there was any reason why a London paper which reported at a length corresponding to yours should not combine with you in order to have a joint report?—I do not know that there is any particular reason, excepting that I do not think it would be practicable.

1060. Do you allow your reporters to report for provincial papers?—No.

1061. Is it a standing order with you that your reporters are not to report for provincial papers?—Yes.

1062. Have you any idea how a provincial paper, a Scotch paper, for instance, which wished to report the debate to which I have referred (and which I may take as an example of several), could get a report of a discussion of interest in Scotland when the reporters' seats are occupied entirely by the London Press, and the London Press prohibit their reporters from reporting for provincial or Scotch newspapers?—I do not know that they do prohibit them generally.

1063. You have not any suggestion to offer as to how the provincial newspapers, or the Scotch, or Irish newspapers, could have reports of discussions which they think of interest to their readers under the present circumstances, assuming that the reporters of the London newspapers are prohibited from reporting for provincial newspapers?—No, if they were all prohibited, I have not.

1064. Do you tell us that your reporters do not report for any of the provincial newspapers?—No, not generally; they may perhaps occasionally, but, as a matter of fact my reporters do not.

1065. You are able to say that your reporters do not give reports to the provincial newspapers?—Yes.

1066. Could the summary writer discharge his duties sitting in the Speaker's Gallery?—He could, no doubt, but not so perfectly.

1067. Is there anything to prevent a summary writer doing as much reporting as you produce in your newspaper, leaving out the reporter altogether; is there anything to prevent the summary writer giving an abstract of a speech as much as you usually give?—One person could not do it, certainly.

1068. Colonel *Arbuthnot.*] How many reporters do you employ in the House of Commons?—Upon an average, six; between five and seven.

1069. And how do you obtain that information which you require, after the time at which you have to give up your seat?—We do not give up our seat until the House closes; our use of our seat commences at six o'clock.

1070. How do you obtain your information until six o'clock?—In the best way we can from the back seats, which is a very imperfect way.

1071. Will you kindly say what the circulation of your paper is?—I should rather decline answering that, though I can fairly say it is a large circulation, and a very increasing one.

1072. Mr. *Hutchinson.*] You were asked by the honourable Member for Newcastle whether your paper had not assumed a national character, and you replied that it had?—Yes.

1073. Afterwards you explained that debates upon purely Scotch and Irish questions are not fully reported in your paper, because they are not of much interest to London readers?—I did not mean to convey that; I meant generally, either Irish, English, or Scotch; I meant to say that they were reported according to the interest to the public generally.

1074. But you used the phrase "not to London readers," from which I may conclude,

Mr. K. Lloyd.
5 July 1878.

conclude, I suppose, fairly, that the bulk of your circulation is in London?—Yes.

1075. Then I am to understand that, in your judgment, a paper acquires a national character by the fact of its being published in London, and that if it be not published in London it has not a national character?—No, I did not intend to convey that at all.

1076. Sir *Alexander Gordon.*] I understood you to inform the Committee that before the change which was made 18 months ago your newspaper was in the character of a provincial newspaper?—Yes, a London local newspaper.

1077. And that 18 months ago you made a change which put it upon the footing, with regard to the reporting of the debates, of a London daily paper?—Precisely.

1078. If a provincial paper took the same steps for reporting the debates as you took 18 months ago, would they not have an equal claim to that accommodation in the Gallery which you seem to have claimed and obtained?—I only claim that as a London daily paper.

1079. But why should a London daily paper have it more than a provincial paper, if the provincial paper publishes the same, or more complete information?—I cannot undertake to say what the accommodation of the House may be, or what not.

1080. Do you see any difficulty in the summaries, which generally consist of a few lines, being written from the reporters' notes after they are written out in long hand?—The summary generally is much more than a few lines; it is something over a column generally in my paper.

1081. Assuming it to be a column (which does not quite accord with my observation), could it not be written out from the reporters' notes?—I think not.

1082. I understood you to say that last night when a Scotch debate took about three hours, your reporter was idle the whole of that time?—He only reported a portion of it.

1083. He did report a portion of the Scotch debate?—Yes.

1084. What portion?—A very few lines, I think.

1085. Do you think it fair that you should occupy a box in which you only report a few lines, when another paper, or other papers, are anxious to occupy that box, in order to give a full report of that debate?—That paper may only give a full report of that particular debate, and its reporters may be idle on other occasions, as ours were on that occasion last night.

1086. But if a paper undertakes to publish a full report of all debates, as some of the provincial papers do, would it not then have an equal claim to accommodation with you?—I cannot say that.

1087. Do you find that six reporters can give full reports of debates up to two o'clock in the morning?—Not always; we have more sometimes.

1088. Then your staff of six is not sufficient to furnish full reports?—Generally, for the length at which they are inserted in the paper it is sufficient; we have more sometimes, as a matter of course.

1089. How do you obtain more when a debate is carried on to two or three o'clock in the morning?—I leave that to the chief of my staff.

1090. You do not know, in fact?—No.

1091. Sir *Henry Drummond Wolff.*] I understand you to say that you apply for admission to a seat in the Gallery, not with a view of getting a position over the provincial papers, but with a view of being placed in the same position as other London papers?—Yes.

1092. May I ask whether, in your opinion, the public interest is still maintained in the reports of Parliament; it has been stated before us that the public are losing an interest in the reports of the debates: what is your experience?—I do not think so.

1093. You think that the debates are an attraction to the readers of your paper?—Yes.

1094. And, therefore, you are anxious to give as long a report as you think will satisfy the public?—Yes.

1095. And that is considerable?—Yes.

1096. Therefore you are desirous of giving a longer report than you are now able

20

to give in consequence of the want of accommodation?—Yes, in most instances.

1097. Mr. *Mills*.] Mr. Hansard told us that a considerable number of Members send to his office copies of their speeches; does that ever happen to you?—No, never.

1098. Mr. *Cowen*.] I understand you to say that you base your application for additional accommodation in the Gallery upon the assumption and the belief that your paper gives as full reports of Parliamentary proceedings as the ordinary London daily papers give?—Precisely.

1099. It is on that ground that you ask for more accommodation?—Yes.

1100. *Chairman*.] You have been asked if you publish a complete report of Parliamentary news, and you stated, I think, that you only published that which was interesting to your readers; do you know of any other rule which influences newspaper proprietors than that of publishing that which is interesting to their readers?—No, I do not. I meant by that that we publish the reports shorter or longer according to the interest of the readers.

1101. So that your report varies in proportion to the interest which the subject reported has in the public mind according to your judgment?—Precisely.

1102. Lord *Francis Hervey*.] You said to an honourable Member just now that it was impracticable, in your opinion, for two or more London papers to combine together for the purpose of reporting the Parliamentary Debates; will you explain why you consider that such a combination would be impracticable?—I do not quite understand the question

1103. You were asked whether it would not be practicable for two or three, or more, London papers to combine together for the purpose of reporting the Parliamentary Debates, and you said that you thought it would be impracticable, but you did not give any reason; and I wish now to ask you what your reason is for saying that it would be impracticable for the London papers to join together for that purpose?—I think I understand the question now; you mean that by combining together they would only want one staff to do the whole. I think that would be impracticable, because we all like to have our own reports. I should not like to have the report of any other London paper.

1104. You are aware that a great number of country papers do, in point of fact, combine for that very purpose, and I believe have reason to be satisfied with the result, is that so?—Yes, I believe that is the case.

1105. Why cannot the London papers do that which the country papers, in point of fact, do, and which they have done for some time with advantage to themselves, and, I suppose, with satisfaction to their clients?—I do not suppose that papers would agree on the importance of the various subjects; one would think one subject of much more importance than another would think it.

1106. The reports in your paper, and in two or three others, at least, of the London papers are exceedingly short, and one would hardly think that they would be very anxious to have their own particular way of putting the few lines, or, it may be, a column, in which they record the debate?—I know that it ran to 16 columns on one occasion in my paper.

1107. That is once, but Parliament sits for six months?—But the subject is not always of that importance.

Mr. *William Saunders*, called in; and Examined.

1108. *Chairman*.] I THINK you are engaged in the conduct of an agency called the "Central News," are you not?—Yes.

1109. You were formerly the proprietor of the "Central Press"?—Yes.

1110. Will you state to the Committee the business which you conduct as the proprietor of the "Central News"?—In reference to Parliamentary reporting, the business which we carry on is that of supplying reports to provincial newspapers, which reports consist of two kinds: one report would be of a general character, which is sent to a great many papers, and extends from one-and-a-half to seven columns daily, according to the interest of the subject; the other class of reports consist mainly of reports of speeches of local members, which are required for publication in the places which they represent; it is

Mr. W. Saunders.

5 July 1874.

is that latter class of reporting which is increasing so rapidly, and which required much larger provision for doing it than we now have.

1111. Do you exercise your own discretion entirely as to the length of the report, with regard to the ordinary summary report which you send to the newspapers?—The reporters engaged exercise their own discretion: sometimes we can anticipate the importance of a report, and on special occasions we are able to say that the report should be so long; on other occasions, they increase or diminish the report according to the interest which may attach to the proceedings in the House.

1112. By way of illustration, do you report a Second Reading debate on an important Bill at considerable length?—It would really depend entirely upon the amount of interest involved in it.

1113. But, I suppose, like the London newspapers, you report proceedings in Committee very briefly indeed?—Very briefly.

1114. Giving only the result practically?—Yes.

1115. And not the conversation which leads to that result?—We do not, excepting that sometimes we take out the observations of local Members which they make in Committee for sending down to the locality which they represent.

1116. You stated to the Committee that the special reports of speeches of local Members were increasing in number?—Very much so.

1117. Has there been an increase this year?—I see that we have sent out about 80 per cent. more of those reports this year than last year.

1118. Does that result from instructions given to you by the particular local paper to report the speaker, or do you exercise jurisdiction?—We get instructions from the local paper.

1119. And I suppose you are paid independently for that?—We are paid independently for that, at so much per column.

1120. With your seat in the front you are still able to execute those orders?—We do it in the best way we can, but it is very imperfectly done; it is the most unsatisfactory part of our business; it is impossible to hear well in the back seats, and consequently we cannot report well from there.

1121. Do I rightly understand you that you have two reporters at one time in the Gallery, one occupying a front seat and one a back seat?—Yes.

1122. And one of the two is engaged upon the summary reporting, and the other in watching for the local Member?—Yes.

1123. I think you succeeded to this business on the demise, so to speak, of the telegraph companies?—That was so. When they were in existence they supplied a condensed report to all the papers in the country, and their charges for transmitting special reports were so high as to be prohibitive, and therefore it was not at that time the custom of local newspapers to get the speeches of their local Members by telegraph; but the Post Office now transmits at a moderate rate of charge, and consequently the system of reporting local Members has, within the last eight years, developed extensively.

1124. And in a very marked manner within the past year?—It has.

1125. Are you aware of any complaints either on the part of the public, or on the part of Members, that the general sense of their speeches in Parliament is not accurately given?—The complaints of the reports that are made from the back bench are very serious; the reports that are made from the front bench I think are generally very accurately given.

1126. Then it comes to this, that the present arrangements are sufficiently good provided you could make the back bench as good as the front?—Exactly, or increase the number of the front seats.

1127. Apart from the desire to obtain the speeches of local Members at full length, has there been an increasing desire for, or any change in the feeling of the public in the country with regard to Parliamentary reports within the last few years?—With regard to the provincial papers, they are published very much more generally than they were a few years since; at greater length, and a much greater number of papers publish them. I see that the number of morning papers that now publish daily reports of the proceedings is 50; 60 morning newspapers in the provinces, exclusive of London.

1128. Has there been a decrease or an increase in the number of those papers within the last year?—I do not remember any changes; I think they are about the same as they were last year.

1129. I suppose the proprietors pay, do they not, both for the report, and also for the cost of transmission?—They do.

1130. Is there any complaint on their part of the cost of the service?—I Mr. W. Saunders.
think the cost of the general service is considered to be moderate and reasonable.   5 July 1878

1131. Is there any desire to diminish the cost, and, therefore, the quantity of
the Parliamentary information which they get?—I think not: the cost is really
very moderate; I have not heard any complaints of it. The cost of special reporting is very serious.

1132. And that you state is increasing?—That is increasing, notwithstanding
the great cost of it, but it is a great burden upon local newspapers.

1133. Has your attention been directed to the question of official reporting
at all; have you formed any opinion upon that subject?—I have considered the
matter.

1134. Do you believe that an official report would take the place of the
private reports which newspapers now give?—I do not think it would take
the place at all of any general reports. Every general report would be done
then by special reporters as now; but I think that a promptly published official
report would supersede the reporting of special Members and special speeches;
I mean if it was published with sufficient promptitude to enable the newspaper
proprietor to use it the same night.

1135. Then do I rightly understand you that the ordinary summary of a
column and a half to seven columns which you speak of as the summary which
you transmit to the newspapers, would be required still?—It would, irrespective
of the official report.

1136. And the advantage you would anticipate from the official report would
be that it would save the agencies which now undertake the duty, the double
and expense of taking down the fuller report of speeches of individual Members?
—Exactly so.

1137. You are of opinion that it would be possible to produce that official
report in the course of the evening as Members are speaking?—The official
report might be published immediately; it might be continuously reported and
printed, and within an hour a Member could be presented with a complete copy
of his speech, which he could then correct if he chose.

1138. Are you of opinion that a complete report of the proceedings of Parliament would obtain any general circulation as a newspaper or periodical?—I
think, if published as an official and complete report, it would obtain a very
extensive circulation, if published immediately, that is, the following morning
at the same time as newspapers.

1139. Have you formed any opinion as to the probable effect of such a report
upon the other reports which appear, and which you, as I understand, are of
opinion would continue to appear in the newspapers?—I do not think is would
make any difference as far as provincial newspapers are concerned.

1139.* But as regards the London newspapers?—If it made any difference
at all it would merely be in respect of one or two newspapers that publish very
lengthy reports; I do not think it would make any difference to the papers that
now publish condensed reports.

1140. What would be the effect, in your opinion, upon those papers which
now produce lengthy reports?—I am not prepared to say; it might induce them
to lessen the quantity and make a more popular report, but I am not prepared
to say that it would.

1141. Do you think it at all probable that the effect of the publication of
this official report would be to produce what we now see in some degree, a
more highly coloured report of the proceedings of Parliament rather than a dry
summary?—The provincial newspapers now publish Parliamentary sketches, and
I do not think that that system would be altered by an official report.

1142. Do you think it would be increased by it?—I do not think it would
make any difference.

1143. Have you formed an estimate of the cost of preparing an official
report and printing it?—The cost of preparing and printing an official report
would be, I think, about 350 £ a week.

1144. That is to say, the cost of reporting, of correction, of composition and
printing, apart from the cost of the paper?—Yes; the paper I have not included
in the cost, because it would be reimbursed by the sale.

1145. That is assuming that no copies were given away?—If any copies were given away, I presume there would be no object in doing that which would be properly paid for.

1146. *Mr. Mills.*] You speak of what you called Parliamentary sketches published by provincial newspapers; now, how would those sketches be furnished to the provincial newspapers; by their own reporters?—By their own reporters in the Gallery, usually; sometimes by a representative sitting in the Speaker's Gallery.

1147. And sometimes, perhaps, it may be by some one in the House; do you know how that is?—If so, I am not aware of it.

1148. It sometimes happens that reports are seen (I have seen myself), for instance, in a provincial newspaper of what has passed in the House, which could hardly have been heard in the Reporters' Gallery; I do not know whether you have noticed that?—I do not think I have; I have never sent out anything of the sort.

1149. Only by way of illustration I will just mention, in order that you may understand the point of my question, that I saw it stated in a provincial paper the other day, which gave a report of a speech of Mr. Gladstone's at the time that Mr. Hanbury's motion was withdrawn, that on that occasion Lord Hartington said, speaking of Mr. Gladstone's speech, that he never heard anything more nearly done in his life. I suppose anything of that kind said casually by one Member to another could hardly have been reported by anyone in the Gallery?—It would not have been considered a Parliamentary report, I imagine, in any sense of the word; it would be a report of a private conversation, which must have been communicated in some way.

1150. A great many of these sketches do consist of matter which could hardly have been reported in the Gallery; but at all events, with regard to that, you have no knowledge as to how information of that sort is obtained?—Undoubtedly reporters do converse with Members in the Lobby; those, I mean, who have admission to the Lobby do converse with them there.

1151. You spoke of the "Central News" as having arrangements with provincial newspapers to a considerable extent; may it be taken that that is an arrangement generally with the provincial newspapers to whatever party they belong, or is it at all special?—There is no distinction of party whatever; the papers on our list are of all shades of opinion, and the reporters in making our report, at any rate, do not regard in any way the opinions of the papers they are writing for.

1152. Do you know at all whether it is the practice, so far as your knowledge goes, of Members to furnish to the newspapers reports of their own speeches?—It is very rarely done in my experience.

1153. *Sir Henry Drummond Wolff.*] May I ask you a question which I asked Mr. Lloyd, whether, in your opinion, the interest in Parliamentary debates is on the increase?—I think so, so far as the provinces are concerned.

1154. And do you think that a full Parliamentary report, of an official character, would find any sale among private people?—I think it would find a large sale. To a great extent it would go to institutions throughout the country, but a great many private persons would take the report, because a large number of people are interested in some special point, of which they wish to see the full particulars.

1155. And then they would buy isolated numbers, would they not?—I think many people would take it in regularly; it might be supplied at a small cost; I d. would be a sufficient charge for it.

1156. You said that the representatives of country papers sit in the Speaker's Gallery: have any representatives of country papers regular seats in the Speaker's Gallery?—They have not; they can only obtain admission there by a Speaker's Order, which is often only to be obtained with great difficulty.

1157. They merely do that sometimes, in fact?—Yes, but there are some representatives of newspapers who endeavour to get into the Speaker's Gallery every night; they do not always succeed.

1158. They get into the Strangers' Gallery, do they not?—They cannot hear there well enough for it to be of service to them.

1159. Your association has a representative who has access to the Lobby?—Yes.

1160. Do you supply country newspapers with any news besides Parliamentary reports?—We do.

1161. Mr.

1161. Mr. *Walter*.] What arrangements have you with the Telegraphic Department of the Post Office for the transmission of the reports of debates?—The charge made by the Post Office is 1 s. per hundred words for the first address, and 3 d. for every hundred words for every additional address.

1162. What do you mean by "address"?—If I send it to one newspaper it is 1 s., and it is 3 d. for every other paper that I send it to.

1163. Is that considered an advantageous arrangement as compared with the ordinary tariff for telegraphic despatches?—The arrangement was based on the charge made by the old telegraphic companies; they supplied us with a Parliamentary report, including reporting, at a certain price; and when the wires were transferred to the Government, they arranged with the newspaper proprietors that the charge for telegraphing should not be in excess of what they previously paid; and it was estimated that the tariff arranged would be equal to the charges made by the old companies.

1164. Then an average, I presume, is struck from the difference between the 1 s. for the first address, and 3 d. each for the subsequent ones, according to the numbers?—Yes.

1165. Sir *Alexander Gordon*.] I understood you to say that the 80 per cent. increase of the last year or two in the reports of speeches which you have supplied was an undoubted indication of the desire of the provincial public to obtain fuller reports of the proceedings in Parliament?—I think so.

1166. It never can arise from any other cause?—As far as my experience goes, it arises from an increased desire on the part of the public to get reports of the speeches of their local Members.

1167. And I understood you to say that there would be no practical difficulty in producing the official publication you speak of on the following morning?—There would be no difficulty whatever; the work involved is very far less than that involved in the production of an ordinary newspaper.

1168. I assume that you have yourself practical knowledge, both of the printing and reporting of newspapers?—Of reporting and of the printing of newspapers.

1169. And you estimate the expense at 350 l. per week?—That is the cost of the reporting and printing.

1170. That would be for 27 weeks under 10,000 l. a year?—Yes.

1171. And as a practical man you think it can be done for that sum?—I think it can be done well for that sum.

1172. Are you aware of the American practice of reporting?—I have no special knowledge about the American reports.

1173. I was going to ask whether you are aware that in America they have arrived at such rapidity in printing the speeches, that on one occasion the beginning of a man's speech was in print before he had finished his speech?—Nothing would be easier than to do that sometimes, when the speeches are long.

1174. I allude to *bonâ fide* reporting; you think it is quite possible that that should be the case?—There is no reason why the printed reports should be more than an hour behind the delivery of the speech in the House.

1175. Therefore if a speech or an address lasts more than an hour, what I am alluding to is quite feasible?—Quite.

1176. Mr. *Hutchinson*.] Having made an estimate of the cost of this official report, which you think, would be generally acceptable, or largely acceptable, will you tell us what you think its general average length would be?—I estimate the average length at 30 columns per day; and by a column I mean 2,000 words.

1177. And do you think that a Parliamentary report of 80 columns per day would be so largely bought up and so much in request that it would be remunerative; would it pay its way?—I think not; I think it would, perhaps, pay for the cost of the paper on which it was printed; I do not think it would pay more than that.

1178. As you have formed an estimate of the cost, and some estimate of the extent to which it would be sold, can you give us some idea of the probable deficit?—I estimate the cost at 350 l. per week, and the only portion of that which I think would be recouped would be the amount received from the provincial newspapers for such portions of the report as they may wish to use, and I think that from them, at least, 100 l. a week might be recovered

Mr. W. SaunBers.
5 July 1878.

1179. I suppose you know the Gallery pretty well?—Yes.

1180. You know the existing space, and how it is appropriated?—Yes.

1181. You told us something about Parliamentary sketches; you said that provincial newspapers are in the habit of inserting Parliamentary sketches, by which I presume you mean accounts of debates that are more descriptive of the manner than a record of the matter?—Quite so.

1182. You are aware that that kind of thing is not confined to the provincial press, are you not?—Undoubtedly it is not; but my observations refer mainly to the provincial press.

1183. Do you not think it is more largely in vogue amongst a certain variety of the metropolitan press than amongst the provincial press?—Very much amongst the metropolitan daily and weekly press.

1184. I suppose you have in your mind's eye a catalogue of journals which might be mentioned, the Parliamentary reports of which are entirely confined to this kind of what you call sketches?—There are many weekly papers of which that might be said.

1185. Now, you have told us that the provincial newspapers that furnish sketches of that kind have representatives in the Speaker's Gallery, and sometimes in the Strangers' Gallery; will you tell us where these London weekly papers get their sketches from?—Some of them have representatives in the Gallery.

1186. And where do they sit?—On the back seats.

1187. Have you any idea of the extent to which the Gallery is occupied by metropolitan gentlemen of that description?—I do not know how many there are representing weekly papers.

1188. Have you any approximate idea?—I cannot say.

1189. Are there a score?—I really do not know.

1190. Colonel *Arbuthnot.*] Do you think that the London press would buy any of the reports to be made officially; you said that the provincial press would: do you think that the London press would also buy them, and do away with their own reporters?—I think that the London press would receive all these reports, and be prepared to pay for them, for editorial purposes, but not for reporting purposes.

1191. Then they would, in your opinion, go to the double expense of keeping their own reporters in the Gallery and also buying this official report?—If each paid a very small sum for these official reports it would, in the aggregate, amount to a good deal; and I have no doubt it would be worth their while to pay a small weekly sum for these reports, in order to have the benefit of writing leaders upon them.

1192. I did not quite gather whether you had gone into the expense of printing, or included that branch of the subject, or whether the figures that you have given simply include the cost of reporting before it was put into type?—They include both reporting and putting into type and printing off those copies that would be wanted for the House itself and for such provincial and London newspapers as might require copies.

1193. On what do you base that calculation of 850 *l.* a week; how many reporters do you allow?—I think about twenty reporters would be required.

1194. And how often would you think it necessary to relieve them in order to get the report rapidly printed?—They should be relieved every five or ten minutes.

1195. In that way it would hardly take, would it, so much as you said before, namely, an hour, to produce the matter that was spoken?—Not to report it, but to get it into type and to have it read and printed an hour would be required.

1196. Will you be so good as to tell me about those seats in the Gallery; I think your agency occupies one of the extreme seats, right or left?—It does.

1197. Are the acoustic qualities of that part of the Gallery good or bad?—By no means good; but some experienced reporters are able to hear there. There are many reporters who could do nothing in a seat of that kind.

1198. You have been, I suppose, in all parts of the Gallery?—I have tested it, and I must confess I could not hear myself in that part of the Gallery, but there are reporters who can hear there.

1199. Are the centre seats very superior to those?—Very superior.

1200. Do you think that there would be any way for the country press to be
enabled

enabled to obtain their Parliamentary reports except through the means of *Mr. W. Saunders.*
agencies like the "Central News"?—I think it is essential that there should be
agencies; but there are often cases in which provincial papers should have their
own reporters in the Gallery. For instance, if they could send in their own
reporters when any local matter is under discussion, it would be a great
advantage.

1201. It is obvious that you could not accommodate there the whole of the
provincial press; do you not think that it would produce heart-burnings and
jealousies if some were admitted and others were refused admission?—I think
it is very hard upon the provincial press to exclude them altogether; and if
proper accommodation were afforded, I think that all who had a fair title to
come, and wished to come, might be admitted.

1202. Can you suggest any means by which accommodation could be supplied for them?—Several seats in the Gallery are occupied now by men who do
not do any reporting, and it might be wise to require that seats so occupied
should be used for reporting; but I think it would be necessary to increase the
accommodation, and I would suggest that the seats in the front of the two Galleries adjoining the Reporters' Gallery be thrown into the Reporters' Gallery on
each side as far as the first doorway.

1203. Could speakers be heard from those seats?—Yes, very well from the
front seats.

1204. Whom do you refer to when you speak of these persons who occupy
the front seats, and do nothing in the way of reporting?—I refer to people who
write summaries, and those who superintend a staff of reporters without doing
any work themselves. The superintendence of a staff could be done just as well
from the back seats.

1205. Then that is the case, is it, that some of the summary writers and some
of the superintendents are occupying front seats now?—Several of them occupy
front seats, and never take a line in the shape of a report.

1206. How many should you say?—I think six seats are occupied in that
way.

1207. *Mr. Barclay.*] I understand you to say that there is a steadily growing
desire in the provinces to have detailed reports of the speeches in Parliament?
—Of local Members.

1208. That is, each local newspaper desires to have a full report of the
speeches of the Members who represent the localities in which it circulates?—
Exactly.

1209. Can you say whether there is an increasing or decreasing desire on the
part of people in London to have detailed reports of the Parliamentary speeches?
—I have no experience on that point.

1210. Is the space devoted by the London press to the Parliamentary reports
increasing or decreasing?—I think the space is the same as it has been for a
long time that is occupied in the London press by Parliamentary reports.

1211. With all the daily papers?—Yes; there has not been any substantial
increase of the number of London papers for many years.

1212. And do they continue to devote as much space in their newspapers to
Parliamentary reports as they did 10 years ago?—I think not; I think the
general tendency is to shorten the reports in the London papers.

1213. The enterprise which you conduct is a private enterprise, I understand?
—It is.

1214. And the Press Association is also a private enterprise?—I am not sure
what you mean precisely by a private enterprise. The Press Association is a
company of newspaper proprietors.

1215. They supply other newspapers, and make a charge for it?—They
do.

1216. And, of course, the charge that they make to papers which are not
members of the association goes in deduction of the cost to themselves?—
I suppose so.

1217. Then, so far as the provincial newspapers are concerned, you and the
Press Association have a monopoly of the supply of Parliamentary news to
them?—No, there is another association; and many of the newspapers in the
provinces obtain reports from gentlemen who represent London papers.

1218. We have had evidence given by the superintendent of the reporting
staff

Mr. W. Saunders.
5 July 1878.

staff of the "Times," and also by the proprietor of the "Daily Chronicle," that their reporters are prohibited from giving any reports to the provincial newspapers; can you say in regard to the other newspapers what their practice is?—I would rather not say, if you will excuse me answering that question.

1219. Supposing that other newspapers prohibit their reporters from giving reports to the provincial newspapers, how are the provincial newspapers to get news except through you and the Press Association?—There is no other mode.

1220. Then, except so far as the House is concerned, by getting them in a certain sense surreptitiously, the provincial press cannot get reports, except through the associations named?—I would not call it surreptitious; it is done so openly that it can hardly be considered so in any light.

1221. These reporters for the London newspapers have seats in the Gallery by virtue of being reporters, and on the sole ground of being reporters for the London newspapers?—Yes.

1222. There is no obligation upon them, so far as the House is concerned, to give reports to provincial newspapers?—No obligation whatever; they simply do it for payment.

1223. Then the reporters of the London newspapers who are allowed to give these provincial reports have, to a certain extent, a monopoly which they hold in virtue of being reporters of London newspapers?—Yes.

1224. Does not it come to this, that they profess to be reporters of London newspapers, and then take advantage of that position to supply the provincial newspapers, with profit to themselves?—It might be described in that way.

1225. Have you a list of the newspapers which you supply with news?—I have not it here.

1226. Do you supply any Scotch newspapers?—We do.

1227. How many dailies do you supply?—I supply 44 daily papers, 59 weekly papers, and 23 clubs, with regular reports of Parliament, and I telegraph important Parliamentary announcements to 93 daily papers, weekly papers, and 143 clubs.

1228. How many of those are Scotch?—I supply six daily papers, 13 weekly, and 6 clubs in Scotland with Parliamentary reports, and 3 daily papers, 15 weekly, and 9 clubs with important announcements in Parliament.

1229. Can you tell us some of the principal ones which you supply?—I scarcely know whether the papers would like their names to be mentioned.

1230. Did I rightly understand you to say that you never gave out a daily report of less than a column and a half of the proceedings in Parliament?—I said that our report varies from a column and a half to seven columns.

1231. Does that mean that you never send less than a column and a half?—There are some occasions on which the reports are of extremely small interest, but it would very rarely be less than that length.

1232. Have you any idea how often you send out as much as seven columns?—Perhaps half a dozen times during the Session.

1233. Then as regards reporting the speeches of Members discussing Imperial questions, Members in regard to whom you have not special instructions from the locality which they represent, do your reporters exercise absolute discretion whether they are to be reported or not, and, if so, at what length?—Excepting as to local Members, they exercise their discretion.

1234. Would many of the provincial newspapers desire to have seats in the Gallery, do you think; perhaps I had better put it in this way: would many of the provincial, or Scotch, or Irish newspapers be at the expense of maintaining a full staff of reporters if they had a seat in the Gallery?—I think eight or 10 provincial newspapers would do that if they had the opportunity.

1235. You do not think that more than 10 provincial newspapers would go to the expense of maintaining a complete staff in the Gallery?—I think not, but several others might wish to have a representative there who would not, perhaps, be entitled to a front seat, but should be there to watch the interests of their paper.

1236. Do you consider that there would be an essential difference between a newspaper which was ready to maintain a full staff of reporters in the Gallery and a newspaper which only wanted to put in a reporter when it suited their convenience?—The difference would be in the expression of their wishes; some newspapers would not wish to have a full staff, and others would. I take

it

is that any newspaper proprietor or any agency applying to the Serjeant at Arms for accommodation would explain for what purpose they required it. The Serjeant at Arms requests us to give him at the commencement of every Session the number of papers which we represent, which we do; and any other applicant would probably be asked in the same manner for what purpose he required accommodation.

1237. I will put it in this way: If a newspaper proprietor wished to have a reporter or a summary writer in the Gallery he would require a box as much as if he had a full staff of reporters, would he not?—I think the summary writer should be entirely excluded from the front boxes; he would require the seat behind.

1238. Such a newspaper, which only wanted a summary writer occasionally in the House, would occupy as much space as a newspaper that had a staff of ten or a dozen reporters?—A newspaper that had a staff of ten or a dozen reporters would require a front seat, and also one in the back for a man to wait his turn, and also space for a summary writer on the back seat; so that a staff would require three seats always occupied.

1239. There is only one daily newspaper that has three seats at present, I think?—There would be only one front seat, the two back seats necessarily occupied on account of the staff; I think no newspaper ought to have more than one front seat under any circumstances.

1240. I thought you wanted two front seats for your association?—I should want two front seats unless there is an official report, because I have two things to do; but if there were an official report published there would be no necessity for a second seat.

1241. What are the two things that you have to do?—The two things I have to do are to prepare a general report which occupies one seat continuously, and to report fully local members, for which duty one reporter must be always prepared.

1242. Is not the one you first named the summary writer?—A general report is not a summary in the sense I mean; the general report I refer to could not be written from the back seat; it is a very different matter from the brief summary which appears in the London papers and in some provincial papers.

1243. Did any of the provincial newspapers give lengthened reports of the speeches in Parliament before your agency was organised?—The "Manchester Guardian," I think, at one time had seats in the House, but I believe they did not continue them.

1244. Did none of the Scotch papers give a lengthened report of the debates when the telegraphs were in the hands of private companies?—I really have not had my attention directed to that.

1245. I asked the question, because I thought you said that there were no lengthened reports in the local papers until you and the Press Association organised this new business?—There might be exceptions, but generally speaking there were no long reports or special reports in the provincial newspapers until the charges for telegraphing special reports were reduced.

1246. Then as to the official report, you would propose to have it out in time for the early morning trains as a general rule?—Yes.

1247. The early morning trains start at five o'clock?—I think some of them start earlier than that now.

1248. Then up to how late might the House sit, and you be able, under this official report system, to forward the reports by the morning train?—Certainly the proceedings of the House might be reported up to half-past two or three o'clock.

1249. And the reports prepared and sent out by the trains at five o'clock?—Yes.

1250. Your idea that the provincial press would not require such long and detailed reports is founded on this, that the provincial newspapers would be furnished with the speeches in detail from the official report the second day?—Not the second day, but the first day; they would receive the report the same evening and telegraph it immediately.

1251. How so?—If any Member made a speech in the House the full report of that speech in print would be presented to the representative of the newspaper, and he would immediately hand it in to the post office, and it would be telegraphed.

1252. Have

1252. Have you any difficulty in getting your messages over the wires when there is a long debate?—There is great difficulty sometimes, but as a rule the work is done very well.

1253. Then I understand your idea would be this, that the official report should be handed to the representative of the newspaper, and that he would hand it to the post office, or send it over his own special wires to his own newspaper, and so a special report on their own behalf would not be required?—Exactly.

1254. If there were official reports, do you think the desire would be any the less to see the reports in the "Times," for instance, of the debates in Parliament?—I think not at all less.

1255. The public would desire to have as lengthy reports as at the present time in the newspapers, you think?—I think that they would desire to have the same reports, and that the newspapers in their own interest would give the same reports. There may be some reasons why the very long reports now given should not continue to be given in the newspapers.

1256. Now, have you any detailed estimate of this 350 l. a week, which you say would be the cost of the official report?—Roughly speaking, I should estimate it in this way: I would estimate the cost of reporting 30 columns per night for 5 nights per week at 1 l. per column, which would amount to 150 l. per week; I would then estimate the expenses of putting it in type at 1 l. a column, which would also amount to 150 l. per week; and then I would estimate the expenses of superintendence and sundries at 50 l. per week, which would make the 350 l.

1257. How late can the provincial newspapers take news from you in order to publish them in the morning?—The time of publication varies very much in different localities, but these local reports, generally speaking, might be sent off as late as 12 or 1 o'clock, and set up in the provincial papers.

1258. What hour of going to press are you assuming?—Say 4 o'clock; and it often happens that newspapers publish special town editions, so that they could get in the speeches of their local Members after the general edition had been printed.

1259. Lord *Francis Hervey*.] The sum and substance of your complaint, I suppose, is, that the associations which represent the provincial press, and the Scotch and Irish press, have not due facilities for reporting the debates in Parliament, as things stand?—That is the sum and substance of my complaint; and I think it will appear clear when I remind the Committee that something like 15 good seats are appropriated to 10 London papers, and three very bad seats to 60 provincial papers.

1260. Now if, instead of having three bad seats, you had three good seats, would that give all the facilities that you think would be necessary?—I think that many more seats should be provided for the accommodation of the provincial papers.

1261. What number of seats do you consider would be necessary for that purpose?—I think at least 12 front seats should be provided.

1262. Do you mean to be distributed between these three associations that now represent the provincial press?—No, because, with an official report, one seat might be enough for each association; but several provincial papers should have staffs of their own in the House; they would wish to have them, and they spend perhaps quite as much on Parliamentary reporting as the London papers do, and I do not see why they should not have the accommodation.

1263. If the summary writers were caused to retire from their present position on the front bench you would gain six seats?—Yes.

1264. Would not that be all that is necessary for the provincial press?—We want 12 more good seats at least.

1265. You suggested that you should come round the corner and take the Members' seats?—I do not see any other way of enlarging the Gallery.

1266. Do not you think that Members might object to those seats being occupied?—They are rarely occupied by the Members themselves.

1267. But they are very valuable on certain occasions; for instance, on the Budget night I go up there, because you can hear the Chancellor of the Exchequer so well from there?—They are very valuable to Members on certain occasions, but to the press they would be very valuable always.

1268. Do

1268. Do you think that a reporter in one of those seats could hear other speakers than those just opposite to him?—I do not think that there would be a difficulty in taking from there a report of a speech made in almost any part of the House.

1269. My experience is that when you are listening to a Member whose face is opposite to you, you can hear very well, but when endeavouring to listen to a Member who is speaking on the same side of the House, especially a Member under the Gallery, and on one of the back benches, you can hardly hear him at all?—I am sorry to hear it.

1270. If you take that as the fact, perhaps you would be less anxious to secure those seats?—I suggested them as the best to be had. An official report would relieve the matter very much, because it could be turned to for the speeches of Members who were indistinctly heard.

1271. I will take you to that question of an official publication; you said that if there were an official publication, the associations representing the provincial and Scotch and Irish press would be discharged from the obligation of supplying a full report for the local papers of their Members' speeches?—Because those reports would be supplied by the official report.

1272. That is, assuming that they could be got in time for the publication of the local press?—They could be got as quickly from the official report as they are now from private reports.

1273. Now, on the subject of the cost of the publication, you would expect that some part of that cost would be recouped by the sale of the publication?—By the sale of the report the same evening.

1274. But do you not think that there would also be an opportunity for recouping part of that course by the publication of debates on special subjects in a separate form at the end of the Session, or during the Session. I will take you to a particular point: Mr. Hansard produced to us a full report of the debates on the Factories Bill; I want to get your opinion on the matter as far as you have been able to test it; that might be of great use and interest to persons connected with factories, whether workmen or masters, or inspectors, and so forth?—Quite so, but I think those occasions would be so rare that they would not substantially produce any income that could be regarded.

1275. Are you aware that the debates in 1870 on the Education Bill were published in a separate form?—But the utmost any one could pay for those reports would be the mere cost of putting them in type, because they are open to any one to put them in type, and republish them; and therefore the official reporter would get no payments worth speaking of from that source.

1276. Dr. Lyon Playfair.) The general reports that you send to the provinces are identical reports?—They are.

1277. Now, of course, they are necessarily partial, and are mere abstracts of the speeches which have been given in the House?—They are.

1278. If they were uniform, I suppose there could be no objection to their being identical reports; but when they are only partial, does that give the Provincial Press a fair representation, or the best representation of what has proceeded in the House?—It gives a fair representation, but not a full representation.

1279. That is to say, it gives a fair representation of the mind of the reporter; but where there are abstracts made of a speech, are there any two reporters acting independently who would give really a fair impression of the person who spoke?—I think so. If you had two good reporters, the summaries which they would give would be very much alike; of course there would be a difference.

1280. But taking two abstract reports, such as you see in the London papers, of a man's speech, they may be perfectly fairly given, but do they not give a totally different view of what was said by the person, because one reporter is struck with some passages in his speech, and the other reporter with others, and the impression conveyed to the public is altogether different?—I should not consider that, with a good condensed report, that would be the case; the London papers have generally a special object in their reports, which we, as agencies, have not.

1281. Do not you think that identical reports are apt to depress the energy of provincial papers which are anxious to report debates fully to their subscribers?—They have that disadvantage; and to meet that I think there ought to be greater facilities for each paper giving special reports when they require it.

Mr. W. Saunders.

5 July 1878.

1982. The fact that the special reporting of the speeches of local Members has increased 80 per cent. during the last year, shows that there is a demand on the part of the localities for full reports upon matters which interest them? —Yes.

1283. Now what would be the result of what you have recommended, namely, an official report; you say it requires 30 reporters; would not that be shutting out 20 reporters from the gallery of the London and Provincial Press?— It would supersede the work of those reporters who are now engaged in making special reports of speeches of local Members, but it would not supersede the work of any reporters who are now engaged in making general reports.

1284. What I mean is this: there is a very limited space for the reporters altogether, and if you bring in 20 reporters to make an official report, 20 must push out 20, must they not?—The number present at the same time would not be more than two, and I think it would be essential that those reporters should be on the floor of the House.

1285. In that case it would not shut out any from the gallery?—No.

1286. I suppose you consider that any official report must be immediate; that it would be of no use if published two days subsequently, or even in the afternoon of the day?—Not the least use; I think it must be immediate to be of any value.

1287. Must it be accurate to be of use?—Undoubtedly.

1288. You have suggested that the speakers should be allowed to correct their reports?—Yes.

1289. What would be the consequence of that. Take a Cabinet Minister who makes a speech, and is very busily engaged in watching proceedings; would it be possible for him on the same night to correct any report of his speech?—Probably not, and I think it would be quite unnecessary, because a Cabinet Minister would be almost sure to be reported with that degree of accuracy which would render it unnecessary for him to look at the copy of his speech.

1290. Then you think it would be officially correct as regards Members who had not responsibilities, but it must be correct according to the views of the reporter in the case of men who had responsibilities?—It would be correct in the case of all speeches that were clear in themselves.

1291. Suppose that a Member uses an argument which is demolished by the Member who succeeds him in debate; in the correction of the first Member's speech, is not the passage likely to vanish that was demolished?—I should not allow any alterations of that kind.

1292. To whom would you give the supervision and the power to prevent the corrections of a Member being accepted?—The editor in charge of the work.

1293. You would make him supreme despot of what the Member had said? —I should; in sending the proof to the Member it would be explained what kind of corrections would be admitted, exactly in the same way as it is explained to us when we get proofs of the evidence which we give here, as to what corrections will be admitted.

1294. Certain newspapers, but especially weekly newspapers, in their Parliamentary reporting, seem to rejoice more in describing the personal peculiarities of the Members than their speeches?—That is not reporting at all.

1295. Would it not be possible for those persons to get another place equally good; perhaps, if the public wish that kind of reporting, it is desirable that they should have it, but would it not be possible to get that done in the opposite gallery, say the Speaker's, and to leave their places for the true reporters?—I think so.

1296. Then I think I gather that your opinion decidedly is, that the provincial papers of such energy that they are inclined to go to the large expense of employing a full staff of reporters for reporting ought to be treated on the same basis as the London newspapers, and to have these facilities?— That is my view.

1297. Mr. Dunbar.] I think you said that 12 seats in the front ought to be set aside for the agencies and the country papers?—I was asked the question

tion without having given it much thought, and I think 19 would perhaps not Mr. be sufficient.

1298. How would you occupy those seats?—They would be occupied first of all by the agencies which now exist, and also by the representatives of the provincial newspapers, which send their own staff to the gallery.

1299. I think you said that there were more complaints made of inaccuracy in speeches reported from the back bench in the House of Commons than from those on the front bench:—We rarely got complaints as to speeches reported from the front benches, but frequently so to those reported from the back bench.

1300. Could you give me an instance of a case of any complaint of that kind? —I might mention Dr. Cameron as having frequently complained, and Mr. M'Laren.

1301. You would have 20 reporters for the official report?—Yes.

1302. What would you give each man a week?—I think seven guineas.

1303. Do you think it would be possible to bring out a full report in the morning in time for the early train?—There would be no difficulty.

1304. You said that each copy would produce a penny; I suppose the official record ought to be on good paper and a handy size; could you turn it out for a penny? — Yes; 30 columns would make a four-paged newspaper, rather larger than the "Times," and that could be sold for a penny, and leave a handsome profit on the sale.

1305. Mr. *Mitchell Henry.*] In regard to the official report which you contemplate for a sum of between 8,000 *l.* and 9,000 *l.* a year, how many copies would you distribute for that sum?—I merely meant to supply copies for the use of Members in the House, and also for the use of newspapers requiring copies in the evening; additional copies would be printed by a different machine, and would be sold in the ordinary manner like other newspapers; and I estimate that the results of that sale would pay the cost of machining and the cost of the paper.

1306. Now with respect to the sum; who would pay or guarantee the 8,000 *l.* or 9,000 *l.* requisite?—The Government, I take it, if they undertook an official report: no other party, I presume, would have any interest in producing an official report.

1307. You would then have to keep a debtor and creditor account between the Government and the newspapers which took some of these reports and paid you?—Yes, unless the Government chose to supply the newspapers without cost.

1308. That is an arrangement that might possibly be contemplated in the official report?—It might.

1309. Would that be in any sense a subvention to the newspapers?—I should not recommend it; I think it is right that they should pay for it.

1310. How far would the official report that you contemplate be in the nature of a verbatim report, or an edited report?—It would be a verbatim report, with the exception of obvious repetitions, and such matter as could be obviously omitted without detriment to the report.

1311. It would then be very nearly a verbatim report?—Very nearly a verbatim report.

1312. In respect to the corrections which you would admit into that report, you would only, as I understand, admit such corrections as the Committee admit in the evidence taken before us?—Exactly.

1313. Now, you were asked about reports of a different character, reports which describe rather the personal appearance and manner of Members, and so on, which you might call sensational reports; and you suggested, I understand, that reporters of that kind should be removed to a different part of the House?—I was asked if they could do that work in the other part of the House, and I said that I think they could.

1314. Then there are in existence reporters whose occupation it is to give these sensational reports only?—I think not exclusively.

1315. Are the sensational reports then supplied by gentlemen who report more prosaic matter also?—They are, but I think it would be quite as well if they were relieved of that work.

1316. Do you think, then, that if the matter could be arranged, you would find

find any gentlemen admitting that they were sensational reporters, and therefore could be removed from the working staff of the newspapers; do you think that there are any such gentlemen who would admit that they could be so removed? —I think that there are gentlemen in the Reporters' Gallery who could not give a good account of the reporting that they do, and I think that such gentlemen should be excluded from it.

1317. You are aware that the Serjeant at Arms gave us a list of a very considerable number of gentlemen attached to different newspapers under the name of reporters; do I rightly gather from your answer to that question that some of these gentlemen can hardly be considered as reporters?—Many of those gentlemen could not make any pretension to be working reporters.

1318. Then, if we are told that one newspaper has 11 reporters, another 15, another 17, and so on, is it within your knowledge that some portion of those gentlemen are not reporters at all?—I would not say that they are not reporters, but they certainly do not do any reporting in the Gallery.

1319. But they have the right of entrée into the Gallery?—Yes, they have.

1320. And they come and go?—Yes, and they occupy front seats.

1321. That, of course, is outside of those gentlemen who are called summary reporters, who write the summaries?—Not altogether so; there are cases in which persons who occupy front seats do not write anything.

1322. Then, would it be possible to obtain some fresh accommodation for the provincial newspapers in the Gallery, by a more careful selection of those gentlemen who are admitted under the name of reporters for the London papers?—Quite possible.

1323. With respect to the telegraphic reports to the newspapers which are done at a cheap rate, am I correct in supposing that the public have equally the privilege with your association of sending a telegram to a newspaper for publication at that rate?—There is no exclusive privilege to any one; everybody can send to a newspaper at the Act of Parliament rates.

1324. An open letter, or an open report can go from any member of the public to any newspaper in England, Ireland, or Scotland, for the sum of 1 s. per hundred words, and 2 d. for any second delivery to another newspaper?—Yes, any matter for publication may be sent at those rates.

1325. Sir Henry T. Holland.] I understand that the speeches would be almost reported verbatim in the official report which you contemplate?—They would.

1326. Now have you formed any opinion as to the number of volumes to which this official report would extend in such case?—I calculate that there would be 30 columns per night of 2,000 words each column; 30 columns of a newspaper about the size of the "Times."

1327. Taking a volume of the size of Hansard, what number of volumes would the official report extend to?—I am afraid I could not answer that offhand; it would depend so much upon the size of the type.

1328. I am assuming the type and the size of Hansard?—I am not prepared to say offhand; it would require some calculation.

1329. Can you give us some notion; it would be considerably larger in extent than Hansard?—Mr. Hansard, I think, estimates his report as increasing from five to nine volumes under his new arrangements; and no doubt the report which I contemplate would add several volumes more.

1330. Beyond the five?—Beyond the nine.

1331. Then have you formed any opinion as to the probable price which a private purchaser would have to pay for each official report?—They might be supplied at a penny per day, and consequently the cost would be very trifling.

1332. You think that the charge of a penny a day would cover the machine expenses, I think you called them, and the paper?—Yes, the machining and the paper.

1333. Now leaving out of consideration Members of Parliament who, we may trust, would be supplied with these copies gratis, do you think that the official reports would be regularly taken in by many persons?—I think that they would be taken in by a great number of persons, and by a great number of institutions. Every club and every news-room would have them throughout the country.

Mr. E. Saunders.
5 July 1878.

1334. Of course I can understand that on particular occasions when questions of special interest arise, a great number of copies would be taken in by those who were interested in such questions; but I am applying my question to the regular purchasers of official reports; do you think there would be many?—I can only say that I should be very glad to have such a report myself, and I think a great many other gentlemen would; and it would be a great comfort if they were given in an official shape independently of a newspaper, because we want a newspaper to give us more varied and interesting matter rather than a long report.

1335. If there is to be an official report you consider it necessary that the reporters should be officers of the House and not belong to any newspaper?—Yes.

1336. And that they should be accommodated with seats in the body of the House?—I think that would be essential.

1337. I think you said that there should be two sets of reporters; one to make a general report of the speeches, and the other to report specially speeches of local Members?—That last is requisite if we have no official report.

1338. But why cannot the reporter who is reporting the proceedings of the House, if he is instructed, take a report of the speech of some particular Member?—He could not do that and do a condensed report at the same time.

1339. Why; is it because there would not be time to condense the report afterwards?—He could not take what we call a full note and write a condensed report at the same time.

1340. But could he not condense the report from his full report?—No, there would not be time for that; if we waited to condense from the full report we should lose our chance altogether.

1341. Mr. Crum.] I think you had a great deal to do in arranging the transference of the conveyance of news from the old telegraph companies to these new associations; you were concerned in making those arrangements?—Yes, in connection with other newspaper proprietors.

1342. Therefore you are familiar with the old system as well as the new?—Yes.

1343. And from your experience, as the head of a reporting establishment during these last seven years, your opinion is that the demand for Parliamentary reports has increased in the provinces?—Yes, very much.

1344. You are clear on that point, because we have had evidence before the Committee in exactly the opposite direction?—I speak merely from my own experience.

1345. How do you account, then, for this apparently contradictory position of affairs; some of the papers in London with the largest circulation give a gradually decreasing report of Parliamentary proceedings?—They undoubtedly study the wishes of their readers; and I very much doubt the wisdom of any newspaper giving very long reports, except with regard to local Members; and it is merely with regard to the reports of speeches of local Members that that increase of which I spoke has taken place.

1346. There are two reports, then; one the report of the general Parliamentary proceedings, which you do not think there is an increased demand for throughout the country; but the other, the reports of the local Members, there is a demand, and an increasing demand for?—That is exactly it.

1347. Then the want which is to be supplied is a want of reports of speeches of local Members for provincial constituencies?—Exactly so.

1348. Your Association supplies reports to about 103 papers?—Yes.

1349. Are any of these 103 daily papers?—Yes, a considerable number of them.

1350. The Press Association gave us in evidence that they supplied something like 50 or 60 daily papers, and a proportionate number of weeklies, as well, I suppose?—I do not know what their number would be.

1351. Your calculation is that something like three-fourths of the population of the country are supplied with reports of the Parliamentary proceedings through the Press Associations?—I have reckoned 14 counties as being supplied with the London papers, and I find that the population of these 14 counties is about 7,800,000; the remainder of the population of the United Kingdom

Mr. W. Saunders.

4 July 1878.

Kingdom receives its Parliamentary reports mainly from the provincial papers, and the whole population at the last census was something over 31,000,000; so that you see that more than three-fourths of the population receive their reports of Parliamentary proceedings from the provincial papers.

1352. And those reports are supplied by the agencies that you represent, by the Press Association and the Central News?—Chiefly.

1353. And the representation that they have in the Gallery consists of three seats?—Of two seats, the Central Press has one seat also.

1354. Is there not one for you, one for the Press Association, and one for the Central Press?—Yes.

1355. There are, therefore, three seats for those agencies?—Yes.

1356. And in the worst part of the Gallery?—In the worst part of the Gallery.

1357. Therefore your evidence is to this effect, that three-fourths of the population of the United Kingdom receive their reports of Parliamentary proceedings through these organisations which are represented in the Gallery by three seats in the worst part?—Three bad seats.

1358. Your object is to obtain better accommodation for the representatives of these associations?—Yes.

1359. And you wish to accomplish that in this way: to have two seats for reporters to represent your association; one to report a general account of Parliamentary proceedings, and another to report the local speeches required?—Yes; it would be essential for each association to have two seats unless an official report is promptly published.

1360. And you propose to get that accommodation by moving the summary writers from the front seats now occupied by them and putting the reporters in their place?—That should be done I think, but that would not provide sufficient accommodation; you would require an extension of the accommodation as well.

1361. You think that the summary writers could sit behind and pursue their avocations without much trouble if the associations had the space which they now occupy?—Yes.

1362. Now the general report of the proceedings that you give is just according to the judgment of your reporters?—Yes.

1363. But the special report of local Members is in consequence of the demand from the local press?—Yes, in consequence of instructions that we have from the editors of the provincial papers.

1364. You mean that if you are not specially instructed, you probably report the speech of a Member at the length of 10 or 12 lines, but if you receive special instructions you report it fully?—Yes.

1365. Therefore it is the judgment of the editor that applies for the report, and not the judgment of the head of the association that determines the length of it?—Entirely so.

1366. We have had from Mr. Lloyd, and we have also had, I think, from Mr. Ross, a statement that the London reporters in connection with their own journals, do not send, or are not known to send, special reports to the provincial papers?—I do not think that the proprietors of newspapers know so much about that matter as some other people do; but I should rather not say much more about it.

1367. The fact is, that the practice does exist, but is winked at?—I do not think it is winked at; it is looked at openly.

1368. Ignored; but the testimony of Mr. Lloyd was that his reporters would not be permitted to supply them?—I do not know Mr. Lloyd's reporters personally.

1369. Has not this occurred to you, that the double work that the reporters on the London newspapers are called upon to perform decreases their opportunity of discharging, or prevents them from discharging, their work in London as efficiently as they otherwise would have done?—I should be very sorry if any reporter of mine appointed to do one work undertook another.

1370. In the discussion which took place in the House of Commons last year, a statement was made by Mr. Gladstone that after 40 years' experience, he found the reports gradually getting worse, and that they were worse now than they had ever been in his life time; does your experience go to show that it is the increased demand upon the London reporters that prevents them from giving that

that attention which they formerly did to their reports?—I cannot say from my own experience that it is so.

1371. You were asked some questions about the ornamental reporting that takes place; have you, in connection with your association, in addition to the mere report of the proceedings that you send to the papers, a description of what takes place in Parliament?—Yes.

1372. And that description is practically a summary; something like the summary that appears in the London papers, is it not?—It is not intended to be a summary; it is intended to give an idea of the different matters that take place in the House; it would mention, for instance, whether a speech was well received or otherwise.

1373. The fact is, that it fills in the lights and shades of the picture, I suppose?—Exactly so.

1374. A question was asked you about information being supplied by Members to the papers of what takes place in the House of Commons; there are instances when the reporters are turned out of the Gallery; a case of that kind recently occurred in the discussion on Lord Leitrim's death, and full reports appeared in the London newspapers afterwards; necessarily these must have been supplied by Members?—I expect so.

1375. They could not have been supplied by anybody else?—I imagine not.

1376. By the ladies, someone suggests; but I think that is scarcely likely?—In America they have lady reporters in the Gallery, and, I think, ladies in the Ladies' Gallery here, would be quite capable of reporting if they were allowed to do so.

1377. You have considered the question of an official report, and have arrived at the conclusion that such a report could be published at an expense of 850 £ a week?—Yes.

1378. And you think that in the course of an hour after the speech was delivered, the Member could have a proof of it to read?—Yes.

1379. Some surprise has been expressed as to the rapidity of that, but is it not the fact that in the French Assembly it is made a condition of the report, that within 20 minutes of the last word being uttered the report should be in the hands of the Member; are you not conscious of that?—I am not conscious of that, and I think that refers to a condensed report.

1380. I believe that that is one of the clauses of the contract by which the reporting is conducted?—I am not surprised; I asked the printer of the "Pall Mall Gazette" how soon he could supply a report after he had the copy, and he said in 10 minutes.

1381. Your opinion, I think, is to this effect, that an official report would not necessarily, as far as your opinion goes, decrease the amount of space that is now given to Parliamentary reports by the London papers?—I do not think it would decrease it with regard to the majority of the London papers; what effect it would have on those papers which now publish very long reports I could not undertake to say.

1382. Has it not struck you that the present space given to Parliamentary reports by the London papers is to some extent accounted for by the larger area of interest that they are taking in the shape of getting reports from foreign capitals and distant countries by telegraph; has not that, to some extent, decreased the demand for Parliamentary news?—That may be so; but my impression is that long reports are not valued by the public now in their newspapers.

1383. That is to say, where the newspaper has intelligible summary or report. But what the Members may require, or the House may require, is an official report for historical purposes, and for purposes of reference?—Yes.

1384. Mr. Forster.] I want to find out how far Ireland and Scotland are represented by your agency; take Ireland first; could you state that?—We send reports to eight daily papers in Ireland.

1385. Could you give the towns?—Dublin, Belfast, and Cork.

1386. Do you think that the Press Association would send reports to any more?—I think that they supply some papers in Ireland, and I am not sure whether some of the papers do not get their own reports.

1387. Would it, or would it not, be true that your agency, and the other agencies, represent the provinces and Great Britain more than they represent Ireland?

Mr. W. Saunders.

5 July 1878.

Ireland?—I think every Irish paper gets a report, either from my agency or from the Press Association; there may be one or two exceptions, but I am not certain that there is an exception.

1388. The same remark would apply to Scotland, I suppose?—There are one or two exceptions, I know, in Scotland, where they do not take reports from us, or from the Press Association, but from their own reporters.

1389. You have mentioned that you send reports to 103 papers; do you think that some of those papers take reports from the Press Association as well as from you?—I should hardly think so.

1390. You mentioned in reply to an honourable Member that you thought the effect of an official report would be, that the papers would give more interesting and varied news rather than long reports; do you think that the effect of an official report would be to shorten the present reports in the papers?—I think that as a rule the reports have come down to a minimum now, with the exception of those long reports which have been mentioned before.

1391. You mean in two or three of the papers; the "Times," the "Morning Post," and the "Standard"?—Yes.

1392. Have you formed any idea whether it would be likely to shorten those reports?—I cannot form any idea.

1393. I suppose that it is part of your business to look at a great many of the country newspapers?—Yes.

1394. Is it not the case that several of the larger country newspapers have quite as long a report as any of the London papers, with the exception of the three you have mentioned?—Quite as long.

1395. And in some cases, even independently of the importance of the local Members, longer?—Yes, frequently.

1396. How do you think they get those long reports that they put in; if, for instance, I take up a paper in Yorkshire or Lancashire, and I find, as I sometimes do, that a debate of great interest upon foreign affairs is reported quite as fully as it would be in several of the London papers, how do they get that?—We supply ourselves reports up to six, seven, or eight columns on nights of great interest.

1397. Do you think that they get them from the reporters of the London papers?—I do not think they get those reports to which you refer from the reporters for the London papers; I think they get them from the Central news, or the Press Association.

1398. Sir Henry Drummond Wolff.] Did I rightly understand you to say that there are 2,000 words in a column of the "Times"?—I think there are 2,300 words in a column of the "Times," but I take 2,000 words as a column.

1399. And you say that a full official report would amount to about 30 of those columns a night?—Yes; I include the House of Lords as well as the House of Commons.

1400. Do you think that report for 1 d., the price you suggest, would produce a bad paper or one neatly printed?—I would have a neatly printed paper.

1401. And that would cover all the expenses except the reporting?—Yes, except the reporting and putting into type.

1402. It would not cover any of the expenses of reporting?—No.

1403. Merely the paper and printing?—Just so.

1404. One honourable Member asked you as to the difficulty of deciding whether things are to be put in the official report or not; of course if the editor had that control he might be controlled again, or there might be an appeal from him to a Committee of the House in a case of difference with a Member as to the corrections he wished to make?—All the persons engaged on this official report would be officers of the House, I take it, and would be subject to their instructions.

1405. That might be arranged, in fact!—Yes.

1406. You said just now that you thought there should be more room for the provincial papers in the Gallery; you referred to the associations who represent provincial papers; you did not refer to the additional reporters that might be sent by individual provincial papers, did you?—Yes, I intended to include the reporters of all such papers as would send a staff of their own to the Gallery.

1407. You think there are some papers that would like to dispense with the services of the associations and have their own reporters?—They would like to have their own reporters, certainly.

1408. There are several papers that would like to have their own; but it is done not

not follow that they would not take our report; they would supplement it, I Mr. W. Saunders. imagine, with their own.

1409. *Chairman.*] I want to ask you one question; are you aware whether   6 July 1878. there is any demand on the part of the public outside Parliament and outside gentlemen in your own profession for an official report?—I do not know that there is.

1410. Has there been any complaint on the part of the public of the absence of that official report?—The matter has often been discussed, and surprise expressed that we should be almost the only country in the world without an official report, and I have heard in many instances persons complain that they cannot find in the reports which are now published that special business in which they are interested.

1411. When you speak of persons, what class of persons are you referring to; men who are engaged in the business of Parliament?—I am speaking more of men of business in the country, for instance, who perhaps may have special interest in some particular thing, and they do not get it sufficiently reported to give them the information they require.

1412. Do you believe that these men of business in the country of whom you speak would regularly subscribe to an official report if it were accessible?—I think if they could get an official report for 1 d. a day, they would subscribe to it for the purpose of looking at those special points in which they are interested.

1413. An honourable Member asks whether they are not more likely to take in a special number, rather than to take in the paper daily?—It would often happen that things turned up unexpectedly which they would wish to know, and a man of business would glance through that report in the morning to see if there was any topic in which he was particularly interested.

1414. Then is it the fact that all men of business do glance through the longest possible report that they can now obtain of Parliamentary proceedings? —I think they frequently do; it is a mere glance; I think there are very few persons who read them in full.

1415. Are you aware that we have had evidence that nobody reads a long Parliamentary report?—I quite agree that nobody reads a long Parliamentary Report; but most people like to glance at it, to pick out some particular point or some particular person.

1416. Which of the two is more important; to provide ample facilities for newspapers which desire to report the proceedings of Parliament, or to provide an official report?—I think an official report would supply more perfect reports of speeches of local Members than could be obtained in any other way, and therefore I look upon that as a most important point in connection with the subject, as far as newspapers are concerned.

1417. Then you are prepared to say that it is not in your judgment necessary to provide increased facilities for newspapers desiring to report local Members, but that it is desirable to provide an official report?—I think both are desirable, but I think an official report is the most desirable.

1418. Would there be any more inconvenience to Members if their speeches were accurately reported and printed without their correction than now arises from the evidence of witnesses before a Committee being printed without correction, as your evidence to-day will be?—I think the reports in the way I propose to take them would be very much more accurate than it is possible to make the reports of the proceedings of Committees as they are taken; because I would arrange for each reporter to read his own copy, which he could only do in the case of an immediate publication. I should just like to say, that for an immediate publication it would be necessary to have accommodation in the building, in the House itself, and for that purpose there is a room specially available, which was formerly used for bathing purposes, and which is not now used; it is under the central lobby, and it is a room extremely well adapted for the work.

1419. You would propose that there should be accommodation for two reporters at the Table of the House?—Yes.

1420. And that there should be a communication between the Table of the House and the space below?—Yes.

1421. So that the reporters could be frequently changed?—Yes.

1422. And that they should have accommodation in the House in which they could write out their notes?—Yes.

M 4   1423. That

1423. That there should also be accommodation in the House for the printers?—Yes.

1424. To take proofs, at all events, of the type as it was set up?—Yes.

1425. Do you go so far as to say that the actual printing ought to be carried on in the House?—I think that the actual printing should be carried on elsewhere, as far as the copies for sale are concerned.

1426. But everything up to the completion of the publication for press should be done in this building?—Yes; I have just prepared a sheet which strikes me as an illustration of the mode in which sheets might be presented every 20 minutes to the House (handing in a copy).

1427. Under your plan the size of the newspaper would, of course, vary with the amount of speaking?—It would, and therefore the pages should be rather small to allow of the number being varied.

Mr. *Charles Alfred Cooper*, called in; and Examined.

1428. *Chairman*.] I THINK you are the Assistant Editor of the "Scotsman"?—I am.

1429. Have you had any experience as a Parliamentary reporter?—I was at one time in the Gallery as a Parliamentary reporter.

1430. In the Gallery of the House of Commons?—Yes.

1431. And you are, therefore, acquainted with the system of reporting, and with the telegraphic arrangements by which newspapers are supplied with reports?—I am, and have been for many years.

1432. We have had evidence that at the present moment the provincial newspapers are not given seats in the Gallery, but that their reports are furnished by associations?—That is to a certain extent true; the associations, however, do not supply the reports which appear in the "Scotsman" every day.

1433. Will you state to the Committee the way in which you obtain reports?—We are able to secure the services of reporters who are engaged by London newspapers, and who undertake to report for us, not regularly, but as they are wanted. In that way we frequently get out very long reports indeed of Parliamentary proceedings; much longer, I believe, than are furnished by any of the press associations. I should say that that plan has very serious inconveniences. The reporters are not our servants, and therefore if they make any mistakes they are not amenable to any reproof. Then being at the call of the London newspaper which engages them first, they may not be able, and are often not able, to do what we want. One instance of that kind occurred not long ago: what in Scotland was regarded as a very important debate on ecclesiastical matters came on in the evening; it happened that on that evening several of the reporters on whom we were accustomed to rely for reports of the proceedings in Parliament had been drafted by their proprietors or editors to an engagement out of the House of Commons altogether, and we experienced extreme difficulty in getting such a report as we wanted of that debate. Then another evil connected with the arrangement is this: these reporters having also to report for their own papers have necessarily to give their first services to their own papers, and we can only get their second; so that on a night when an Imperial debate is on of great interest, and of which we want a long report as well as the London papers, we are not able to get it from them as we want it; they have to write their own report, and they have not time to do our report as we would like to have it done.

1434. I think you applied for admission to the Gallery some three or four years ago, did you not?—Yes; I believe an application was made about six years ago, but, about four years since, I myself had a long interview with Lord Charles Russell and Colonel Forester on the subject, and I was then met by the same objection which I think has been taken in the Committee now, that if one provincial paper were admitted to a seat in the Gallery, several others must be. I was not able to remove that impression from the mind of the then Serjeant at Arms, and it appears to prevail yet. I think it is a mistake.

1435. But what would be your answer to that objection?—My answer would be that there are not many newspapers in the country which would care to go to the expense involved in keeping a staff of reporters in London; they would prefer

prefer to take the reports of one or other of the press associations; these would suit their purposes and their pockets, and they would not want more; but I believe that if all the accommodation were made that was actually applied for, with certain guarantees taken from the newspapers, it would probably be found that eight or ten newspapers at the outside would ask for admission to the Gallery.

1436. Then you advocate provision for eight or ten newspapers in the Gallery, making it a condition with those newspapers that they should make a *bond fide* use of the space allotted to them: is that what the Committee are to understand?—That is it. I would admit no paper to the Gallery that did not undertake to keep a staff of its own, and to publish independent reports of the proceedings as far as it was possible with that staff.

1437. An honourable Member asks in what way you would exercise, or suggest that there should be exercised, a check or control over a newspaper claiming the privilege?—At present there is an exercise of a certain control; if there were not we could get into the Gallery; you have the Serjeant at Arms, as I suppose, the representative in that matter of the Speaker, exercising authority over the Gallery, and having it in his power to send from the Gallery, if he pleases, any one who is not doing what he thinks ought to be done. I think that the fact would be easily known to the Serjeant at Arms, because I think there would very soon be complaints made, and the attention of the Serjeant at Arms would be called to the fact if any one were abusing the admission that had been given him.

1438. But I think you have yourself stated in evidence that although the "Scotsman" has not any representative in the Gallery, it obtains very full reports of the proceedings in Parliament; how, therefore, could a control be exercised by the Serjeant at Arms over the agent of the "Scotsman," which is not at present exercised over the action of the London papers which receive admission to the Gallery?—I think there would be a difference. At present the condition of things in the Gallery is so extraordinary that if any watchfulness were to be exercised over the London newspapers, I mean any action of the House or the Serjeant at Arms, to the extent of preventing their reporters from furnishing to the provincial newspapers a report, it would raise a very great hubbub, a much greater hubbub than people think about, and therefore it is let alone, I think.

1439. But has it ever occurred to you how it would be possible to exercise this control of which you speak?—I do not think I should have any difficulty in exercising the control. I remember perfectly well that when I was in the Gallery there used to sit in the Gallery a very stately representative of the authorities of the House; and I think he might very well take an account as to whether there was any abuse of the privileges given to papers.

1440. How would he exercise this control; I understand you to suggest that the "Scotsman," or any provincial newspaper possessing the privilege of having a staff of reporters in the House, should be bound to use that privilege for its own newspaper and for no other; is that what you mean?—That is what I should require in my own case. I did not exactly go so far as that; I did not say that I should require each reporter to report only for the paper which he represented, but I should require it in the case of the reporters who came into the Gallery for the "Scotsman," undoubtedly.

1441. How would you secure that?—I should have to rely to a great extent upon the honour of the reporters; and I think that the Serjeant at Arms would probably have to rely to a great extent further upon the honour of the newspapers.

1442. I should not wish to question their honour, but it has been stated to the Committee, and you have stated to the Committee, that the reports in the "Scotsman" are furnished by gentlemen who are nominally, I suppose, in the Gallery as the representatives of London newspapers; and it appears to me to be difficult to see how you can secure that your representative should act only for you, seeing that at the present moment that is not the rule in the Gallery?—But I do not understand that the reporters now in the Gallery are under any restrictions from the authorities of the House not to furnish this report; therefore, surely, that objection falls.

1443. You suggest, as I understand, that they should be under such a restriction?—I do not really suggest that at all; I would leave the authorities of the

House to settle it; indeed, I think that the authorities of the House would do best to let them alone. But what I do mean is, that the newspaper proprietors who got boxes in the gallery should give guarantees that they would occupy those particular boxes which they got with a staff of reporters, who should be engaged by themselves, and paid by themselves, to do their work.

1444. You would impose no restriction whatever as to the work that they should do for anybody else?—I should, as being connected with a paper, but I do not think that the Serjeant at Arms or any one else could do that.

1445. You were present when the last witness gave evidence as to the importance of an official report: are you of opinion that an official report would supersede the necessity for the full and extended reports which you now desire to obtain?—Certainly not; it would not have the least effect in the world upon them, and it could not harm. An official report taken in the manner in which Mr. Saunders suggests could not, I venture to say, in the case of one late debate in a thousand be got through to the papers in Edinburgh in time to be delivered the next morning.

1446. The last witness relied especially upon the importance of providing an official report, in order that the speeches of the local Members might be accurately transmitted to the local newspapers; from your experience would the speeches of the local Members, the Members for Edinburgh, and for Glasgow, be received by the "Scotsman," under that arrangement in sufficient time for the publication of the paper?—Certainly not; and we should not care to receive such reports at all; that would be to impose upon us the full official report of the Member's speech; it would mean, therefore, the cost of telegraphing a great deal of matter which we might think uninteresting, and which could have been put quite as well into much less space. I, speaking for the "Scotsman," certainly do not believe for one moment that the official report would be taken for anything in connection with the reporting for the "Scotsman."

1447. With your knowledge of the mechanical arrangements connected with a newspaper you admit, I suppose, that the official report of a speech could be prepared as rapidly as Mr. Saunders said?—No, I do not think it could, to be put into the hands of the reporter to go to the telegraph office; of course all would depend upon the amount of the turn. Supposing that a man had taken a turn of five minutes, it would take him from 20 to 25 minutes, we will say 20 minutes, to write it out properly, doing it with care, and when he had got it done it would make a piece the third of a column long or rather less. That would probably be in type very nearly by the time he had done writing; but not only would it have such imperfections as he had left in it, but it would have such imperfections as the compositor had left in it; and it would require to be read by the reader for the press, and to be corrected before it was fit to be sent out to the telegraph office.

1448. What would be the difference in time?—I should not like to say; but it would amount to a very considerable time in the course of the night.

1449. The objection to it would be that the process of setting up and correction would be done twice over; it would be done in the House of Commons, and it would be done again in Edinburgh?—Yes.

1450. And the delay would amount to the difference between the transmission of a reporter's notes by telegraph, and the transmission of the report from the printed copy supplied by the House?—Yes.

1451. And that might be half an hour?—It might be half an hour, and I should think in most cases it would. And I think that this also should be borne in mind, that in all cases of official reports of that kind there is not and never would be the same expedition as there is in the case of private work. You would find, first of all, that the reporter, as he would be an official of the House, would be under no special urgency to get through his work; then you would find the printer very much in the same way; and the result would be that the reports would not come to hand in good time. We have, I may say, already an instance of that in the case of the press associations. I believe they do their work very well indeed; their reporters I have no doubt are very good men; but as a matter of fact we can get through our special wires our own reports very much quicker than we can ever get the reports of the press associations. I have known cases where the Press Association reports which have been ordered by us as "stand byes," have come to us hours after we have gone to press, with the report which they profess to give.

1452. The

1452. The Press Association is a co-operative society, in point of fact, is it not?—It is a co-operative and trading society, I should say; it sells its news to proprietors of newspapers who are not members of the company.

1453. But if you subscribe to it you have a voice in its management, have you not?—I do not know how far a mere subscriber to it would have any voice in it; I apprehend that the shareholders in it would have some voice.

1454. Then are the Committee to understand that even if there were an official report delivered to the newspapers as soon as it could possibly be set up, which would be within a very few minutes of the conclusion of the Member's speech, the newspapers in your position, you representing the "Scotsman," would still desire to have a report taken in the Gallery by a staff of their own?—Unquestionably.

1455. You would not rely upon the accurate and official report furnished by Parliament?—No, for several of the reasons that I have given, one being that it would often involve the telegraphing of far more than we wanted.

1456. Are you of opinion that the interest which the outside public take in the proceedings of Parliament would be increased by an official report?—I do not think so; I believe that the official report is a matter between the House and its Members, for the most part; I myself should certainly want the official report, if there were one published, for purposes of reference, and I suppose that several other newspapers would; and, undoubtedly, some institutions would want it, but that the general public would read it I cannot conceive.

1457. It would, in point of fact, simply be a work of reference?—It would be a work of reference.

1458. For persons who are specially interested in the work of legislation?—Yes, it would be a work of reference and not of news.

1459. Mr. Cowen.] I understand that the managers of the "Scotsman" are dissatisfied with the Parliamentary reports which they now get from the Press Association?—We never use them; we get a report from the Press Association in case there should be at any time a break down of the wires, and in that case we should have it as a "stand-by." I do not think that we have used twenty lines from it in the whole course of the Session.

1460. When you say that you do not use them, is that because the reports are not sufficiently long, or is it because they are inaccurate, or for what reason is it?—Of their inaccuracy I cannot say anything, for I really have never taken much trouble to look at them; but they are reports identical with those which are furnished to other newspapers, and we do not think that it is in the interest either of the newspapers or of the public, that there should be identical reports of anything so important as Parliamentary proceedings. They are insufficient because they frequently leave out much that we want, and they put in sometimes on the other hand, some (very little) that we do not want.

1461. I can understand that newspapers may be anxious to have an independent account of a descriptive matter, but I cannot see how there can be any difference between the report which you would get from the Press Association and that which you would get from your own reporters, if it were simply a transcript or an account of what a man says?—But these reports never are simply an account of what a man says. I remember lately being very much puzzled with the form of an answer given by a Minister to a question with regard to Scotland. When I looked at the papers I found only two of them alike; the "Times" had one report, and I think two of the other papers were alike, but the others were all different; and obviously the two reporters in that case in which the papers agreed had written side by side. The Press Association had one report of it, the Central News, if I remember rightly, had another, and our special report gave a different one. The difference was very great, and I could not ascertain what was exactly the answer, or the meaning of the Minister who had given the answer; what was his intention, in fact.

1462. Does not that make against the argument which you are using; you are contending against an official report, and you complain of five or six different accounts being given of one transaction; now if you had an official report, you would have one dependable account?—That official report might also be inaccurate. The official report would come to us, I suppose, uncorrected at its best.

Mr. G. A. Cooper.

5 July 1878.

1463. Passing from the subject of an official report, we understand that you do not use the reports which you get from the Press Association or the Central News, but you do give reports and very long ones in the " Scotsman," and you get those reports from the reporters who represent the London papers in the gallery?—Yes.

1464. Now is that an arrangement made with the reporters individually, or is it an arrangement made with the proprietors of the newspapers which those reporters represent?—It is an arrangement made with the reporters individually.

1465. We have had it in evidence here from Mr. Ross, the representative of the reporting staff of the " Times," and from Mr. Lloyd, the proprietor of the " Daily Chronicle," that the reporters of neither of those papers are permitted to engage in that description of labour; are we then to understand from you that in all probability this arrangement which the reporter makes with you is made by him without the knowledge of the proprietors of the newspaper on which he is engaged?—I do not really know whether it is so or not; but I do see that the answers of Mr. Ross and Mr. Lloyd point in the direction of giving us access to the gallery with a staff of our own reporters; because if it pleased the proprietors of the London newspapers to insist to-morrow that no members of their reporting staff should do any reporting for a provincial newspaper, we should be cut off altogether from the reports which we now get; and, as a matter of fact, that has in part happened to us more than once.

1466. Then the arrangement is a private arrangement between the " Scotsman " and the reporters of the London papers?—Yes.

1467. You wish to have accommodation in the gallery for the " Scotsman " separately from other papers?—Yes.

1468. I understood you to say to the Chairman, that if you had that accommodation, you would make a bargain with your reporter that he should not supply other papers with the result of his labours in the gallery?—I mean to say that I should regard it as part of the terms of his engagement, that he should serve us alone.

1469. In other words you are quite willing to take the services of London newspaper reporters for the " Scotsman," but you would not allow the " Scotsman " reporter, if you had a box of your own in the gallery, to supply like reports to other papers?—I would not. We get what we can; we buy what we find in the market.

1470. The point which I wish to bring out is this: that if you could get admission to the gallery yourself, as the representative of the " Scotsman," you are utterly indifferent as to what arrangements are made for the reports of the other daily newspapers?—I am not indifferent, but I should have nothing to do with them, just as I have nothing to do with them now; it is no business of mine.

1471. But you would take the reports furnished to you by the reporters of the " Daily News " for example, and you would use them in the " Scotsman " without the knowledge of the " Daily News " proprietors, and yet you would not allow the reporters of the " Scotsman " to report for a Bristol paper, for instance, if they had an opportunity of doing such work?—I object to that question in its form altogether. I know nothing whatever of the reporters of the " Daily News," nor do I know that any member of the " Daily News " staff reports for us. I would not take a report from one of the reporters, knowing it to be contrary to the wishes of the proprietor of a particular paper which had engaged him. If the proprietor of a particular paper does not think it worth his while to put a stop to his reporters reporting for provincial papers that is his business, and not mine; I take what I find ready for me in the market.

1472. I make no complaint as to what you take, but that is scarcely the point; it does not appear to me that it is altogether fair that, if the House gave you a box of your own in the gallery, you should impose upon the men who occupied that box stronger restrictions than are now imposed by the proprietors of the London newspapers?—It is surely a question between the man who engages to report for us and ourselves.

1473. I should suppose that the proprietor of a newspaper ought to deal with the proprietor of another newspaper, so that if the proprietors of London newspapers have any objection to their reporters acting in that capacity for provincial

provincial papers, the proprietors of the provincial newspapers had better communicate with the proprietors of the London newspapers?—I do not really see that, but it may be my obtuseness.

1474. That, however, is scarcely the question which we are considering; the point is simply this: you wish a box in the gallery for the "Scotsman," and if you got a box for your newspaper, you are prepared to prescribe that your reporters should report for no other newspaper?—I should ask that of them, certainly, just as I ask a sub-editor engaged upon the "Scotsman," and just as I ask every one in fact engaged upon the "Scotsman," not to work for any one else.

1475. Supposing that the "Scotsman" got a seat in the gallery, and that there were eight or ten daily papers which wanted seats also, with your knowledge of the gallery, how would you set about preparing for those eight or ten without altering altogether the structure of the House of Commons?—I agree with Mr. Saunders in what he said with relation to that subject, that the summary writers might very well be put on the back seat, and I think that a little examination of the plan of the gallery before you will show you that that would leave at least six seats in the front row. I believe that the reporting accommodation in the gallery might be increased and improved, if that which has been called the back seat, and which I remember very well, with a knife-board sort of thing in front of it, were raised three or four feet, and a kind of writing desk put in front of it. I believe that if that were done, you would find room for reporters there where they would hear almost as well as they hear in the front seat.

1476. The arrangement which Mr. Saunders, and I think which Mr. Lovell also suggested, of getting front seats was for the whole of the Provincial Press; it was not for one special paper?—Certainly.

1477. And if the accommodation which they want is accorded to them, I do not myself see how it would be possible, with the present gallery arrangements, that individual papers could be represented?—Four years ago I made to Lord Charles Russell the very proposition which Mr. Saunders has made now that the gallery might be turned round the corner. I felt that it was very delicate ground, because we should be infringing upon the seats of Members; but I thought that in consideration of the services which they would get from the Press in reporting their speeches, they would not be unwilling to submit to the inconvenience for one or two nights in the Session.

1478. But your calculation is that only eight or ten provincial papers would send a staff of reporters of their own to the gallery?—I do not believe myself that so many would; and I will tell you my reason for coming to that conclusion. I think that the right of saying what papers should be represented in the gallery, if there was not sufficient accommodation for all the provincial newspapers, might be left to the Speaker. At present you admit to the gallery, by a process of selection, and your process begins and practically ends with the London newspapers: you say that the only paper which shall have admission to the gallery shall be a London newspaper. Now, that was quite intelligible at the time when the arrangement was first made, but it has ceased to be applicable now, and there are certainly other parts of the country that ought to have representatives there, and particularly, I think, Scotland and Ireland ought to have representatives there. England is, to a great extent, interested in questions which are reported pretty fully, say in the "Times," but neither the "Times" nor any other London newspaper ever troubles to report at particular length the proceedings on a Scotch question. I have had two or three instances of that. We had the Roads and Bridges Bill debate the other day, and the "Times" (having, I have no doubt, a perfectly just appreciation of the wants of those who read it), reported that at the length of a column and a half. I think there were two other newspapers that gave nearly a column: one gave about half a column, and another, 80 lines; whereas the report in the "Scotsman" that morning ran to over ten columns. When reports of that kind are wanted, there surely should be some accommodation provided for the papers that want them.

1479. But supposing that the House of Commons should give you, the "Scotsman," a box, there are two other daily papers in Edinburgh, three in Glasgow, one, if not two, in Dundee, and one or two in Aberdeen; is there any reason why, if all these papers apply for accommodation, we should not accommodate

Mr. C. A. Cooper.

5 July 1872.

modate them all?—I think there is a reason. As you apply a process of selection now, you might continue that; if you have not room for all, you might take those which the country would be most likely to take an interest in.

1480. You would depute, then, to the Speaker the duty of saying which papers he would admit to the gallery, and which papers he would refuse?—I would give him some facts for his guidance.

1481. But are you not aware that the process of selection now followed by the House is perfectly intelligible; the papers which now have seats in the gallery are the London papers, because they are published on the spot, and they are represented directly; and the provincial papers are represented by an association; that is an intelligible line, but if you depart from that where are you to stop?—I do not think, practically, it would come to anything; I object very strongly, and I think the Members of the House ought to object very strongly, to have all the provincial newspapers represented by press agencies. Supposing that this Committee were to lay down the rule which is indicated in the question which you have just asked, namely, that the provincial newspapers shall only be represented by associations, and supposing that that were carried out to the refusal of the London reporters to report specially for provincial newspapers, what would be the result? Not only would newspapers like the "Scotsman" which wanted a full report of a debate, be at the mercy of the average of the papers which got their reports from the Press Association, but Members themselves would be at the mercy of the Press Association, and what their reporters chose to report would be the only report that would go into the country for the public reading; and I think that that is far too great a power to put into the hands of anybody.

1482. I do not think there can be any doubt (at least there is not any in my mind) as to the difficulty which you have pointed out of vesting in the hands of two or three associations the right of reporting for the whole of the Provincial Press; but the question rather is how to obviate the difficulty, considering the necessarily limited space at command?—If we are to suppose that all the Scotch papers, and all the Irish papers, and all the English daily papers, would apply for seats in the gallery, then I personally should be prepared to go the length of suggesting that the House of Commons should be altered to let them in; but that is not likely; I think you need not expect that the sky is going to fall; I think, in short, that there would not be so many of these people applying for admission as you imagine. Nothing is more certain than that a great number of the papers in the country could not afford to keep up a staff of reporters in the gallery.

1483. You have law courts in Edinburgh?—Yes.

1484. And you sometimes have interesting trials there?—Yes.

1485. Supposing that the provincial papers were to send reporters to those trials, take for instance such a trial as you have recently had, the Chantrelle trial, the space of the court is necessarily limited; when they demand admission, how would you act?—As we did. They did apply, and they did get in, and the "Scotsman" only got a single ticket of admission along with the others; there were reporters from England, and they got admission; all the reporters who presented themselves got admission, so, at least, I am informed; and we, as I have stated, only got one ticket; and I was informed distinctly that the reporters from England all got admission.

1486. I will not contest that point with you, though my impression is different from yours; but supposing that they did not all get in, supposing that the space was limited, would you not then give an Edinburgh newspaper the first claim; if it came to a case of this sort, that only six could get in, and eight applied: if two of the eight were from outside Edinburgh, would you not give the six Edinburgh newspapers the preference?—I am not at all sure that I would in that case; but I do not see that a case of that sort, or any trial in a court of law, is analogous to the case of an Imperial Parliament, which deals with very great interests, not only here, but in every county of England, and in Scotland and Ireland.

1487. It might not apply to England, but it would apply to all the Scotch newspapers, because they were distinctly and directly interested; it was a Scotch trial?—You see that we manage things rather better there; we did find room for the reporters when they came.

1488. The

1488. The question was put to Mr. Lovell, "Would it not be fair to allow those papers that have a special wire and a London office of their own, to have admission to the gallery, and his answer was, that it would be handicapping the poorer papers and placing them at disadvantage; what do you say to that? —I do not see that it would be handicapping them at all; it simply means that the people who have capital and enterprise shall have the benefit of it; and I do not see how Parliament, or any one, is interested in keeping up an undertaking. People who want to do their work as cheaply as possible are quite right to do it so; but I do not see that Parliament has any need to assist them in that.

1489. I merely asked the question with a view to convey to your mind the fact that such an objection would necessarily be raised by the poorer papers? —But I do not see how the poorer papers could do it; the poorer papers, if they choose to pay for a special report, would get the same as we get; there is no Parliamentary disability; it is simply a question of capital and expenditure. As a matter of fact, we have two special wires at work every night.

1490. You propose a division; you think that the Scotch papers and the Irish papers should be specially represented?—I do.

1491. Because they have special interests that are peculiar?—Because they have interests that are never attended to by the London papers; the Scotch suffer more in the London press than the Irish do; their interests are never attended to by the London press.

1492. Is it not possible to suppose that the division could be carried farther, and that it might be said that the papers representing the cotton district, or the papers representing the coal and iron districts, might conceive that they had interests requiring to be represented as well?—You could conceive that; but I should think it extremely unlikely.

1493. In the event of the " Manchester Guardian," or the " Leeds Mercury," asking for admission to the gallery, on what ground would you exclude them; would you exclude them because they were provincial English papers, and not Scotch or Irish papers?—I would not exclude them at all; I would give them admission.

1494. But supposing that there is not room?—Parliament, I thought, was powerful enough to make room, if it wanted to do so.

1495. You do not think that it is of any importance for the House of Commons to spend a little money in printing an official report (you have not a very elevated idea of an official report), and yet you would have no objection to Parliament incurring an expense in order to facilitate newspaper reports?—I do not know what the expense of an alteration in the building might be; but you had it in evidence from Mr. Saunders that his official report would cost the Government about 10,000 l. a year; it would be a little less perhaps, but very nearly that; with an expenditure of 10,000 l. on the alteration of the building (always assuming it to be architecturally possible), you would get reports for many years to come in the provincial newspapers, and you would get in the provincial newspapers such reports, not only of Imperial debates, but of local debates, as would go very far to render any special official report unnecessary. The official report being compiled as it has been hitherto, would be furnished with a great deal more material than has hitherto been available for it.

1496. Of course the report which you get in local provincial papers would be too voluminous and cumbersome to be of use as records, and those reports would necessarily be coloured by the locality in which the newspaper circulated?—I do not think there would be any question of colouring at all; they would be fair reports of what took place in Parliament.

1497. How many reporters would you propose to have here as your staff?—I have not considered that question, but I should think six or eight probably.

1498. You would maintain six or eight reporters if you had a box set apart for you?—We should support a sufficient staff to give us a much longer report than that which appears in most of the London papers now.

1499. Would you require a staff of London correspondents and summary writers?—No, we do not want London correspondents there.

1500. You make a demand for the facility of getting an increased Parliamentary report, upon the assumption that there is an increased interest in Parliamentary proceedings?—I am certain that there is; we have the best evidence of that in the world. The circulation of the " Scotsman " invariably rises

Mr. C. A. Cooper.
5 July 1878.

rises with the sitting of Parliament, and we, I suppose, report the proceedings of Parliament much more fully than any other paper out of London, and much more fully than any paper in London, excepting the "Times," and, I believe, the "Standard."

1501. You believe that the advance in the circulation of the "Scotsman" in February, and its comparative decline in August, are attributable to the reporting of the Parliamentary proceedings?—I did not say that there was any decline in August: I said that there was an increase when Parliament sat. There is, in point of fact, an increase in the circulation every year; and I have no doubt that it is because of the Parliamentary reports. I have the means of tracing that distinctly; we know the interest that the Scotch people, who are very intelligent and politically intelligent, take in all political matters, and that they read the debates.

1502. The long speeches which you wish to be reported would be read by those intelligent Scotch people, you think?—There is no question about it; they would be read by the weavers in Galashiels and Hawick, and all the places round, not a doubt of it.

1503. You speak with considerable positiveness upon that point; but that scarcely accords with the views of other witnesses whom we have had; their testimony goes to the point that the interest in Parliamentary proceedings has decreased rather than increased of late years?—They may know, and no doubt they do know perfectly well what has happened in London; some very extraordinary things in that way do happen in London, but I am speaking of Scotland, and I am certain that the political interest taken in Parliamentary proceedings in Scotland has become stronger of late years than it was, and that there is now certainly a demand more than ever for Parliamentary reports.

1504. The largest London newspapers give the smallest Parliamentary reports, and their circulation increases, I think, even as rapidly as that of the "Scotsman"?—Yes; a taste has arisen in this country for special correspondents, and things of that kind, and Scotland has not yet taken that fever.

1505. Scotland has not yet got so low as that, you think?—I do not say that it has not got so low as that. If I might compare one thing with another, I would say that London has taken to champagne, and Scotland prefers to stick to its old whisky.

1506. The testimony which you give the Committee is that the interest in the reports of the proceedings of Parliament has increased, and is increasing, and that is why you wish this accommodation in the gallery?—Yes, it is a pure matter of business; if the interest in Parliamentary reports had not increased there would be no necessity for us to print long reports in the newspapers; we should not think of forcing upon our readers that which they do not like; our readers do like it, and we want to have an opportunity of giving it to them.

1507. Would not that go to show that an official report would also find a sale?—I do not think that, because the official report would only be a report of the proceedings of Parliament, and the "Scotsman" has other features besides its Parliamentary report.

1508. Mr. Forster.] How soon do you think that an official report could come out?—I have not the shadow of a doubt that an official report could be produced as soon as the morning papers.

1509. So as to come out at the same time as the "Scotsman"?—Yes.

1510. Still you think that those Scotchmen who were interested in politics would prefer taking the general papers, to taking that report?—Yes; they could not get that official report until it was several hours old.

1511. That is what I ask; would the "Scotsman" still come out before the official report?—Undoubtedly.

1512. You feel confident of that?—Yes, no doubt of it; we should give the public what they want.

1513. Supposing that there was an official report, how early do you think that official report would come out in Edinburgh?—Not possibly until four o'clock in the afternoon, supposing it to be sent down by the morning newspaper trains; and then by that time everybody knows what has happened in Parliament.

1514. That difference would entirely take away the probability of those who cared about politics going to the official report, rather than to the newspaper?—I have no doubt that, in the case of an official report of that kind, if some
private

private Bill had been discussed or some Edinburgh question, there might be a few members of that particular day taken. I have very little doubt that the literary institutions there would subscribe to it; we should certainly want it, but I do not think the general public would.

1515. Then the Galashiels weaver, of whom you spoke just now, would still get his political information from the newspapers?—No doubt of it.

1516. Am I to understand from what you have just stated that, when we take what may be called Scotch Bills, such as for instance the Hypothec Bill, the London papers (I suppose for their London readers) give scarcely any report?—Almost nothing.

1517. Is the final upshot of the reporting of a debate on a Bill which has so very much interest for Scotchmen as that, and yet does not interest Englishmen, that you do not get in Scotland full reports of it?—We very rarely do get full reports of it, but the longish reports that we do get for the "Scotsman" are got under very great difficulties.

1518. They are not got through these three agencies which we have heard of?—No; the reports of the three agencies would not be so long as we should require, to begin with, and we should not get them, as a rule, so early as our own.

1519. I suppose I am to understand that with the present arrangement with regard to the reporters in the gallery, you consider that Scotchmen do not get as much knowledge of what interests them that happens in Parliament as Englishmen?—They have not the same facilities for getting it that Englishmen have.

1520. But do they get it?—They get a great deal more than Englishmen often get, just because of the enterprise that we show.

1521. They get it at the cost of putting the purveyors of information to much greater trouble than the purveyors of corresponding information in this country are put to?—Yes; you give all the facilities on one side, and on the other none; and the people who have facilities do much less than the people who have no facilities.

1522. As regards English questions, all the London papers have reporters, have they not?—I believe so.

1523. Then you would consider that any attempt at monopolising information is impossible as far as London is concerned, because it can be checked by one paper as against another?—Yes.

1524. And one of your objections to the present state of things is that if you hand over the Provinces, and Scotland, and Ireland to these three agencies, there might be a much greater monopoly than there is in London?—Yes; a worse monopoly and a monopoly of a different kind.

1525. In what way of a different kind?—The present monopoly is a monopoly confined to the London newspapers; but this would be a monopoly confined practically to two associations.

1526. And those associations going over the whole country, what you would fear would be, that Scotland would get only just as much as the West of England, for example?—As to Imperial questions, that would exactly be the case; and Scotland takes a great interest in Imperial questions as well as Scotch questions, and wants to know more about them than, as a rule, the press associations give.

1527. You have stated that not unfrequently the "Scotsman" publishes longer reports of debates of interest than any but one or two of the London papers?—I know that to be the case.

1528. I will ask you to put in not picked numbers, but several numbers illustrating that statement?—You mean, that I should hand in the newspapers; I shall have pleasure in doing that; I will take care that the Committee have them.

1529. Have you any idea how many Scotch papers would claim seats if there were a possibility of getting them?—No, I have not.

1530. When my honourable friend the Member for Newcastle put to you the difficulty of selecting amongst all the newspapers in the Provinces, and in Scotland, and Ireland, and the impossibility of admitting them all, you said that you thought the expense would make a natural selection; would you give us any idea of what a paper would have to do in order to have a seat for itself; in the first place it would have to have a staff of reporters in London?—Yes.

1531. That staff, in order to make it worth while to do their business, would not be less than, how many?—Six or eight.

1532. Then it would have to have a special wire?—Certainly, to do the work properly.

1533. Supposing that these seats were offered to papers that would keep a staff and would have a special wire, have you any idea how many such papers there would be?—I have not at this moment; I thought the numbers were put in the other day; my impression is, that there would be all over the country about 14 or 15, perhaps.

1534. How many do you think there would be in Scotland?—There are, I believe, six or seven papers that have special wires in Scotland.

1535. Do you not think that if there was room to admit papers in this way several papers would unite together, and take the same wire?—I have not the shadow of a doubt about it.

1536. But you think that the final result of that would be that Scotch business would be better reported than at present?—It must; you would have an opportunity of doing the work which now you have not.

1537. Sir *Henry Holland*.] I think you said that the reports of the three agencies are not as long as you require them to be?—They are not.

1538. But if you required longer reports on any special subject would they not furnish you with them?—I should think not; they would only furnish us with special reports every night, the same as the special reports which were furnished to other newspapers: if they were to write out a special report for us at our length every night, it would come very much to our having a box with the Press Association engaging our reporters.

1539. Mr. Lovell said that he thought they published everything required, "because everything we are asked for we are ready to supply"?—What he may think important is one thing, and what we may think important is another; I do not mean Parliamentary reporting alone.

1540. I am speaking of Parliamentary reporting alone; is it not the fact that if a paper like the "Scotsman" required on all Scotch subjects a full report, they could obtain it?—They would obtain the same report as was sent to any other Scotch paper applying for a full report; but that is not what we want.

1541. You mean to say that they would not furnish to the "Scotsman" a special full report?—I have never understood that they would do anything of the kind; if they did, it would be putting a staff into the Gallery for the "Scotsman," and letting them be employed by the Press Association.

1542. Not quite so; because the "Scotsman" would not desire on every subject to have one of these full reports?—It certainly would.

1543. The "Scotsman" might, but every Scotch paper would not?—No; but I am speaking for the "Scotsman" on this occasion.

1544. But supposing that a Scotch paper which did not desire a full report on every subject has a great desire for a full report, for instance, on the Roads and Bridges Bill, would not that paper be able to obtain it from the central agency by stating their desire?—I believe so; I believe the Press Association have supplied special reports of that debate; and having seen all the reports that have appeared, I say that they would have been insufficient for the "Scotsman."

1545. As to your having now reports from the London reporters, that proceeding, in the first place, is not against any rule of the House, nor, as far as you know, not against any rule of the newspaper?—It is against neither, so far as I know.

1546. Mr. *Dunbar*.] I suppose sometimes in a debate you would require a report rather different from another paper?—We require all our reports as far as they can to be different; I mean to be specially ours.

1547. You might wish to report on one side very fully, and on the other side not quite so fully?—Not at all; that is a very great mistake. The object we have in view in our reports is to secure a full report of everything; anyone who knows the "Scotsman," knows that it is perfectly free in the expression of its political opinions, but it never confounds its political opinions with its news columns, and the last thing it would desire would be that

that any report should be coloured, or be any better on one side than the other. Mr. C. A. Cooper,
It has happened sometimes that some appearance of that has been given
through break down in the reporting, but when that has been the case it has
been matter of great complaint and regret.

1548. Some papers are more lax in their practice than others are?—I am
not much inclined to judge any other paper.

1549. If you report so fully, one copy from the association would meet the
different wants of two papers; take the "Scotsman" and some other Edinburgh paper: If you both seek only an accurate and full report, would not one
report do for the two papers?—It would not answer the views of the
"Scotsman"; it would not want to have the same report as any other paper
has.

1550. Dr. Lyon Playfair.] Practically, you are of opinion that if accommodation was given to the provincial press that accommodation would not be
extended to an unreasonable amount?—I do not believe it would.

1551. Supposing you were to say that accommodation would be given to any
provincial newspaper that chose to employ five reporters or four reporters, would
that limit very much the demand that would be made?—Certainly.

1552. You have said that it is a question of natural selection, as the honourable Member for Newcastle said: in the law of natural selection is there not
another development of the law which is called the survival of the fittest?—
Certainly.

1553. And therefore the energy of the newspapers would soon limit their
position?—No doubt of it.

1554. Now, the honourable Member for Newcastle asked you whether it was
just for the "Scotsman" to employ the whole time of its reporters when it
takes reports from the London reporters at the present time; was not your
meaning this, that the "Scotsman" wants such full reports that it will employ
all their time, and that they would have no time available for doing other work?
—That is distinctly my meaning.

1555. And was not that the answer which Mr. Ross, the reporter of the
"Times" also gave, that the "Times" could not allow its reporters to use their
services for other newspapers, because they were all required for their own?—
Yes, that is required for them to do their own work properly; that is my conviction.

1556. Is it not the case, that the reporters whom you employ now of the
London newspapers are from the newspapers which do not give full reports?—
I am scarcely able to answer that question, because I have never nicely inquired
into who the reporters were; I should think that was probable.

1557. Supposing that the reporter of the "Pall Mall Gazette," or of the
"Daily Telegraph," which give short summaries, and not full reports, were employed in the Gallery, their whole time would not be occupied, and they might
be able to report for you?—Yes, undoubtedly.

1558. Now was not the present system of reporting, when the London press
got a practical monopoly of the Gallery, established when London papers were
practically the only daily papers in the country?—They were; they were the
only daily papers in the country.

1559. And now, with the facilities of communication, the whole system is
altered; is not Edinburgh as near the House of Commons now as London is
near the House of Commons, so far as sending the news is concerned?—Yes; I
could give you a curious instance of that. I suppose we may fairly take the
"Times" as being the best in all its arrangements for reporting; on the morning
when the debate on the Indian troops closed here, the Marquess of Hartington
spoke; the "Times" went to press with its first edition (which was the only
edition that came down to us) with a break in the Marquess of Hartington's
speech, and the numbers of the division only given in its summary; the
"Scotsman" went to press with a report of the Marquess of Hartington's
speech and the division, and everything in its proper place. So that we, I
should say, are at least as near for practical purposes as the "Times."

1560. Is it not the fact that whilst certain London newspapers are reporting
less and less Parliamentary news, certain provincial papers, especially the
Scotch papers, are reporting more and more Parliamentary news?—Undoubtedly that is so.

1561. If that is the case, does it not appear to be unjust that the facilities
are in an inverse ratio to the requirements?—It appears to me.

Mr. C. A. Cooper,
5 July 1878.

Mr. C. A. Cooper.

3 July 1878.

1562. An honourable Member asked you whether a long report which would be given in a provincial newspaper, say in a Scotch newspaper, upon Scotch business, would not be wholly disproportionate to the general interest; but are you aware that Mr. Hansard gets up his excellent reports largely by culling from the provincial newspapers?—I believe that to be the case.

1563. I know in my own case that when Mr. Hansard sends me a report I find it cut out from a Scotch newspaper, and not from a London newspaper; now, does not that fuller report in the provincial papers help to make a more complete record in Hansard?—Yes; and I believe that if the provincial papers had facilities given to them it would probably make an official report altogether unnecessary. I mean an official report in the sense in which we have heard about one to-day.

1564. The political education in Scotland is such, is it not, that it demands a very much fuller report than the penny London papers supply?—Unquestionably; we have some very remarkable instances of that. I said a little while ago that the circulation of the "Scotsman" increases always at the beginning of the Parliamentary Session; I should, perhaps, also have stated that on the occasion of any important Imperial debate, which it is pretty well known that we shall report fully, there is an extra demand for that paper; and that is all over Scotland.

1565. You need not answer this question unless you like; but is it not the case that a newspaper which has some 60,000 circulation is a very important agency for distributing political news, and ought to have an opportunity of obtaining that news?—I think so; a circulation of 60,000 means one to every 56 of the inhabitants of Scotland, men, women, and children; and I certainly think that a paper that has a circulation of that kind is entitled to recognition here.

1566. Mr. Barclay.] I should like you to give the Committee some idea of the extent to which the "Scotsman" reports the proceedings in Parliament as compared with the London papers?—If I may take one or two Scotch questions, I could give very striking instances of that. This morning I have noticed that the Scotch Roads and Bridges Bill that was on last night is disposed of in a few lines in every paper in London. I understand by telegram from Scotland that we have about two columns report to-day of that which took place after midnight last night.

1567. And you think that a matter of considerable interest to the people in Scotland?—Undoubtedly; there cannot be a question of it.

1568. Are you willing to state what proportion your report of Parliamentary proceedings bears to that of other papers in Scotland?—I am scarcely able to do that. I know, just looking at it roughly, that it is invariably longer than that of the other papers, unless there has been some extraordinary breakdown; and that is all I can say. I should think that if we were to look at it it is fully a third longer than in any other paper.

1569. You aim at giving longer reports of the Parliamentary proceedings than any other paper in Scotland?—We aim at giving the best Parliamentary reports that we can get; and in the result it appears that what we get are longer than the other papers in Scotland get.

1570. Is it your opinion that, of the papers in the United Kingdom, with regard to the report of Parliamentary proceedings, you stand third in the length of the reports?—I believe we do.

1571. That is including the London papers?—Yes, including the London papers. I have only a doubt as to one newspaper, and I have looked at that lately a great many times, and found our report longer than theirs.

1572. Do you aim at giving full selected reports on all Scotch subjects?—Yes.

1573. And full selected reports also on Imperial questions?—I am not sure that I understand what you mean by "selected"; do you mean for ourselves alone?

1574. You said that an official report would not suit you?—No, it would not.

1575. An official report would be a report of all the speeches of Members, while you would only profess to give a full selected report?—That is, we should give a report which should not be full in the sense of an official report.

1576. You would select the speeches which you would think your readers would

would desire to read, and so give the full report which would be the case if the official report were given?—Certainly. I would rather not put it that we should select the speakers, but that we prefer to elect at what length we shall report speeches.

1577. Can you give any explanation as to the cause of the differences in the reports of the Scotch papers?—I cannot; I suppose something may be due to the indistinctness of the utterance of the Minister; he may not have given his reply quite clearly; something must be due also to the fact that many of the reporters in the Gallery do not understand Scotch questions in the least, and therefore are very likely to make mistakes over them.

1578. Would the reporter for a London paper be able to apprehend at once a point which might be of very considerable importance to Scotchmen, though it did not appear to him to be so?—I should think it would be very unlikely; and that is one of our causes of complaint now; we believe that Scotchmen understand Scotch business best.

1579. Then as to the practicability of getting the "Scotsman" supplied by the news agencies, do we understand that the report of Scotch matters in the "Scotsman" is almost invariably longer than that of any of the other Scotch papers?—I believe that to be the case.

1580. Perhaps you will not be able to answer the question, but have you any idea whether the other Scotch papers would be prepared to devote as much space to the reporting of the Parliamentary proceedings as you are?—I have no means of knowing what the other Scotch papers would do.

1581. But as the matter at present stands, if you were going to get a report such as you want from the Press Association, or the Central News, it would practically come to be a report exclusively for the "Scotsman"?—It must, to be satisfactory to us; but they could not do it; it would be impossible; as I have already said to do that would mean that they would have to set apart a staff of reporters for us; they would in fact put into the Gallery a staff employed by them to do the work of the "Scotsman" alone, and no other work.

1582. Speaking of the reports which appear in the "Scotsman," and the reports which appear in any of the other newspapers, in order to produce the same reports under the new system, it would practically come to be a special report for the "Scotsman" itself?—I am not sure that I follow you.

1583. If we assume that the other newspapers give as full a report as they wish, and you want to continue to give as full a report, or a still longer report than you have at present, would it be necessary for the Press Association to employ a special staff of reporters for you?—Undoubtedly.

1584. In regard to the question of selection, you propose that one condition of access to the Gallery should be that the newspaper should maintain a full staff of reporters in the Gallery?—Yes.

1585. Would it be practicable to make a stipulation also in regard to results, such as that each newspaper which had a box should at least, on an average over the Session, give a certain number of columns and devote a certain amount of space to reporting Parliamentary debates?—It would be quite possible to make such a stipulation; but I do not think it would be a very wise stipulation to make; the reports must depend to a great extent upon the interest partly in the locality and partly in the particular questions.

1586. Do you think it would be practicable to state the minimum below which a newspaper should not be entitled to have a box in the Gallery?—Perfectly practicable.

1587. That is, that not on a particular day, but over the whole Session, they should at least afford a certain number of columns?—It would be perfectly practicable.

1588. Then if those two conditions of selection were applied, you think there would not be many provincial newspapers which would ask to have special seats for themselves?—Very few.

1589. The newspapers which did not apply for seats would be supplied in future by the Press Association and the Central News, and otherwise, as they are at present?—I suppose so.

1590. By such arrangements, and with such conditions, the real wants of all the newspapers might be met by only a very limited addition to the number of seats?—I think so.

1591. It suits a great many newspapers to have their reports provided by the Press Association better than to have reports of their own?—Undoubtedly.

1592. And it would suit you better to have reports by your own people?—Yes.

1593. Do you think a reporter could do justice to two newspapers at the same time, giving what you would consider two full satisfactory reports of the proceedings in Parliament?—Do you mean write two reports for different newspapers? All would depend upon circumstances. If a reporter went into the box and had a turn of say a quarter of an hour, which he had to write out fully for one paper, if he was not called upon to go on again for another turn and had time to write it out, he could write a second report of it very well. For my own part I think the first would probably be the best report; it would be the freshest, and most likely in every respect the best. That would be possible.

1594. Would you object to your reporters doing other work than yours on the ground of exclusiveness, or upon this ground, that the reporter could not then do that justice to your newspaper which you would desire he should do?—Certainly not on the ground of exclusiveness; it is simply a matter of minding one's own business and not trying to do other people's.

1595. You have stated that the reporters of the London newspapers do supply you with reports: do you think that if they gave a full report of the proceedings in Parliament, nearly as full as the "Times," for instance, they would be able to supply you with these reports?—No, they would not, and I do not believe that we should get them if another state of circumstances existed. I am informed that at present the salaries of the reporters in the Gallery in London are much lower than I at any rate think they ought to be, and that they report for other papers really to eke out their income. I think that if the provincial papers were admitted to the Gallery it would have an effect in that way also; as they could earn little from the outside they would get more for the work they did; the work would be a great deal better done, and they would be a great deal better off.

1596. Do you think it would improve the status of the reporters?—I have no doubt of it. I have no doubt that if Mr. Ross is able to carry out his rule on the "Times," the status of the "Times" reporter must be better than that of the man who has to hunt about for other things to do.

1597. Do you think the London newspaper gets his report more cheaply done in consequence of allowing its reporters to report for the provincial newspapers?—That is what it comes to; no doubt about it.

1598. And a reporter by being on the staff of a London newspaper has the advantage of being able to sell his services to a provincial newspaper upon such terms as he can make out of it?—A reporter who gets an engagement in the Gallery, and is able to do work for other papers, has the means of earning an income in addition to that paid to him by the paper which he represents, or which he is supposed to represent in the Gallery.

1599. Now, as regards the desirability or the necessity of having a special representation, if I might say so, of the Scotch and Irish newspapers in the Gallery, the honourable Member for Newcastle put to you the case of Manchester and Leeds, and asked whether it was not possible that they might desire to be represented in the Gallery, on the ground of the cotton and iron interests; but is there any separate legislation for Manchester and Leeds as there is for Scotland and for Ireland?—No, they are wholly different from the case of Scotland and Ireland.

1600. There are public Bills before Parliament relating to Scotland only, and also some relating to Ireland only?—Yes.

1601. And the London newspapers, considering (justly, I presume) that their readers do not care much about Scotch and Irish questions, give very meagre reports of debates on such questions?—Yes.

1602. And on the ground that there is separate legislation for Scotland and Ireland, you think that they ought to have representatives in the Gallery to report the discussions on such Bills as relate to Scotland alone, or to Ireland alone?—For the reporting of the separate legislation of Scotland and Ireland, I think that the admission of Scotch and Irish newspapers to the Gallery is necessary.

1603. The fact is that there are public Bills which relate only to Scotland, and other public Bills which relate only to Ireland, and the English newspapers justly hardly consider that the discussions on those Bills are not of much importance in the eyes of English readers, and, therefore, do not report them; do you consider it necessary in the public interest that under these circumstances Scotland and Ireland should be represented in the Reporter's Gallery by such newspapers as would give a report of the discussions on those particular questions?—I do.

1604. Then as to the question of an official report, do you think that it is worth the while of Parliament to go to the expense of an official report?—I think that is a matter for Parliament; my personal opinion is that it is not, but I really have thought very little about it. The only use, as it appears to me, of an official report in the sense of one specially taken and reported for you is that it would be there for reference; and, practically, I can find in the "Times" as much as I want for reference on any question.

1605. You do not find sufficient in the "Times" on Scotch questions, I understand?—No; I find it in the "Scotsman."

1606. Do you really not think that this official report is worth 10,000 l. a-year?—I do not myself; but that is my private opinion. If Members think it is, that is another matter. As for the public outside I do not think it is worth sixpence.

1607. Do you think that libraries, and institutions, and public news-rooms would take copies of it?—I have no doubt that the best of them would.

1608. But the circulation throughout the country would not be large, you think?—It would be no service whatever for the purpose of political education; and that I understand is the great use of publishing the debates of Parliament, that you are to get them read.

1609. Would it be of any service for making a somewhat condensed summary which people would read?—Not the least, because the papers must go to press at a certain time in the morning, and the time occupied in condensing would be so much time lost.

1610. I was referring to a separate publication, which should be a condensed report of the proceedings in Parliament, and which would be valuable as a work of reference, and where you might readily find what had been said on a particular question?—I do not think it would be of much service—of very little indeed. Those who want to find what has been said in Parliament are able to get it pretty well now, though not so perfect as Members might desire.

1611. Then do I rightly understand that you would prefer the 10,000 l. being expended in improving the accommodation for reporters in the House?—If it were put as a question between the two, I should; because the 10,000 l. in the one case would only be spent for one year, while in the other case it would go on every year.

1612. Colonel Arbuthnot.] Did I rightly understand you, in your answer to the last question of the right honourable Member for the University of Edinburgh, to infer that the amount of circulation of a newspaper should be the principal test of the right to a seat in the Gallery, supposing that there were only a certain number of seats to be divided amongst the provincial press?—I think it would be a very fair test.

1613. What is your opinion as to the practicability of dividing the country up into districts, and allotting seats to certain sections of the country, leaving it to the newspaper proprietors of those districts to settle among themselves how the seats should be occupied?—I do not think there is any necessity for that; I think that in 99 cases, certainly in 90 cases out of every 100, you would find that the newspapers would be perfectly satisfied with the reports that would be furnished to them by the press agencies, and that therefore there is no occasion to enter into fresh arrangements, which would be in the nature of co-operative agencies.

1614. I thought, a little earlier in your evidence, you expressed yourself as dissatisfied with identity of reports?—I am.

1615. That is as it affects your own papers, but not as regards others?—No, not if they are satisfied with it; I think they are wrong in being satisfied with it, but that is their business, not mine.

1616. Is there any reason why the press agencies which now exist, or others, should not be sufficiently well organised and improved to suit the wants of everybody, yourself included?—I think they are very good as they are; but if they were sufficiently organised, and if they were improved ever so much, the result would be that they would print an identical report; and it is to identical reports that I object.

0.121.   O 4   1617. Would

Mr. C. A. Cooper.
3 July 1878.

1617. Would not an identical report imply perfection of report?—No, it would not by any means; it might become the very worst report in the world, and I should think it would be very likely to become the worst report in the world if it were to get the monopoly which might be given to it.

1618. Do you think that an official report, such as has been spoken of, would be largely used by the weekly provincial press?—No, they would never look at it; they can get all they want from the papers which are published every day. The official report would, I will be bound to say, in the case of nine out of ten of the weekly newspapers, never find its way into their offices at all.

1619. I will assume that the official report would be a correct report; I think it is generally admitted that the newspaper reports could not be accurate?—I do not admit that; I think they could be accurate without much difficulty.

1620. But is it possible to give an accurate description of a speech of half an hour in ten lines?—No.

1621. Is it necessary to do that sometimes in order to economise space, and to enable the paper to be brought out in time?—Not to enable it to be brought out in time; of course if the House sits till three o'clock, any paper going to press at three cannot get in time for publication the report of a speech delivered at that time; but any speech delivered before two o'clock would be almost sure of getting a longer report than you mention, viz., ten lines for a speech of half an hour. I am speaking of what I should do, and what the paper would get, not of what it does get.

1622. Mr. Hutchinson.] I understand you to say that you can get whatever you like from the Press Associations in the way of Parliamentary reports; whatever you choose to order from them you can get?—I do not think we could do that; we could not get, for instance, from the Press Association every night in the week a special report which should go to no other newspaper than ourselves.

1623. Supposing that you were to order the Press Association to send to you a report of all the speeches on a certain night in the first person, could you get that?—I do not know; I have not asked the question, and could not tell you; but I should very much doubt it.

1624. But even if you could get a report perfect in point of accuracy, if that same report were supplied to any other newspaper than yourselves, that would not suit you?—If it were perfect in point of accuracy that might make a difference in one way; but what we want is that we shall have our own report, and the perfection in point of accuracy is much more likely to be got by having two reports.

1625. But I understood you to say just now that you thought the newspapers were wrong in accepting identical reports?—That is my impression.

1626. And I understand you also to say that you would have your own report from your own reporter?—Yes.

1627. That comes to the same thing as my question. Now, there must be very few newspapers that want a report of that kind?—I should think very few.

1628. Your argument, in fact, is that there are very few such?—Yes.

1629. In that case, does it not strike you that you are asking the Committee and the House of Commons to legislate for exceptional instances?—No; it strikes me that it is the other way, that if we do not get it we shall be driven into the arms of a monopoly, and because 69 people do not want a particular thing, which it is lawful to want, it will be refused to us.

1630. Does it not strike you that it is in the nature of a monopoly if the newspapers which are to be tacitly favoured, are to be the Speaker's nominees, because there are very few, according to your evidence, that want this accommodation, and they are to be the subject of nomination; does it not strike you that it is in the nature of a monopoly?—If it is, who is injured by it? Not the people who do not apply for the accommodation.

1631. You tell us that you publish Parliamentary reports because in your opinion they are interesting matter, and cause the paper to sell?—Yes.

1632. I have a list of newspapers here in Scotland, and in Ireland, and in England, comprising the newspapers of Newcastle, Liverpool, Manchester, Leeds, Birmingham, Belfast, Cork, Dublin, Aberdeen, Dundee, Glasgow, and Edinburgh (I mention them in the reverse order perhaps to their importance); does it strike you that if the fashion were set of an influential paper like the "Scotsman,"

"Scotsman" making great exertions to obtain these reports, and it became a   *Mr. C. A. Cooper.*
point of honour among leading newspapers to vie with each other in this matter,
the number of applications to the Speaker for seats in the Gallery might be   *2 July 1878.*
much more numerous than you at present imagine?—I do not think so, because
there is always the question of expense.

1633. In that case I must take my choice, and you must take your choice
between two alternatives; either you are asking for special legislation on behalf
of a few newspapers, or you are setting up a demand which, from the number
of applicants, could not possibly be complied with?—I do not think either.
We are not asking for special legislation, but we are simply asking that we shall
not be excluded from a position in which we have the right to be put; we are
rather the victims of special legislation than people asking for it. I have no
doubt that the circulation of the "Scotsman" is much larger than that of any
other paper in any one of the places you have mentioned.

1634. Phrases have been used in the course of the inquiry to-day, such as
that of "natural selection," and "survival of the fittest," but in this case, does
it strike you that the present state of circumstances is the consequence of a
natural development of the state of things which took place when the London
newspapers were the only daily papers, and the consequence was that being the
only daily papers, they occupied the only available space, and since then there
has been the rise of an influential provincial journalism which finds itself not
excluded by preference, but simply by want of space; so that you are not, as
you say, the victims of special legislation, but the legislation has not developed
concurrently with the rise of this journalism of which I speak?—It does not
make any difference to me whether I am excluded because I have developed,
or whether I am excluded by special action.

1635. It makes this difference, that you are not the victims of special legislation, but that it is simply because the legislation is in arrear?—I do not
admit that at all; it is a matter of argument; I contend that we, the provincial
newspapers, are specially excluded.

1636. You are excluded in this sense, that you have not been specially provided for?—That we have not been put on the same footing as those that have
been specially provided for.

1637. Supposing that you took the two things together, the Press Association
which gives you a very full report of Imperial business, and the special reports
of Scotch business, that would not satisfy you?—It would not; not the reports
that they would furnish; we want our own report.

1638. Sir *Alexander Gordon.*] I understood you to say that you give
summaries of debates in the "Scotsman" from the reporters' notes?—No, I do
not think I said so; as a matter of fact we do not.

1639. Do you not give summaries?—We have a summary of the report, but
it is not written from the reporters' notes, it is written from the copy after it
has reached Edinburgh.

1640. That is what I mean; you find no difficulty in producing a summary
without having a summary writer for that special purpose in the Gallery?—Not
the least.

1641. Therefore may I assume that those papers which have summary
writers might adopt the same course for their summaries?—I think so.

1642. You said something about the special wire accommodation which you
have to Edinburgh; will you state what that is?—We have two special wires
going from the office in Fleet-street to the office in Edinburgh; they are at our
disposal from six o'clock at night till six o'clock in the morning, but as a rule,
we do not use them after three o'clock in the morning.

1643. In the day time are they available for other places?—Yes, they are
coupled up by the Post Office for us at six o'clock in the evening.

1644. Do you know at all why the London papers report Irish debates more
fully than Scotch debates?—I suppose there is an impression here that the
Irish debates are more amusing.

1645. You consider that in Scotland people read the debates and political
matter more than they do in England?—I do not know so much what they do
in England, but if I may take the evidence which has been given here as
correct, then certainly the Scotch read the debates much more generally than
people here.

0.121.   P   1646. Did

Mr. C. A. Cooper.
4 July 1878.

1646. Did you hear the evidence given that readers in the country like to have full reports of speeches of their own Members?—I did not hear the evidence, but I know there is a feeling of that kind.

1647. Do you consider that the class of people you speak of, who like to read the debates, are satisfied with a paper merely giving reports of the speeches of their own Members?—No; I would rather put it that they would be satisfied without getting the reports of the speeches of their own Members if they got a good report of the debate generally.

1648. I have in my hand a Scotch provincial paper giving a report of the adjourned debate of the Cattle Diseases Bill the other day, and there were 16 speakers, among whom were Dr. Lyon Playfair, Mr. Chamberlain, Mr. M'Lagan, myself, Mr. Clare Read, who spoke for more than an hour, Mr. Barclay, and some other speakers; and the only two that are given in any detail are my own speech and the speech of the Member for Forfarshire; the speech of Mr. Clare Read, who spoke for more than an hour, occupies three lines; Dr. Lyon Playfair's speech occupies a little more, and Mr. M'Lagan's occupies four lines; do you consider that the readers of that paper would have preferred having a more full report of all the speeches than simply a detailed report of two?— Undoubtedly.

1649. Then that is a want which is not provided for at present?—Just so.

1650. If they had an official report sent down to institutions, and reading rooms, and clubs, would not that supply in some respects the want which this illustrates?—I do not think so; the object is to get a report of what takes place into the hands of the public; I do not think they would go after an official report.

1651. But if they do not get any more report than that which I have described, how are they to get it unless it is from an official report?—They would get it by going to some other newspaper which gave a better report, and the result would be that the paper which systematically gave short reports of that kind would lose its hold of any district, and some paper which gave better reports would come in.

1652. Is not it a question of demand and supply; if more were wanted now, this paper would give more, would it not?—I can only say that, in my opinion, that paper neglects its business.

1653. Would it not be in accordance with your views of the representation of the people that England, Scotland, and Ireland should have a proportion of the Gallery accommodation in proportion to their Members?—I think that would be a very fair arrangement.

1654. You said that official reports would be unnecessary if the local papers published the speeches in full; how could that be the case if the local papers only published individual reports?—I do not seem to have made myself very clearly understood; what I mean is this, that the more independent reports of what takes place in Parliament you can get, the more certain you are of having the materials from which an official report, such as that of Hansard now, could be compiled.

1655. You alluded to the importance of an official report for reference but not for news, and you said that you yourself certainly would have one for your own use as the editor of a paper; would not the editor of every provincial paper of any consequence also find it of use for reference?—He would find it of use undoubtedly; whether he would get it I do not know.

1656. Would not that of itself procure a certain sale for such a report?— Certainly it would, 200 or 300 copies.

1657. Sir Henry Drummond Wolff.] You were saying that you did not think there would be any difficulty from the competition of newspapers for accommodation in the Gallery on account of papers of a large circulation only being able to afford to have a special staff of reporters; but still there might be cases in which papers are at present small; papers might fall into the hands of rich men who would wish to improve them by this means; do not you think that might happen?—I do.

1658. But what would you do with these papers if there were not any room for them in the Gallery?—If they could make out a good claim they would soon find their way in; I am not going to assume that every available inch would be occupied at once, if good arrangements were made.

1659. But still this might go on indefinitely; a newspaper might go on
wanting

wanting places for their reporters? - So they will; you may keep the number of the Members at 658, but you cannot keep the number of newspapers at a particular point.

1660. Do you not think that the newspapers ought to do something for Parliament, as well as Parliament something for the newspapers?—Yes.

1661. Do you not think that there might be an arrangement made by which all the Scotch newspapers, for instance, might join, to have a report of the debates?—I fail to see how that would do anything for Parliament, except an injury. Parliament is not interested, I think, in having an identical report. If it is good in Scotland, then it is good in England also, I suppose. Now apply that to the case of the "Times." The "Times" would not be satisfied with a less report than that which it now gets; but the other papers, if they were ever so anxious, could not print that report or take it, and difficulties would arise at every turn; and so it is with all the provincial papers; and besides, there is always the other danger which I indicated a little while ago, that when you set up an identical report, you put too much power really into the hands of a reporter.

1662. If the idea were carried out which was put to you just now by an honourable Member, and if you divided the country into districts, you would have two or three English districts, and two Scotch districts, and two Irish districts, and each would have their own staff of reporters; there would be a sufficient diversity in those districts not to have a monopoly for any one staff; and if you had an official report besides, you would stimulate these different districts to have a good report to be as near as possible to the official report, would you not?—I do not think that the official report would have any influence in stimulating the newspaper reports; but suppose you began by making London a division, for the purposes of that co-operation, what would come of it?

1663. You might have two or three districts for London?—I have no objection to that if you make me a district in Scotland.

1664. Is your objection to the official report this, that you object to there being an official report, or is it that you do not think there is any object in having one?—I do not object; my personal opinion is that there is no necessity for an official report.

1665. You do not think it would do any harm?—No, not the least; it is a harmless thing.

1666. Mr. *Mills.*] In answer to the questions that were put to you as to the expediency, or otherwise, of having an official report, you used the expression, "An identical report": and I understood you to say that it would not be a good thing if there should be one uniform report. In the paper you are connected with, for instance, you would not wish to see precisely the same report as appears in another paper published in some other part of Scotland. Now, supposing that you could be sure of having, not from an official source, but from a set of reporters employed for the papers in Scotland, a perfect, and consequently an identical report for all papers published in Edinburgh, Glasgow, Dundee, or elsewhere, do you think that any injury or mischief would arise from having that report the same for all?—Yes; the question would be then who should be entrusted with the getting out of the report to begin with, and there jealousies and difficulties of all kinds would arise. But this difficulty would certainly arise, that whereas we should want for the "Scotsman," say a report of 10 columns in length, another paper would, perhaps, want one only of eight columns, another, say, six or four, or whatever it may be, and yet you would have them all stretched to the end of the one bed. In that way the man who wants four columns must take ten, or the man who wants ten must take only four.

1667. Do you think there might be value to be attached to the mutual check by having a diversity?—Yes, great value: I think it keeps the reporting much better than it would be.

1668. There has been a great deal of evidence given by you and by others, on the point of the probability of there being any large number of purchasers for an official report; I mean for a verbatim official report?—My impression is, that there would be very few indeed.

1669. Mr. Ross was asked, "I think you have stated it as your opinion that no large amount of the public would take in this paper containing an official report,

Mr. C. A. Cooper.

5 July 1878.

report, or read it," and he said, "I do not think anyone would"?—I do not agree with him there.

1670. You do not go so far as that?—No, but I think the number of official reports circulated would be so small as not to be worth taking into account in estimating for expense.

1671. I think Mr. Ross spoke to this effect, that speaking generally of verbatim reports of speeches made in the House of Commons, he did not think any one read them except the Members who delivered them?—I think that was a great mistake; there was very much in Mr. Ross's evidence which I do not agree with.

1672. You think that with regard to the speeches of a great many Members of the House of Commons full report would be valued by others than those who have made the speeches?—I am sure of it; or the report would not be printed in the newspapers.

1673. Evidence was given of the loss sustained by the "Times;" Mr. Ross said he thought a loss of 20,000 l. a year was sustained by the "Times" by giving such full reports as are now given; do you think that any newspaper which undertook to do that on its own account, if I may say so, would not also lose considerably, supposing that a newspaper attempted to do it?—I think, to call it "loss," as all, was a great mistake. It is a matter of the expense of getting out the paper. If they choose to spend 20,000 l. upon Parliamentary reporting that is a part of the general expense of the paper which they must take into account; I would not call it loss at all. For instance, the printing of the paper you might call a loss, which would cost you 10 l. a day; I mean the machining.

1674. But, I suppose, if the public did not appreciate a full report of the debates to such an extent as to make it valuable to the proprietor of the paper that he should put them in to the exclusion of other matter, there would be a falling off in his gains?—I do not think so. If the Parliamentary reports were more valued than the other matter he would gain by it; if it were less valued than the other matter he would not print it.

1675. Then I think that your opinion is against any subsidised official report of the proceedings in Parliament?—I should not like to express a strong opinion about it; I do think that there ought to be available for the Members of this House some record of debates, and I think that if some money were spent upon that in one form or the other it could not be better bestowed.

1676. I think you said the money would be better employed in improving the accommodation for the reporters in the Gallery?—I was asked whether I thought 10,000 l. spent on a particular report, which was described, would be better spent on the Gallery, and I said yes, and I think so; but it does not follow that there might not be a less sum given to some one person to get up an official report.

Monday, 8th July 1878.

MEMBERS PRESENT:

Colonel Arbuthnot.	Sir Henry Holland.
Viscount Crichton.	Mr. Hutchinson.
Mr. Dease.	Mr. Mills.
Mr. William Edward Forster.	Dr. Lyon Playfair.
Sir Alexander Gordon.	Mr. Walter.
Mr. Hall.	Sir Henry Drummond Wolff.
Mr. Mitchell Henry.	

THE RIGHT HONOURABLE WILLIAM EDWARD FORSTER, IN THE CHAIR.

The Right Honourable Mr. *Speaker*, Examined.

1677. *Chairman.*] WE have had a great deal of evidence with regard to an Official Report of Parliamentary proceedings, some of the witnesses strongly urging that there should be such an Official Report; I suppose your attention has been directed to that matter?—Yes, my attention has been directed to that matter.

1678. And, upon the whole, do you think it would be an advantage?—On the whole I think it would not be an advantage. I think there are many objections to an Official Report. In the first place, if we have an Official Report, it is to be assumed that that report is either to be what has been called a verbatim report, or a full report.

1679. We will first take it upon the supposition that it is a verbatim report?—In my opinion, a verbatim report would not be largely read, except upon occasions when the debates were upon very important questions, and sustained by debaters of high standing. If you had reports of that character published under the authority of the House, it would be necessary in order to have them correct, that they should be sent previously to the different speakers for correction; and it is obvious that the delay would make the reports so given of a stale character; and in these days readers will not read stale news.

1680. Of course such reports would have to be furnished under the orders of the House, and at the public charge?—Undoubtedly.

1681. I suppose that you would not consider that the question of expense was one that ought to rule the decision of the Committee, or of the House, although it ought to be considered?—The question of expense is one of importance, but no doubt there are other considerations of still greater importance.

1682. But there is an important question which I understand you consider ought to be borne in mind, and that is the question of privilege; will you kindly give the Committee your opinion on that?—As the Committee are aware, all papers now published under the authority of Parliament are privileged. If the House were to order its reports to be published day by day, the question would arise whether public opinion would approve of such papers so issued day by day by the House being protected by privilege.

1683. Could you give us any illustration of how that would work?—According to the law as it at present stands, newspapers publishing libels contained in a speech of a Member of Parliament, would be liable to the penalties of the law, unless they can show that such reports were made *bonâ fide*. I apprehend that the House, if it undertook the publication of its own reports, would probably be guided by the principle which applies to all its publications, that those reports so published day by day should be protected by privilege; but a doubt arises in my mind whether public opinion would sanction the protection of privilege of Official Reports so published by the House.

1684. You

1684. You have stated one objection that you see to verbatim reports, namely, that they would be so long, and, in many cases so unreadable, that no attention would be paid to them; but would not the objection of privilege that you now state apply even more strongly to full reports? To make my question understood, I will suppose that a Member corrects the report of his speech, and that, therefore, it is not precisely what he has spoken; would not the House then be in the difficulty of having to protect him, or to determine not to protect him, for words which he did not actually utter in the House?—That is so.

1685. And that brings up another question with regard to full reports; how do you imagine, supposing it was decided to have an Official Report, but not a verbatim report, that the House would ensure that the correction was not different from the actual speech?—I see no means of ascertaining the difference between the actual speech and the corrected speech.

1686. I understand you to say that if there be an Official Report it must be a report sanctioned in some way or other by the House of Commons?—Certainly.

1687. If that Official Report be not a verbatim report, but a full report corrected by the Members, do you see any inconvenience likely to arise from the House of Commons having sanctioned the report of a speech that was made by a Member, that report being not precisely the words that he used?—There would be inconvenience arising from a conflict of evidence.

1688. My question goes a little further than that, because it appears to me that there would be no conflict of evidence, inasmuch as the only authoritative evidence would be the report of the speech delivered; but inasmuch as that might be contrary to the recollection of Members, would there not be an inconvenience in the House having sanctioned, as the speech to which the Member might refer, or to which his opponents might refer, that which was not the actual speech that he made?—Yes, no doubt there might be that inconvenience.

1689. With regard to the present system of reporting, of course it has its advantages and disadvantages; but on the whole do you think that it is as good a system as we could have?—I think it has many advantages.

1690. Would you kindly state what advantages it appears to you to have?—I think one important advantage is that which I have already stated, that the question of privilege would not be raised. Again, I think it is a great advantage that Parliament and the press should be mutually independent; whereas, if Parliament published its own reports it would be entering into competition with the press, and possibly driving it off the field of Parliamentary reporting; and that would be a very serious misfortune. There is another great advantage in the present system, namely, that the newspaper is a convenient medium for conveying with marvellous promptitude, and at slight cost, to hundreds of thousands of readers, the reports of proceedings and debates in Parliament.

1691. There are, I suppose, countervailing disadvantages; what have occurred to you?—No doubt there are countervailing disadvantages. They appear to me to be these. First of all, the reports that are given by the newspapers at present are very meagre with respect to private Bills, with respect to proceedings in Committees of the House, and with respect to proceedings after midnight; but as the Committee are aware an arrangement has been lately entered into with Mr. Hansard with a view of removing those disadvantages. There is another disadvantage in the present system which has been brought to my notice frequently since I have had the honour of being Speaker, and that is as to the incompleteness of reports, especially on subjects of local interest.

1692. A great deal of evidence has been given to the effect that there is a difficulty in obtaining reports, not merely on questions of local interest, but on questions of Scotch and Irish interest?—When I spoke of local interests, I had Scotch and Irish questions in view.

1693. Those are the two defects in the present system; the meagreness of the reports upon certain occasions, and the incompleteness of the reports on matters of local interest, giving the word "local" a very large interpretation?—Quite so.

1694. Have you any suggestion that you could make which would enable specially that last-named defect to be met; because the first defect, I understand, is now attempted to be met by the arrangement with Mr. Hansard?—I have had frequent communications from different Members interested in the local press

press (including in that term the Scotch press and the Irish press), desiring that accommodation should be given to reporters for the local press in the Reporters' Gallery. I have been myself very anxious to meet those applications, but I have been prevented by the consideration that the Gallery is now and has been for many years fully occupied; and I did not feel warranted in taking up space now allotted to Members, with a view of accommodating reporters for the local press, without the express sanction of the House. I may say that I have suggested upon several occasions to Members advocating the interests of the Scotch and the Irish press, that the Irish press and the Scotch press should be respectively contented with a seat for two reporters, the one representing the Scotch press and the other the Irish press; and I engaged that if the press of those two countries would be satisfied with an arrangement of that kind, I would endeavour to find in the existing Gallery accommodation for such reporters.

1695. Even as the seats are at present arranged?—Even as the seats are at present arranged.

1696. That, you think, could be done without taking any seats from the Members' Gallery?—I think that could be done; but I am bound to say that that proposition does not appear to have met with favour; at all events my offers have not been accepted.

1697. I suppose that the reply which is made by the Irish and Scotch press is, that it is almost as unreasonable to ask them all to unite as it would be to ask the London press to unite in a report?—I have no doubt that those are difficulties in the way of such an arrangement.

1698. We have had evidence given showing that there are three provincial agencies represented in the Gallery, those agencies including to a certain extent Ireland and Scotland as well as the English provinces?—Yes, and I have always been in hopes that through those agencies the wants of the local press might be satisfied.

1699. But, I suppose, you have rather reason to believe that that does not give full satisfaction?—Yes, that is so.

1700. The reasons given to us why that does not give satisfaction are twofold; first, that there are some newspapers which are anxious to give a very full report, and do not wish to be fettered by the average report, which might be smaller than they would give; and also that giving the work to agencies of this kind is giving them more or less of a monopoly, and more or less of a complete control over the report which is given?—Yes, I can well understand that that would be a difficulty in the way of the arrangement.

1701. Could you make any suggestion to the Committee as to what would meet the difficulty in the shape of an extension of the Gallery if the House was to assent?—If one newspaper connected with the local press is admitted to the Reporters' Gallery, all may claim a like privilege, and I do not see my way to a limitation of the number. I understand that the local press amounts to 140 or 150 different newspapers. It is quite obvious that they could not all be accommodated in the Gallery.

1702. What has been stated to us is that there would be a natural limitation, in this way, that only a very small number of those newspapers would find it worth while to have a separate staff and to incur the expense of a separate wire, and, in fact, to provide themselves with reports without joining with other papers?—That may be so; but I think the House will have probably to take in view the likelihood of the applications becoming very numerous.

1703. How many seats do you think could be given to the reporters, without seriously inconveniencing the Members, in the present Gallery?—That is to say, assuming the present Gallery to be enlarged?

1704. Yes?—The space between the Reporters' Gallery and the door that goes into the Members' Gallery might be available for the purpose, provided Members were willing to sacrifice the accommodation; but the Committee must observe that those seats are not nearly so good for reporting as the present seats. I cannot state precisely the number of those seats.

1705. We have been told that it is not quite so important for the summary writers to have the best seats as for the actual reporters; has it occurred to you whether those extra seats might be allotted to the summary writers?—I presume that the summary writers themselves would hold that it was equally necessary that they should hear the debates; but should an arrangement of this kind

kind be carried out it certainly has occurred to me that the summary writers should be placed in a different position from that in which they are now placed.

1706. Behind the present reporters, do you mean?—Some of them, as I understand, are in front.

1707. Yes; but do you think that those who are now in front might be put in the row immediately behind?—Yes, certainly.

1708. Although it is absolutely necessary for them that they should be able to bear the debates, yet the hearing of every word is not of so much importance for them as for the actual reporters?—It would be desirable to accommodate equally well both the summary writers and the reporters, but the two things seem to be impossible; and of the two it strikes me that the reporters should have the front seats. Perhaps the Committee will allow me to add, that it would be desirable, if the reporters from the local press are to be admitted, that specific and clear instructions should be laid down as to the number or the conditions under which they are to be admitted.

1709. I suppose there are very clear regulations now with regard to the London press, are there not; no London paper is allowed more than a certain number of seats, which is fixed?—That is so; but supposing a resolution were to be passed by the House, that reporters for the local press should be admitted to the Gallery, inconvenience might arise, because there would be great difficulty in finding accommodation to meet all the applications that would be made to the Serjeant at Arms.

1710. May I ask you what you found to be the established custom with regard to the preference given to the London press over the provincial press; it has not been made quite clear to us whether, in case of a vacancy arising from one of the London papers ceasing, the custom as established would give that seat by preference to a fresh London paper, or to the local press?—As the Committee is aware, ever since the House of Commons assembled in this palace, reporters from the metropolitan press have alone been accommodated in the Gallery, with the exception of certain members of the Central Press Association and other similar associations recently admitted. If any vacancy should occur by the accident of a newspaper ceasing to exist, or from other causes, I certainly should not feel myself bound in any direction that I might think it right to give to the Serjeant at Arms upon this matter to limit those seats to the metropolitan press.

1711. That is to say that, supposing there were two applicants, one a fresh London paper, and another a combination of provincial or Irish or Scotch papers, you would weigh the different claims according to what appeared to be their merits, irrespective of any rule?—There is no rule laid down, and I should judge each case upon its merits.

1712. I suppose, in fact, this claim of the local and the Irish and Scotch papers is so far a new claim, that it came in with telegraphic communication?—I believe that is so.

1713. That before that time, knowing that they could not get a report in the morning, they took, in fact, the London reports?—Yes, that is so, no doubt.

1714. Excepting in the case of matters specially interesting, there would be even then some questions specially interesting to Ireland or Scotland, do you at all know how the report on those occasions was obtained?—The local press since the date to which the Right honourable Chairman refers, has been largely developed; and there are many matters of local interest, many matters especially relating to Scotland and Ireland, that local newspapers desire to publish as interesting in their respective localities, but which are, comparatively speaking, of lesser interest to the metropolitan papers; and for my part I think it desirable on many grounds that encouragement should be given to reporting of that character.

1715. We are also informed that several of the papers, for instance, the principal papers in Yorkshire and Lancashire and in Scotland, appear, and most appear, before it is possible that the London papers can arrive, and that they find so much interest taken in politics by the populations for which they are published, that they would not be content without as full a report of Parliamentary proceedings as is given in some of the London papers, perhaps even including the "Times"?—I can well understand that to be the case.

1716. And I suppose you would consider that it is a matter of public advantage cage that that desire of those populations should be met?—Certainly it would be a very great public advantage; and, moreover, I think that healthy competition between the metropolitan and local press would benefit both the one and the other.

1717. Have you had many representations made to you by Members with regard to incomplete reporting at present?—Yes, I have, but principally from Scotland and Ireland.

1718. To go back for a moment to the official report, there is one question I should be glad to ask you; evidence has been given tending to show that if there could be an official report it would be an advantage for historical reference, both on constitutional questions, almost, we may say, for posterity, and also for immediate use, that is to say, within a year or two, by Members and others who are interested in the debates: I suppose you would admit that there would be an advantage in that?—There would be advantage in that no doubt, speaking of the speeches delivered in the House; but, as the Committee are aware, all the acts of the House are recorded in the Journals.

1719. On the other hand, this fear has been expressed, that the effect of an official report might be to diminish the present newspaper reports, and by that means to leave the general public less informed by the newspapers than they are at present; and then the fear is also expressed, that if that be the case, as the official report would be but little read, what may be called the sympathy between the country generally and what goes on in Parliament would be less able to be realised than it is at the present moment; do you think there is any reason for that fear?—If the official report were to prove a success (which is not likely) it would probably drive Parliamentary newspaper reporting out of the field; and I think that would be a public misfortune.

1720. The misfortune being this, that as the public generally take their newspapers for very much else besides Parliamentary reporting, only those who bought the official report would know what was going on in Parliament?—That is so.

1721. And that would lessen the knowledge by the public of what is going on in Parliament, and, to some extent, lessen the influence of Parliament upon the public?—Yes; that is no doubt true. The education of the people through the newspapers, in fact, would be materially diminished.

1722. But now supposing that it was not a success, do you think that it then would have any effect upon the present reporting?—I do not think it would, because I apprehend that it would become, after the lapse of a certain time, a dead letter or obsolete, and would not be carried on.

1723. Mr. Mills.] You have alluded to the arrangement just made, I believe, with Mr. Hansard in reference to a report of the proceedings on Private Bills and proceedings in Committee, and, I think, the proceedings which take place after a certain hour of the night. I presume that those arrangements will necessarily involve the publication of that part of the proceedings of the House of Commons at a later period; that is to say, that they will involve a delay in their publication beyond the time at which the ordinary reports of the daily newspapers come out?—No doubt.

1724. Then I want to ask you whether you think any practical inconvenience is likely to arise from that circumstance from the reports of proceedings on Private Bills and proceedings in Committee being delayed some days after the publication of the other proceedings in the ordinary daily newspapers?—I do not apprehend any inconvenience resulting from that arrangement, and for this reason, that it is proposed that Mr. Hansard should occupy ground that is not now occupied by the press.

1725. And, therefore, that unless the public had the reports through that process they would not have them at all; I mean, as matters stand at present it would be the only means by which the public could have full reports of those proceedings?—I understand that arrangement with Mr. Hansard to have been made because the reports to which the honourable Member refers were in the daily newspapers incomplete.

1726. With reference to what has been said about the proposal which was made to the representatives of the press in Scotland and Ireland that there should be a report specially taken for them, and that they should have one representative of the press in the Reporters' Gallery for Scotland and one for Ireland,

Ireland, evidence has been given before us as to the objection to what has been called an identical report; for instance, in the case of Scotland, one witness said that he thought it would be undesirable that there should be one report for all Scotland, because he said that Scotland then would be deprived of the advantage provided by competition in reporting; has that difficulty or objection presented itself to your mind as a reasonable and well-founded one?—No doubt that may be a fair objection. Of course I could only offer the accommodation that was at my disposal. I should have been very glad to offer further accommodation to the Scotch and Irish press if it had been available.

1727. But as a general principle, do you think that in the interest of the public it is desirable to have the check, as it has been called, which is provided by competition in reporting?—Yes, I think it very desirable.

1728. We have had evidence before us as to what I may call the structural difficulty in providing sufficient accommodation for the reporters; we have also had evidence as to the present use of the back seats in the Reporters' Gallery; I think they have been stated to be in some instances filled by what are called leader writers and Parliamentary sketch writers; has it at all occurred to you whether it would be possible to find some space for reporters in the back seats by utilising some of the seats now occupied by those gentlemen I have alluded to?—That might be; but a back seat is not a proper place for a reporter.

1729. Then you think that practically the only means by which sufficient accommodation could be provided would be by some means which at all events would give the reporters front seats?—I think the reporters should have front seats to report effectively.

1730. Sir *Henry Drummond Wolff*.] Is the Reporters' Gallery under you, and not under the Serjeant at Arms?—I consider that, under the authority of the House, everything within the four walls of the House, that is to say, from the entrance door of the House of Commons, is under my jurisdiction while the House is sitting; the precincts of the House are left exclusively to the Serjeant at Arms; I have never interfered with the arrangements of the Serjeant at Arms with regard to the Reporters' Gallery; at the same time he consults me, and no doubt that any directions that I gave would be attended to.

1731. I thought that the theory of the Serjeant at Arms was that he was an officer of the Crown appointed to look after a Royal palace in which the House of Commons assembled, and therefore I did not quite understand whether the Serjeant at Arms was actually under the jurisdiction of the Speaker, or had an independent jurisdiction of his own?—The Serjeant at Arms is appointed by the Crown to attend upon the Speaker; but while the House is sitting, and the Speaker is in the Chair, he is, under the authority of the House, supreme as to the Chamber in which the House assembles.

1732. Mr. *Walter*.] In regard to the question of privilege, can you state what cases, if any, of libel or action for libel have occurred within your experience in consequence of reports in newspapers of speeches delivered in Parliament?—I am not able to give the precise case, but there is a case within my recollection in which proceedings were taken against a newspaper for reporting a speech of a Member of the House, that speech containing libellous matter; and, if I remember rightly, it was held that the report being *bonâ fide*, the verdict must be for the defendant.

1733. If that be a rule of law, I presume that, practically, in case of an accurate report the privilege of Parliament would cover reports in newspapers?—I am not prepared to say that.

1734. What is the status of reporters at the present moment; are they looked upon as simply strangers, to be excluded at any moment, or have they any sort of recognised status?—As the honourable Member is aware, when strangers are excluded the reporters are excluded also.

1735. Then I wish to know whether, in your opinion, the same rule should apply to an official reporter, or should apply to one of Mr. Hansard's reporters under the new system; should he be excluded, or should he be retained while the newspaper reporters were excluded, in case of an order being given for strangers to be excluded from the House?—The case has never arisen; but I apprehend that Mr. Hansard's reporter would be called upon to withdraw.

1736. Then you think that the case of an official reporter, under any new
system

system which might be adopted, would be precisely the same as that of an ordinary newspaper reporter?—No, I am not prepared to say that.

1737. But do you contemplate that in the case of a system of official reporting being adopted those official reporters should be protected by an Order of the House, while newspapers reporters were liable to be excluded; that is a very important matter on which I should like your opinion?—It would be for the House to lay down its own rules upon that matter. I apprehend that an official reporter would be protected by privilege, or by Order of the House.

1738. Are you prepared to give an opinion whether in such a case the public who at present read the newspapers would be satisfied that the sources of information upon which they depend should be liable to be shut out, while the official reports, which they would not care to read, should be privileged and protected?—I think that is one of the many difficulties which would arise in case we had official reports.

1739. Is it your opinion that the system at present adopted, under which the reporters claim the right of exercising a certain discretion as to the length of the reports which they give to different speakers is a good one or not?—I think that sometimes the reports in the newspapers are marvellous in respect of accuracy and fullness and promptitude; but occasionally they are very defective.

1740. But a good deal has been said before the Committee as to the discretion claimed by the reporters in reporting speeches according to their supposed merit, and the importance of the speakers. In the case of an official report I presume that there would be no such discretion; but the speeches would all have to be literally and fully reported?—Under a system of an official report there would be no such discretion.

1741. Is it your opinion that full reports would have any influence one way or the other, either upon the length of debates or upon the quality of the speaking?—I think that a full or verbatim report would have a prejudicial effect upon the quality of speaking. I think it would tend to lengthening speeches, and that in many instances we might have pamphlets published under cover of the official report.

1742. To what extent do you think, in the case of official reports, a Member should be allowed to correct them; should they be merely corrections of clerical errors for the sake of accuracy, or should they be allowed to give their second thoughts in the official report?—I do not think second thoughts ought to be allowed, nor any substantial alterations. Grammatical and structural corrections might be allowed.

1743. When you spoke just now of the possible, though not probable, success of a system of official reporting, what did you contemplate as constituting success in a system of official reporting?—I think is possible that if official reports were published at a very low rate indeed, and largely circulated at the public expense, a forced circulation might in that way be obtained.

1744. It would be necessary in the first place, would it not, that they should be brought out early in the morning at the same time that the newspapers come out?—I apprehend that that would be impossible, because they must be subject to correction.

1745. But any system of cheap publication at the public expense would be precisely the same kind of bonus as that which the French pay for the exportation of refined sugar to compete with the home-made article, would it not?—No doubt it would be a premium upon one class of reporting.

1746. Do you think that that in itself is a desirable system to recommend?—No, I do not.

1747. With regard to additional accommodation, can you state to the Committee what seats you think would be available; what additional space is available in the House without seriously interfering with the accommodation of Members; do you think that the end-seats in the Members' Gallery might be appropriated to reporters?—I think that those seats to which I have referred might be appropriated to reporters if the House wished, but they are by no means so convenient as the existing seats.

1748. But supposing a system of what may be called wholesale competition with the newspaper reporters were not thought desirable, would it, in your opinion, be desirable to have an official record of the speeches of the same class as Hansard's Reports, published weekly, or anything of that kind, merely as a record

record of the Parliamentary proceedings?—But Hansard's publication fulfils that object.

1749. It does not come out weekly; but there would be no difficulty whatever, I presume, in its being published weekly?—If it could be published weekly no doubt it would be a great advantage.

1750. You think that would be an advantage to the public, and would not be attended with the inconveniences which you have mentioned as interfering with newspaper reports, and as entailing any of the other objections to which you have referred?—The honourable Member is speaking of the Hansard Report, as I understand?

1751. Yes, I mean a report of that character?—A report of that character published weekly would, no doubt, be an advantage.

1752. Do you think that would be sufficient to meet the requirements of the public?—I think it would; qualifying that observation with the statement which I have already made, that I think some accommodation should be afforded for the local press.

1753. Sir *Alexander Gordon*.] Would the difficulty about privilege to which you have alluded be greater in this country than in the other countries where official reports are published?—I am not prepared to say, because I am not aware how the question of privilege applies in other countries.

1754. It was stated to us by Mr. Hansard, when he gave evidence, that the answers of Ministers when the House meets are not included in the arrangement for which he is paid now by Government: do you think it would be an advantage if an accurate record of the answers given by Ministers were preserved?—The answers of Ministers are very important, and so far as my experience goes those answers are generally speaking very efficiently reported.

1755. But it depends upon the reporter of the newspaper whether he puts the answer down or not at present?—That is so, no doubt.

1756. And few papers put down all the questions and answers that are given?—Probably if an answer happens to be one relating to a subject of no great public interest that answer is not reported.

1757. As the questions are all recorded in our Minutes, is it not desirable also to have the answers recorded in our Minutes?—It seems to me that the object is sufficiently attained by the present practice.

1758. You stated that you thought it would be very convenient if Hansard, as now carried on, could be published every week, would it not be still more advantageous if it could be published, or printed rather, in a form such as he has given us a specimen of for one day's work, in time to be delivered to Members at 4 o'clock the next day when the House meets?—I do not see how that can be done, having regard to the necessity of correction on the part of the different speakers.

1759. It has been stated by two or three witnesses who are thoroughly conversant with the subject, that there would be no practical difficulty whatever; and upon that subject I would ask, do you see any reason why the speech of a Member should not be recorded and printed as he delivers it, precisely the same as now in the House of Lords the evidence before a Committee is printed by 9 o'clock the following morning for the use of the House of Lords?—It might be done, no doubt; but whether it would be to the public advantage I am not prepared to say.

1760. Would it not be an advantage that Members should have the next day a record of what had passed on the previous day, especially in the case of an adjourned debate?—It might be an advantage so far as that goes, but there are many attendant disadvantages.

1761. Would you mention the disadvantages of having a report, such as Hansard would publish a month later, published the next day at four o'clock?—But I maintain, with all respect to Mr. Hansard, that he could not do it; for this reason, that time would not admit of Members correcting their speeches.

1762. Do you see any objection to a Member of Parliament, who comes forward to represent a large number of persons, having the words which he makes use of in a speech recorded precisely the same as now the evidence given before a Committee in either House is recorded, without his correcting it?—I see no objection to that in itself, but there are many attendant disadvantages, its cost among others.

1763. The

1763. The expense has been stated to us as under 10,000 l. a year?—I have no doubt that it would also increase the length of debates.

1764. Would it not have this effect, that it would make Members cautious how they spoke when they knew that every word was put down?—I cannot contemplate such a result as that.

1765. But you are aware that it is now done when any Member of eminence speaks; his words are taken down as he delivers them?—His words, no doubt, are taken down.

1766. Do you not think that a person who comes forward to represent in Parliament a large constituency ought to be able to speak in such a manner that his words are entitled to be put down?—No doubt.

1767. And if he found the next day that his speech was a jumble of nonsense, he would be cautious how he again addressed the House?—No doubt.

1768. And that would be an advantage, would it not, as tending to improve public speaking in Parliament?—I do not think that that advantage would result from an official report; on the contrary, I think it would tend to render public speaking not so good as it is now.

1769. In the event of Hansard not being able to be continued by private subscription, would not that be a loss to Parliament?—No doubt Hansard's publication is a very valuable publication, and in the interest of the public I hope it will be maintained.

1770. But as it is now, it is entirely maintained by contributions of private Members, is it not?—No, that is not so.

1771. A subsidy has been given this year, but up to the present year no public subsidy has been given to Hansard?—There has been an engagement to take a certain number of copies.

1772. One hundred and fifty copies?—Yes.

1773. With regard to the seats in the Gallery, if the six seats now given to summary writers of the London papers were placed at your disposal, two for Scotch papers, and two for Irish papers, should you feel any difficulty in selecting the papers which should be represented in the Gallery?—Yes, I should feel great difficulty in selecting papers for that purpose.

1774. Would it be a sufficient guarantee if the proprietors of the papers showed that they were able to keep a constant staff of reporters for transacting the business properly?—No doubt that is one consideration that might be required on every application of that character. If the applications were limited to two, of course there would be no difficulty, but I am contemplating the possibility and the probability of a very large number of applications, and I should not know how to select amongst so many applications.

1775. With regard to continuing Hansard's Debates, Mr. Hansard stated that he had printed a debate on Women's Disabilities at much greater length and more fully than he usually did, on account of the importance of that debate: does not that show that it rests with a private individual to give more prominence to some of the debates in Parliament over others; that is to say, that in that case Mr. Hansard gave prominence to that debate?—Yes.

1776. Is not that rather objectionable, in what is supposed to be a record of our proceedings, that a private gentleman should be able to give prominence to a subject which he happens to think important?—Of course it is open to every member of the press to take the same course if he thinks proper.

1777. But as "Hansard" is practically the only record that we have, is not that rather an inducement to have it under official control?—If it is put under official control, then the question arises of the character of the report that is to be made, and all the objections follow to which I have already adverted.

1778. Mr. Hutchinson.] I understand that you give it as your opinion that Hansard, as at present conducted, if issued weekly, is sufficient for the purpose of a permanent record, and that if additional facilities be afforded to the provincial, and Scotch, and Irish press, enough may be done under the existing arrangements to maintain the connection which should subsist between the House and the reporters?—Yes, I think so.

1779. You have been just asked, supposing all the additional accommodation were given that could be provided without large structural alterations, what you would think of the proposal that you yourself should select the newspapers to be admitted, and I understood you to say that you would prefer some other arrangement?—I should find great difficulty in making the selection, among many applications, of such newspapers as were entitled to preference.

1780. The reason why I ask that question is, that we had before us the other day a gentleman who is the assistant editor of the " Scotsman," and at Question 1480 this is put to him: " You would depute, then, to the Speaker the duty of saying which papers he would admit to the Gallery, and which papers he would refuse?" and he answered, " I would give him some facts for his guidance:" meaning that he would put that power in your hands, and would at the same time supply you with information to enable you to arrive at a conclusion. The question I have to put to you is, whether you would not prefer some other arrangement?—The responsibility which would rest in the Speaker in a matter of that kind would be of an invidious character, and if it could be equally well done by any other agency than through the Speaker, it would be better, I think, in the public interest.

1781. Colonel Arbuthnot.] May I ask you a few questions with regard to the accommodation in the House, as bearing very much upon what has been put to you. I asked a question of a previous witness to this effect: " What is your opinion as to the practicability of dividing the country up into districts, and allotting seats to certain sections of the country, leaving it to the newspaper proprietors of those districts to settle among themselves how the seats should be occupied?" With a view to the limited number of seats that could be available for the local press, the Scotch and Irish, and the provincial press, does that suggestion commend itself to you as practicable, and likely to remove the difficulty of a selection of individual newspapers?—That idea is new to me. It would involve, it appears to me, a very large change; it would involve the displacement of a considerable number of the present occupants of the Gallery.

1782. I only referred to any seats that might be made available: whether that would be an alternative suggestion to choosing individual, local, or provincial papers?—In the event of any seats being available, and the appropriation of those seats being placed at my disposal, I should feel bound to consider the claims of different newspapers.

1783. But do you think it would be fairer to give the sole occupation of a seat to an individual newspaper, rather than to the district in which that newspaper might circulate, but in which other newspapers might also circulate, leaving it to the proprietors to arrange for a report by what means they pleased?—If I understand the question of the honourable Member correctly, I may explain it by an illustration. Assuming that Scotland, for instance, desires to have a certain amount of accommodation in the Reporters' Gallery, the honourable Member contemplates that a certain number of seats should be appropriated to the Scotch newspapers; I apprehend that there would be great difficulty in carrying out this plan, because the Scotch newspapers would not agree among themselves as to the occupation of those seats.

1784. Could not this, to a certain extent, be decided for them by the imposition of certain conditions, such as having a private wire, and a certain circulation, and a certain staff of reporters?—But supposing that a large number of the newspapers fulfilled those conditions beyond the accommodation available, I do not see how the arrangement is to be carried out.

1785. I might explain my object by stating that, probably, it would be the case that the two largest, and the two most important papers, would be published in the same district; does it not seem desirable that other districts should benefit as well as the metropolitan district of any particular country?—I think it most desirable that other districts besides the metropolis should benefit.

1786. When I speak of the metropolis, I mean Dublin for Ireland and Edinburgh for Scotland?—Quite so. I think that the provincial newspapers, speaking of the provincial newspapers in a broad sense, should be as far as possible accommodated in the Reporters' Gallery.

1787. As regards the seats available, a previous witness stated that if the back seats which have been spoken of as the seats occupied by the leader writers, were raised, they would be as good for the purposes of hearing and reporting proceedings of Parliament as the seats in front of them; is that your opinion?
—I should

—I should be very glad to think that the reporters themselves held that the back seats were as good as the front ones, because then our difficulty would be very much lessened.

1788. That they could be made so is what I meant to suggest?—I should be very glad to think that they might be made so, because in that case our difficulties in accommodating the reporters of the press would be much diminished; but I apprehend that the reporters would hardly entertain that opinion.

1789. I do not know whether I made myself quite clear that it would require structural alterations, and that the seats would have to be raised two or three feet?—No doubt some advantages might be obtained in that way.

1790. And there would be no objection to making that alteration if the case is as that Witness supposes?—I apprehend that there would be no objection to that.

1791. Mr. *Hall.*] If the side seats, as has been suggested, were given to reporters, would not that be a very great inconvenience to Members on nights of important debates?—No doubt; the House is already small, and taking away even those few seats would be to a certain extent an inconvenience.

1792. Would it be possible on the other side of the House, over the clock, for instance, to accommodate any reporters?—I do not think the other end of the House is so convenient for the reporters, and for this reason, that, according to the rules of debate, every Member ought to address himself to the Chair, and if he does so, he would be speaking with his back to the reporters, if they were over the clock.

1793. Supposing that an official report were determined upon, have you considered the possibility of accommodating the official reporters on the floor of the House?—That is the place where they are usually accommodated in foreign assemblies, but in our assembly I do not think there is space for it.

1794. Is it true that there is underneath the floor of the House a room available for copying out such a report?—I am not aware of it.

1795. Mr. *Dawber.*] Do you think it would be possible to advance the front seats of the Gallery as was done in the House of Lords some years ago?—That is a question of structural arrangement upon which I do not feel competent to give an opinion.

1796. You were asked some question by the honourable Member for Aberdeenshire about the reporting of the debates, and he referred to the debate on the question of Women's Disabilities, of which Mr. Hansard had a full report taken; now I believe there are a good many societies who take precautions to have a full report on particular subjects in which they are interested; there is a society, for instance, for promoting Women's Suffrage, which take care to have a report of a debate on that subject; and there are societies interested in questions relating to intoxicating liquors, which in the same way would take care to have a report of debates on those questions?—There are, I apprehend, many questions upon which full reports are given.

1797. By private societies?—By private societies.

1798. I think the honourable Member for Christchurch asked whether the Serjeant at Arms had not said that he was responsible for the arrangements in the Gallery, but I think that in answer to Question 17 he stated that he received orders from you to find Mr. Hansard a place in the Gallery?—I did give him directions to provide a seat for Mr. Hansard.

1799. Mr. *Mitchell Henry.*] Recognising, as I understand you do, the desirability of keeping the newspapers dissociated from the House of Commons, I understand you to approve entirely of what I may call the improved Hansard of the present Session?—Yes, I do.

1800. And do you think that if that publication were to appear once a week, somewhat enlarged, it would answer all the purposes of a permanent record for the House of Commons?—I think a weekly publication of Hansard enlarged under the present arrangement would be an advantage.

1801. Have you examined that specimen which Mr. Hansard put into our hands (*handing the same to Mr. Speaker*)?—No.

1802. That I understand to be a full but not a verbatim report of one day's proceedings

The Right Hon.
Mr. Speaker.

8 July 1878.

proceedings of the House of Commons, being in point of fact the Hansard improved as is at present contemplated, but somewhat more fully than can be done now?—I am not sufficiently acquainted with the publication to give any opinion upon it, but we all admit that Hansard is hitherto published has been a most valuable publication, and if it were brought out weekly and enlarged I think it would be an advantage.

1803. And that would not involve the objection which you feel towards official reporting: you would not regard that any more as an official report than you do now?—No, I should not.

1804. You would simply regard it as a subvented report?—As a subvented report.

1805. In reference to the back seats in the gallery, would it be possible to raise those seats about two feet, and to make an entrance into them from the back, and in that way to afford better provision as to hearing for the persons who were there?—I cannot say; that is rather a matter for an architect to determine than for me; but I am bound to say this, that both the Serjeant at Arms and I have at different times tried to find means of increasing the accommodation, but we have hitherto failed.

1806. I presume you would be willing to receive from the provincial press collectively any proposals that they might make for a structural alteration in the present seats, or for facilitating their entrance into the gallery?—Certainly. I wish to say that any structural alterations of the House of Commons would be made by the Minister of the Crown responsible for public works; but any suggestions that the House might give upon the subject would, as a matter of course, be carried out.

1807. Sir Henry T. Holland.] I think you said that if it was decided to admit the reporters for the provincial press you would wish to see special conditions imposed; is there any other condition which you would wish to see imposed beyond the limit of numbers?—Supposing that the selection of the reporters who should be admitted were vested in the Speaker, I should be glad to have special conditions laid down for my guidance, because I apprehend very considerable difficulty hereinafter in making the selection of such newspapers as shall have admission.

1808. Then the conditions that you would wish to have laid down are with reference to the selection of newspapers?—Yes.

1809. Chairman.] As it will be desirable for us to know what number of seats could be added to the Reporters' Gallery by including in it the seats which you suggested between the Reporters' Gallery and the doors in the Members' Gallery, would you inform the Committee of the number of those seats?— The number of seats added to the Reporters' Gallery by the alterations referred to would amount to 14, of which eight would be front seats, and six back seats. I submit a tracing (vide Appendix, No. 7) of the alterations in question. It is right that I should point out that the accommodation for Members would be reduced by this arrangement to the extent of 22 seats; the discrepancy between the figures arising from the fact that reporters require more room in the exercise of their work. As the Committee is aware, the existing accommodation for Members amounts to 476 seats, of which 352 are in the body of the House, and 124 (including the 22 seats above referred to) in the galleries.

1810. Hansard's Report, though not an official report, is one that by the mode in which it has been conducted is found to be a dependable report, and is admitted generally in the House of Commons to be one that can be referred to. I suppose from your answers that you consider that there is an advantage in having such a report, and that it avoids the disadvantages which you mentioned of an official report?—Yes, I think it of great advantage to have a report of that character, not being official.

1811. But obtaining its authority by the manner in which it has been conducted?—Quite so.

Mr. *William Henry Gurney Salter*, Examined.

Mr. W. H.
Gurney Salter

8 July 1878.

1811.* *Chairman.*] You are one of the firm of Messrs. Gurney?—I am; Mr. Gurney, with whom I am associated in the firm, and who filled the office of shorthand writer to this House for a great many years, is unfortunately not well enough to attend.

1812. In fact, you are the head of the staff?—I am the shorthand writer to the House, and the acting member of the firm.

1813. Will you just explain to the Committee what your duty as shorthand writer to the House is?—It is our duty to take notes of all evidence given before Committees of this House, and also at the Bar, whenever occasion arises. We have been directed at various times to take notes for the House of proceedings also at the Bar; those have of late years become very rare; but 40 or 50 years ago it very frequently happened that we were called upon to report, not only the examination of witnesses, but also speeches at the Bar.

1814. The gentlemen who report the questions and answers in Committee (and I think I am speaking the opinion of every Member of the Committee when I say that they are remarkably well reported) are from your staff?—Yes.

1815. It is your business, as I understand it, with Mr. Gurney, to superintend that reporting?—It is.

1816. Do you know anything about the reporting in France?—Yes, from personal observation of the shorthand writing at Versailles, and also, I may say, in Germany; and to a less extent in Italy, not to any extent probably that would be useful to this Committee.

1817. We will take France first: what sort of accommodation is there for reporters in the French Assembly?—The reporters have seats close to the tribune at Versailles. By permission of the President of the Assembly I had the opportunity of sitting beside the reporters, and actually watching their operations, and in fact I, myself, wrote close to the tribune for a short time; so that I know intimately how the work is done.

1818. Comparing their facility for hearing with the position of our reporters, to which would you give the preference?—The opportunities in Versailles are immensely better than any in this country.

1819. Would that apply to the Chamber generally, or merely to those speakers who addressed it from the tribune?—The speakers all did address it from the tribune at the time when I was there. I subsequently sat at a distance, in two of the more remote parts of the building, and I observed that the opportunities for hearing there were no better than they are in the Gallery of the English House of Commons.

1820. Then the advantage there was rather owing to their custom of speakers addressing the House from the tribune than to greater advantages being given to the reporters?—Very much so. Perhaps I may be allowed to say that I have also written on the floor of the House of Commons; that is to say, at the Bar of the House, and that I am therefore able to institute a comparison with that position. Undoubtedly the position in France, from the fact of there being a tribune there, is better than the seat at the Bar in the English House of Commons, because in France the speaker is necessarily close to the reporter, whereas in the House of Commons he may be at some distance from the Bar.

1821. There is an official report in France, is there not?—Yes; published in the "Journal Official."

1822. Do you know how many reporters are engaged on the staff for the official report?—The number has varied from time to time. At the time when I was there the report was originally prepared by 12 *stenographes*, taking turns of two minutes each. Their work was afterwards read through and revised by what are called the *stenographes réviseurs*, of whom there were at that time six. I believe the number has been increased since.

1823. When were you there?—The time when I had an opportunity of becoming intimately acquainted with the process was in the last Session of the *Assemblée Nationale*, immediately before the *Assemblée Nationale* was dissolved; that is to say, about two years ago. I have not been present during the sittings of the present Chambers at all for the purpose of examining the shorthand writing.

R   1824. I suppose

Mr. *W. H.*
Gurney Salter.

8 July 1878.

1824. I suppose there are many other reporters besides those who furnish the Official Report?—There are others; but the newspapers and the public appear to depend mainly upon the Official Report in one or other of its forms. I was introduced to some others, so that I know that there are others.

1825. Do you think that the newspapers obtain their reports at all from the Official Report?—I am not able to speak much about the newspaper press in France, but I believe that they do obtain them very largely from the Official Report.

1826. I rather gather from your answer that the newspaper reporting is not conducted there on anything like the same scale as it is in England?—Certainly, it is not.

1827. Do you know what opportunities are given to members of the Chambers for correcting this Official Report?—Yes; after the Official Report has been prepared originally by the shorthand writers writing for two minutes, and after it has been revised by the *stenographes réviseurs*, each of whom writes for half-an-hour, during the time that the other men are writing for two minutes, there is an opportunity for revision by the Members in the course of the same evening, and their revision is again revised by the head of the staff.

1828. Will you just describe how they are able to avail themselves of that opportunity?—In another part of the same building there is a room in which the proof sent up from the printer is submitted to the Members, or is available, rather, for the Members, in case they choose to revise their speeches.

1829. Did you have access to that room?—Yes, I was present during part of the time that the process was going on.

1830. May I ask whether it was an important debate?—Yes, it was a very important debate upon the electoral law.

1831. Did you observe to what extent the Members made use of this opportunity of correction?—I observed that very few came in on that particular evening to make corrections. M. Gambetta had made a speech that day; I was rather anxious to see to what extent he revised it; I found that he did not look at the proof at all.

1832. Had you any means of getting information on the point, so as to satisfy yourself whether Members did or did not make use of the opportunity of correcting their speeches?—Yes; I ascertained from the official shorthand-writer, with whom I had very long conversations, that some Members revised to a great extent. I may, perhaps, mention that M. Thiers almost re-wrote his speeches; he could never be satisfied with anything that had been taken down; but that M. Gambetta, on the other hand (who, however, was no better reported), never touched his speeches. Perhaps I may mention that the reason given to me why M. Gambetta never revised his speeches was, that he was then able to say that he had not revised them.

1833. And upon the whole, do you think, taking Members of note, that they generally revise their speeches or not?—On the whole I understood from what I was told that the extent to which the speeches as reported were corrected afterwards by the Members at Versailles, was not greater than the extent to which the evidence taken before the Committees of this House is ordinarily corrected by the Members and witnesses.

1834. Then I think I understood you to say that after the Member had revised his speech, his revision was submitted to some other person?—To the chief of the stenographic staff, M. Lagache.

1835. For what purpose is it submitted to him?—He had the power at that time (I believe it has been somewhat curtailed since) of objecting to any alteration which he considered to go beyond an alteration of form, and to amount to an alteration of substance.

1836. Do you know whether he made use of that power?—Yes; I have memoranda of a conversation with him in which he told me that he had repeatedly refused alterations proposed even by Ministers, indeed, by Prime Ministers, but that he had never really been brought into unpleasant relations with any Member in consequence.

1837. Now you have been in Germany also?—Yes; I am not able to give quite as much information as to that country, but I have made myself acquainted by personal observation with the process of reporting there. I know in some detail the arrangements for shorthand writing in both countries, but probably the Committee would not care to enter into them.

1838. There is no tribune in Germany, is there?—In the Herrenhaus at Berlin, where

where I was present, there is not exactly a tribune, but the Members very often speak from a place where they are very well heard.

1839. And what sort of accommodation is there for the reporters there?—The reporters there sit immediately under the President. I think I may qualify my former answer by saying there is a tribune, but it is not always used.

1840. But the Herrenhaus is their House of Lords?—Yes.

1841. We will take their House of Commons: have you any information to give us as to the reporting there?—I did not actually see the reporting going on in the Chamber, but there again the reporters have the best seats for hearing.

1842. Have they an Official Report?—They have.

1843. And have the Members opportunities for correction?—There are opportunities for correction. I am only able to say in general terms that the correction is not carried to any great extent.

1844. Do you know when the Official Report comes out in Germany?—I cannot speak of the practice at the present time. I believe it used to be not until two days after the debate.

1845. Going back to France, when does the Official Report there come out?—The "Journal Officiel," which contains it, may be purchased the next morning at the bookstalls.

1846. Do you think many people buy it?—I asked the official reporter, and he said, Yes. I am not able to give any more precise information.

1847. It has, I suppose, a gratuitous circulation to a large extent?—Yes.

1848. Now, taking our House of Commons, supposing an Official Report were required, or desired, how do you think it could be produced?—I apprehend that although it would be a difficult and responsible duty, it could be done by shorthand writers of the highest professional ability and standing, whose work might afterwards, according as the House might think fit to direct, be subject to revision by the speakers themselves; I mean, by shorthand writers whose practice it is to take down, not only the greater part of what a fast speaker says (which is sufficient for what is ordinarily called "revision reporting"), but the whole of it with the same minute verbal accuracy with which a slow speaker is reported. They ought also to be well informed and trustworthy gentlemen.

1849. Have you formed any idea as to how many seats would be required for such an Official Report?—I think two seats in good positions would be necessary. Perhaps I may venture, as the House would certainly desire that an Official Report should be produced with every advantage for hearing, to assume, what has been assured by other witnesses, that the House would feel it necessary to assign to the shorthand writers seats at, or near to the Table, if so, at the most two seats there, or one there and one in a good position elsewhere would be ample.

1850. But supposing that they had to be in the Gallery?—I have written sufficiently often in the Gallery to be able to say that the opportunities of hearing there are not all that could be desired; and, therefore, of course, an Official Report would suffer to some extent if taken there.

1851. Then your notion would be that if the House determined to have an Official Report, it would probably put the reporters in the body of the House?—I think the House, if it had an Official Report, would be likely, sooner or later, to place them there; because I am confident that if the shorthand writer were placed in any other position there would be occasions when he would not be able to do complete justice to the speakers.

1852. I suppose the report would have to be very quickly furnished?—That would depend upon the system which the House determined to adopt as to the expedition of the delivery of the manuscript. I think I may say that it is generally considered that keeping the shorthand writer in his place for a sufficient time to enable him to follow the thread of the speech or discussion, is advantageous; and if two or three days were allowed for the production of the report, it would undoubtedly be desirable to keep the shorthand writer longer in his seat than would be possible, if the report had to be produced by the next afternoon.

1853. Now would it be your idea that such a report would be a similar report to what is given of questions and answers in Committees?—I should venture to suggest that that would be the necessary basis for any such report.

1854. That it should be a verbatim report you mean?—However the report might afterwards be revised or abridged, throughout or in particular parts, I think the

Mr. W. H.
Gurney Salter.

2 July 1878.

the basis should be a verbatim report, subject to the correction of any grammatical errors, or any such slips as most speakers occasionally fall into. Sometimes a speaker adds to a sentence, by way of an afterthought, a clause which obviously should be introduced at an earlier stage; an intelligent shorthand writer would correct that when it was copied out.

1855. Then whether the Official Report was to be finally a verbatim report, or a full report not verbatim, a verbatim report, subject to these grammatical corrections, must be the basis of it?—I should venture to suggest that such a verbatim report must necessarily be the basis, because a "full report," by which I understand a report abridged to some slight extent, would be much better produced if the process of abridgment were performed afterwards than if it were performed at the moment of reporting. If you require a shorthand writer, at the time when he is taking down a fast speaker, to engage his thoughts also in literary improvement of the style, or in anything beyond the merest matter of form, you are asking from him more than you would be likely to succeed in obtaining.

1856. What you mean is, that it is much more difficult for a reporter to condense than to report verbatim?—No; what I mean is, that if the result is to be an Official Report, I think that it would be almost more than could be expected from any man, that he should condense at the same time when he is called upon to report. The tendency of combining the two operations is to give a well-rounded sentence rather than to give a sentence containing more matter, and to depart unnecessarily from the *ipsissima verba* of the speaker.

1857. If the reporter was to be told, "Now you may, or rather, it is expected that you shall, abridge the report; you must take care to omit no fact of importance, and no argument, and you must shorten by condensation;" that would be almost more than ought to be expected of a reporter?—It is more than ought to be expected of him at the moment of reporting. Condensation is really a distinct work from reporting, and it would be much better done at a subsequent stage; and by one experienced person condensing the whole than by each shorthand writer condensing his own manuscript. Then any one who afterwards wished to appeal to the report could do so, and see to what extent the condensation had taken place, and that really nothing material had been omitted. For instance, if it were desired that the verbatim transcript should be condensed throughout, or abridged very much at some parts and much less at others, that might be done by an alteration of the transcript, which could be referred to, possibly in the Library, with the alterations appearing in red ink.

1858. I think you have stated that the corrections by Members and witnesses of questions and answers in Committees is carried to but slight extent?—I do not remember stating that, but ordinarily that is the case; it varies. There are often some obvious clerical errors and misprints to be corrected, but as the Committee may be aware, some witnesses correct what they have themselves said to a very much larger extent than others; some are more punctilious in matters of style, and more desirous to give a literary finish to their evidence. Perhaps I may be allowed to mention, as bearing upon the general question, that there are some Committees in which the usual opportunity for alteration of the print is not given. For instance, there was a Committee about two years ago on Foreign Loans; the Committee in that case said to the witnesses, that if they had anything to correct or alter, they must come forward and state it publicly; and I believe that nothing of the kind was done, and the evidence now stands in the Blue Book as the shorthand writer left it.

1859. That was to guard against the witnesses rather than the Members?—It was. The same has happened in Committees of the other House on public subjects, before which there have been counsel present, and also in Committees before which there have been no counsel. There are repeated instances of evidence taken before Committees being published in the words in which it was given, subject only to a right on the part of the witnesses to come forward and make any correction if they liked in public; that is to say, there was to be no correction done by a mere stroke of the pen.

1860. But leave was given to the witness to ask to be re-examined, if he wished to correct or explain any statement?—Just so; and I may say that in those cases I believe no such request was made, or it was to a quite inappreciable extent, if at all. There have been also other cases in this House, not only of

private

private Bill Committees, but of important Select Committees, in which the same thing has been done.

1861. With regard to the time of furnishing the transcript, have you anything to say?—That would be as the House might direct. I am speaking of what might be done in case the House at any time decided upon having an Official Report.

1862. How quickly do you think it could be done?—It could be done undoubtedly, so as to be produced, I may say at almost any speed. What has been done, could be done again. The evidence taken before Private Bill Committees is very frequently in print the next morning at eight o'clock; and of course if the House desired that pressure to be put on, it could be put on. I am not prepared to say that there would be no greater difficulty in furnishing an absolutely satisfactory report so quickly.

1863. Do you think it would be at all possible for the Official Report to appear at the same time as the "Times" does?—If the House were prepared to let the Official Report so published be as it were a "proof," it would be possible, undoubtedly, so far as shorthand writing and printing are concerned.

1864. I think I understand you to say, that the "Journal Officiel" does appear in the morning?—Yes, but the circumstances are different.

1865. The debates in France end, as a rule, very much earlier?—Very much earlier, and the total quantity produced in the sitting there would be very much less.

1866. We have been informed that when a sitting at Versailles is protracted beyond eight o'clock in the evening, the report does not appear till the next day but one?—That is so; but it should be added, that in that case the report has been already corrected by Members; and when the question was put to me I was answering rather with regard to that what might be done, so far as shorthand writing and printing are concerned, independently of the time given for correction.

1867. Sir *Henry T. Holland*.] Have you read the return that was made with reference to the proceedings in France, a return of the 30th March 1674?— I have, and I have talked over that return with the official shorthand writer at Versailles.

1868. Is that return correct?—The official shorthand writer at Versailles told me that there were one or two small matters in which it was inaccurate.

1869. Are they of sufficient importance to bring before us as corrections?— I think not. I have looked through the return carefully on purpose to see.

1870. Then from that return it appears that the printing of the reports ceases at a quarter to six in the afternoon, and that if the sitting lasts after that hour, the part of the report still unprinted is only completed the next day?—May I ask whether that applies to the report in *extenso*?

1871. These are the analytical reports which are referred to in that passage of the return?—I think that statement would hardly be considered as applicable to the *extenso* report, because I know that is going on all night, and the *bon-à-tirer* is generally given at about two in the morning.

1872. Then the report in *extenso* is furnished to the newspapers the next morning?—The report in *extenso* is published in the "Journal Officiel;" the representatives of the newspapers may see it in Paris at an office provided for that purpose, but if they see the report of the proceedings of any day up to the completion of that day's proceedings, it must be at an hour far advanced in the night, and practically, I believe, they do not avail themselves of it.

1873. You propose that if there is an Official Report the reporters should sit in the House; now as the Members do not speak from a tribune here, in what place in the House could the reporters be put so that they should at all times face the speaker, which of course would be desirable?—I think it would be impossible to put them in a position in which they could at all times face the Member speaking, but if they sat at the Table, inasmuch as most Members address their observations towards the Chair, or towards the two front benches, which are in the same direction, probably the shorthand writer would have no serious difficulty in hearing.

1874. Except in the cases when Members of the Government and Members of the ex-Government were speaking, the two reporters in almost all cases would have their backs to the speaker?—In many cases they would, as indeed they have sometimes in these Committee rooms. That is not an insuperable

difficulty in itself, provided that the seat is in other respects favourable for
hearing.

1875. You think, upon the whole, that if the reporters were placed at the
Table they would be able to hear sufficiently well?—I feel no doubt of that,
because I have listened to debates frequently, occasionally at the Bar, and often
under the Gallery.

1876. And there would be some difficulty, would there not, in supplying
fresh reporters, each one of them having to walk up the House and take
his seat at the Table?—That would be a great difficulty; I felt bound to
mention the point of hearing, although I was aware what difficulty it would
occasion, because I was satisfied that the House would not wish if there were
an Official Report, that it should be produced under such unfavourable circumstances that it could not be a perfectly accurate report.

1877. Mr. Mills.] I take it for granted that the evidence which you have
given about proceedings in France, where they have a Tribune, does not bear
upon our arrangements here, since we have no Tribune?—I think it bears upon
them so far as to show the great advantage which a seat near to a speaker
confers upon any reporter.

1878. But nothing that we could do here could bring us the same advantages
which you think exist at Versailles now unless we had a Tribune?—Not to the
same extent, undoubtedly.

1879. You alluded to the proceedings at Berlin; is that "Kammer Correspondenz," the paper they publish there, an official paper or not?—There is
an Official Report produced; it is distinctly official, that is to say, that the shorthand writers hold official positions, and have salaries from the Government.

1880. Sir Alexander Gordon.] Do the reporters employed by your firm write
out their own notes?—No, that would delay the proceedings far too much, and
therefore the practice is that clerks who can copy the note should transcribe it.
By that means greater dispatch and economy are obtained in cases where only
shorthand-writers of the highest qualifications can be employed. It takes six
or seven hours for a fast writer to write in longhand what is uttered and taken
down in shorthand in one hour.

1881. But the evidence we have had before us lead us to suppose that
reporters for the newspapers write out their own notes?—I believe they do
ordinarily.

1882. Your system is different in that respect from theirs?—It is. I may
say that the difference does not by any means arise from the fact that in writing
speeches a different kind of shorthand is adopted, nor does it arise from a
difference in what is technically called the system of "shorthand" used by the
one or the other: it arises from our arrangement that the same shorthand
writer should continue writing without interruption as long as possible, which
is found to be a great convenience to Committees, and advantageous for the
report.

1883. Does it not indicate very great accuracy of work, that the shorthand
notes of one writer should be read and written out by another?—The shorthand
writer must write with great accuracy and skill, undoubtedly, for that to be
possible.

1884. Do you know what the papers published, for instance, at Marseilles or
Lyons, do to obtain reports of the debates in the French Assembly?—No, I
have not interested myself really in the reporting either in England or in
France, except so far as the shorthand writing is concerned, and that which
touches the newspaper press I am very imperfectly informed upon. It is only
upon the shorthand writing part of the question that I feel myself at all competent to give evidence.

1885. Assuming there to be an Official Report, how long do you propose
that each gentleman should sit in the seat for the purpose of reporting?—That
would depend entirely upon the degree of speed with which the transcript is
required. I should think it desirable to keep him there as long as was con-
sistent with sufficient dispatch in the production of the manuscript.

1886. Assuming that it was only wanted to get it out by the next afternoon,
how long would you keep the reporter in the seat?—In the early part of the
evening he would be there certainly, I should say, for an hour, or perhaps an
hour and a half.

1887. Do you find reporters for the Committees of the House of Lords as well as for the Committees of this House?—Yes.

1888. I believe I am correct in stating that the proceedings of a Committee of the House of Lords, including speeches by counsel, are printed through the night without any correction by the witnesses or counsel?—The proceedings of a Committee on a private Bill in either House are printed during the night, and are produced the next morning at eight o'clock.

1889. Without any correction whatever?—Without any opportunity for correction by anyone.

1890. Is the type broken up then?—I believe it is in most cases.

1891. So that there are no means of a witness, or a speaker, making any correction of what he has said?—The practice in the case of those Committees is for anyone who conceives himself to have been inaccurately reported, or who wishes what he said to be altered in any respect, to come before the Committee at its meeting the next morning and say so; that is done when it is considered necessary, but the necessity rarely arises.

1892. That must be done by a reprint, then, I suppose?—No, it is not done by a reprint, but the next day's evidence will contain a question and an answer at the beginning, setting right anything that may require to be set right.

1893. Then do you see any difficulty in reporting and printing in a similar manner speeches delivered in the House of Commons?—There is no physical difficulty of any kind. The responsibility would be exceedingly great; it would be of the very utmost importance that the Members should be represented with perfect faithfulness and accuracy, and probably the Members themselves would desire to have some opportunity of correction, which in that case, I think, it would be hardly possible for them to have; quite impossible, I may say.

1894. Would it not be a test of good speaking if a Member had his speech produced as he said it to a great extent, as those gentlemen who speak before the House of Lords Committees are obliged to have theirs?—Perhaps I may be allowed to say, with regard to that, that a shorthand writer in Germany, who has had probably as much experience as any other in reporting in some of the kingdoms now included in the Empire, and also in the Imperial Parliament, I mean Dr. Zeibig, who is also a professor of shorthand, and knows the art better probably than any other man, told me that the effect in Germany had been decidedly in that direction: that Members were much more careful about their utterance, and the form in which they expressed themselves, when the Official Report was introduced than they were before. I believe his chief experience was at Dresden; he could speak of the state of things at various places where there were not official reports, and also of the state of things where there were.

1895. Therefore the result of an Official Report abroad has been found to be to make Members more careful in their speaking; to make them study the art of speaking more carefully?—According to the statement of Dr. Zeibig that is so. Of course it is not a matter on which I can say anything.

1896. Mr. *Mitchell Henry.*] When you speak of the reporters sitting at the Table in the present House of Commons, what part of the Table do you refer to; do you mean with their backs to one of the two front benches?—I cannot say that I have thought of it sufficiently to be prepared with any scheme of any kind. I merely ventured to express an opinion generally from what I have seen of reporting here and elsewhere, and what has been told to me by the official reporters elsewhere, in fact it is what every shorthand writer must know, that the opportunities of hearing require to be the very best possible. Hearing is a very important element in the question, and I am able to say that even the Bar, where I have written sometimes for the House, does not afford an equally good opportunity with a seat in Paris close to the Tribune. I have not really thought exactly what part of the table would be appropriated to the shorthand writer if the House thought fit to assign him a place there.

1897. Then as far as that matter goes, your evidence is of a general character, and does not refer to the present House of Commons?—It only professes to be of a general character throughout.

1898. It merely amounts to this, that as Members ought to address themselves to the Chair, the nearer the reporter is put to the Chair the better he could hear?—Yes, on the general principle that the shorthand writer ought always to be between the person speaking and the person spoken to, as far as possible.

1899. But you are not prepared to say that by any arrangement that could be

0.121.   N 4

be made in the present House of Commons reporters could be placed at the Table of the House?—I would not presume to say so.

1900. I mean you have not formed any idea as to that?—I merely ventured to express the opinion that if the House had an Official Report it would be sure to want to have as good a one as could be produced, and that anything that could be produced without the very best opportunities of hearing would not be as good a report as the House would desire for an Official Report.

1901. Mr. *Dunbar*.] I think in Versailles the reporters sit close under the Tribune?—Yes: there are two writing at the same time; the one who writes for a two-minutes turn may be said to be underneath; the *stenographe réviseur* writes more at the side.

1902. Your reporters who report Committees are on duty the whole day?—Usually.

1903. The reporter sends away his book every half hour?—Yes.

1904. And then it is read by clerks?—By clerks who are accustomed to read the shorthand, and who dictate it to writers who write it out; and when the shorthand writer returns home in the afternoon he compares the whole of the transcript so produced with his original shorthand, to see that it is accurate; a process which occupies many hours.

Friday, 12th July 1878.

MEMBERS PRESENT:

Colonel Arbuthnot.	Sir Henry T. Holland.
Viscount Crichton.	Mr. Hutchinson.
Mr. Dunbar.	Mr. Mills.
Mr. William Edward Forster.	Dr. Lyon Playfair.
Sir Alexander Gordon.	Mr. William Henry Smith.
Mr. Mitchell Henry.	Mr. Walter.
Lord Francis Hervey.	

THE RIGHT HONOURABLE WILLIAM HENRY SMITH, IN THE CHAIR.

The Right Honourable Viscount *Eversley* (attending by special permission of the House of Lords), Examined.

1905. *Chairman.*] I THINK you were Speaker of the House of Commons for many years ago, were you not?—For 18 years.

1906. And during the period you had charge of, and were responsible for, the Reporters' Gallery as well as all other parts of the House?—I never had much trouble with the Reporters' Gallery, because at that time there were not so many reporters as there are now, and the provincial press was hardly represented.

1907. In point of fact it was before the time of telegraphs, I think, was it not?—Precisely.

1908. Have you considered the question of official reporting?—I have, but I cannot say that I think any advantage would be gained by an official report; but on the contrary, I think it would be very disadvantageous to the House.

1909. Might I beg you to state what, in your opinion, would be the principal objection to a system of official reporting?—I may be wrong, but I consider that if you have official reporting you must have verbatim reporting; everything that goes on in the House must be noted down in detail. The inconvenience of that would be considerable, because if these reports were to be published on the morning after the debate had arisen there would be no time for correction; and if you give time for correction I am afraid that you will be no better off with official reporting than you are now with " Hansard."

1910. With the great experience that you possess of Parliamentary life, do you think that the influence and authority of Parliament would be increased by a verbatim official report of the deliberations of Parliament?—No, I think it would not. I think the authority of Parliament is maintained to a great degree now by the present system of reporting; the reports in all the public papers are very full and wonderfully accurate, and the accuracy really is secured by the competition amongst the variety of newspapers which do report.

1911. Would there be danger, in your judgment, that an official report would lead to an absence of the accurate representation, on the whole, of the proceedings in Parliament which newspapers would give?—I think it would be open to this objection, that everything would be noted by the official reporter that passed in the House. Very often in debates, as we all know, intemperate expressions are used, what we commonly call words of heat, which are much better allowed to be forgotten; those would all be recorded by the official reporter.

1912. You would not think it possible that discretion should be left to an official reporter to omit remarks made in debate which would not conduce to the dignity of Parliament?—Certainly not; if you have an official reporter you cannot leave him any discretion; he must report faithfully what he hears.

1913. Are you aware of any complaint out of doors as to the sufficiency of the reporting?—No, I never heard any.

The Right Hon.
Thomas Erskine.
10 July 1878.

1914. Not in your time as Speaker ?—Not in my time. You must remember that in my time there were not so many reporters, and there was ample space for them in the Reporters' Gallery.

1915. Then, speaking for the public out of doors, I understand you to express your opinion than an official report is not desirable, and certainly not necessary ?—That is my opinion.

1916. Do you consider that there is any occasion for it, so far as Members of Parliament are concerned ?—I think not.

1917. Your view is that it is not necessary that there should be a record, for the satisfaction of Members, of the words which they themselves have uttered ? —I am assuming that everything remains as at present; that you have newspapers reporting the debates, as they do now, every day; and that you have also "Hansard," in which the Members correct the reports of their own speeches, and that would always remain as a record, and a very faithful record, of what passed in the House, provided the corrections are not allowed to be too numerous.

1918. Am I correct in assuming that your view is that competition between newspapers secures independent and, on the whole, accurate reports ?—That is exactly my view.

1919. That "Hansard," compiled from the best sources of information which the newspapers supply, secures the permanent record which is alone required by Parliament ?—Precisely. I am told that there are complaints made at present that there is not a sufficient report of the private business of the House, or of the proceedings in Committee. All that ought to be supplied by "Hansard."

1920. You are probably aware that, tentatively, an arrangement has been made with Mr. Hansard this year, under which he supplies reports of proceedings in Committee of the House, reports of local Bills, which are debated before public business commences, and reports after 12 o'clock, under which, in fact, he supplies the deficiencies which have been remarked as existing in the reports of the London press ?—I have heard that such an arrangement has been made, and I think it will supply all the deficiencies that are now complained of.

1921. Are you of opinion that it would be possible to retain official reporters in the House when strangers are excluded from the House ?—That must depend entirely, I think, upon the regulation of the House itself. Of course the House has it always in its power to remove everybody, and an occasion certainly might arise when an official reporter might be ordered to withdraw. I think that must rest entirely with the House.

1922. But have you considered the question whether inconvenience would arise from the exclusion of strangers reporting for the press, and the presence of official reporters who would report the proceedings in Parliament for Parliament itself ?—The withdrawal of strangers must of course be caused by the House wishing its debate to be in secret, and I think that, therefore, the presence of any reporter would then be an inconvenience.

1923. Sir Henry T. Holland.] There are two points of view, are there not, from which we have to consider that question, that of the public and that of the Members ?—Precisely.

1924. Now the amount of reporting done in the newspapers is a sure test of what the public desire, is it not ?—Certainly.

1925. Because any paper in its own interest would follow the wishes of its readers, and if longer reports of the debates were wanted, longer reports of the debates would be furnished ?—Yes.

1926. Therefore, as regards the public, we may assume that they are satisfied with the present reports and the summaries ?—Yes.

1927. You are also probably aware that if a paper requires a full report of some special debate of local interest, it can secure that by an arrangement with the reporters ?—I understand such to be the case.

1928. And also that any paper can secure a full report of the speech of any special Member ?—Yes.

1929. Therefore that has to be considered in judging whether the public are satisfied ?—Yes.

1930. Then as regards Members, your Lordship is doubtless of opinion that a full and accurate report of proceedings in the House should be secured for reference in future ?—Yes.

1931. And

The Right Hon.
Visconut Eversly

12 July 1878.

1931. And may I ask you, from your experience, are you satisfied that "Hansard's Debates" do secure us that full and sufficiently accurate report for purposes of reference?—I think that "Hansard's Debates" do secure such a report.

1932. Mr. *Mitchell Henry*.] Your Lordship is of opinion that the reporting of proceedings in private business, and of proceedings in Committee of the House, and also after 12 o'clock, should be supplied by "Hansard"?—Certainly.

1933. That has involved a subvention to "Hansard"; would it not be an advantage then that "Hansard" should appear somewhat more frequently than it does now?—It would be an advantage certainly; but if Members are to correct their speeches, time must be required between the report and the publication of the report.

1934. If "Hansard" were to appear once a week, for instance, would that meet your Lordship's view as to what is necessary?—Quite, I think.

1935. With regard to provincial papers, of course there is a great demand now for the admission of provincial papers, particularly papers in Scotland and in Ireland, and in the large towns of the country; that, I presume, you would regard as a legitimate demand?—Certainly; but I am not prepared to say how it could be complied with; because the number of papers requiring accommodation in the gallery has so very much increased since my time, that I do not know what accommodation there is in the gallery for them.

1936. But if it is a legitimate and proper demand on the part of the public, it is a demand which we may hope that the House will be able to supply?—Certainly.

1937. Mr. *Dealer*.] I think that in your Lordship's time there were no country papers represented in the gallery?—I do not remember any.

1938. Colonel *Arbuthnot*.] In the event of its being decided that an official report is requisite, do you think that the newspapers should be allowed to continue to have their own reporters in the gallery; or should they be compelled to use the official report, or such part of the official report as they might desire?—I think it would be a great misfortune if you interfered with the newspaper reports in any way.

1939. Sir *Alexander Gordon*.] With reference to the question just asked you, it has been stated by, I think, most of the newspaper proprietors who have been before us, that the publication of an official report would in no way interfere with the reporting for public newspapers; it has been stated, for instance, by the gentlemen who appeared on behalf of the "Times," and on behalf of some of the other leading newspapers, that an official report would make no difference in their report; but that does not agree with your opinion, if I understand you rightly?—I am not prepared to say what would be its effect; my own opinion is that it would be very undesirable if it interfered with the reporting in the newspapers.

1940. I understood you to say that "Hansard" compiled from the best sources, that is to say, from the best newspapers, was a sufficient publication of the debates of Parliament for the use of the House?—Yes; it is a sufficient record of what passes in Parliament; it is very seldom quoted, but when it is quoted it is generally found to be accurate, because Members have had the opportunity of correcting their speeches.

1941. But is it always right that Members should be at the trouble of correcting their speeches?—That I think depends very much upon themselves. If they wish to have a perfectly true report of what they have said in Parliament, it is well worth their while to take the trouble of correcting their speeches.

1942. But does not the system of a private individual selecting from such newspapers as he thinks proper the reports of debates, open the door to prejudiced reports. The proprietor of this publication, like all other human beings, has his own views upon matters; and does it not open the door to his giving more prominence to some debates than to others?—I should think not; it is too much to the interest of the proprietor of "Hansard's Debates" to publish perfectly fair debates without leaning on the one side or the other, because it really is a sort of Parliamentary history.

1943. Mr. Hansard told us in evidence the other day that he has published some debates at greater length than others, because he considered the subjects of great importance?—I think he ought to publish the debates with perfect fairness, without reference to his interest in the subject.

1944. But that is matter of opinion on the part of an individual? —Certainly.

1945. What I may think fair another man may think unfair, according to our political bias?—Yes.

1946. I think you said that the public were satisfied with the present reporting arrangements; but we have it in evidence that the provincial public, as represented by their press, is very much dissatisfied with it?—I am not aware of that.

1947. And the object of many of the witnesses has been to obtain greater accommodation for the provincial press; do you think that a fair demand on the part of the provincial public?—It would be almost impossible, I suppose, to provide for all the provincial press; but I think a fair selection might be made, so that there should be a general representation of the press throughout the country.

1948. Would a means of giving the provincial public that accommodation be obtained by giving any what they call press associations the same accommodation that the London press has?—I am not prepared to say that. I did not know till two days ago of the existence of press associations.

1949. Your experience is anterior to the present state of things?—Yes, I am speaking very much upon recollections of what occurred 90 years ago.

1950. Mr. Mills.] We have had evidence as to an arrangement made with Mr. Hansard about the publication of proceedings of the House in Committee, and proceedings on Private Bills, in respect of which there is a subsidy made to Mr. Hansard: that will involve, of course, some delay in the publication of the proceedings in Committee and the proceedings on Private Bills; that is to say, I presume it would be delayed till the time when it may be possible to bring out Hansard's numbers. I wish to ask you whether you think that any practical inconvenience will result from that delay in those reports which will come out some days after the daily papers' report of the other proceedings in Parliament?—I presume that there will always be some delay in the production of Hansard's reports, because of the time it would take to enable Members to correct their speeches. I should not think that that delay, to which you allude, would operate unfairly in any way, or that it would be inconvenient in any way to the House. I look upon "Hansard" as more like a Parliamentary history than anything else. I think the debates in the newspapers are very fairly and accurately given, and in a very short space of time, so that almost everybody is in possession of all that has happened in the House on the previous day. I look upon the value of "Hansard" to be this: you want some record, a faithful record of what passes in the House when there is no exciting question before it, when there is no question which would lead to the newspapers reporting it in extenso; and if "Hansard" will supply that, I think you have all that you want, and you do not want an official reporter at all; and by that means you escape the responsibility which the House would incur if it employed an official reporter.

1951. And you think with reference to those two portions of the reporting which I alluded to, namely, the Reports of Committees of the House, and the Reports on Private Bills, that practically no inconvenience would result from that delay?—I think that, practically, no inconvenience would arise.

1952. Do you think that it is an advantage under the present system, when we have no official reporter, that there is some competition between the newspapers in giving reports of proceedings in Parliament; do you think that an advantage results to the public from that competition?—A very great advantage. I think that the competition of the newspapers is the great security that you have for accuracy of reporting.

1953. And that this advantage would be to some extent interfered with by the creation of an official report?—Certainly.

1954. Chairman.] I am asked by an honourable Member to put this question to you: has your Lordship ever heard any complaints of inaccuracy in reports of speeches and evidence given before Committees of the House of Lords, which are printed during the night without any correction by the speakers or witnesses, and delivered the following morning at 9 o'clock?—I have never heard any complaint of inaccuracy; I have sometimes seen slight inaccuracies in those printed reports of evidence given before Committees, but not any great inaccuracy, or any inaccuracy that anybody could complain of. But there are great facilities for reporting evidence given before Committees, which do not exist in the House itself. The one is done in a comparatively small room, and the other is done in a large room, where it is difficult to hear.

1955. So that you would draw a great distinction between the report of a speech made in Parliament by a speaker from his own seat, and that of evidence given at a table, with the ear of the reporter close to the witness who is giving that evidence?—Certainly.

The Right Hon. Viscount Eversley.

11 July 1878.

Sir *John Rose*, Bart., K.C.M.G., called in; and Examined.

1956. *Chairman.*] I THINK you were a Member of the Canadian Parliament for many years, and held office in the Government of Canada?—Yes, for a good many years.

1957. Will you be kind enough to state to the Committee what the practice is as to reporting the proceedings of Parliament in Canada?—I have noted down briefly an answer to the question which you were kind enough to send me as to the present state of Parliamentary reporting there, and I daresay it will be the shortest way if I read the substance of what has taken place. In Canada there has been a kind of semi-authoritative report for some years, but it is still experimental rather than otherwise. It cannot be said to be exactly official, its aim being to fulfil the purpose that Hansard does here, namely, preserving the substance of the debates in a convenient form for reference, although in Canada they likewise deliver a number of copies to Members for gratuitous distribution, and also supply a considerable number free to local newspapers, societies, &c. The metropolitan press of Canada, by which I mean the papers of two or three of the larger cities, by arrangement among themselves, have for a good many years furnished admirable reports of all debates of general interest, which are transmitted by telegraph from the House, and appear in these papers in *extenso* next morning. In matters of local concern the reports are, perhaps, less extended than the special interest affected would desire, although much fuller than they are here. The proposal to have the debates printed in a form to serve as a permanent record naturally found support on the part of Members who were less fully reported than they desired. It was strengthened by the argument (I think an unfounded one) that the reports of the papers which gave the debates in *extenso* were more or less tinged with party bias, and also that in local matters (which in Canada are relatively more important) they were not as ample as was necessary. Another argument was, that speeches in Canada, as in the legislatures of most new countries, are necessarily longer, being often largely made up of facts and figures, containing information of value to the country, but difficult of access owing to the less perfect and mature statistical returns, and which it required the industry of the Members to produce in a readible shape. Under these and other influences various plans were suggested from time to time since 1870. I may add that there was a special report of the debates preceding Confederation, but that was altogether an exceptional thing; the importance of the subject was considered to justify the House in authorising a special report of the debates that might affect opinion in the various provinces as regarded coming into Confederation or not; but it was a special report on the question of Confederation only. These plans all encountered considerable opposition; they have not been uniform, and they have only existed from Session to Session. It was at first proposed by the joint Committee of both Houses on printing that the work should be done by contract, and a person who furnished Parliamentary reports for his own newspaper was selected, it being supposed that the reports used by the press might be utilised in making up the "Hansard," and thus save expense. It was proposed that 2,900 copies should be furnished; that Members should have six hours to revise their speeches, but that in order to give the reports a popular character, and enable the distribution to be made before the interest of the debate passed away, publication should take place within 36 hours of delivery. This proposal was, however, negatived by the House, and in 1871 a second one was made, that the Speaker, in conjunction with the Committee which regulates the internal economy of the House, should take measures to have the debates officially recorded; but this also ultimately fell to the ground. However, in 1874, I think, a recommendation was adopted, though not without division, in favour of procuring by contract 2,600 copies of reports similar to "Hansard," at an estimated expense, including translation, of about 2,500 *l.* to 3,000 *l.*, and the following rules were prescribed by the Joint Committee of the two

Sir J. Rose, Bart., K.C.M.G.

Sir J. Rose, Bart.,
K.C.M.G.

11 July 1878.

two Houses: (1.) That the contractor for the reporting should keep a book, in which an entry shall be made of the copy sent to the printer, the hour at which each copy is sent, the receipt of the copy to be acknowledged by the printer when received. (2.) That the contractor for the reporting be responsible for a fair and impartial summary of the debates, for a prompt delivery of copy; and that the contractor for the printing be held responsible for accurate proof reading according to copy. (3.) That no written speeches be received by the contractor for the reporting. (4.) That Members shall be allowed to make any verbal corrections in the report of their speeches as they first appear in sheet form (I may add that it was intended to have a certain number of copies distributed in sheet form and a certain number of bound copies), such correction not to involve any variation of idea or sentiment, or any lengthening of their remarks. These corrections being intended for the book form of the reports cannot be entertained unless made on the same day as the reports are delivered at the post office (this was afterwards extended to 24 hours). The Committee further recommend the following as the basis of distribution, both of sheets and bound volumes: Daily sheets—Members of House of Commons, five copies each, 1,030; Members, Senate, one copy each, 60; Privy Council, 13; Press, 400; Reporters, 30; Reserve, 47; total, 1,600. Bound volumes—Members of House of Commons, two copies each, 412; Members, Senate, one copy each, 80; Privy Council, six; Departmental, 20, making 518; Library and Reserve, 82; total, 600. This system it appears by the Parliamentary journals was but tentative also, and next Session a new plan was adopted, apparently by the Commons alone, under which the work was to be done by a staff of reporters appointed by the Committee, and who should have the qualification necessary to "revise and condense the speeches, and preserve their sense, tone, and spirit." Any corrections proposed by Members were to be subject to the approval of the Committee, and to be made before the report was in type. It will thus be seen that Canada has rather aimed at securing something like "Hansard" than an exact official report. Some of the objections to verbatim reports which exist here were felt there, although there were wants to be supplied in Canada which either do not exist in England, or, if they do, are supplied by the press and by the abundance and cheapness of statistical reports, which are by no means so great there as they are here. It will also be seen that a large proportion of the copies were intended for free distribution among the local press in Canada. There are a great many small papers there in remote districts which could not afford to send reporters or even to get the debates by telegraph; and the gratuitous distribution was doubtless to give facilities for preparing a summary for their readers, and to enable them to keep a permanent memorial of the debates. One of the objections felt there, as here, was the question of privilege; another question, the tendency it would have to prolong the debates and to give a forensic rather than a business character to the House. The comparatively limited use that could be made of the copies when circulated was also felt, because it was impossible to issue them until the general public had read all they wanted to read in the newspapers. Their interest once satisfied could not be revived, and I believe also the opinion that the debates were all the better for being subject to an æsthetic process in the Reporters' Gallery was generally accepted. In other words, the system which Canada has been trying to establish is very much what "Hansard" has long provided here; they have aimed to have a publication of the nature of "Hansard," but nothing more; and in order to effect this, they have found it necessary to do it at the public expense, which I am informed is now about 3,700 l., and that some 2,500 copies are distributed gratuitously. It was felt that to have exact official reports, for which Members could be held responsible, you must give them an opportunity of revising their speeches. Those Members who would naturally speak most frequently, and whose speeches would necessarily be of most importance, viz. Members of the Government, could not, from the pressing character of their official duties give any time to revision; and it seemed, therefore, impossible to ensure the approval, as regards a most important part of the debates by those Members, of the accuracy of the reports. It may, perhaps, be interesting to the Committee, as an evidence of the views of public men in Canada, if I quote the language of two of the oldest and most experienced Members of the House, sitting, however, on opposite sides; I mean Sir John McDonald and Mr. Holton. Mr. Holton, who has been for 30 odd years a Member of the House, states in the Session of 1876, when the Committee brought

in

in a Report in favour of the continuance of the Report for another Session, "I believe that the majority of the House are opposed to the continuation of "the 'Hansard.' If I were not of that opinion, certainly I would not assume "the responsibility of taking the course I am now pursuing. With reference to "the manner in which the reporters have discharged their duties, I have no fault "whatever to find. I think that those duties have been fairly and faithfully per- "formed. I strove with others for many years to have this system tried. It has "been tried, and to my judgment, it is a failure. We are better without than "with it; and I think that this is the present sense of the House." Sir John McDonald takes the contrary view, and speaks as follows: "My honourable "friend says he feels that the majority of the House are against the 'Hansard.' "I beg leave to differ with him, and to say I believe that when the House meets "next Session, the majority will be found to be in favour of its continuance. The "country is in favour of it, and will not be willing to give it up. This will be a "retrograde step in respect of a most important subject. I am convinced, now "the country has had the advantage of an official record, it will insist on its con- "tinuance. The people have a right to have a report of the debates of their "representatives which has some official character, and which is not tainted by "the supposed political proclivities of the different newspapers, which would "otherwise be the sole repositories of the proceedings of this House." There is no doubt that party feeling runs higher there than here, but my individual opinion is that the debates have been very fairly and impartially reported. Now and again there might be a little prominence given to the views of par- ticular persons. I think that is all that I have to say generally as regards Canada; and I will give a brief summary now of what I believe to be the condi- tion of things in the United States.

1958. The Committee would be glad to hear it; will you favour us with it? —As regards the United States, there exists an official verbatim record of the debates and proceedings in Congress. The debates were originally published in a paper called the "National Intelligencer," which was almost entirely devoted to them; they were afterwards done by contract by the "Congressional Globe;" but in 1873, I think it was (it might have been a year earlier or later), Congress undertook the work itself appointing official reporters, the publishing being done in the Congressional Printing Office which is a very large establishment, as you are aware. There are five official reporters for each House, and I learn that of the daily, or sheet edition, some 6,000 copies are supplied gratis to Members of the Congress, and about 3,300 more either furnished to the departments, or sold. About 7,000 of a bound edition are also supplied, mostly to Members of Congress. The public may buy them at a cost of about 10 dollars per copy for the long, and five dollars for the short Session; but I learn that comparatively few copies are actually purchased. The cost varies according to the length of the Session: some Sessions terminating, as the Committee are aware, in March and some in August. The appropriation in 1877 for printing was 100,000 dollars, and the reporting amounts, I am informed, to about 25,000 dollars in each House; say 150,000 dollars, or 30,000 £ sterling in all. I learn that the cost last Session of the printing did not amount to so much, only, I think, to about 85,000 dollars.

1959. Will you state, for the information of the Committee, the length of the Session in which is cost 85,000 dollars?—From November to about three weeks ago, I think.

1960. The six months, do you mean?—There was a considerable interval; they had a longer holiday than usual. I shall probably get the details soon. I am informed that the appropriation has been about 100,000 dollars every year, and it may fairly be estimated that the expenditure has not come much short of the appropriation; and the salaries of the reporters are about 5,000 dollars each, there being five reporters for each House.

1961. Sir Henry T. Holland.] Putting a dollar at what?—Four shillings and one penny, or 4 s. 2 d. The gentleman who gave these figures to me has very great experience, and he says that the cost of the reporting in each House is about 25,000 dollars, in addition to the printing.

1962. Chairman.] For a Session of about four to five months, taking the actual sitting?—The Session that goes into August is longer. They usually meet on the 1st Monday of December and sit until the beginning of August during the long Sessions. It will be seen from an inspection of the publication of which I have spoken, that it is not only a record of the debates, but of every proceeding in

Sir J. Rose, Bart., K.C.B.A.

13 July 1878.

Sir J. Ros, Bart.

10 July 1878

in Congress; of the Members present; of every petition presented; of every notice, vote, Bill, message, and document read or laid before it, I daresay the Committee are familiar with the character of it; and it contains nearly all the information and matter supplied to Members and the public here in the form of separate Parliamentary Papers, and of the Votes and Proceedings. I may add, also, that it is a sort of Dod's and Vacher's publications combined; it gives the Members' names, their ages, their residences, and their particular opinions. Then there are a great many matters which are supplied by these informal publications here which are found in the "Congressional Record"; and also information as to all the foreign legations in Washington, and a great deal of other matter which does not properly appertain to the proceedings of Parliament, but which is useful there. But as bearing on the origin and continued existence of the "Congressional Record," the peculiar circumstances of the United States are to be kept in mind. The whole government of that country is practically a legislative one; the Members of the Government have no seats in either House, having executive functions only. There are, comparatively, few questions of general interest and still fewer of foreign policy which newspapers would find it worth while to report at great length. Local and sectional affairs mainly engage their attention, but these are of great diversity and importance, and what may deeply interest one state or region has often comparatively little interest elsewhere. The question of Chinese immigration, for example, is a vital one to California, but it is confined to that State. The debates in Congress have rarely been reported by the press in America at anything like the same length as those of the English Parliament by the press here, a fact which is due, perhaps, in part to the causes I have mentioned, namely, the immense variety of sectional interests in localities very remote from each other which almost wholly engross its attention. It must also be borne in mind that the character of the debates there is very different from those in the House of Commons. The speeches are often more like essays, containing information difficult of access in the Member's state or district, and are addressed less to the Assembly than to the Member's constituents. Then in America appropriations of money may originate with any member of Congress, and items may be added to or reduced. In a country where local improvements are very important, and the grants for them correspondingly large, discussions on such subjects have naturally a keen interest, and the efforts of the member are closely watched by his constituents. These local elements and interests are aggravated by the fact that the members are themselves local, being elected, as the Committee are aware, from their own district. Then there is no metropolitan press at Washington, as in London, and even if there were it would be impossible for it, however enterprising, to give as much space to the varied local discussions, and the documents affecting them, as their importance really merited. Nor must it be lost sight of that there is a distinct class in the United States who adopt politics as an occupation, and that a position or reputation in Congress is a stepping-stone not only to a position in the Federal Government or Legislature, but to every State office, and that speeches are often made in Congress as much with the purpose of influencing State politics and elections as for any other object. The influences and condition of things I have alluded to all operate on the minds of Members to favour a system of formal reports, and a liberal distribution among their constituents of copies, as well as of the Congressional documents they contain, at the public expense. The speeches are generally carefully revised by the leading members of Congress, often written beforehand, and sometimes printed without being delivered at all, as they may be with the leave of the House, a leave which, to save time, it is generally ready to grant; but the practice leads to the evil of great prolixity, as well as the dissemination of facts and arguments which must remain for a time unanswered. Another inconvenience, which sometimes arises, is a doubt whether the corrections proposed by Members are really in harmony with the words used in the House. The official reports are delivered to the clerk, and if any question arises it must ultimately be referred by him to the Speaker, on whom is thus entailed a responsible and onerous duty. It would, however, I presume, hardly be a possible thing for Members of the Government here, under the constant pressure of ministerial, as well as Parliamentary duties, to revise their speeches; and, therefore, as regards them, no official report could be pointed to as accurate. Official verbatim reports may suit

in

Sir J. Eer, Bart.,
K.C.M.G.

12 July 1878.

in some countries, but here they would, I think, hardly be possible, and even if possible, would produce far from an unmixed advantage, and they would entail great inconvenience. If the experience of other countries with representative institutions of a popular character is any guide to opinion, I believe that it would lengthen the debates, and not operate, as some imagine, as a deterrent to unnecessary speaking. The reports would not, I think, be used by the public at large who would still rely on the prompter reports of the newspapers, and they would only be valuable as a convenient record for occasional reference. I am assuming that an official report and its distribution at the public expense would not interfere with the present fullness of the newspaper reports. If it did I should consider it a great evil, for it is impossible that Parliamentary intelligence can reach the public at large except through the press. Few men would, as a rule, take up "Hansard" to peruse a debate two or three days old, even if it were given to them, and still fewer would buy it in an isolated form for the purpose of reading only those debates.

1963. I understand you to say that the practice in Canada is to give a summary only, and not a verbatim report?—Clearly so. I cannot give the Committee the last reports which were adopted by the Commons House of Parliament in Canada in reference to their improved system, but I believe they practically amount to what I have summarised in my evidence.

1964. And that the aim of the Canadian House of Commons was to obtain the nearest possible approximation to the "Hansard" which we have in England?—Quite so.

1965. Recognising the fact that "Hansard" does not pretend to be an official report or a verbatim report?—Quite so.

1966. And I gathered from you just now, that looking at the condition of this country, with the very intimate acquaintance which you possess of Parliamentary practice here, you entertain a strong opinion against official reporting, or verbatim reporting, as far as the British Parliament is concerned?—I think, to carry it out, you would have to alter the genius of the House of Commons and the mode of conducting business; I mean if you are to have a thorough complete official report, such as exists in America, or, I am told, in some other countries. I should consider it a great evil if the press did not continue to report Parliamentary proceedings, and I think that they do it now at as great length as the public are inclined to make use of. Considering that telegraphic communication has brought us into such intimate contact with the affairs of all parts of the world, I think that there is as much space devoted to Parliamentary reports as the public at large are inclined to use.

1967. Do I rightly understand you that you would prefer to leave the measure of the information to be given to the public at large to the appreciation on the part of competing newspapers of the demands of the public rather than to supply a report from day to day on the authority of Parliament itself?—I am not, of course, aware of the extent to which there is any foundation for the complaints as to the imperfect nature of the reports of the proceedings of Parliament in reference to local matters, or the proceedings of the House in Committee; but assuming, as I think to be the case, that it were possible to supply any want which experience might have shown in reference to those two matters, I certainly should leave things very much as they are, keeping "Hansard" as a record of the substance of what takes place in Parliament, and if possible devising some means by which perhaps a larger amount of information as to what takes place in Committee of the House and with reference to local measures could be given.

1968. I understood you to say that the Canadian "Hansard" was set on foot in the first instance with a view to the great importance of the questions which were before the Canadian Parliament at that time, those relating to confederation?—Yes.

1969. I apprehend that you have there no newspapers which occupy at all the position of the older newspapers in this country; in Canada there are powerful and important newspapers, but they do not occupy the position of our older newspapers, do they?—To remove any misapprehension with reference to the Confederation Debates, I ought to repeat that the debates of which the Canadian Parliament authorised the publication then, were confined exclusively to the question of confederation; they were not debates on the general affairs that took place in the House, but merely with reference to that single matter.

T   As

Sir J. Rose, Bart.,
and T.O.

11 July 1878.

As regards the position of the newspapers, the three or four leading news-papers now have, I believe, come to an arrangement among themselves to produce one report, and it is done at great length, and I think very accurately. For instance, the "Toronto Globe," the "Montreal Herald," and the "Mail" and "Gazette," may unite among themselves to have a common staff of reporters; and I think the reporting is done with great impartiality, and very great accuracy.

1970. As a matter of fact there is very little competition in reporting in Canada itself?—It is confined to three or four of the leading papers in Montreal and Toronto.

1971. Would it be right to say that there was no foundation whatever for the impression that there is a colour to the reports which appear in those news-papers, or in other newspapers in Canada?—My own experience is rather against it, but I know how high party spirit sometimes runs there, and Members who are more of party men than I was have made complaints that they were less per-fectly reported than the Members whose views were in harmony with the particular newspaper in which the reports appeared. I have not heard many complaints of unfair reporting or of mis-reporting, but I have heard occasional complaints of imperfect reporting.

1972. Have you heard any such complaints with reference to the proceedings of Parliament in this country?—None whatever of unfairness.

1973. The impression left upon your mind, then, is that, on the whole, a fair report of the proceedings of Parliament is given in the newspapers?—I have never heard otherwise than that it was done with the greatest accuracy and very great impartiality.

1974. That could hardly be said, I suppose, of the United States?—I think not. But, as you are aware, the press of Washington is comparatively unim-portant as compared with that of New York, or Philadelphia, or any of the larger towns, and there is no local metropolitan press there which corresponds to the press here.

1975. There is no press which concerns itself with the interests of the United States as a whole?—Not of general circulation.

1976. And, therefore, which would feel it to be its duty, or to its interest, to report the proceedings of Congress as a whole?—No.

1977. There is, therefore, no record of the proceedings of Congress, as a whole, apart from the "Congressional Globe," or "Record," which is published with the authority of Congress?—There is really none, no adequate one.

1978. No adequate publication of the deliberations of the Legislature in the United States, excepting that of the "Record"?—That is so. It originally began with the "Globe," afterwards the "Congressional Reporter," and now the official paper which Mr. Forster has, at this moment, in his hand.

1979. So that the two countries, Great Britain and the United States, are not at all parallel in that respect?—Not at all; in no respect in regard to the publication of the reports of the debates of the Legislatures.

1980. Mr. Mills.] Your evidence, I think, applies, in reference to Canada, to the proceedings of the Dominion Parliament?—Entirely so.

1981. Can you tell us whether any arrangements at all are made in the Provincial Legislatures for an official report?—I think not. I am sure there is none in Ontario, which is the most populous and most important of the provinces of the Dominion; there are none in Quebec, and I think none in any of the smaller provinces. There may possibly be some arrangement to preserve the reports of the press, but there is no official report in any of them, as far as I know.

1982. A report has been laid before Parliament (in the year 1874) in reference to Nova Scotia, and the system of reporting there; it is stated that "A contract for the sessional reporting is awarded every year by the Government. This contract embraces every expense connected with reporting and publishing the debates. The contractor engages his own assistance, and enters into his own arrangements with the newspapers; his contract usually obliging him to furnish copies of the debates to at least two leading journals, one Government, and one opposition." Can you tell us whether, so far as you know, that arrangement exists now in Nova Scotia?—I should not like to accept that as an accurate statement of the condition of things in Nova Scotia without further inquiry; and I am sure that any reports that are authorised there must be of an extremely

·limited

limited and restricted kind. They would have come under my eye in some form, I think, if they had been of any great length or importance.

1983. You have told us that a special arrangement was made in reference to reporting the debates in Canada on the confederation question; was there no other special arrangement like that made for reporting, besides that with reference to the confederation?—Not in Canada. I am not sure that on the occasion of the union of the provinces of Upper and Lower Canada, in the time of Lord Sydenham, with a view of influencing public opinion, and giving the public a proper means of forming their own judgment as to the advantage of an union, there was not some official report; but I cannot charge my memory at the moment; I think not.

1984. May it be taken that the sum which you have stated as the cost is now the arrangement in Canada?—The latest information I have is, that it was from Session to Session.

1985. I think you said that now the Canadian newspapers (and you mentioned the "Toronto Globe" and other newspapers) make an arrangement between themselves to have a common system of reporting; did I understand you to say that?—Yes, they did so, and I think the practice continues still, because I see reports of the same sense, and almost in the same words in all the leading papers.

1986. Have you heard any objection raised to what are called identical reports resulting from that common arrangement between the newspapers in Canada?—No, none whatever; on the contrary, I have heard an argument in favour of its being evidence of its impartiality and fairness; that the best men on the staff of the various papers take their turn in the Reporters' Gallery, is being for a common object.

1987. Would those reports so furnished or arranged for by the different newspapers furnish reports, say to Nova Scotia and New Brunswick, and to all the provinces which are comprised in the Canadian Dominion now; would they supply all those provinces?—All those papers circulate largely in all the provinces, and of course the local press would take their own summary from these papers which appear from day to day; and I have been told, though I cannot assert it from my own knowledge, that the smaller newspapers in the remoter districts take their summary more from the reports of the daily press than from the copies of the authorised reports which are sent to them, and which rarely reach them in time for the publication of their own local papers.

1988. With reference to the United States, I think you said that practically there was no metropolitan press worthy of the name at Washington?—That is so.

1989. Now with reference to the other States, with reference, for instance, to New York and Philadelphia, and the States of the Union generally, are there now any newspapers that you know of that give full reports of the proceedings in Congress?—Not of the proceedings in Congress. I think the debates in those papers occupy but a comparatively small space; the debates of the Assembly of the State of New York are given, I think, at greater length in the New York papers than the debates in Congress when they are sitting together, because the matters are of more local interest to the readers.

1990. The newspapers in the different States report the proceedings of the State Legislatures but not those of the Legislature at Washington, in fact?—They report the former to a greater extent, undoubtedly.

1991. Anybody in the United States who wants to have a full report of what takes place in Congress depends, in fact, upon the official report?—He does.

1992. Which, as I understand you, has no sale at all?—I think it has very little sale; it is offered at a very moderate price; but the information, which I derive from gentlemen connected with Washington, is, that there are very few copies indeed sold. There may be occasional copies purchased by Members for distribution among their own constituents in excess of those which are given to them.

1993. Mr. Walter.] The volume which I hold in my hand, and which is entitled "Debates of the House of Commons of the Dominion of Canada," I think represents what you call the semi-authoritative report of the business of a whole Session, as far as the House of Commons in Canada is concerned?—I think so.

1994. I see it runs from the 11th of February to the 19th of April, two months?—Yes.

1995. What length are the reports of the other House, the Senate; is there a similar report for that?—There is a report. May I ask whether that volume is one of the reports which took place under a joint Committee on printing?

1996. This appears to be a report of the House of Commons only?—Then the Report of the Proceedings of the Senate would be not as large, but a very considerable size.

1997. Does two months constitute the usual length of time of the Session?—I think three months generally would be nearer the duration of the Dominion Parliament.

1998. And therefore this is, in fact, a shorter record than even "Hansard?"—Undoubtedly it is.

1999. This being one volume for two months, "Hansard" would be five volumes for five months, about?—It would.

2000. Nearly as thick as this volume?—Very nearly.

2001. What are the usual hours; the House meets at 3 in the afternoon, does it not?—Yes.

2002. And how late does it generally sit?—Very much the same hours as the House of Commons here; they meet at 3 and sit till 1, 2, or 3 in the morning.

2003. Do they ever sit through the night?—They have occasionally done so, and I think this very last Session. I remember once the House sat three days and three nights almost without a break.

2004. Up to what hour is it found practicable to report the speeches for the press in Canada?—I should say that midnight might be taken as a fair time. There are, of course, cases where an important debate goes on very much later, and in those instances a special addition would be made to the staff of reporters.

2005. But in case the newspapers are unable to give an account of the business of the day's work in consequence of the lateness of the hour, do they continue it the following day?—They do, the next day.

2006. There is nothing actually lost?—There is nothing lost; but I ought to add that the debates generally appear next morning, and in a very full form indeed, no matter how late the House sits; the telegraphing there is cheap, and the distances are great, and the wires are used almost entirely for the purpose of reporting; the sheets are sent off at once as the debates go on.

2007. With respect to the identical reports to which you have referred, I presume that it is entirely optional with the newspapers how far they should avail themselves of that identical report, or whether one should give it at greater length or another shorter, according to their respective interests?—Entirely so; the arrangement is confined probably to two or three of the leading newspapers; but there is room in the Reporters' Gallery for the provincial press, and they may send off their own reports as they please; and, as a matter of fact, Members are frequently reported by the reporters of the press for papers in their own locality when any subject of special local interest engages the attention of the House.

2008. Colonel *Arbuthnot*.] You spoke of the contractor for the report in the Canadian Parliament; to whom is he responsible for the accuracy of the report?—He would be responsible to Parliament; he would be a contractor with the Houses of Parliament.

2009. But is he under the jurisdiction of the Speaker of the House?—The contract is entered into, I think, by a joint Committee of both Houses, and he would consequently be responsible to the Speakers of both Houses for the proper performance of the work.

2010. Is the space assigned to the press in the Canadian Houses of Parliament, and in the United States, very large and convenient?—A difficulty arose when these debates were authorised in the Canadian House of Commons as to where the official reporters, or the reporters who were to report the debates in the authorised form were to be, and eventually it was allowed as a compromise that they should be on the floor of the House for one Session, until it was seen how the experiment would answer, and whether it should be continued; but the space in the Reporters' Gallery was already occupied by the reporters of the different papers; and I see on reference to another volume that a conversation arose between Mr. Mackenzie and Sir John M'Donald as to where the official reporters should

should be; Sir John M'Donald objected to any one being on the floor of the House excepting the Members and the officers of the House; but, as a compromise, and in order not to raise objections to trying the experiment, the clerk's table was lengthened, and a couple of reporters were allowed to sit there for one Session.

2011. How soon are the semi-official Canada reports ready for circulation after the speeches have been made?—Theoretically they ought to be so within 36 hours, but practically I believe they are not ready so soon; it may be one, two, or three days; it would depend a great deal upon the length of the debates, I should think.

2012. Then except for the purpose of reporting in individual local cases, they are comparatively useless to the press of the country?—I think so, except to some of the remote local press who may make use of them for the purpose of giving a summary of the reports.

2013. But if they do not appear for nearly two days after the speeches have been delivered, they would hardly be of any use for the daily press?—No, not for the daily press; but many of the small newspapers in the country parts of Canada are only published weekly; and it would depend a great deal upon whether the local weekly paper was supplied beforehand by the other papers with which it exchanged, or whether the official report came to hand first, which they would use.

2014. Do you know whether in the United States the newspapers obtain their reports through the instrumentality of press agencies?—I think most of the leading papers in the United States have their own representatives, and their own offices at Washington, and I think their own reporters as well; more for the purpose of correspondence, I think, than reporting.

2015. You spoke, in the paper which you were good enough to read, about the question of privilege; did it ever occur in Canada that the official reporter was excluded from the House?—I cannot speak from personal knowledge, because we had no official reporter while I was in Canada; but I know that whenever the question of official reporting came up, as it frequently did under the pressure of various causes, the question of privilege was one which gave us all concern; that we should be authorising, under the authority of the House, that which might be possibly libellous, but I do not know of any instance in which the difficulty has practically arisen.

2016. Have you ever known a case of the ordinary reporters being turned out of the House?—The galleries are very frequently cleared in Canada.

2017. Is it your impression that it is in contemplation that the official reporter should leave the House when the others are turned out?—I think so. I should say so certainly. It is, however, only in very exceptional instances where domestic matters are to be settled without the public knowing anything about it, that the galleries would be cleared, and the Reporters' Gallery as well.

2018. Mr. Mitchell Henry.] I observe that in the Canada "Hansard" some of the speeches are reported in the first person and others in the third person; how is that?—I have no doubt that the speaker himself had a great deal to do with the form in which the speech was reported. Although there is a rule that no written speeches shall be received, and that the sense shall not be altered, yet I am afraid that it is very frequently broken; and I may add that reporting there is not so much of a science as it is here, not so uniform in the form in which it is done; one reporter may take a speech in the first person and another in the third person.

2019. Is there a quorum of the House in Canada?—If you mean a certain number of Members required to be present, there is.

2020. What is that number?—I think 20; at least it was originally 20 under the Union Act, and I do not think the number has been altered. The House there has 206 Members, I think, at present; the Members increasing with the population.

2021. I ask the question, because your "Hansard" being a correct account of what takes place, my eye caught a very singular passage; an objection was made, I see in that report, to going on with the subject, because there was not a quorum of the House, and the answer made was, "The Government represents the House"?—It is a very singular answer, I must admit.

2022. It is near that passage which you read just now?—As a matter of fact, I know

Sir J. Rose, Bart.,
R.C.M.G.

12 July 1876.

I know that the House is very frequently counted out. You will observe in reference to this, that in a very few moments the Usher of the Black Rod appears; probably there were only some dozen Members sitting; it was just previous to prorogation, and I see that this very conversation (rather than debate) was brought to a close thus: "The Gentleman Usher of the Black Rod entered and informed the Speaker that his Excellency the Governor General requested the presence of the House in the Senate Chamber, to which the Members repaired with the usual ceremony." I see that it was Mr. Mitchell who said, "The Government represent the House;" I presume it was more in badinage than anything else.

2023. The Government in Canada have no other position in that respect than the Government here?—No, the positions are entirely analogous. We endeavour to follow in every way, even in the most literal way, both the system and the forms that prevail here as far as it is possible to follow them.

2024. Sir *Henry Holland.*] As far as you know, does the Rule of May 1874 as to the supplying of the provincial papers still hold good, namely, that one copy of the "Dominion Hansard" shall be sent "to each newspaper' in the Dominion; the sheet to be delivered in the post office wrapt up and ready for mailing not later than three o'clock upon the day after each speech is delivered;" that is the Report of a Committee of May 1874, adopted by the House?—I think the basis of distribution must remain the same.

2025. And that it is not necessary to deliver the sheets at the post office till three o'clock upon the day after each speech is delivered?—Not before that, certainly; I think it was extended to 24 hours.

2026. But I understand you to say that practically the distant provincial papers, as in British Columbia and other distant places, take their reports of the debates, not from the official reports, but from the reports of papers which have private reporters?—I should say so.

2027. And that is because the official report comes too late?—Yes; the others are sent by telegraph.

2028. And, perhaps, the official report may be also too long for them?—Yes, rather.

2029. So that they would have all the trouble of condensing that report to suit their newspaper?—Undoubtedly.

2030. Did I rightly understand you to say that in Canada the corrections of speeches of Members are made subject to the approval of a Committee?—Theoretically they are, but I am afraid that they are very often made without any reference to the Committee, and I have little doubt but that there are cases in which the sense has been somewhat altered.

2031. Still there is a court of appeal as to those corrections?—Yes, undoubtedly.

2032. And what constitutes that court of appeal?—In one instance, under one report it would be the Committee, and in the other undoubtedly the Speaker, the reports being delivered to the Clerk of the House.

2033. But, in the first instance, supposing that a Member finds fault with a correction which has been made by another Member, would be bring it before the House, or what steps would be take?—I should think he would bring it before the House as a question of privilege almost; and if the power of deciding what was a verbal alteration, or an alteration in the sense, was to be determined by the Committee on reporting, then that might relieve Mr. Speaker; but in ordinary instances, unless it is relegated to a Committee, the reports are delivered to the Clerk of the House, and it would be for him, under the authority of Mr. Speaker, to say whether it was an exact report which ought to be printed, or not.

2034. Is it your experience that Members are in the habit of correcting their speeches?—Undoubtedly they are; extensively, I should say.

2035. Mr. *Forster.*] In answer to my honourable friend, you said that if one Member complained of the corrections made by another Member, you think he would state so in his place in the House; did you ever know any such complaint?—Before the days of the quasi official reporting I have known attention called and complaints made as to the difference between the delivered speech and the speech as reported by the press; that difference may either have been due to the fact that the speaker himself had suggested the alterations, or to his being misunderstood.

2036. I suppose

2036. I suppose that kind of complaint or remark is made much more in the *Sir States, with reference to the reports in the "Congressional Record," than it would be in Canada?—I do not know, because I think that the reports in the United States are mainly for distribution among their own constituents, and are often written beforehand.

2037. I observe here in these two or three members of the "Congressional Record" which you have given us, one or two speeches which, I suppose, would be sent in written?—No doubt.

2038. I will not ask the name of the speaker, but take such a speech as that (*pointing to a speech*); that would be written, I suppose?—Undoubtedly that speech must have been written beforehand. I do not wish to trouble the Committee with them, but on a great many days they are three times the extent of that; particularly speeches on the currency question, which are nothing more nor less than elaborate essays prepared days beforehand, and probably never spoken in Congress at all.

2039. I suppose that the result of that is, that nobody looks at the "Congressional Record" as a record of debates; and that if they have any interest in looking at it, it would be to see what any person thought upon a particular subject, and to read his essay?—I think that is the object, and almost the only object that it fulfils.

2040. How soon do the reports of the Dominion Parliament appear in the "Toronto Globe," for example?—A debate finished at four o'clock this morning would appear by six o'clock, or the ordinary hour of publication; it is transmitted continuously by telegraph; the wires come in to the basement of the House; there are a great many wires there, and it is sent on as the sheets are copied.

2041. Those reports are telegraphed to Toronto and to Montreal, or anywhere else?—And to Halifax and Quebec; I think with Montreal and Toronto, London may perhaps be named. Occasionally an important debate on the Budget, or any other important question, will appear in the Halifax papers, the St. John's papers, the Montreal papers, and the Quebec, Kingston, Toronto, London, and Hamilton papers.

2042. I imagine from that reply that the interest of the inhabitants of the Dominion is strong in the debates that take place at Ottawa?—Undoubtedly, on matters where the public interest is centred; and, as a rule, party feeling runs tolerably strong.

2043. Would you imagine that there would, or would not, be a longer report of Parliamentary proceedings in the principal Toronto or Montreal papers than there would be in the New York or Pennsylvania papers?—Undoubtedly I think that the proceedings of the Canadian Parliament occupy a much larger space in the Canadian press than the proceedings of Congress do in the press of the places that you have just mentioned.

2044. And do you think that any part of that difference is owing to the fact of your having gone upon the lines of a larger Hansard, as we may say, rather than of an official report as they have in America?—I think it is partially due to that, and partially due to the other causes which I enumerated in the first instance.

2045. But you imagine that an official report, however necessary it may be in America, has had some effect in diminishing the reports in the newspapers there?—I think so. Of course it is a mere matter of opinion, and the press would be guided by what is best for their own interest; but I should imagine that if there were no official report there the press would have given a larger space to the proceedings in Congress than they have done.

2046. Take, for instance, the "New York Herald," and compare it with the "Toronto Globe;" generally speaking, which would give the longest report?—The "Toronto Globe," beyond all question; four or five times as much, I should think.

2047. I will take the "Toronto Globe"; I suppose that the character of their report of the debates would be a long report of very well-known speakers, and quite a summary of others?—Yes, I think preference would undoubtedly be given to a well-known speaker, but it would depend a great deal upon the character of the speech; I think there is a very honest appreciation among the reporters of what is worth reporting and what is not worth reporting.

Sir J. Rose, Bart.,
K.C.M.G.

19 July 1878.

2048. I think you said that there was a combination between some of the papers in order to obtain a report?—Yes, between some of the leading papers.

2049. For instance, the "Toronto Globe" and a paper at Montreal?—The "Montreal Herald," and the "Montreal Gazette," and the "Mail," might probably all combine.

2050. Is it necessary for papers to unite together that they should be of the same politics?—Not at all, on the contrary.

2051. The fact of papers of different politics uniting together would prevent there being a colour in the report?—That is exactly what I stated.

2052. Now, you have great experience, and you are kind enough to give us the benefit of it; take the "New York Herald" or the "New York Tribune," on an important debate in Congress; is the length of the report according to the politics of the speakers, do you think?—I should hardly like to give an opinion upon that; I really have followed so little the reports of the debates in Congress in the American papers that I should hardly like to hazard an opinion upon that point.

2053. Take a matter of detail; are the reports in the Canadian papers ever in the first person?—Yes, they are sometimes; it would depend a great deal upon the reporter, I think.

2054. Do you remember whether they are ever in the first person in the newspapers in the States?—I think not in the papers, but they are in the "Record" almost always; I have known a Budget speech reported verbatim in the newspapers in Canada in the first person.

2055. Looking at your "Hansard," I find it varies very much; sometimes the speeches are in the first person, and sometimes they are not; I suppose it is, as it is in our "Hansard," according to the importance of the subject?—A great deal that, undoubtedly.

2056. This "Dominion Hansard" is not official; there is no official responsible for your "Hansard," is there?—I am not prepared to say that; because you see that the reporters one year were on the floor of the House, and they were named by the Committee as persons who were competent to give a fair and impartial summary of the debates, and to that extent they would be official. It is rather difficult to give a precise character to the present Canadian reports; I think it is quite an anomaly which has been forced upon Canada from the absence of a person like Mr. Hansard, of public spirit and enterprise, disposed to risk his own means in producing a publication of the debates. I think it would be much more convenient, and less calculated to entail the anomalous responsibilities that that publication does, if they had a person like Mr. Hansard, who would take the responsibility of doing it himself.

2057. The reason I ask the question is this, that some most important witnesses whom we have had have stated that one danger of an official report here would be the possible question of libel and of privilege?—Undoubtedly.

2058. That there would arise the question of whether the House by sanctioning the report did or did not guard the speech from any action of libel; has that difficulty at all occurred in Canada?—It is a difficulty which we always felt when the subject of official reporting was approached; a difficulty which I have frequently spoken of, because there has been occasional pressure to have reports in a more enlarged form, which might be distributed by Members among their own constituents; but that was one of the difficulties that always encountered us at the threshold.

2059. It was a difficulty which you feared, but in practice have you had it?—I am not aware that it has arisen, because it is only a year or two since the reporters were allowed on the floor of the House.

2060. Has it been a common thing for the question to arise in Canada, how far a speech is privileged in an action for libel?—That has arisen in courts of justice, unquestionably.

2061. You have stated very clearly that one very great difference between Canada and also the United States and England, is, that both Ottawa and Washington, being small towns compared with other towns, the important press in both cases is in the provinces, and not at the seat of Parliament?—Quite so.

2062. Do you imagine that in the States there is anything like the constant telegraphing of speeches that you say goes on to Toronto or Montreal; do you think

think that speeches are telegraphed to Cincinnati, for instance?—I think not.
If they are, it is in a very brief form indeed. In any American newspaper you
take up in any of the larger towns like Chicago or Cincinnati, the reports of
Congress occupy but a very small space indeed, and you may see, " Mr. So-and-So
supported the Motion," or " dissented from the Motion."

2063. If you excerpt New York and Pennsylvania, and Boston, I suppose the
report would, as you say, be very meagre?—Very meagre indeed.

2064. And even for those papers, except in special cases, it would be far
shorter than the shortest reports that we have here?—Very much more so; I
do not pretend to enumerate all the causes to which that is attributable; but
the fact is undoubtedly so.

2065. Chairman.] The honourable Baronet, the Member for Aberdeen, has
asked me to ask you what becomes of the 7,000 bound copies of the American
debates which are distributed; do you know what class of persons seek to
obtain those copies?—They are, I presume, distributed by the Member among
the institutes and reading-rooms, and in such channels as he thinks would best
promote his re-election to Congress, or improve his status in his own locality.
No doubt they are put on the shelves for reference. I do not know whether
they are very often referred to, or not; but each Member who gets a certain
number of copies, will distribute them in the way he thinks most calculated
to sustain his political influence in his own State among reading-rooms, societies,
and the libraries in different towns. They are distributed in that form, I should
think, in a great measure.

2066. I think many of the speeches in the Dominion Parliament are delivered
in French, are they not?—They are.

2067. And does the reporter report in French or in English?—A difficulty arose in consequence of that; whether the speeches should appear in the
language in which they were delivered and reported, or whether they should
afterwards be translated by the sworn translators of the House (there are a
certain number of translators, a large staff of translators, in fact, because
all the reports of proceedings and various documents have to appear in both
languages), and it was for some time a matter of controversy whether they
should all be reported in English, and afterwards translated, or be reported
and printed only in the language in which they were uttered; and they have been
done sometimes in one way and sometimes in the other. The whole thing,
so far as Canada is concerned, is tentative.

2068. Does that book which you have produced contain a French report or
an English report of the speeches of French Members in Canada?—The volume
is only in English. I see in the Report of the Committee of 1877, the ninth
condition is, " The speeches shall be reported in the language in which they are
spoken, and translated by the official translators of the House, according to the
editions for which they are required, at a cost not to exceed one dollar 25 cents
per page. There is a French edition and an English edition.

2069. I think you stated that very full reports, sufficiently full reports of
the proceedings of the Dominion Parliament, were published every morning
at Hamilton and London at one end of Canada, and at St. John's and
Halifax at the other end of the Dominion; a distance of some 2,000 or
3,000 miles apart, are they not?—Yes, certainly more than 1,000, very
nearly 2,000 some of them; Halifax from London would be nearly 1,200
miles.

2070. So that under the present system in Canada an interest in the proceedings of the Dominion Parliament is maintained notwithstanding the enormous
distances which separate the two ends of that great Dominion?—I think public
interest is very amply and adequately supplied by these reports in the press,
which are very admirably done, I think.

2071. And that condition of things does not exist in the United States?—No,
it does not.

2072. Speaking as a man having taken a great share in the Government of
the country during the last 20 years, is it your opinion that the system prevailing
in Canada is to the public advantage?—Do you mean with or without this volume,
the " Dominion Hansard "?

2073. I mean the system of publication of Parliamentary proceedings
throughout the whole country?—I think it is very much calculated for the

Sir J. Ross, Bart,
K.C.B.
10 July 1878.

public advantage. A record in a convenient form, of the character of Hansard, I think, would however be very useful; but I am not prepared to say that I should like to encounter the dangers which may some day or other attend an official report. Perhaps I might be disposed to sanction it in this form rather than to cut the slips out of the newspapers and be dependent upon them for the only record of the Parliamentary debates; but I should certainly not go further than this; I should not have an official report, and I should rather endeavour to give a subsidy to someone who would be willing to take the responsibility, very much as Mr. Hansard does here, and to aid him more from the public purse, if it were necessary, by taking a larger number of copies, or even by a money grant-in-aid, of such a record in an independent form.

Mr. T. Wemyss Reid, called in; and Examined.

Mr. T. W. Reid.

2074. *Chairman.*] You are, I think, the Editor of the " Leeds Mercury " ?—I am.

2075. Have you been acquainted with the system that prevails of furnishing reports to newspapers of the proceedings in Parliament ?—Yes; I was at one time a reporter in the Gallery, and for the last eight years I have had the management of the Parliamentary reports in the " Leeds Mercury."

2076. Will you state to the Committee your views as to the character of that report which is required for the provincial press. You probably are aware that Mr. Cooper, the sub-editor of the " Scotsman," gave evidence the other day; has your attention been drawn to that evidence?—Yes, I have read that evidence.

2077. The Committee have had evidence that the principal difficulty in the way of affording accommodation to provincial newspapers is the absence of space in the Gallery; have you any suggestion to make with regard to the selection of those who should obtain admission to the Gallery :—I think that accommodation might be provided in the Gallery for those provincial papers which are prepared to publish independent reports of the proceedings in Parliament.

2078. It has been stated to the Committee that provincial newspapers are in the opinion of some persons, adequately supplied with reports by the Co-operative Association, by the Press Association, by the agency of the Central Press. and by another agency of that character; have you any opinion to express with reference to those agencies?—We have found that they do not supply what we want, and, as a matter of fact, we have gone to very large expense in order to provide what we could not obtain in a satisfactory manner from them.

2079. I do not wish to ask you any secret of your business, but if you think it right to do so, will you state to the Committee in what way you have obtained the reports which you find to be necessary for the " Leeds Mercury " ?— We have the services of gentlemen in the Gallery who are employed for some of the London papers, and who get admission to the Gallery in that way. We supplement that by ordering large numbers of special reports from the " Central News," and from the Press Association, and in that way I believe that the report of the debates in Parliament published in the " Leeds Mercury " is longer than that published in any other English provincial paper.

2080. Then do I rightly understand you that you have first of all the report of the Press Association on which you depend ?—No, we do not depend on that.

2081. Perhaps you will explain to the Committee the order in which you proceed ?—We get our ordinary report from reporters of our own; at least so far reporters of our own, that they are employed by us as fully as possible; but owing to the Gallery regulations, we are compelled to take gentlemen who work also for London papers, who give us our report; and we supplement that on special occasions by the reports of the " Central News " and the Press Association.

2082. Then is your report identical with that which is given to any one of the London newspapers ?—No; quite distinct.

2083. So

2083. So that a gentleman employed for a London newspaper makes two reports; one for the paper which he is supposed to represent in London, and the other a fuller report for you; is that so?—No, hardly so; he is employed for us at a time when he is not employed for the London paper.

2084. You are of course aware that it would really be quite impossible for Parliament to find accommodation for every one of the London, and every one of the provincial daily newspapers?—Quite.

2085. The space which is at the disposal of the House of Commons would be insufficient for a reporting staff which would produce about 100 independent reports?—Quite.

2086. Have you any suggestion to make as to the conditions under which the reasonable requirements of newspapers desiring to give an independent report could be met?—I think that, in the first place, the Gallery might be slightly enlarged, as the Speaker, I think, suggested in giving evidence on Monday, so as to admit a certain number of additional reporters; and in the next place, I think there would not be so large a number of applicants for admission as seems to be generally supposed by the officials of the House who have given evidence.

2087. On what ground do you base that opinion?—On the ground of the great cost at which an independent report is supplied to a provincial paper.

2088. Then you would make the condition of admittance into the Gallery that a bonâ fide independent report should be given?—I should.

2089. You would give discretion to the officer, or to the Speaker, to exclude a newspaper which did not give a considerable and independent report?—Certainly.

2090. That is the suggestion which you make to the Committee?—Yes.

2091. You would include, I suppose, as part of that condition, that there should be special means of communication between London and the office of the newspaper desiring to obtain a report; a special wire or special wires?—Yes; as a matter of fact that is necessary in order to make use of a report.

2092. So that unless a newspaper had a special wire from London to its office or town, it could not properly avail itself of a separate report?—No, it could not.

2093. The special wire is not to the office of the newspaper, but to the Post Office, is it not?—No; to the office of the newspaper. Up to a few weeks ago I had a wire from my room in Leeds to the London office of the "Leeds Mercury," in Fleet-street, and another wire from that office in Fleet-street to the Lobby here, so that I was in direct communication practically with the Lobby.

2094. Has that ceased now; because you say it was so " up to a few weeks ago "?—We have been compelled to abandon that for a time, because of the unsatisfactory way in which it was worked by the Post Office; I speak of the wire from here to our London office.

2095. I suppose the cost of such an arrangement as you describe would be very considerable, would it not?—Yes; if the Committee wish, I have no objection to state the cost.

2096. If you desire to state it, the Committee would have no objection to receive the information?—The cost of such a report as we publish in the "Leeds Mercury" is about 780 l. a year; the cost of telegraphing is at least 400 l. a year; so that we get a total sum of 1,180 l. as the cost of a special report; and as opposed to that, the "Central News" and the Press Association supply their ordinary report of Parliament, which satisfies a large proportion of the country papers, for 55 l. a year, including telegraphing.

2097. The Committee have had evidence that the Press Association supply longer reports whenever they are requested to do so, and especially longer reports of local Members; do you pay separately for those?—Yes, we pay separately for those.

2098. And does that largely increase the charge to those newspapers containing separate reports?—We have paid during the present Session for the reports of local Members, or rather we shall have paid by the end of the Session, taking an average, 160 l. for that alone.

2099. Are the Committee to gather from what you say that the full report of the Press Association would cost something like 220 l. a year, and that your special arrangements would cost 1,200 l. a year?—I am not prepared to give

Mr. T. W. Reid.

11 July 1878.

the figure for the Press Association, but I should say that possibly it would be that; perhaps a little more.

2100. Why cannot you employ an agency like the Press Association to get what you require. I only ask you to give the Committee the information, because it is desirable that they should have it?—There are many reasons against our employing a news agency in London; one being, that by employing that agency, we publish the same news as that supplied to papers much inferior to our own in position and circulation; another being that we find we can do the work in a more satisfactory manner by having our own staff. Of course we have no control over the staff of the Press Association. And a third and very important reason is, that we find by practical experience that we get our own reports of Parliament much more quickly to our office in Leeds than any of the association reports are sent.

2101. But the Press Association is really a co-operative association of proprietors of newspapers, is it not?—Yes, in which however the smaller newspapers naturally, being more numerous, have the largest representation.

2102. Then you are not able, as a member of this partnership, to obtain through the agency of the association what you want?—No.

2103. Your own servants will not give you what you want; is that a correct representation of the fact?—We find that we do not get what we want; we get it in a more satisfactory manner, and in a way more suitable to our needs from our own servants who are specially our servants; and we are willing to pay a much larger sum in order to get it in that way rather than take the stereotyped news supplied by one or two agencies in London.

2104. When you say that you are willing to do so, the Committee may understand that you find it to be your interest as the conductors of a newspaper to do so?—Yes, speaking generally; it is not, perhaps, to our pecuniary interest, but we have a position to keep up which we desire to maintain, and we find that we can do so best by taking that course.

2105. I suppose you will say that the pecuniary results are due to the position which you maintain?—Ultimately, no doubt.

2106. Then it is your opinion, I infer, that great interest is taken in proceedings of Parliament, greater interest than formerly, in the districts supplied by the "Leeds Mercury"?—I can hardly say that a greater interest is taken than formerly; I think the interest is as great as it was, but the enterprise and competition of newspapers are very much greater than they were.

2107. Your desire to supply full reports, I suppose, arises from the fact that you believe they are desired and read by the public?—I have made some inquiries as to the effect of the publication of the Parliamentary reports upon the circulation of the "Leeds Mercury," and I find that they very seldom raise the circulation after a great debate more than 5 per cent.; so that the giving of good reports does not affect the circulation; but it maintains the character of the newspaper, to pay attention to what we consider, and what everybody considers, a very important matter.

2108. But you would not insert, on an average, four columns a day of matter in your newspaper if that matter were not interesting to your readers?—No, certainly we should not.

2109. You believe it to be interesting to your readers?—I believe it to be interesting to the intelligent readers.

2110. And that that justifies the expense which you actually incur for it?—Yes.

2111. Has it ever been suggested to you, or have you ever proposed, to associate yourself with other newspapers at a distance from Leeds, in order to lessen the cost of a report?—Yes; and I ought to explain that we are associated with another newspaper for a part of our report at this moment. In that way we reduce the expense to some extent, but not to a considerable extent.

2112. Is the expense which you have mentioned the proportion of the cost which devolves upon you?—No, the cost which actually falls upon us at this moment is about 250 l. less than the 1,200 l. that I mentioned; but that is the cost of providing such a report as we give.

2113. Then the result would be, I suppose, that if there were two newspapers publishing a report similar in character to that which you produce, only one sent would be required in the Gallery in order to produce that report?—Yes.

2114. Mr.

2114. Mr. *Forster.*] When you say that your combining with another newspaper reduces the expense by 250 *l.*, I suppose that that does not imply that out of that expense of 1,300 *l.* you pay the 950 *l.* and the other paper the 250 *l.*, but that there are special expenses for each paper?—Yes, special expenses for each paper, and the cost to both papers is about the same.

2115. You have told us that you give, as compared with other provincial papers, a very full report; but I suppose the real fact is that you give quite as full a report as some of the London papers?—A much fuller report than some of the London papers which have seats in the Gallery.

2116. And although it is quite true that you cannot measure the increase of circulation by an important debate, and that it does not rise by such a debate, as I suppose it does by a murder or by a battle, yet you imagine that your character as a political paper, and not only your position, but the extent to which your paper is bought, in fact, by the inhabitants of Yorkshire, does to some degree depend upon your giving such a good report of Parliamentary proceedings?—Undoubtedly we find that it pays in the long run in that way.

2117. You stated that you obtained at present your reports, to a considerable extent, from reporters employed for London newspapers; but it has come out to us in evidence that the reporters for almost every paper are very quickly changed; how do you manage to get your report if the gentleman upon whom you rely leaves his seat, and is replaced by another?—Because we do not make use of gentlemen who are engaged in that way. Occasionally we are compelled to do so; but the gentlemen who supply our reports regularly are not changed in that way.

2118. I clearly understand why you prefer getting your own report to relying upon the reports furnished by the agencies; but would you tell the Committee in what way you think you would be benefited by a change in the arrangements, so that you got your own seat?—Because we should then have a reporting staff more directly under our own control, the system at present compelling us to make use of the partial services of gentlemen who are partially engaged upon other newspapers; because we believe we could do our work better; because we could insure its being done more rapidly; and because we hope that possibly there might be some slight diminution in the expense in consequence.

2119. But I suppose your chief wish to make the change is not from the hope of pecuniary saving so much as the being able to do it more easily and more perfectly?—Certainly; the pecuniary question may possibly turn out to be the other way.

2120. At what time does your paper appear at Leeds?—The first edition goes to press at one o'clock; that contains a report of Parliament up to a few minutes before midnight.

2121. That is the edition which goes to the villages around Leeds, does it not?—Yes.

2122. But for Leeds itself, when does your edition appear?—I think four editions are published during the night, and the last edition is published at 10 minutes past five in the morning.

2123. And that contains the report up to what time?—Up to half-past four, if the House is sitting till then.

2124. In fact it contains a complete report up to the time that most of the London newspapers do?—Later than the London newspapers which reach Leeds by the first train.

2125. In fact you give to the Yorkshire public the Parliamentary information as fully as, and much sooner than, most of the London newspapers?—We do.

2126. Sooner than any of the London newspapers?—They reach Leeds about 10 o'clock.

2127. Therefore it would be proper then to expect that those Yorkshiremen who wished to have Parliamentary reports would not rely upon the London newspapers; because they would take in your newspaper for its general local information, and get it so much earlier?—Yes; I do not think the London papers are now bought in the country so much for their Parliamentary reports as for their foreign intelligence.

2128. Although it is the case, I believe, that Leeds is one of the towns in which there has been a very great effort to get the London papers early?—Yes, they now reach there at 10 o'clock in the morning instead of 12 as formerly.

0.121. U 3 2129. Would

J. T. W. Reid.

14 July 1878.

2129. Would you be content with one seat in the Gallery, or do you think that you ought to have both a seat for a reporter and a seat for a summary writer?—We should be very glad to have one seat, and as much more as we could get.

2130. You think you would be able to give what you want to give to the Yorkshire people by having one seat?—By having one seat.

2131. Sir *Henry T. Holland.*] I suppose that you get, through your special wires, other information than the mere report of the debates?—A great deal.

2132. I can understand that you would object to having an identical report upon general subjects of interest and information with other newspapers; but do you object to having an identical report of debates?—Yes. The report of a debate, for many reasons, may not be suitable for us; we may wish to have a fuller report of certain speeches, or of a debate dealing with a certain question, than appears in other papers.

2133. I quite understand that, on certain occasions, on questions of local interest, you would desire to have a fuller report; but I mean rather as a general rule, should you object to have an identical report of debates with other newspapers?—Yes, we should, even if the report were a very good one.

2134. Mr. *Mitchell Henry.*] When you speak of 700 l. a year for the reporting, do you refer to the Session during which Parliament sits?—Yes, to the Session.

2135. That is the extra cost for the report now transmitted to the "Leeds Mercury"?—It is rather more than 700 l.; it is 780 l. for the Session.

2136. The 400 l., which you spoke of as the price of the wire, is for your general wire, available for all purposes?—No, I beg your pardon; I gave 400 l. as the cost of telegraphing the Parliamentary intelligence alone; our wires cost more than that.

2137. When you spoke of admitting newspapers to the Gallery which gave separate reports, how does that tally with the answer which you gave, that you unite with another newspaper?—I think that I ought to explain perhaps that we only unite for a part of our report with another newspaper; but I think that a syndicate of newspapers, whether it consisted of two, or three, or four, might claim a seat in the gallery on the ground of giving an independent report, just as a single newspaper might.

2138. Then you would attach the report rather to the seat than to the newspaper; that a seat given for the purpose of a reporter in the Gallery would be given only if an independent report was supplied from that seat, although that particular report might go to many newspapers?—There are limitations of course to that rule, but, under certain conditions, it would practically amount to that.

2139. Do you think that the Speaker would have no difficulty in exercising his discretion to that extent in only admitting a reporter to the particular seat placed at the disposal of the provincial newspaper, provided that the report was entirely independent?—No; and provided that it amounted to a certain length in the course of the Session, I think that that might be made a condition. I find that, so far as the "Leeds Mercury" is concerned, the report every Session averages very nearly the same length; we generally have about 400 columns during the course of the Session telegraphed of the report from Parliament.

2140. Have you formed any idea as to the number of seats which you think would be claimed in that way by the provincial press?—I do not think there are more than ten newspapers in the provinces which would be likely to incur the expense of keeping up a staff in London for the purpose of supplying special Parliamentary reports and Parliamentary intelligence; and some of those newspapers might combine with each other.

2141. Do you refer to England alone, or to Ireland and Scotland as well?—I refer to England, Ireland, and Scotland.

2142. You think that a provision of ten seats for that portion of the press which is not metropolitan would be sufficient?—I think so.

2143. How would it do, in your opinion, if the rule was laid down that every newspaper occupying a seat should be required to have a London office and a special wire?—That rule in the main would answer in the way of selection; but there are one or two, perhaps I ought to say there is only one, important newspaper published very near to London which does not require a special wire,

wire, the "Birmingham Post." Such a rule would exclude that paper unless it obtained a special wire on purpose.

2144. But without making such a rule a hard-and-fast rule, a provision of that kind would be a guide to the Speaker in case of an application being made for admission to the Gallery?—Yes, it would be a very fair test.

2145. You would leave it open to the Speaker, if he saw reason to do so, to disregard that rule technically if he thought the spirit of it was observed?—Certainly.

2146. Mr. Dashar.] How many papers are there in Leeds?—Two morning papers.

2147. Have they both special wires?—No, only the "Leeds Mercury."

2148. The other paper is supplied by one of the associations?—It is.

2149. May I ask how many men you have in the Gallery?—I could not answer that question; I really do not know how many reporters supply us.

2150. You tell me that they are gentlemen who have admission to the Gallery, but do not take their regular turns for the London papers?—They do work for the London papers, but some of them do not require to leave the box, or their place in the Gallery, at the end of each turn.

2151. Dr. Lyon Playfair.] Would it sufficiently limit the number of papers that were likely to require a seat if you defined the number of reporters that should be engaged upon the staff of the newspapers; say that four reporters were generally engaged for the purpose of furnishing a Parliamentary report: would that sufficiently limit the number of newspapers?—No, I do not think that that would be an altogether satisfactory limit.

2152. Then you would make a condition of that kind, plus the private wire?—I do not think the number of reporters employed would be a satisfactory limit at all; you might send dummies into the Gallery, a newspaper might do that, in order to obtain a seat.

2153. But we are going on the supposition that the newspapers which would apply for a seat would generally carry out the conditions upon which they obtained that seat; you do not suppose, for instance, that the Speaker, or any of the officers of the House could be continually watching the newspapers to see whether they were giving the reports; you must rely a great deal upon their honour, must you not?—Certainly.

2154. If a newspaper undertook to say that they would keep four, or, if there were a great demand for the newspaper, six reporters, for the purpose of Parliamentary reporting, and you could rely upon the honour of that newspaper, would not that be a sufficient condition in the way of limitation?—I hardly think it would from my experience of the way in which a staff may be employed in the Gallery.

2155. What other limitation would you put?—I should not object to a limitation as to cost, or as to length of report, or as to a special wire, plus the discretion of the Speaker.

2156. Practically it would be impossible for the Speaker, or the officers of the House, to look after the length of the report, or the character of the report, would it not?—Certainly, it would be impossible, or, at any rate, difficult to keep a constant watch upon it; but if a newspaper proprietor or editor pledged himself to give a certain report, I think it would be a more satisfactory pledge to exact from him than a pledge that he would send a certain number of reporters into the Gallery.

2157. You spoke of the difficulty that you had recently found of transmitting your intelligence from the House to your office; is that on account of your wires being blocked?—I do not speak within my personal knowledge, but I believe it was from the delay which took place in the transmission of our messages from the Lobby to our office in Fleet-street.

2158. Your present practice is now a good deal to send the copy by cab?—Yes, we use cabs instead of the wire.

2159. Do you not think it would facilitate very much newspaper reporting if the Post Office were to lay down pneumatic tubes from the House of Commons to the Post Office with one or two stations in the City, and then you could send down your copy by pneumatic tubes with great celerity?—Undoubtedly it would be a very great advantage.

0.121.   U 4   2160. Chairman.]

Mr. T. W. Reid.
11 July 1878.

2160. *Chairman.*] Is it not a fact that there are such pneumatic tubes at the present moment?—I believe there are; but they are not available for independent newspapers.

2161. Dr. *Lyon Playfair.*] At the present moment I understand the Post Office transmit reports in little cases which are sent to them, through three pneumatic tubes; now supposing they were to transmit copies in the same way, and that they had one or two stations so that the newspaper offices, which are chiefly in the City, could obtain their own copy, would it not be a great advantage?—It would be undoubtedly a facility for the newspapers. I think that the Press Association and the "Central News" copy is now transmitted by pneumatic tube; I do not speak positively, but that is my impression; but it is not available for any of the special wire newspapers which pay the largest sums to the Post Office.

2162. Generally, then, you think that the provincial press when it determines to report the debates of the House of Commons well, has now just as much claim as the London press to be represented in the Reporters' Gallery?—I think they have, subject to certain limitations.

2163. Of efficiency in the transaction of their business?—Yes.

2164. Colonel *Arbuthnot.*] I think you said that in the event of a certain number of seats being placed at the disposal of the provincial press and the number of applicants being too large, a greater number, some papers might coalesce, and have one staff between them; can you say how many papers could work together with convenience; the maximum number, I mean?—I do not think that more than two papers could work conveniently together.

2165. We have heard that in Canada four papers, I think, so combine; but, of course, I am unable to say what the size of those papers is; would you think that in England not more than two could combine?—I think two papers would be the most convenient number certainly.

2166. Would you prefer to coalesce with a paper in another part of the country in preference to one in your own locality?—Certainly.

2167. Would your reason be to avoid the identity of report?—Yes, and to avoid a combination with a rival.

2168. Mr. *Hutchinson.*] You are aware of the accommodation in the Gallery, of course?—Yes; I have my own recollection of it when I was in the Gallery 10 years ago.

2169. You have also told us that if the alteration suggested by the Speaker were made, you think that reasonable accommodation might be provided?—I think that more accommodation might be provided.

2170. Now you are aware that the Press Association supplies Parliamentary intelligence to 60 or 70 daily papers, are not you?—I do not know the exact number, but I should think that was about the number.

2171. It is a very large number?—It is a very large number.

2172. I think you also told us that you do not imagine that above 10 daily papers would apply for seats in the Gallery for a special staff of reporters?—I do not think that more than 10 would do so.

2173. Now the question I have to ask you is this, whether you think that the Press Association, the Central Press, and another agency which supply Parliamentary reports for 60 or 70 daily papers, ought, as a matter of equity, to be provided for, or that gentlemen like you, who ask for a special seat, ought to be provided for?—I say that the Press Association, the "Central News," and the "Central Press" are already provided for, but of course I freely admit that if only provision can be made for them, they must be considered first.

2174. That is the point; you think that when the space available is ascertained, these Press Associations, which supply the 60 or 70 papers, ought to be considered first before individual newspapers are allowed to set up special claims?—I think so; at the same time I should like, if I might, to make this observation with reference to the number of newspapers, that having made a rough estimate of the circulation of the 10 papers which I think would be likely to ask for seats in the Gallery, I am quite sure that the gross circulation of those 10 newspapers is very much larger than the gross circulation of the, say 50, remaining newspapers.

2175. May I take your answer to be this, that if it came to be a matter of competition

competition for the space, in your judgment, as a matter of fair play, these Press Associations, which represent the great bulk of the daily papers, ought to be provided for?—Yes, I admit that.

2176. Now you have told us that the "Leeds Mercury" gives a longer Parliamentary report than any English provincial paper?—Yes.

2177. I know the "Leeds Mercury" pretty well; but will you tell us what the average length of your Parliamentary report is?—The average length during the present Session has been exactly four columns a day; it has sometimes extended to 13 columns, all telegraphed.

2178. Now the question I have to ask is this: have you ever asked the Press Association to supply what you wanted, a report of the length you wanted, and the particular kind of report, and found that that association could not comply with your request?—The Press Association did supply us with a report, and we gave it up, because we found that we could get a better report from our own staff.

2179. Have you ever made a direct application to them to supply a report of a certain length and of a certain character, and found that from any reason they could not, or would not, do it?—I can hardly answer that question; I can say this, that in making our arrangements for news of different kinds we are guided by our experience of what the Press Association can and what it cannot do; and we are decidedly of opinion that the Press Association cannot supply us with a report such as we wish in the time in which we need to have it.

2180. Then I take this as your answer, that you cannot say that you have ever failed to get what you asked for, but you have formed an opinion that you might occasionally want something that you could not get?—No; it is founded upon actual experience of not having got what we wanted from the associations, there being more than one association.

2181. I will put to you a question which I put to the gentlemen connected with the "Scotsman;" are you aware that if you were to ask for a report of any length you like, done in the first person throughout, you could get it?—I have no doubt that the Press Association would be willing to supply it.

2182. Would not that satisfy you in length?—In length possibly; but there are other things of course to be considered.

2183. I observe that you speak much of the desirability of having your own Parliamentary reporters under your control, and you say at the same time that newspapers should combine; does it not strike you that that combination that you speak of is in the nature of the kind of report which the Press Association itself supplies?—I have spoken of the extent to which I thought combination desirable for newspapers; the extent, therefore, is very slight compared with a report supplied by an association over which we have practically no control as regards the internal management of it.

2184. Do not you think that a report furnished by an association which supplies Parliamentary reports to a great number of newspapers, differing as they must do in politics, as in everything else, is very much more likely to be independent, and generally impartial as regards the whole body of the report and the wants of the public generally, than a report which is supplied in obedience to a particular kind of control, and to suit the wishes and politics, and circumstances of one particular paper?—Most assuredly not.

2185. Will you explain why?—Any newspaper which is conducted by men of honour, or men who respect themselves, whatever else it may do, will undoubtedly publish impartial reports; and I may say that I do not know a single case of a newspaper failing to do so.

2186. "Impartiality" is a widish word; it means not only accuracy, but it includes the length of the report that you give to the different speakers, and a report, though it might report with perfect accuracy what every speaker said, might be practically unfair if it gave too large a portion to one man and too little to another?—That is perfectly true.

2187. Do not you think that an association representing a large body of newspapers would be much more likely to be impartial in that particular, than a report ordered by one particular paper for its own purposes?—It would be likely to be impartial in giving everybody with equal brevity; I do not say anything more than that; it would not give any speaker with any fulness; and its accuracy of course I do not guarantee. In all other respects it would not be more likely to be impartial than a report ordered by a single newspaper.

2188. You do not think so?— I do not think so.

2189. Sir *Alexander Gordon.*] With reference to the questions which have just been put to you, practically, does not the Press Association report fully or not according to the local instructions it receives from different local newspapers?—It does.

2190. Therefore the impartiality that has been spoken of rests entirely with the instructions that it receives?—Entirely.

2191. I understood you to say that you now supplement your own wire by information derived from the " Central News" ?—And the Press Association.

2192. Do you publish summaries of debates in the " Leeds Mercury" ?—We do.

2193. May I ask where those are prepared?—They are prepared in the office in Leeds from the reports telegraphed.

2194. Do you or your editors find any difficulty in preparing those summaries from those reports?—No, I think not.

2195. Do you think that the London newspapers would find any greater difficulty in publishing their summaries from the reports which they receive from their reporters?—They would be able to publish summaries from those reports, and probably in most cases those summaries would be as good as they are now; but I do not say in all cases. I think that in some cases the summary derives additional value from the fact that the summary writer is in the House.

2196. Therefore you would consider it essential to the London newspapers to keep their places for summary writers as well as for the reporters?—I think so.

2197. Therefore any accommodation that might be given to the provincial newspapers at the expense of those summary writers, would be an injury to the London newspapers?—I think, so far as the question of boxes is concerned (you know of course the construction of the Gallery), that the summary writers might be placed on the back bench without disadvantage.

2198. But practically they are with one exception, are they not ?—I was not aware of that; if so there has been a change since I was in the Gallery in that respect.

2199. You mentioned 10 large provincial newspapers as being the extent of those that were likely to expect accommodation in the Gallery; do you include England and Ireland in those 10?—I do include Scotland and Ireland.

2200. I did not quite understand your arrangement about the reporters; you stated that you got a full report for the " Leeds Mercury" by employing the reporters of the London newspapers at a time when they are not working for their own paper; but the London newspaper proprietors require a full report for their own paper just as well as the " Leeds Mercury;" how can there be occasions when the reporters are not wanted by the London papers?—As a matter of fact, there are reporters who are not always engaged; who have, whatever the importance of the debate may be, to work only during certain hours actually for the London papers, and we are able to make use of those reporters: but upon the occasion of great debates, we are compelled to fall back largely upon the services of the Press Association, and the " Central News" at present, owing to our being unable to have the other reporters.

2201. Let me take an important debate, of an Imperial character, which you want to have in extenso, and which the London papers also require to have in extenso; on that occasion can you obtain the services of any of the London newspaper reporters?—Not of many of them.

2202. Can you of any?—Yes.

2203. But then the inference would appear to be that the London reporters have more accommodation than they actually require for the purposes of the London newspapers?—You are, perhaps, not initiated into the mysteries of supplying reporting matter; there is such a thing as producing duplicate copies; a reporter may be writing his copy for two papers as well as for one sometimes.

2204. I know that perfectly well; but I am speaking of your employing the London reporters at a time when they are not required for their own paper, on great occasions; even then you can get the services of some of them?—Yes, to a certain extent; I say there are some reporters whom we can make use of even on great occasions; we do not get their exclusive services, however, even then.

2205. Mr.

Mr. T. W. Reid.

11 July 1878.

2205. Mr. Mills.] Speaking of the structural difficulties with reference to the Reporters' Gallery, of giving accommodation, you knowing the Reporters' Gallery, do you think that if the back seats were raised they would then afford such accommodation as would be suitable for reporters?—They would be very bad seats in any case, but they might be improved.

2206. But you do not think that any alteration of the structural arrangements of the Gallery in that respect would make the back seats sufficiently convenient for reporters?—They would not be convenient seats; it would be possible to report there, but the reporter would have to undergo an amount of physical fatigue which would not be necessary if he were sitting in a proper place, and he would be very liable to hear badly, and not to be able to report accurately in consequence.

2207. I think you stated, as one objection to the clubbing together of different newspapers in the same district with a view of getting a report, say through the Press Association, that it would be an objection, and a detriment, for instance, to your own paper that there should be an identical report published by another paper in the same neighbourhood?—Certainly; we wish, of course to publish a better report than is published by any other paper.

2208. Now, supposing an arrangement were made, say, for half a dozen towns at considerable distances from each other; for example, Leeds, Glasgow, Harwich, Penzance, and Plymouth, do you think the same objection would apply to an identical report in reference to its prejudicing the circulation of a particular paper?—No, not to anything like the same extent.

2209. Supposing the difficulty could be relieved in any degree by that sort of combination, your objection to an identical report would not apply to the same extent as it would if the newspapers were in the same county, or in the same district?—I agree to that; but I would point out that papers published in Penzance, to take an extreme place, and Newcastle, say, at the other end of England, would not require the same reports; there would be matters of interest to the people of Cornwall, which were of no interest to the people of Northumberland, and vice versâ.

2210. At present do you consider that the arrangements which you make for getting a full Parliamentary report, and an early Parliamentary report, so as to compete successfully with the London newspapers with regard to full and early Parliamentary information, pay as a matter of business the expense which you incur upon them?—As a matter of business, I am afraid it does not pay.

2211. But what I wanted to know is this: do you think that, supposing for instance, any alteration were not made which would give you greater facilities, it would make any difference in your continuing your present arrangements about reporting?—I am not prepared to answer that question, because it would need to be very seriously considered, and I cannot say what the decision might be.

2212. But at present?—At present we are disposed to continue; we believe that it is for the benefit of our readers, and ultimately for the benefit of the paper.

2213. Chairman.] You have been present in the room when official reports have been spoken of?—Yes.

2214. And probably your attention has been given to the evidence upon the question of official reporting?—Yes.

2215. Supposing there was an official report of the character of that furnished in France, consisting first of all of a very full, almost a verbatim report, next of a summary, and thirdly, of an analytical summary, and that those reports were delivered as they were taken to the newspapers, would there be still a necessity for the presence of newspaper reporters in the Gallery?—Most assuredly. I suppose you are aware that none of the important French newspapers rely exclusively upon the official report; they all have reporters of their own who supply them with summaries of the proceedings in the Chambers, which are published practically 24 hours before those supplied by the Government.

2216. But does the summary which is published by the French newspapers, and furnished by their own reporters, partake of the character of the short report which appears in the English newspapers, or is it more of a descriptive character?—It is enlivened by descriptive writing; perhaps not quite so lively as that in some of the English papers.

2217. But you are of opinion that if there is an official report, and if Par-

X 2

liament

Mr. T. W. Reid.
12 July 1878.

liament should furnish that official report to the newspapers and to their own Members, it would still be necessary to have as complete a system of newspaper reporting as that which now exists?—I believe so; we could not get the official report in time to make any use of it.

2218. That is a question of arrangement, I suppose?—It is more than that. The Press Association, which is very well managed, and which puts forth a great deal of energy in producing its reports, cannot supply the "Leeds Mercury" at this moment with its reports in sufficient time for our use. That is one of our strong objections to taking the Press Association reports. We find that unless we have an independent wire of our own, and a report which is prepared with special regard to the hours at which we require it, we cannot get it in time for our edition; and it would be impossible of course for an official report to be prepared with such regard.

Mr. John Jaffray, called in; and Examined.

Mr. J. Jaffray.

2219. Chairman.] I think you are one of the Proprietors of the "Birmingham Daily Post"?—I am.

2220. And you have been connected with the actual management of that newspaper for many years, have you not?—For 54 years. At first it was a weekly newspaper, and it has grown into a daily; I make this explanation, because daily papers were not in existence in the provinces then.

2221. You have seen the rise and the gradual growth and development of the whole system of Parliamentary reporting for the provincial press?—I have.

2222. How do you procure your reports for the "Birmingham Daily Post"? —Entirely through the agency of the Press Association. At the commencement of each Session we send an order to the Press Association to supply us with their first class (as they call it) Parliamentary report; at the same time we send them a list of local Members, selected, not because of their politics agreeing or differing with us, but because of the repute in which they stand, and the desire of the constituency among which our paper circulates to have information of their legislative proceedings; and we accompany that order with the request that all important imperial questions, such as Budget debates, the exposition of a new policy, all Ministerial statements, questions affecting local interests, and what are called scenes in the House, should be reported in extenso.

2223. Then you treat the Press Association as if it were a corps of reporters of your own?—That is the light in which I look upon their agency, and, in effect, at any rate it is so; they are our reporters and agents, and under our control, within certain limits.

2224. And the manager of the Press Association is the manager of your Parliamentary corps?—He is; and he is amenable to reproof or advice; and I generally find him take reproof, if it is necessary, and advice, and act upon that advice.

2225. You have heard a great deal of evidence as to the necessity of special reports for the provincial newspapers?—I have.

2226. And, therefore, of special seats in the Gallery for those newspapers?—Yes.

2227. Do you consider it to be necessary in the interests of the "Birmingham Daily Post," that you should have the privilege of a seat in the Gallery?—Supposing accommodation could be provided for all who are likely to go to the expense of having a special staff of reporters, we, as a matter of course, of prestige, and probably of convenience, might, indeed would, necessarily apply for accommodation; but up to this point we have never found any difficulty whatever in getting any class of reports, either as to length, selection of speakers, or other matters from the Press Association.

2228. Do you believe that the public are sufficiently well served with the reports of the Press Association through the agency of your newspaper in the districts which you supply?—That is my opinion, or I should take other means of supplying the want.

2229. It has been stated that there has been delay in the transmission of the matter; is that so?—That is true rather in respect of the past than the present;

present; and on tracing out the causes of the delay I have found, in the majority of cases, that the delay is attributable to the telegraph department of the Post Office rather than to the Press Association, which supplies the matter to be transmitted.

2230. Putting it another way, do you apprehend that, with reporters distinctly paid directly by yourself, rather than by your manager, you would obtain your information more quickly or less quickly than you do by the Press Association?—I do not see that we should gain anything in point of rapidity of transmission. We send all our Parliamentary reports by the ordinary public wire. Our proximity to London and a very good train service render it unnecessary to have the ordinary run of news sent by wire to us. Nearly all that we have got to us by wire consists of Parliamentary reports and Reuter's foreign news, and that comes very promptly as a rule. Sometimes the wires are loaded on great occasions, occasions of great debates, but, as a rule, we have very little cause to complain. We go to press very early, too, with our first edition, and of course with an imperfect Parliamentary report when the House sits late. Still, as a rule, the news is transmitted very promptly. Will you allow me to give you an illustration? This morning there was a very late sitting of the House, till 10 minutes past 3, and I brought a paper with me, our own paper, from Birmingham at 7 o'clock in the morning, and I bought one of the London papers on my way at Coventry at 8 o'clock; that London paper did not contain the close of the debate, but the Birmingham paper did. That is an illustration of the promptness with which these things are sent to us.

2231. Sir *Henry T. Holland.*] Have you a copy of the Birmingham paper?— Yes, I have; this is the "Daily Post" (*handing it to the honourable Member*); and this (*pointing to a paper*) is the London paper which I need not name.

2232. *Chairman.*] But as evidenced by the interest which the public take in your district in the proceedings of Parliament, are you of opinion that the ordinary supply is sufficient for the readers of the "Daily Post"?—Yes, I am. My answer must refer to the ordinary business of Parliament, of course. Great occasions of important debates excite considerable interest, and we are considered to be rather a political people in Birmingham; and notwithstanding that I find that the ordinary supply is sufficient for business men and the ordinary run of readers.

2233. Do you find any greater demand for your paper at the commencement or the end of the Parliamentary Session?—I agree with the witness who was previously examined, that the meeting of Parliament adds very little to the circulation. That is the best test that I can apply. At the opening of Parliament there is a little interest evidenced by the increased sale; but, as a rule, we find very little difference between the sale during the sitting of Parliament and that on ordinary occasions.

2234. Will you explain to the Committee how the Press Association is managed; you are a member of the association, I understand?—I am a member of the association, and I was its chairman for the first two or three years of its existence. It is entirely a co-operative association, embracing the proprietor or manager of every important daily paper in the provinces, and of most of the weekly papers; and it is managed by a very large committee; there are 10 altogether in the management committee, and in the consultative committee, as it is called, so that it is entirely under the control of the members of the press. I think the former witness said that it was managed to a considerable extent by proprietors of weekly papers; that is not so. If you will permit me, I will read the names of a few of the papers that were represented on this committee of management during the time I was chairman; they were the "Manchester Guardian" and "Examiner," the "Scotsman," the "Leeds Mercury," the "Freeman's Journal," "Belfast News Letter," "Liverpool Courier," "Sheffield Telegraph," the "Bristol Press," and the "Birmingham Post," and several important weeklies. I quote these names to show that all these important papers have a controlling voice in the management, and that, in fact, it is their own agency.

2235. Do I rightly understand that a newspaper must take the report given by the association, or can the newspaper obtain any report which it may desire through the medium of the association?—That is my experience, that it may obtain any report as to length and selection of speakers that the various newspapers may require.

2236. The manager of the association, I think, gave some evidence to the Committee as to the amount of accommodation placed at its disposal; are you acquainted with the accommodation which the association possesses in the gallery?—Several times I have had occasion to complain of the awkwardness of the reports, hitches in the reports, and a want of continuity sometimes, and I then complained to the manager, and I was very much astonished to find that the accommodation was so bad, and as much astonished to find that the reports were so accurate under the circumstances. I am strongly of opinion that that association, composed as I have shown it to be, of nearly all the provincial newspaper proprietors, has a claim to far better accommodation than it has at present, because on many occasions we have as long a report as any of the London papers probably, except the "Times" and the "Standard"; and representing as we do a very large population, we think we have a claim to be treated in a fashion somewhat analogous to the London papers.

2237. Have you any opinion as to the use of official reports; I asked the last witness whether, if an official report was furnished almost immediately in slips to the newspapers as the speaker spoke, it would be possible to substitute the official report for the news-paper report now in the gallery; have you any view upon that point?—It would be utterly impossible to use it, even if we could get it in time. It is not what we want, and those who are acquainted with the machinery of a newspaper office know this, that there is nothing so difficult as when there is a flood of matter coming in at the last moment, to select with judgment what should go in and what should be left out; and it would be utterly impossible to condense with any amount of fairness and accuracy a long report like that which would be transmitted to us if we had the official report.

2238. That disposes of the question, so far as a verbatim or very full report is concerned?—Yes.

2239. Then what have you to say in reference to an official condensed report?—Simply that our local interests require special reports. Take as an illustration the scheme of King Edward's School lately issued by the Education Department, and, as you are aware, debated in Parliament. That is a matter of very great importance to everyone in Birmingham; it is a large foundation educating a great many hundred scholars, and the official report would take but slight cognizance of a merely local matter, while to us it is of the utmost importance. I am quoting that as an illustration of the uselessness, so to speak, to us of an official condensed report.

2240. Then, speaking from a newspaper point of view, and for the public (because the newspapers may be taken to represent the interest which the public feel in Parliamentary debates), an official report, if there was an official report, must be superadded to the existing system of newspaper reporting, in your judgment?—Yes, I think it would be of no service to us.

2241. No service at all to the press?—No, I think not; we should throw it aside.

2242. Now, if it were proposed to move the gentlemen from the gallery altogether, and give the newspapers these three reports gratuitously, would the newspapers avail themselves of them, or could the newspapers avail themselves of them to give the public as good an idea of the proceedings of Parliament as they now do?—In the first place, I think I am speaking the sentiments of every respectable newspaper when I say that we would not take gratuitous reports; we dislike gratuitous work of any kind; we cannot control it; and if I say so much, I think I answer the whole question.

2243. If that is so, it comes to a question as to how the accommodation required by the press, and by the press for the public, shall be met; have you any suggestion to make upon that point?—Supposing the accommodation can be considerably increased, then the test should be, I think, the bona fide use of the seat appropriated to every provincial paper that would apply for it. There is no principle of selection that I can suggest that would not be invidious, and could even be tolerated. Take the private wire test; we are so situated that we do not want a private wire for the general purposes of our paper, and why should we be compelled to go to that expense in order to buy an official privilege? The only test I can suggest is that which Mr. Reid has already spoken of, namely, the real and bona fide use of the seat by the paper to which it is appropriated; and it follows from that, that you must accommodate every paper that applies, and conforms to the conditions imposed.

2244. Have

2244. Have you any idea from your very extensive acquaintance with the newspaper press of this country, of the number of newspapers which would apply for admission to the gallery upon that principle which you suggest?—I have; and my calculation is more liberal than Mr. Reid's; he spoke of 10; I have the details before me, and I think the probability is that you would have 16 or 17 papers applying for that accommodation.

2245. Does that take account of the number of papers which would find it to be possible in their own interest to work together; just as the last witness told the Committee that the "Leeds Mercury" works with another paper?— The difficulty in working with another paper is this: If you must have a distinctive report, you cannot, according to the last witness, work with a paper in the same locality, because of the, shall I call it, trade jealousies which exist; and you cannot work with a paper published in a remote place, because the news that suits a Leeds paper, for example, has no reference probably to Liverpool, or to Scotland, or to Ireland.

2246. Sir Henry T. Holland.] There are different local interests, in short; —Entirely different interests; and therefore while you remove the jealousy of the same thing appearing in the same locality, you get into difficulty with reference to the character of the report.

2247. Chairman.] Then you see great difficulty in two or three newspapers working together, but you do not see any difficulty in the Press Association acting for all?—If the private newspapers working together published an identical report, then I do not see how they are benefited as compared with the use of the Press Association; and I go back to my original statement, that we have never applied to the Press Association for any description of reporting which they have not been competent to supply, and which they have not supplied. And I supplement that answer with the other observation, that if it is not in a condition to supply all that is wanted now, it is an instrument entirely in the hands of its creators and its managers, and ought to be made to discharge that duty.

2248. Do I rightly understand you to take the view that the Press Association should do for its members anything that any one individual member requires to be done; or is it to do only that which the majority, or the committee governing it, consider to be necessary and desirable?—In practice it does whatever the individual members require it to do.

2249. What is the conclusion the Committee should draw from that, in your judgment, as to the admission of provincial newspapers into the gallery?—I would say this, that if accommodation can be provided in the gallery for all the provincial newspapers that will comply with such conditions as are imposed, the position of provincial newspapers entitles them to that privilege. If that cannot be done, then I think the Association, as representing the provincial press, should be placed in a condition of equality, at the least, with the ordinary London newspapers.

2250. Mr. Mills.] If the Press Association were placed in a position of equality with the ordinary London newspapers, and were enabled to discharge its duties as its committee would think necessary, do you think that all that was wanted would then be done, so far as the provincial press was concerned?— Again, I must say that I, with a great desire to maintain what I think is the character and position of the provincial press, would prefer that accommodation was provided for the principal provincial newspapers. Failing that, the Press Association should be better accommodated.

2251. But supposing the structural arrangements of the Reporters' Gallery did not seem to meet the necessities of the case in providing for the 16 or 17, I think you say, newspapers for which provision would have to be made, then in that alternative you would say, "Let the provincial press be content with the provision made by the Press Association;" is that your view?—Not quite; the provincial press have other means of supplementing the reports of the Press Association, or the Central News, and they must either continue that system or go to the Press Association; they are not necessarily confined to the Press Association.

2252. But at present, as I understand, the arrangement of the Press Association, providing for meeting the special and peculiar requirements of the provincial press, furnishing them with reports of the speeches of their own local Members as they may desire, and thereby securing them against the objections which have been started in some quarters to what are called identical reports; because, for instance, if at Birmingham you required to be furnished to you, through the Press Association, full reports of speeches of the Members of the district, as I understand you do, possibly at Stafford, a daily newspaper which is published there makes its requirements to be furnished with the speeches of the Members specially connected with that district; in that case Birmingham and Stafford are supplied with what they respectively want, are they not?—Yes, that is my experience.

2253. Then, as I understand, you would not think that the circulation, say, of the "Daily Post," would be prejudiced even if a newspaper near you published the same report as you published; do I rightly understand you that that would be the case?—That is my contention.

2254. I think I rather understood you to say that so far as Parliamentary reporting is concerned, you did not regard that as a very important feature as regards the circulation of your paper; I am speaking now of the "Daily Post," and I understood you to say that when the Session began you did not see any perceptible increase, excepting at the very commencement, in the circulation of your paper; and that during the five months, say, that Parliament was sitting, there would not be very much difference in its circulation from its circulation when Parliament was in recess; is that so?—I do attach very considerable importance to Parliamentary debates; but the tendency of the reports is towards closer condemnation, giving the spirit and essence of the proceedings rather than what may be called the verbiage, and that is caused, perhaps, as much by the monopoly of space, by meetings of local bodies which have been created within a short time, by expansion of advertising, and by lengthened Stock Exchange reports, and by that flow of foreign news which is now supplied, and the existence of which is the creation of a very short time; so that we are almost compelled to condense what may be called the ordinary proceedings of Parliament.

2255. Then with the exception of speeches made by the representatives of the district, in which naturally the people of Birmingham and its neighbourhood would take an interest, you do not think that there is any importance attached to full Parliamentary debates?—That is not quite so; on occasions, such as say a Budget speech, as I have previously said, when there are remissions or increase of taxation, or any ministerial statement of an important character, or a party debate, then a great deal of interest attaches to the proceedings of Parliament, and we meet that requirement by verbatim reports in some instances, and very lengthy reports in others, according to the measure of importance which seems to attach to the special debate; but there is a very considerable interest felt in the proceedings of Parliament on those special occasions.

2256. A witness who was examined before us, I think Mr. Ross, said, as his general opinion, speaking of full reports of speeches of Members of Parliament, that he doubted whether any one read them excepting the Members who had made the speeches; you would not perhaps go quite so far as that?—No, I would not go so far as that; it is not for me to indicate certain speakers whose every utterance is read with interest; but verbatim speeches relating to the ordinary business of Parliament would be a perfect nuisance.

2257. Sir Alexander Gordon.] May I ask you what is the particular point that you came before the Committee to press; I do not quite gather what it is?—I came before the Committee to press for a better report than we at present can obtain under the circumstances in which the Association which represents me is placed.

2258. In fact a better seat in the Gallery than you now have?—Yes, two seats, in fact, I should suggest.

2259. Better accommodation is what you desire?—Yes; accommodation equal to that now enjoyed by the ordinary London papers.

2260. You have laid before us a copy of the "Birmingham Daily Post" of this day as a specimen, as I understand you, of the excellent manner in which the debates are reported there, in superiority even to the London newspapers? —No; I think you misapprehend me. I was asked if we experience much delay in the transmission by the Press Association of the proceedings in Parliament,

Mr. J. Jaffray.

12 July 1878.

Parliament, and as an illustration of the speed with which they do their work, I produced this paper containing the finish of the debate, whereas the London paper had it not.

2261. But may I ask whether it is a fair comparison to put the report of a 10 hours' debate, which occupies little more than half a column in your newspaper, in comparison with the London newspapers which give the full speeches?—The London paper to which I refer does not give full speeches; it gives a report as brief in reference to the later proceedings of Parliament as we give.

2262. Do you consider the report which you published of last night's debate, such a report as the provincial public wish to have?—Yes, on the particular subject in debate.

2263. Therefore, a 10 hours' debate that you reported in little more than half a column of your newspaper is a sufficient amount of reporting, you think?—I think so; and for this reason, that the subject debated, however important, had been debated over and over again, and this debate was on a matter of procedure rather than of principle.

2264. You stated that at Birmingham you have great facilities for publishing reports of debates, owing to the telegraphic arrangements and the train arrangements between London and Birmingham?—No, not with regard to the debates. I stated that our proximity to London, and a good train service, enabled us to get everything from London that we wanted, excepting the Parliamentary debates, and that therefore it was not needful to set up a private wire, and incur all the expenses appertaining thereto, for the purposes of getting that.

2265. Mr. Hutchinson.] Is your ordinary Parliamentary report about a column and a half?—Yes, fully that; I should say the average is more.

2266. And when you want it, it is possible, I think, for you to get a Parliamentary report of any length you require?—Yes, we have had reports of 12 columns.

2267. And this ordinary Parliamentary report of a column and a half, coupled with the possibility of getting reports of any length that you require, are in your judgment sufficient means of political information to the large population among whom your paper circulates?—Yes, or I should adopt some other means of obtaining these reports.

2268. You are of opinion that the existing press agencies, with which you tell us you are connected, if provided with better accommodation in the Gallery, would be able to satisfy the requirements of the provincial press?—That is my experience.

2269. And I think you said that the ordinary summary of the length you mentioned satisfied many people; and I suppose that is the reason why some newspapers are provided with seats in the Gallery for the purpose of writing these summaries, because they are sufficient for ordinary men of business?—I think the summaries in the London papers are a very valuable feature, and I should not suggest that the London papers should be deprived of any facility for giving those summaries.

2270. I think you give it as your opinion that the proper test, the only fair and practicable test of admission to the Gallery should be the production of a *bond fide* Parliamentary report?—That is my view.

2271. That is to say, one peculiar to the newspaper applying for the place?—That is my opinion.

2272. Of course, that would be quite irrespective of its length?—Yes; quite irrespective of its length.

2273. And in your judgment, supposing that facilities were provided, there would be 16 or 17 such applications almost immediately?—That is my opinion.

2274. Does that include England, Ireland, and Scotland?—It does; it includes the whole, and although some of these 16 or 17 newspapers might not feel that such an outlay was necessary for their real wants, it would be a mark of inferiority if they did not have this accommodation, and were not able to say that they had the same accommodation as their fellows.

2275. As you say it would become a matter of prestige, and a point of honour to have a seat?—Yes, I think so.

2276. Colonel *Arbuthnot*.] You say that at present you are well served by the

the Press Association; we are told by those connected with Edinburgh and Leeds, that without any reflection upon the Press Association, they do not find that they can obtain either sufficiently lengthy reports, or sufficiently reliable, as regards time of arrival, to justify them in being content with that means of communication: do your attribute your difference of opinion to the situation of Birmingham, or to any peculiarity connected with Birmingham?—No.

2277. Then to what do you attribute the fact that that answers so very satisfactorily with you, which is not found to answer with them?—I must only speak of my own experience; and so far as I am concerned, and the district which we represent is concerned, we are satisfied, or all but satisfied, with the provision which they have made. I cannot say what is the reason that the others are not satisfied, excepting this, that there is a craving for a different report amongst newspapers to avoid the sameness which results from having one agency.

2278. Does the Press Association usually convey its news by the ordinary Post Office wires?—Yes.

2279. Could not several papers coalesce and have a joint staff capable of meeting the requirements of all of them?—That is done by the Press Association; it would just be a repetition of the same machinery.

2280. But do you think that a large co-operative association, such as the Press Association, works better than a small co-operative body, such as two or three papers, or four or five papers?—If well managed, the large associations should do it quite as well, if not better; because having a multiplicity of subscribers and funds they are enabled to extend their organisation, or the field of their operations, as much as opportunity allows.

2281. I asked the last witness what was the largest number that would work conveniently together; now I will put it in the other way to you, and ask, what is the smallest number of papers that could have a staff, and work beneficially?—Each individual paper could have a staff, and two could have a staff. I cannot see the practical drift of the question or answer, if I may be allowed to say so.

2282. Does not the Press Association give identical reports of the Parliamentary proceedings to all those papers?—Their ordinary reports are identical, with this difference, that they have three classes; they have the first class Parliamentary, that is an extended report; a second class for papers that do not go to the expense of the first; and a third, which consists of mere indications of what is going on, and without any details, so that to that extent the reports are different.

2283. Do you happen to know whether the "Birmingham Gazette" belongs to your association?—Yes.

2284. Do you publish the same identical reports of the Parliamentary proceedings on many subjects; are the words on ordinary subjects identical?—I am not sure whether at this particular time the paper you refer to has its report from the Press Association or the "Central News." It may be remiss on my part, but I have not compared them recently, and, therefore, I can scarcely answer the question, but they have the same facilities for expansion and selection as we have, and they exercise those facilities.

2285. And do you think there is any real objection to identity of report in such matters as the ordinary Imperial debates?—I do not.

2286. Mr. Dundas.] I think the manager of the Press Association gave us this list which I hold in my hand, and I see that Mr. Chamberlain is put down in that list as a Member whose speeches are to be supplied in full to the "Daily Post"?—That is so.

2287. Have you any difficulty in getting a special report of his speeches?—We have not; and he is a very rapid speaker who uses somewhat precise language, and I should almost know if there was an inaccuracy even in the manner of his expression; and I should say that they very accurately report him.

2288. Quite sufficiently for your purposes?—At full length as a rule.

2289. Do you consider that there is any desire on the part of some of the proprietors of local papers to outstrip their competitors, and to get a reputation for spending money in obtaining reports?—No doubt there is.

2290. There is a good deal of vanity about the matter?—They are not free from that failing.

2291. Mr.

2291. Mr. *Mitchell Henry*.] I understood you to say that if provincial papers are to be accommodated in the gallery, the test should be the giving of a *bona fide* report?—The *bona fide* use of the seat.

2292. And in answer to another question of an honourable Member, you used the phrase "peculiar report;" that is a report peculiar to the newspaper itself, I suppose?—I did not mean in any sense peculiar from others; if I said peculiar it was a wrong word; I should say an independent report; that was the meaning that I attached to the word if I did use it.

2293. But you also qualified that expression by the words "irrespective of its length"?—I did.

2294. That it should be either a peculiar or independent report, irrespective of its length?—Yes.

2295. In what way can a report of Parliamentary proceedings be *bona fide* or peculiar, if it has no regard to the length of the report?—I spoke of this last as a test to be applied by whoever had the control of those seats; and if a report is complete in itself, even if it is only a summary, that, in my judgment at any rate, would be a *bona fide* use of the seat.

2296. Supposing that a newspaper had a seat assigned to it in the gallery, and that it gave at great length the speeches of the Members representing the place in which it was published, and gave hardly any report at all of the speeches made by other Members who might speak in the course of the debate, would that be the kind of the report that you would think would entitle a newspaper to a place in the gallery?—Yes; and that is what is done every day by those who have the use of the seats; the London papers do so; they give, according to their judgment, preference to certain speakers and certain subjects, and they minimise their report with reference to others; so that those who had the use of those seats, and so used them, would be simply doing what is done already and recognised.

2297. I can understand that it would be an expensive thing to give such a report as is given in the London "Times," for instance, and that if it was required that a provincial paper, having a seat in the gallery, should give any kind of report approximating to that, it would greatly diminish the number of applicants; is not that so?—It would be impracticable almost, and unnecessary.

2298. Still between that and giving reports which would simply name the Members who took part in the debates, and give at length the reports of speeches of the Members particularly connected with the locality in which the newspaper was published, there is room for a very great difference in the quality of the reports?—No doubt. What I would answer to these observations is, that what is done now, say, by the Press Association, is a *bona fide* use of the place they have, and I apprehend that any one who applied for a seat, and used it in the same manner, would comply with the condition of giving a *bona fide* report.

2299. But you are satisfied, as I understand, with the report now supplied to you by the Press Association?—Yes, with this exception, that, as I have said, we find sometimes deficiencies in the report, and that those deficiencies are not greater is a matter of astonishment to me, because of the want of proper facilities for reporting.

2300. We have had it in evidence from a Scotch newspaper, the "Scotsman," and also from a Yorkshire paper in large circulation, that they are greatly dissatisfied with the reports supplied by the Press Association, because they are wholly inadequate to their requirements? That is not my experience; and I should say that these papers that have failed to get the reports have not applied for the reports that they want; that if the Press Association is not able to supply those reports, it being the servant and the machinery of the Members, should and can be made to supply those reports. The Press Association I may say is in the happy condition of having a large balance of profit for the last year; and not being able to distribute that in the way of dividend, as it is precluded by its articles of association from doing, it ought to apply it to the extension of its machinery in such a way as would satisfy the requirements of its members.

2301. We have been told by the managers of the "Leeds Mercury" that his newspaper expends upwards of 700 *l.* in actually getting peculiar reports for itself during the Session of Parliament, as well as 400 *l.* in special wires; do you apprehend

Mr. J. Jeffrey.

12 July 1878.

apprehend, when you say that you think there would be 15 or 16 papers applying for seats in the gallery, that each of those papers is prepared to go to anything like that expense for their Parliamentary reports?—I think so; it is on
that basis that I have made this calculation of the number likely to apply.

2302. Sir *Henry T. Holland.*" Then would you make it one of the conditions
for having a separate seat that there should be a separate wire?—No, certainly
not.

2303. That seems to me rather inconsistent with the last answer you gave;
because you say that there are 16 papers that would have separate wires?—No,
I did not quite say that. With the exception of ourselves in Birmingham, the
papers applying for these facilities must either have a separate wire or avail
themselves of the ordinary wires. There is no mechanical difficulty in transmitting the lengthened report which they might have through the agency of their
own reporters by the ordinary telegraphic wire.

2304. Then the condition would be that there should be a separate staff of
reporters, so as to secure a *bona fide* employment of the seat for reporting?—
Yes, I think that would be an absolute necessity.

2305. Now, every year the position of newspapers may alter; I suppose that
you would reserve a discretion in the Speaker from time to time to re-consider
the allotment of seats?—So long as the conditions of use were complied with, I
think that the holders of the seats must be undisturbed; but, as you say, great
changes take place in the position, financial and otherwise, of newspapers, and
no doubt the number would be subject to revision.

2306. I assume that the conditions are the same, but that they may not be
fulfilled in the course of years by some papers?—Yes, that is possible.

2307. And that therefore the Speaker should then re-consider and re-allot
the seats?—Certainly.

2308. Now you have spoken of the importance of summaries, in which,
I think, we all agree with you; but do you concur in the opinion which has
been expressed by several witnesses here, that the work of a summary might be
conveniently done from the back seats, though not so conveniently, of course,
as if it was done from the front seats?—I am not acquainted with the construction of the Reporters' Gallery, and therefore my opinion would be of very little
value on that point; but I do know that the reporter, who has to take a
verbatim note, must have greater facilities than he who simply takes a catch
note to seize the spirit of the debate.

Monday, 15th July 1876.

MEMBERS PRESENT:

Colonel Arbuthnot.
Mr. Barclay.
Mr. Cowen.
Mr. Dunbar.
Mr. William Edward Forster.
Sir Alexander Gordon.
Mr. Mitchell Henry.

Lord Francis Harvey.
Mr. Hutchinson.
Mr. Mills.
Dr. Lyon Playfair.
Mr. William Henry Smith.
Mr. Walter.

THE RIGHT HONOURABLE WILLIAM HENRY SMITH, IN THE CHAIR.

Mr. *Thomas Senior Townend*, called in; and Examined.

2309. *Chairman.*] I THINK you are the London manager of the " Manchester Guardian " ?—[am.

2310. You have occupied that position for some years, have you not ?—About 10 years.

2311. You attend here to urge that the provincial papers should be admitted to the gallery, I believe ?—Yes.

2312. Will you state to the Committee the grounds upon which you urge that claim ?—According to the present system of admission, the gallery arrangements are practically a monopoly for the London papers. That, it is true, is tempered in some degree by the admission of news associations; but the news associations do not meet the requirements of many of the leading provincial newspapers. The chief difficulty, I take it, in regard to the admission of the provincial papers, has arisen through the want of accommodation in the gallery; but it has now been stated to the Committee that that defect can be remedied, and, therefore, I think that the provincial press should now be admitted.

2313. It has been stated to the Committee that if the House is pleased to surrender a portion of the Members' Gallery on either side of the Reporters' Gallery, further accommodation could be provided; but the Committee have not had it in evidence that that accommodation would be sufficient for any newspaper which might claim it ?—I believe that the number of applicants for admission would be so very few that the difficulty on that point has been considerably exaggerated. I do not believe that more than ten or a dozen provincial papers would really seek for admission if it could be found.

2314. From the information which you possess, you believe that only ten or a dozen provincial newspapers would ask for admission to the gallery, the rest obtaining their supply through the news associations ?—Yes, I base that belief on the supposition that not more than 10 or 12 would care to go to the large expense which would be entailed in supplying a better report than is now supplied by the news associations.

2315. How is the " Manchester Guardian " now supplied with its Parliamentary report ?—It is supplied in part by one of the news associations, and in part by arrangements made with gentlemen in the gallery, on a somewhat similar plan to that which was explained, I believe, by the editor of the " Leeds Mercury," as having been adopted for his paper. We are supposed to have a special report of the entire debate, but we cannot always accomplish that; and when we cannot succeed in that object we supplement our service with news that is contributed by the Press Association.

2316. It was given in evidence by the proprietor of one of the newspapers supplied by the Press Association that the arrangements of that association are, in his judgment, sufficient for the supply of news to the provincial press;

Mr. T. A. Toward.   Mr. Jaffray, I think, gave that evidence?—Yes, I heard Mr. Jaffray's evidence,
15 July 1878.   and I should have been much surprised at it but for the knowledge that his
circumstances are very different from those of many other newspapers. The
"Birmingham Daily Post" goes to press at a much later hour than the
majority of the leading provincial papers; it has the advantage of having little
competition, and it would therefore be satisfied, I daresay, to take from a news
association a quality of report that would not satisfy papers where competition
is very keen, as it is in Scotland and in Ireland, and in the larger towns of the
north of England.

2317. But if the quality of the report, and the delay in the report, prevents
the "Manchester Guardian" from relying exclusively upon it, are there not
many more newspapers than the 10 or 12 which are exposed to competition,
and which, if facilities were afforded to provincial newspapers in the
gallery, would claim accommodation in the gallery?—I do not think so,
and for this reason: there are two classes of journals in the provincial
press; there are those that have a purely local circulation; there are others
which have not only a local or a district circulation, but a circulation
extending from the north to the south of the country. Those papers which
have a purely local circulation could well afford to submit to the loss of
time that is involved in the transmission of the reports supplied by news associations; those papers that have a circulation extending to more distant areas are
bound to go to press at such an early hour that they cannot afford to wait for
the delivery of the Press Association news. The news associations have to
rely (and this is one of the chief causes of their weakness) upon the Post
Office for the transmission of their reports. The leading provincial papers that
would be likely to ask for admission to the gallery would rely upon the use of
their special wires. I will give you a striking illustration of how the Manchester
papers suffer from the fact which I have mentioned. Whenever the House has
a morning sitting, the Manchester papers which reach London, that being their
chief edition, contain not a word of Parliamentary news, as a rule, after seven
o'clock at night. That is a condition that no enterprising newspaper would care
to continue. What I mean is this, that we just get up to the rising of the
House at seven o'clock, and we got nothing of the evening sitting. Of course
if there is a count out we may get the count; but if there is a prolonged
debate it is the rule rather than the exception, that we get nothing of the
evening sitting. That occurred only so recently as Friday last; and it has
occurred three or four times in the course of this month. That observation
applies only to those papers in Manchester which rely upon the associations.
I believe the other two papers rely upon them pretty exclusively; we do not;
and in a case like that the "Guardian" would appear with a report of an evening
sitting up to half-past eleven.

2318. You go to press at 1 o'clock, do you not?—Before 1. We cease taking
copy at a quarter to 12. We may run a division through the wires up to
possibly 12, or a minute or two past 12; but the rule of the office is that no
copy shall be sent to the printer after a quarter to 12 o'clock.

2319. The Committee is to understand that you believe that a newspaper
that would have the advantage of its contemporaries by three hours, because
that is the statement that has been made, that the "Manchester Guardian" is
able to give information up to a quarter to 12, and that the other newspapers
in Manchester receive news not later than 9 o'clock by the aid of the associations?—That is so in regard to this particular class of news.

2320. You are of opinion that the "Manchester Guardian" will continue to
be the only newspaper in Manchester which would have a special arrangement
for the supply of news?—I cannot answer for what the other papers might do.
I daresay that if facilities were given for admission to the gallery they would
seek to enjoy them.

2321. Does not that point to a much greater extension of the facilities than
that which you have suggested yourself, 10 or 12 newspapers?—No, I do
not think it will be so, because, in the case of some of the newspapers, they
would be satisfied to take a joint report; one or two papers might join, and,
in that case, the officials of the House would not be asked to provide more than,
perhaps, one box for two papers; or it might, in some rare cases, be for three
papers. The expense would be a serious difficulty with many of them.

2322. Have you any suggestions to make as to the accommodation itself in
the

Mr. J. S. Townend

15 July 1878.

the gallery; I think you have been in the gallery a great deal, have you not?—I have not the *entrée* to the gallery, but I nevertheless know the gallery very well; and I have had conversations with men who are in the gallery daily, and the suggestion that I have thought of, as being the most practicable, would be the extension of the gallery round each side as far as the side doors, as I believe has been already laid before the Committee, and the raising of the back seats in the present gallery. It has been urged that the summary writers might be removed from the front seats and put in the back seats, or probably put in the side seats if the gallery were extended; but two or three of the London papers give such genuine summaries that a consideration of that kind should be approached rather delicately. The "Times," for instance, has so excellent a summary, that whatever accommodation may be wanted for a work of that kind should be provided, I think, if it can possibly be found.

2323. How would you distinguish between newspapers which applied for the advantage of a seat in the gallery; have you any proposal to make of that kind?—I think it has been suggested that there should be a special privilege for the Scotch and the Irish newspapers, by reason of their distance, or by reason of some special questions that relate to those parts of the kingdom; that the Scotch and the Irish papers should be allowed either a box or boxes. I must say that I do not quite see the wisdom of that suggestion, except in the interest of those who make it. There is no reason for saying that the Scotch papers or the Irish papers have any special claim to special privileges. Besides, if that suggestion were adopted by the Committee, it would be a great injustice to many of the English papers which already circulate in Scotland and in Ireland. For instance, if the English papers were excluded because an arbitrary rule was laid down for the admission of Scotch papers, those English papers (and there are several in the North of England) which circulate largely in Scotland would suffer a decided disadvantage. The Newcastle papers, the Manchester papers, and the Leeds papers, circulate largely in Scotland. A rule like that would be very detrimental therefore to English papers so circumstanced.

2324. But are you prepared to leave the selection absolutely to the officers of the House, or are you prepared to suggest any conditions under which the newspapers should be entitled to have this privilege?—I think whoever makes the selection, whether it be a Committee of the House, or the officials (the officials would, doubtless, be entrusted with it), should be influenced in the first instance by the consideration as to which papers had special wires and London offices; and, in fact, no provincial paper could very well avail itself of the advantage unless it had one or more special wires. The loss of time in transmitting news over the Post Office wires is, as I have already explained, a weak point of the present news associations, and, in order to remedy that, it is necessary that the provincial papers should employ one or two, or in some cases I dare say three, wires for the transmission of the Parliamentary news. I would admit none that had not a special wire. Then if it were necessary to continue the selection, the number of applicants still being larger than the gallery would accommodate, I would give the preference to those papers which had two or more wires. I cannot quite say that the Committee ought to make a bargain with provincial papers because they are customers of the Government, by hiring two or more wires; but the fact of their having two or more wires is a proof that they would be likely to use this privilege more than a paper that has only one; and in dealing with the papers that had single wires it might be a rough test, but not an unfair one, to give the advantage to those which had held the single wires the longest time; they are the papers of the greatest enterprise, and it is only the more enterprising papers that would be likely to make the most of the facilities that the House would give.

2325. Are you prepared to add to that condition that the report of the newspaper should be evidently a good report?—It must be a genuine, and a special report, undoubtedly; and in order to secure that end one Member of the Committee has suggested to cross-examination that no papers should be permitted to use this privilege which would not promise to employ a certain number for its staff of reporters. I think that rule would not be an unfair one. My object is to give the privilege to those papers that will make a genuine use of it.

2326. Evidence has been given before the Committee that an official report could be very rapidly prepared indeed, so rapidly that a speech could be printed within

within a very few minutes after the speaker had done speaking; would such a report be of use to the provincial press?—I very greatly doubt it; partly from the fact which I think I have already brought out, that many of the provincial papers go to press at an exceedingly early hour; and partly also from the general consideration, that no papers of substantial position care to publish the same report that appears in other journals, which is one objection that many provincial papers already have against the news agencies. Their report is supplied all round, and it suits very well the purposes of smaller journals. If you were to apply the same rule to the London papers, I think you would at once see the weakness of it. The "Times," for instance, would not care to publish the same report that appears in the "Morning Advertiser" or the "Daily Telegraph."

2327. Then one principal objection would be the delay?—That is a strong objection.

2328. And another objection would be the fact that the reports would be identical if they were published in the newspapers as they were sent by the news agencies?—Yes; and on that head I may observe that, of course, the conductors of newspapers do not desire to be tied down to publish exactly what other papers publish, any more than they would in any other department of the newspapers. Another point, I should add, would be that by the admission of our own reporting staff we should be able to adapt the report to the requirements of each particular day. To a large extent that can now be done by the news associations; but conductors of newspapers have always experienced this difficulty, they never know till probably the middle of the day before publication what demands are likely to be made on their space for the ensuing day. If they have the control of their own reporting staff they can so summarise the report that although it may happen to be shorter on any particular day, nevertheless it preserves a uniform quality.

2329. And it would not be possible to summarise the report from the extended report that was handed to you; is that what you intend to convey? —The element of time there again comes in. The Parliamentary reports already arrive at a very late hour, and it is exceedingly difficult to make condensation from what is called flimsy copy. A provincial sub-editor must have enormous difficulty under the present system, having reports from special wires which are laid into his own office through one door; the Press Association and the Central News, or whatever service supplies him, contributing its quota, perhaps, through another door, and the newspaper parcels arriving by train, there is very little time to discharge duties like those in an efficient manner; and the object, therefore, is to give the sub-editor precisely what he wants, and no more than he wants.

2330. With your experience, do you believe that it would be possible for that service to be conducted by an official report?—I do not.

2331. Do you believe it to be impossible for the agent of the country newspaper to summarise the extended matter in London with a view to transmission into the country, or for the editor of the newspaper in the country, when he receives the extended report, to summarise it himself before the paper goes to press?—It would certainly not be possible for the sub-editor to summarise it at the other end, and if it were done at this end it would require an enormous staff to condense it. Much, I should say, would depend on the hour at which the official report was issued. If Parliament rose as early as the French Chambers there might possibly then be some chance of carrying that scheme out; but Parliament sitting to the late hour it does, I regard it as utterly impracticable.

2332. Mr. *Mills*.] In reference to the accommodation in the Reporters' Gallery of the House of Commons, you alluded to the effect of raising the back seats, which, I think, you said you thought would be a useful thing to do?— I do not know of my own knowledge, but I have been at some trouble to ask probably a dozen, or possibly more, reporters who use the gallery, and they tell me that it would be a very great advantage indeed to have the back seats raised; some even go to the extent of saying that if the back seats were raised the chances of hearing would be as good as in the side galleries, supposing the House determined to extend the Reporters' Gallery round the sides.

2333. Then at all events, judging from some of the opinions you have heard expressed by qualified persons, you would, if I understand you, go the length of of saying that for the use of reporters, the back seats, if raised, might be made available; would you go so far as that?—I should hesitate about using the word "reporters"; there are those who have business in the gallery, and who have to write there, in addition to reporters; there are summary writers and leader writers, and in their case where it is not absolutely necessary to take a dead note, as is sometimes necessary with the reporters, the accommodation in the back seat, supposing it were raised, would be a very great advantage. As a matter of fact, the news associations now have to take some of their reports from the back again; and I dare say that that circumstance will account for some of the deficiencies of their reports.

2334. If you had always a good and complete summary, perhaps rather fuller than that which is contained now in the "Times," would that summary, do you think, generally satisfy your clients and customers in Manchester?—No, it would be too short; occasionally we have to give five or six columns of a debate.

2335. Do you adopt the same plan which is adopted by other provincial papers, of getting full reports of the speeches of your own local Members?— Yes; those are obtained in two ways, partly through the associations, and if we can secure them by our own special arrangements we do so, naturally preferring our own report to that of an association, because the association sends a report of the same speech to our contemporaries.

2336. You agree with the gentlemen who represented the "Leeds Mercury," and with those who represented other provincial papers, when they gave evidence to the effect that identical reports published in the same district in different newspapers would be prejudicial to the circulation of the newspapers concerned; that is, that if, for instance, there were published in some other newspaper exactly the same report as that published in the "Manchester Guardian," it would damage your circulation?—I do not know that it would be prejudicial to the extent of damaging the circulation. If newspapers are to join in identical reports, they would prefer to join with papers that are published in some distant part of the country, I should take it, but the more influential and the more wealthy provincial papers would not join at all, I think, if they could possibly get the accommodation without joining.

2337. If that joining or clubbing together by newspapers in distant parts of the country could be accomplished, you do not, as I understand, think it would be open to the objection that it is now open to if attempted in the same district; suppose, for instance, that a newspaper in Dorsetshire arranged with a Manchester paper, and also with three or four others in distant parts of the country, then do you think it would be open to the same objection as it would be open to if there were two or three newspapers in Manchester and its immediate neighbourhood clubbing together to get reports which were identical?—The objection would be less no doubt in working with a distant paper than to working with a local contemporary; but I think that every newspaper that could possibly do so would avoid joint arrangements.

2338. Supposing the stipulation were made which you have suggested, namely, that on paper should have a representative in the gallery which had not a special wire, do you think that would reduce the applications to the number you have mentioned, 10 or 12?—I do; and in fact I believe that in the case of most of the applicants it would not be one but more wires that would be wanted, a circumstance that would further reduce the number. Papers going to press at an early hour must hurry the copy through quickly; a telegraph wire cannot take more than a column in an hour and a half; therefore, if they desire a long report, they must be prepared for it by making special arrangements; and the Post Office is very little use to those papers which go to press at an early hour unless the copy be handed in by half-past eight or nine o'clock.

2339. Perhaps you might be able to say what the cost, taking an average of years, of a special wire is to newspapers?—It is laid down by the Act of Parliament; each wire is 500 *l.* a year, but there are incidental expenses, which make an enormous difference.

2340. That was what I meant; I did not know whether you could say at all, taking an average of years, what the incidental expenses, added to what I may call the statutory cost, would be?—It would depend upon the enterprise of the paper. When a provincial paper opens a London office, and starts a special wire or more special wires, it is tempted to embark in other enterprises than just the reporting of the proceedings of Parliament; for instance, the transmis-

... sion of leaders, the collection of general or imperial news; in fact the expense may almost be regarded as limitless.

2341. In short, the expense would be so considerable that it would operate so as considerably to reduce the number of applicants for admission to the gallery you think?—I do. Something was said upon the question of expense by Mr. Reid, of the "Leeds Mercury," on Friday night last. I may say that his figures are rather a low estimate.

2342. Mr. *Walter.*] You stated, did you not, that your first edition goes to press at one in the morning?—A little before one.

2343. What is the object of going to press so early?—Because the circulation of the Manchester papers is in remote areas; it is not a local circulation either in Lancashire or Cheshire, but it extends as far north as Glasgow, Edinburgh, all the way down the Lake district, down the North Western line, also to Bristol, London, and Dublin; and we are so situated with regard to the railway service, that we must catch particular trains as they pass through Lancashire, the Scotch express going downwards, and the London express coming from Scotland, which I think happen to pass very nearly together at the same point.

2344. What time do you go to press with your second edition?—We have a lift at half-past one.

2345. I mean for the Manchester and Liverpool circulation?—We can take copy for our first edition up to 11.46: at that hour we stop taking copy. At 1.30 we stop taking copy for what we call the first lift. Then, I think, the next lift is somewhere between three and four o'clock in the morning.

2346. Is that the edition which chiefly supplies the local circulation?—Yes.

2347. And how late can you get Parliamentary news from London in order to meet that edition?—Not later, I think, than about four in the morning.

2348. Do I rightly understand you to say that you can get news from London as late as four o'clock in the morning, including the Parliamentary debates, for the supply of your local edition?—I believe that is so.

2349. Sir *Alexander Gordon.*] What o'clock does the "Manchester Guardian" reach Edinburgh and Glasgow?—I am afraid I cannot speak to that very distinctly, for my business is in London; but I think about eight o'clock in the morning.

2350. And with regard to Dublin, what time does it get there?—I cannot answer that; I know they go about the same time.

2351. I understood you to say that the arrangement is to catch the Scotch and the Irish express?—Scotch and English, and the Irish too; they are all about the same time.

2352. Those copies of the "Manchester Guardian" that go off to Scotland and to Dublin by those express trains could not have Parliamentary news up to a late hour?—No; so I have explained, if we relied exclusively on the press associations we could not have a Parliamentary report when there is a morning sitting, after the seven o'clock rising. When the House meets at four and sits through, we should then possibly get the debate up to about half-past nine o'clock, or on special occasions perhaps 10.

2353. But if you have to go to press so early for the Scotch and Irish mail, even with a wire of your own, you cannot give Parliamentary news up to a late hour?—We can only give it up to about 20 minutes to 12.

2354. Therefore your readers in Scotland and Ireland must depend upon other sources for the Parliamentary information?—Yes, or take it next day from our own paper.

2355. Have you any information about the Central Press Association?—No.

2356. Do you employ them?—No.

2357. Colonel *Arbuthnot.*] Would you be satisfied with one seat in the gallery, supposing arrangements to be made by which you could have one seat?—Yes, quite content.

2358. Mr. *Barclay.*] Would you be prepared to accept, as a condition of getting a seat in the gallery, that on the average you would bind yourselves to devote a certain space of your newspaper to Parliamentary reporting, taking an average of the whole Session?—I am afraid that is a question which I could not

not answer; and I should like to point out that it would be a very unusual and
a very hard condition for Parliament to suggest how much space a newspaper
should give to those reports.

Mr. T. S. Townsend.

13 July 1878.

2359. Would you accept it as a test of service to the House of Commons, in
exchange for a seat in the gallery, that you should keep a full staff of reporters
to occupy that seat?—It would depend upon what you considered a full staff.
Three or four reporters would be a pretty good staff for a provincial
paper; some papers require 10 or 12 reporters. As a matter of fact we once
had the *entrée* to the gallery, and on that occasion I think we had four or five
reporters.

2360. You propose that the test should only be a special wire or wires in
order to get a seat in the gallery?—That should not be the exclusive test. If
the number of applicants who had one wire exceeded the accommodation in the
gallery, then other tests should be applied. I suggested that provincial papers
employing two or more wires should have a preference in the choice; and then
if the number was still too great, you might adopt some rough test such as
this, giving the box to that paper which has had the wire the longest time;
that would be a proof that that paper at any rate had been longer in the field
in search of Imperial news.

2361. But seeing that the object of having a seat in the gallery is to report
the proceedings of Parliament, would not the essential test be the amount of
space devoted by the newspaper, extending over the Session, to the reporting
of Parliamentary proceedings?—I am not prepared to say that that would be
the best test. Much would depend upon the size of the paper and the amount
of space that it could devote to such a subject. For instance, some provincial
papers give shorter reports because they have not the same space for Parliamentary news that younger papers have. I remember a Scotch paper which
was recently started, which made an enormous feature of its Parliamentary
reports; I should not like to say that paper was in any respect whatever a
better paper than the "Scotsman," which happened to give a few columns
shorter, because the demands upon its space in respect to other news were
greater than those upon the new paper.

2362. Speaking for the newspaper which you represent, would you be prepared to undertake to devote a minimum amount of space, extending over a
Session, to the reporting of Parliamentary proceedings?—I am afraid that
I am not in a position to give the undertaking; that would be a matter for the
editor; but I have little doubt it would meet with his views.

2363. Supposing that there were two newspapers having one wire each, and
we had to choose between the two, would you see any objection to the House
of Commons choosing the newspaper which devoted the most space to reporting
the Parliamentary proceedings?—I do not think that that rule ought to be
applied in all cases. I have suggested a case where it certainly should not
apply. There is one provincial paper that has two special wires; I believe
those two wires are hired for a particular purpose, not for Parliamentary
reporting, and it is merely a local paper of very little influence. Were your
rule to be applied, you would give that paper an enormous advantage even over
any Scotch or Irish paper, because it could throw open the entire of its columns
to a Parliamentary report.

2364. Dr. *Lyon Playfair*.] I think you clearly see that the question is not
whether room should be found for the 134 provincial newspapers, but whether
room could be found for the limited number of newspapers that are willing to
take conditions, however high, for efficient Parliamentary reporting?—That
is so.

2365. And if those conditions were laid down with sufficient severity to
obtain an actually good report, you think only a limited number of newspapers
would comply with them?—Decidedly, that is my opinion.

2366. Do you think that ten or twelve newspapers, appearing in different
parts of the country, would adopt a good system of Parliamentary reporting?—
Yes, bearing in mind the papers which I suppose would make the application.
I know the character of the papers, and I am sure they would use a privilege
like that to the best advantage.

2367. The ten or twelve papers that you speak of are not confined to
any one part of the kingdom, but are distributed all over the kingdom?—Yes.

2368. *Mr. Dunbar.*] Would the other papers in Manchester require accommodation in the gallery?—I am afraid I cannot answer that question; I do not know what they might require; it is very possible that one, perhaps two, would.

2369. Do you think that with the Scotch and Irish papers the number would only be a dozen that would require accommodation in the gallery?—I still think that the number would not be more than a dozen.

2370. *Mr. Cawes.*] The practice of the House with respect to the admission of reporters is, that the London papers are to have the preference, and to be represented directly, and the provincial papers indirectly: they have followed that practice, not because they object to provincial papers having reporters in the gallery, but because their space compelled them to follow it; you would extend that by giving admission to the gallery to papers that have London offices and special wires?—Yes. I should consider it no more arbitrary to lay down a rule for the admission of provincial papers than the present rule in regard to London papers. If five London papers were to be started to-morrow they could not get access to the gallery, and the limit of admission would stop at the number of seats that could be spared. I cannot see that it would be any greater hardship to lay down a rule for the provincial papers, to this effect: "We will admit 12 or 15, and any paper desiring admission after that number has been exhausted, must wait its turn just as any new London paper would now have to wait its turn."

2371. But as a matter of fact all the London newspapers have been accommodated?—Yes.

2372. How would you provide for any additional demand for provincial papers, should it arise?—Do you mean in case the metropolitan papers increase also.

2373. Yes?—I think the character of the metropolitan papers should be considered just as it would be in the case of the provincial newspaper.

2374. That is the point I wished to get out; you would admit the representatives of papers that had London offices and special wires, but you would stipulate as a condition that these papers should give special reports. reports at a special length, or should have a certain number of reporters representing them?—Yes, certainly.

2375. Do not you think that the newspapers would consider that an interference with their editorial or commercial management?—To a certain extent it would be so; but there must be some restriction; you must apply some hard-and-fast rule, and the point is to make the rule as gentle as possible.

2376. Then if you specified that the provincial papers should report at a certain length, or should maintain a certain number of reporters, would you apply the same rule to the London papers?—I am not particularly in favour of applying either of these rules; but if, as has been suggested by one of the Members of the Committee, the rules are laid down by the officials of the House, we must accept them.

2377. If you apply that rule to the London daily papers, some of the present daily papers that have admission to the gallery give very limited reports, do they not?—Yes; and that is a very strong argument, I think, in favour of the admission of provincial newspapers that are prepared to show their enterprise.

2378. The point I wish to convey is this, that it is quite possible for the officers of the House to act upon the principle of the London papers, being represented directly, and the provincial papers indirectly, through the press agencies; but if you ever called upon the officers of the House to pick and choose you would call upon them to make a selection which would be extremely invidious; do not you think so?—To some extent undoubtedly that is so.

2379. It has been suggested that the Scotch papers should have a special box in the gallery, and that the Irish papers also, because those countries have special questions; do you see any objection to that?—I think they would see an objection to it. All the Scotch papers would not care to join in one report; and I do not see the necessity of having a special Scotch staff; we do not require reporters from Scotland to teach us to grapple with the mysteries of hypothec.

2380. But there are only some three or four debates in a Session that are specially interesting to Scotch readers?—That is so.

2381. There

2381. There are occasions when a debate is specially interesting to the Lancashire readers, and when the Lancashire papers would like special reports of them, are there not?—Yes; I think there is no substantial ground for an application of that nature from Scotland.

2382. Your opinion is, that the proposition to assign a box to the Scotch papers, and another to the Irish ones, would not be satisfactory to the English provincial papers?—And further, that it would not be satisfactory to the Scotch or Irish papers themselves, on the ground that they would object to joint reports.

2383. Your opinion is, that there are only about 10 papers that have special wires that would be likely to apply to be represented?—Ten or twelve; more probably 12.

2384. Supposing an increase were to take place, how would you deal with that?—In the same way as if there were an increase in the London papers; they must wait and take their chance of an empty box.

2385. You have been asked a question about summary writers; do you think there would be any objection to the summary writers being sent to the back seats or to other parts of the House?—No, but I think that the claims of those summary writers who wrote a genuine summary should be fairly considered. For instance, there are three London papers at least that give a really genuine summary, and for which good accommodation should certainly be provided; in the case of the other London morning papers, I think they might very well be accommodated in the back seats, or in the front of the new side galleries.

2386. You would assume, therefore, that a paper like the "Times," that gives a very ample summary, should have special accommodation, and that those which do not give such an ample summary should not have the same accommodation?—I think so. The "Times" gives an excellent summary; the "Morning Post," the "Standard," and the "Morning Advertiser" give genuine good summaries.

2387. Do not you think that, considering the enterprise that has characterised the provincial press of late years, if you admitted 10 papers into the House of Commons to report the proceedings, the very fact of their being admitted would create a demand amongst other papers, and they would wish for the same privilege?—I daresay that might happen in course of time; but the provincial papers that have already hired special wires have already shown that they are prepared to embark in enterprise of this nature, and I do not think that the number of applicants for special wires has been very great of late.

2388. You do not think that they would increase?—I do not think that they would largely increase.

2389. As far as your knowledge goes at the present time, about 10 or 12 would probably be the number of applicants, and these 10 or 12 might possibly be further reduced by combination?—I think so; and I think that the admission of these 10 or 12 papers might lead to an extension of the Parliamentary reports in the papers that applied for the privilege.

2390. Chairman.] I am requested to ask you this question: are you of opinion that the desire for Parliamentary reports is increasing in the provinces?—Yes, I think it is.

2391. Not only for summaries, but for extended and fuller reports?—My answer related more particularly to extended reports.

2392. You think that there is an increasing desire for Parliamentary reports in the provinces?—I think so.

2393. I am also requested to ask you this question, whether the fact that there is special legislation for Scotland and for Ireland does not constitute an essential difference between Lancashire and Scotland and Ireland?—I confess I do not see that. The only ground, I think, upon which an Irish or a Scotch paper could have its claim according to that principle would be, that the character of the subjects dealt with by the House was above the intelligence of the reporters who usually frequent the House. We have no end of Scotch and Irish reporters there, and they are quite equal to dealing with special questions.

2394. The reporters themselves may be able to deal with special questions, but the question arises whether a special report of subjects not ordinarily reported for English newspapers is not required for newspapers circulating in Scotland and Ireland?—If a Scotch paper had admission to the gallery, it would

Mr. T. S. Townsend.
14 July 1878.

give a longer report to those special questions, no doubt. If an English paper had admission to the gallery, and it had a local question to deal with, in that case also it would give that local question at greater length. I do not see any difference between the two cases.

2395. I suppose you are not able to point to any legislation which affects Lancashire exclusively which is not of general interest throughout England, and which would not be reported in the London newspapers, are you?—Yes ; factory legislation certainly is a very special subject to us.

2396. A special subject which interests, does it not, a very large population throughout the whole country; factory legislation affects Glasgow as well as Manchester, and Bristol as well as Glasgow?—It affects in a less degree each of those places, because the population of Lancashire is employed more in factory work ; and I may say, of Yorkshire as well.

2397. There is a large factory population in parts of the east of London, is there not?—Yes, but relatively it is a small one compared to Lancashire.

2398. And shipping questions are interesting to a large number throughout the country?—I think if these questions of special legislation are to be considered, papers which have to attend to shipping intelligence might set up a claim, and you would have no end of special questions.

2399. Mr. Barclay.] The point I wish to put to you is this; that there is special legislation for Scotland affecting Scotland alone, and for Ireland affecting Ireland alone, and which is not of such general importance to be reported in the London newspapers which have reporters in the gallery, and I wish to ask whether that does not constitute an essential difference between Scotland and Ireland and Lancashire; inasmuch as the reports in regard to legislation affecting Lancashire, probably, and, indeed, undoubtedly, would be reported at fair and proper length in the London newspapers?—The special questions arising out of special legislation would constitute no stronger claim to Scotland or to Ireland than would special questions arising out of local interests or trade interests to any particular paper in any part of England; on the contrary, there are many questions that the Scotch papers would not touch at all that are dealt with by the English papers.

Mr. Edmund Dwyer Gray (a Member of the House), Examined.

Mr. E. D. Gray,
M.P.

2400. Chairman.] You are one of the proprietors, or the proprietor, of a Dublin newspaper?—Yes, the "Freeman's Journal."

2401. Is the "Freeman's Journal" in the habit of reporting the proceedings of Parliament at length?—At very considerable length; I have had a summary made out for the month of June, and I find that in the "Freeman's Journal" there were 69¼ columns during the month. I have compared that with some of the London papers, and I find that in the "Daily News" during the same period there were 41 columns, and in the "Daily Telegraph" 80¼ columns. The average of the "Freeman's Journal" was low that month; the previous month it was 83 columns. There might be a slight difference in the columns; possibly 10 per cent. to the advantage of the London papers; I should think there would be.

2402. Ten per cent. more matter you mean?—Ten per cent. more matter probably.

2403. Is this a special report of your own, or is the report obtained through the medium of the Press Associations?—The two combined; the greater portion of it would be special Irish matter. The Press Association reports a considerable amount, but two-thirds of that are probably cancelled in the Dublin office as not being suitable for the requirements of an Irish paper.

2404. So that you cancel a considerable portion of the report which you receive through the Press Association, and you substitute for the matter so cancelled your own special report?—Quite so; the Press Association, of course, is not in a position to report special Irish matters at any length; and these are the matters which we require to have reported at length.

2405. But the Committee have had it in evidence that the Press Association acts upon the directions given by individual proprietors?—No doubt; and some of the special reports of which I speak would be supplied at the special order of the

the "Freeman" by the Press Association. I referred to the ordinary report of the Press Association. Other parts of the special report, as I think you have already got it in evidence, would be prepared by the reporters of other papers, who do special work for the "Freeman."

2406. Has the system of reporting changed within the last few years?—It has been revolutionised by the introduction of the telegraph. In olden times the provincial papers and the Irish papers would take all their reports cut from the London papers; now they require to compete with them, and to publish simultaneously with them.

2407. May I ask if that change has taken place since the transfer of the telegraphs to the State, or did it exist before the transfer?—It existed before, but to a comparatively very small extent; the old telegraph companies supplied a telegraphic summary to all the papers in the United Kingdom, which averaged about three-quarters of a column, I think; and then the Irish papers scarcely reported anything by telegraph themselves; occasionally they would a little, but practically the change has taken place either within a very short time previous to the introduction of the Government telegraph system, or since it.

2408. Is the present system satisfactory?—It is most unsatisfactory; the "Freeman's Journal" has constant complaints from the Irish Members. Our instructions to our representative are to spare no expense in the supplying of such reports as he can procure, as good as he can get them, but it is obviously impossible to supply good reports at the present, do what we will, and the Irish Members (the "Freeman" represents politically a majority of them) constantly complain of the inefficiency of the reporting in the "Freeman's Journal," although the "Freeman's Journal" reports at greater length than any other Irish paper; but it is impossible to give good reports under the present system.

2409. That is to say, either through the agency of the Press Association or by the reports which you obtain from reporters acting for other London papers in the gallery?—Quite so; we do the best we can, but to give a really good report is impossible. A Member who speaks very early in the evening may be fairly reported, the others cannot be. There is no dependence to be placed on the report; sometimes it may be done by a thoroughly competent reporter, and fairly and promptly done; at another time there may be a delay of one, two, or three hours before the report is delivered to us, and it may be done by an incompetent reporter.

2410. So that your complaint is both as to time and as to quality?—Yes. I may point out that the Irish papers suffer exceedingly with regard to the quality, because the reporters do not understand Irish subjects as well as they do English subjects; they are not accustomed to deal with them in the same way. A report may be done at considerable length, and still may be a very bad report; and a report may be done shortly, and be a very good one.

2411. Are you able to urge any special responsibility or necessity for reports for the Irish press?—If you take an Irish paper like the "Freeman's Journal," which circulates throughout the entire country; it represents politically a very large section, a considerable section of the Members of the House, say 60 or 70 Members, and it is looked to in Ireland to give full reports. The Irish Members at present labour under very grave disadvantages, because the English papers practically do not report them at all, and the Irish papers under the present system are unable to do them justice; they are placed in such a position that they cannot report them satisfactorily.

2412. The last witness was unable to see any special reason for the admission of either Irish or Scotch reporters into the gallery, on the ground urged by the honourable Member for Forfarshire; do you concur with the last witness; I presume you do not?—No; I think it is very evident that there is considerable difference. Irish questions of primary importance are constantly discussed in the House; matters are discussed which are said by opponents to be of an almost revolutionary tendency; they are of such importance; they are of great interest to the Irish people, and they naturally desire to see the views of their representatives on such questions of great importance, Home Rule, the Land question, the Education question, Grand Jury Reform, and similar matters, reported at length. No such vital questions ever arise with reference to any particular locality in England.

2413. So that you would urge that the political position of Ireland is such as

Mr. E. D. Gray,
M.P.
15 July 1878.

to make a report of the deliberations and the debates of Parliament of great importance in Ireland?—A number of Irish Members have complained to me that their speeches in the House are practically of little use, because they cannot be reported efficiently in Ireland; and they throw the responsibility upon me until I am able to show them that it is really impossible for us to do more than we do under the present system.

2414. We have had evidence that the Press Association is perfectly ready to give any report which any newspaper can require; is there any reason why it should not supply the want which you describe?—The Press Association, no doubt, does the very best it can, and it is perfectly ready to undertake to give any reports that any newspaper requires; as a matter of fact, however, it very often fails to give them.

2415. Is that saying more than that we very often fail in what we ought to do, or try to do?—They do not do it at all efficiently. I will give you the latest sample that occurs to my mind, the Sunday-closing debate the other night; we ordered a report from the Press Association of the Irish speeches; the English speeches on the subject were only of secondary interest to Irish readers; they did supply us with a report, but it consisted principally of the English speakers: if they were doing reports simultaneously for the English provincial papers, they naturally for them would report the English speakers.

2416. It comes to this, that you want a special report; is that the case?—We want a special report.

2417. You are not satisfied with a report which will suit the wants of, and is admirably suited for, the great majority of the customers of the parties of the association; you must have one for yourselves?—We must have one for ourselves to have it done effectively.

2418. To meet the wants of your readers?—To meet the wants of our readers, and of the Irish Members.

2419. Have you many complaints of the present system; you have spoken of Members who have complained, but are you aware of any complaint on the part of the public?—The public are not in a position to judge whether the reports are well done or not; they have nothing to compare them with, because, as I have said, the English papers do not give the Irish debates as we want them given.

2420. The English newspapers do not give the reports that you require?—They do not.

2421. Have you represented at any time the necessity for better reports, and special reports to the Speaker?—We have frequently applied to the Serjeant at Arms, and we did address a special letter to the Speaker in April last; perhaps I might be permitted to give it in, as it really represents our position.

2422. Are the Committee to understand that that is a letter written by yourself, as proprietor of the "Freeman," or representative of the "Freeman" newspaper, or is it a collective letter representing the Irish papers?—No, it is a letter written by the manager of the "Freeman"; I did not care to write it personally, being a Member of the House.

2423. Does that letter state anything which you have not stated to us to-day?—I do not know that it does.

2424. Would you wish yourself to read it?—I do not wish unnecessarily to take up the time of the Committee. I may mention that the Speaker replied, saying, that the question was under the consideration of a Committee, and that therefore he did not desire to take any action on it. The letter which the manager of the "Freeman" wrote was as follows: "Freeman's Journal Office, Dublin, 19th April 1878. To the Right Honourable the Speaker, House of Commons, London. Sir,—We perceive, by paragraphs in various newspapers, that it is your intention to reconsider the present arrangements for the accommodation of newspapers in the House of Commons; and it is also stated that it is contemplated to afford accommodation for the representatives of the Irish and Scotch newspapers. We beg therefore respectfully to repeat the application which the proprietor of this paper, Mr. E. Dwyer Gray, made two years ago to the Serjeant at Arms, for accommodation in the Reporters' Gallery for the 'Freeman's Journal'; and, in doing so, to bring under your notice our claims therefor. The 'Freeman's Journal' has the largest circulation in Ireland, and is recognised, without question, as being the organ of the party with which the majority of the Irish Members of the House are identified. Notwithstanding

Notwithstanding our utmost endeavours and sparing expense, it is absolutely impossible for us to give accurate reports of the debates in which the Irish Members take part, owing to our not having any representatives in the Reporters' Gallery. We are constantly receiving complaints of inaccuracies and imperfections, which it is quite beyond our power to remedy unless the present arrangement be modified. We publish all our reports by telegraph, and thus require extreme promptitude and accuracy, and particularly a knowledge by the reporters of the subject and the speakers. This latter quality it is impossible for us now to secure; we are compelled to depend upon the services of members of the staffs of other papers, when they are not at work for those papers. However competent they may be for the work for which they are specially engaged, they lack that intimate knowledge of Irish affairs and Irish Members which members of our own staff would possess, and without which proper reporting is an impossibility. When the 'Freeman's Journal' is placed in the position of not being able to give really accurate reports of Irish debates, the result is that there is no means by which the Irish people can obtain them, as the English papers do not circulate to any appreciable extent here, and, at all events, do not report Irish debates at any length. Should we be given accommodation in the House, we are prepared to use it for a special staff of our own for reporting Irish matters; and we respectfully submit that this is the only way in which satisfaction can be given to the Irish Members. The 'Freeman's Journal' is the only paper which devotes itself to reporting at length those Irish debates in which the majority of the people of this country take so deep an interest. Our reports of Imperial matters frequently exceed those of the London metropolitan papers, while in reports of merely Irish subjects we always exceed them. But on Irish subjects these reports can never be sufficiently accurate unless done by our own staff. I may state that I am informed that while the Irish metropolitan press is not given any accommodation in the gallery, the English metropolitan newspapers are given from two to three seats; and even such papers as the 'Globe' and the 'Pall Mall Gazette,' which go to press early in the evening, are given seats which, if I am correctly informed are, by a private arrangement, subsequently utilised by English provincial newspapers. The present arrangement amounts to this, that one or two provincial newspapers can, by arrangement with the evening papers I have mentioned, purchase seats in the gallery either by money or money's worth; and that a seat in the Reporters' Gallery becomes a valuable property owing to the monopoly enjoyed by its possessor to report at a very high tariff for those papers that are excluded. I respectfully submit that, however it is possible it may be to afford general accommodation to the press, owing to the limited room disposable for reporting purposes, such of the Irish metropolitan press as are ready and willing to incur the heavy expense necessary for the proper reporting of Irish matters should, if possible, be afforded facilities for that purpose. I have the honour to be, Sir, your most obedient servant, J. H. Verdon, Manager." The reply to that letter was as follows: "7th May 1878. Sir,—The Speaker desires me to acknowledge the receipt of your letter of the 19th ultimo, which shall receive his consideration. As, however, a Committee of the House is about to be appointed to consider the whole question of 'reporting,' he would prefer to postpone his reply to your application until the Committee has expressed its views on the subject. I am, Sir, your obedient servant, C. W. Campion."

2425. What is your view of the present arrangements with regard to the London press?—The present arrangements as regards the London press are most unfair; and even if the Committee decided on no other change I think that it would be well worth their while to revise the London press arrangements and to make them more stringent. There are many of the seats at present in the gallery which are nominally occupied for one purpose, and used for another. For instance, the "Globe" has a seat: now, as I am informed (it will be easy for the Committee to correct this evidence if it is inaccurate), that seat is used by the "Glasgow Herald" after six o'clock in the evening; that is to say, one provincial paper by a special arrangement of which the officers of the House have no cognisance, has a seat in the gallery for all practical purposes.

2426. I think Mr. Hansard gave evidence that the seat allotted to the "Globe" was occupied by his reporter after six o'clock?—I think not; I have taken great care to make my evidence accurate.

2427. Mr. Hansard has the "Globe" sent after six o'clock, I am informed?—Then it must be by some very recent arrangement, because I made very careful inquiries. I believe that it is as I state. The seat which is allocated to the summary writer of the "Morning Advertiser," I am told is practically used by the representative of the "Manchester Guardian."

2428. That the summary writer of the "Morning Advertiser" uses the seat for the "Manchester Guardian"?—And really does the work of the "Manchester Guardian." Then the "Times" chief reporter, Mr. Ross, I am inclined to think does no reporting (I am merely pointing out that three seats could be utilised). The "Daily Telegraph" summary, I am inclined to think, is non-existent; they have a seat for a summary, but I do not think that they do any summary, or scarcely any; therefore, if the Committee did not consider it right to afford any further accommodation, they might, by re-arranging the present seats, and taking care that they were utilised for the purposes for which they were given, be able to appropriate some seats to other papers. There are some papers, for instance, the "Standard" and the "Morning Post," and of course the "Times," which give very admirable summaries, but except a paper really does use the place which is got for the purpose for which it gets it, I do not think it ought to retain it unless there are seats to spare.

2429. Retain it to the exclusion of others, you mean?—To the exclusion of others.

2430. Your evidence goes to this, that there are two provincial newspapers, representing probably a third or a fourth portion of a seat, that have admittance to the gallery at the present time?—I think so. I think the "Manchester Guardian" and the "Glasgow Herald" practically have admittance to the gallery at the present time.

2431. The "Glasgow Herald," I think we had it in evidence, works with the "Leeds Mercury"?—I think there is some arrangement of that kind.

2432. Have you ever formally applied for admission to the gallery for the "Freeman" besides the application in April last?—Yes, frequently. I may mention a curious thing which I ascertained the other day: that in 1843 the "Freeman" was, as the "Freeman," represented in the gallery. I think the Serjeant at Arms gave evidence here the other day that no provincial newspaper was ever admitted, or something to that effect. His memory may not extend back so far as 1843; but as a matter of fact the "Freeman" was represented in 1848, when Irish matters of great importance were before the House; O'Connell was at the zenith of his power just then. I cannot say how we got the admission, but we were represented; and I cannot say how we lost it.

2433. You did lose it, at all events?—It is gone.

2434. Is there an increased demand for Parliamentary reports in Ireland?—No doubt there has been a very largely increased demand since the present Irish party were returned, that is to say, since the commencement of the present Parliament, because matters of vital importance to Ireland are constantly discussed; certainly two or three times a week questions of great interest to Ireland arise.

2435. And is it your opinion that that interest in Parliamentary debates will continue?—That depends upon Parliament. If the questions were settled I suppose the interest would abate; I do not see very much prospect of that at present, I am sorry to say.

2436. Have you mentioned to the Speaker the facts which you have stated to the Committee, that the "Freeman's Journal" is excluded, while two or three other provincial newspapers are admitted?—Yes, I did mention that in the letter which I put in. I did not go into any details, but I stated that some of the papers were represented indirectly.

2437. Is it probable that a number of newspapers in Ireland would agree upon a joint report?—No, I am quite certain that it is impossible.

2438. That is to say, that no newspaper in Dublin would concur with you in publishing the same report?—No.

2439. Would any newspaper in Cork and Dublin take the same report?—With reference to the last witness' evidence as to the number of papers that would probably require to be specially represented, my opinion is that not more than two or three papers could establish any such claim from Ireland. They certainly could not by any possibility work together; and if there were any combination

Mr. E. D. Gray,
M.P.

15 July 1878.

combination between a large number of papers it would simply mean that the wealthy papers which could afford to give proper reports would be supporting the poorer papers which could not afford it.

2440. You would refuse, in point of fact, in all probability, to combine with any other newspaper?—Yes. If you want to work effectively you must have one of two things; you must either have an official monopoly, which would be supplied to every paper; or you must leave to the healthy action of competition for the carrying out of efficient reports.

2441. Would you be prepared to accept a full official report in lieu of your own arrangements?—If it were effectively done, and if it were promptly done, I do not see such strong objections to it as some of the former witnesses have urged. Of course, as the witness who was examined last said, it would require a large staff in the London office of the paper to summarise that report; but that would simply mean that the staff which at present would be occupied on behalf of that paper in reporting in brief, would then be occupied in the office in cutting down, as it is called. It would all depend upon whether the official report were promptly supplied; if it were, I think, as far as I am concerned, we could work it.

2442. You see no difficulty whatever in rapidly summarising, to suit the necessities of every newspaper, a full extended official report?—I see great difficulty, but no insuperable difficulty. Of course, the most efficient plan would be that we should have our own reporters and direct them what amount to report, and not have a longer report than we required, but I can see that, of course, the accommodation is limited, and it would be very difficult to make that arrangement. I can see no insuperable difficulty in summarising an official report, if it were promptly supplied.

2443. Do you see any objection from your own point of view, either as a Member of Parliament or as representing the newspaper press, to the exclusion of reporters from the gallery, and the production of a complete official report, which should be handed to the newspapers for their use?—I have a strong objection to the work of Government departments in connection with newspapers; I confess that my experience of the working of the Government telegraphs is not satisfactory; but if we could have some guarantee that it would be really effectively done, I could see no objection to it. Your question, as I understand, really goes to this, whether I could see my way to a certainty that it really would be effectively done; and I have doubts upon that point.

2444. Mr. *Forster.*] What time ought you to receive that official report, in order to get it into your paper the next morning?—It should come by degrees; if it all came at once, we could not get it in; it should be supplied page by page.

2445. Would it not be almost impossible for you to get it in time to condense it for the next morning's issue?—The witness who proposed the plan stated (and I see no reason why it could not be done, if the money were spent upon it), that that report could be supplied in print within an hour. Now, from the News Associations I do not think we get our reports in manuscript so promptly as that; sometimes, at least, we do not.

2446. Do you subscribe to all three associations?—Not for Parliamentary work.

2447. You have an office in London?—We have an office in London.

2448. I suppose unless you got that report out the following morning it would be practically of no use?—Quite useless; it is always cancelled, in fact, now after a certain hour.

2449. At what time do you issue in the morning?—We go to press very much later than the Manchester papers, for instance; we go to press about half-past four, Irish time, that would be five o'clock English time.

2450. I understand you to say that there would be no chance of an Irish Press Association?—No.

2451. Has there ever been one attempted?—I do not think so; you see there are very few leading Irish papers that go to any large expense.

. 2452. We have had a suggestion made of something between an official report and the present system; that is to say, what might be called an improved "Hansard," giving Mr. Hansard, or somebody in his place, the power of making reports very quickly; giving him the facility of staff, and so forth, with the understanding that the House of Commons should not pledge itself to the accuracy

accuracy of the report, but should allow it to gain its circulation by its merits; now, supposing that system were established, would that meet your object at all?—No; it might be a useful thing for the Members of the House, not for the press; I do not think it would do at all; we should resist the supplying of any report which was not either a verbatim report or written under our control.

2453. I do not know whether you read or heard Sir John Rose's evidence, stating that a full "Hansard" was the report in the Canadian Dominion Parliament?—I looked at a summary of that evidence, but I did not understand that the report in question was for the press.

2454. No; but my question is whether, supposing that it was arranged that it should come out very quickly, it could be made use of for the press?—No; I am certain that it could not, and I am certain that it would provoke insuperable and ever-recurring disputes as to favouritism, and as to who was reported at length, and so on.

2455. Take, for instance, an Irish debate of great interest, a Home Rule debate, how do you get your report; you have one of some length, I presume?—On such occasions we have often 12 or 13 columns of report; we get it first by telling the Press Association to do as much as they can of it, and next by employing as many reporters of other papers as we can get; as a rule, they would not be busy on their own business that night, because the English papers would not devote much attention to such a debate. But I may point out that after this investigation, if no reform is to result, we shall probably be very much worse off than ever, and for this reason: the "Times" already has a stringent rule that no reporter belonging to it shall do any work for any provincial paper; and I understand that it is the intention of some, at least of the other London papers, to give similar orders to their reporters. Now, if we were deprived of the facility that we at present have of employing reporters belonging to other papers, and if at the same time we were unable to obtain information otherwise, we should be infinitely worse off than at present; and I am afraid that there is a probability of that being the result next Session.

2456. Then I understand your statement to be this, that in the Imperial Parliament debates on questions greatly affecting Ireland cannot be reported fully, or, in fact, at all fairly, unless you go to some London newspaper, and get from them the help you require?—Quite so.

2457. And, in fact, for reports on questions of Irish interest, you are dependent upon the indirect, and I may almost say, underhand arrangements which you make with the London press?—Quite so, except that they are not underhand. I believe it is thoroughly well understood by the conductors of the other papers that this arrangement is made, and probably their reporters are not paid as highly as they would be if their services were retained exclusively by those papers.

2458. Mr. Cowen.] I think you said that in making the arrangements for reporting the Sunday-closing discussion, you asked the Press Association to supply a full report, and that they promised, but did not fulfil their engagement; what I want to ask is, is the blame attachable, or was it attached to the Press Association, as a reporting body, or to the Post Office authorities, for not sending the report quickly on; was it the reporting arrangements of the Press Association, or the Post Office Telegraph that were to blame?—It was the reporting, because we wanted it delivered in London, not in Dublin, for us to take it over ourselves by our special wire.

2459. I ask the question, because it has been given in evidence that the reports that are published by the Press Association are very frequently delayed in being transmitted; that was not the case in this special instance?—No. My experience with regard to the transmission of long special reports is, that the Post Office constantly delivers them about six o'clock in the morning, when they are quite useless. But I do not wish to make too strong a complaint against the Press Association. I believe that under the disabilities under which they labour they do as well as can be expected. On this particular occasion they did not do very well; but I do not wish to make anything in the nature of a sweeping charge against them.

2460. Then the special reports which you get in the "Freeman" are got by the combination of the services of the Press Association, and of the reporters of the different London newspapers?—Yes. Our representative here, who has

carrie

carte blanche in the matter, does the best he can night by night; if he can get the London reporters he dispenses with the Press Association; if he cannot get the London reporters, as sometimes he cannot, they being occupied with special reports for other newspapers for instance, then he falls back upon the Press Association.

2641. The fact is that you do exactly the same as the "Glasgow Herald" does, and as the "Manchester Guardian" does with the use of the "Globe" box?—Quite so.

2642. You do not complain of the "Glasgow Herald," or the "Leeds Mercury," or the "Manchester Guardian," having this facility?—I do not complain of them at all. All I want is to have the same myself.

2643. I understood your evidence to imply that it was an abuse of the gallery accommodation that these papers got admission?—I do not think I used the word "abuse," but I certainly pointed out that the box was given for one purpose, and was utilised for another.

2644. But supposing that the "Freeman" could get that box instead of the "Glasgow Herald"?—I think it would be perfectly justified in taking it, and no doubt it would.

2645. With respect to the "Morning Advertiser," as far as my knowledge and information go, the "Morning Advertiser" gives a very excellent and ample summary of Parliamentary proceedings, one of the longest given by any newspaper; and in the evidence of Mr. Townend he quoted the summary given by the "Morning Advertiser" as one of the best?—My impression with regard to the summary of the "Morning Advertiser" does not coincide with yours; but I believe that the gentleman who sits in the "Advertiser's" box is an employé of the "Manchester Guardian."

2646. Still there is a summary in the "Morning Advertiser"?—Yes, I think there is a summary, but I do not think it is anything to be compared to that of the "Standard" for instance, or the "Morning Post," or the "Times."

2647. The "Morning Advertiser's" staff, practically, only use their facilities in the same way as the staff of the "Daily News," or any other London newspaper do?—The "Daily News" gives less summary than the "Morning Advertiser."

2648. And the "Telegraph"?—The "Telegraph," practically, gives none at all, though each of those papers has a box for that purpose.

2649. The point I wish to bring out is this, that even if these gentlemen do not supply their own London newspapers at great length with a report, the provincial press is benefited by that, inasmuch as they are able to engage their services?—I do not know that you are exactly accurate in saying that the provincial press is benefited. Individual provincial newspapers are no doubt benefited.

2670. It is a question whether these provincial papers are not active in commanding their services; but still they are commanded by these provincial newspapers?—They are, but I do not think that that is a desirable arrangement.

2671. The desirability of it is scarcely the point; the fact is that that arrangement exists?—Yes.

2672. Would there be any difficulty in such a summary as that in the "Morning Post," for example, being written by one gentleman, and at the same time that gentleman summarising or reporting for another newspaper?—No, I scarcely think there would: I have no practical experience, you understand, in reporting work, but I do not see that there would be much difficulty in a man writing a summary and doing some other work.

2673. Do none of the "Times" reporters supply special information to the provincial newspapers?—I understand that they do not supply reports.

2674. And you anticipate, from the information which you have got, that the probability is that, in consequence of the explanations which have taken place before this Committee, the privileges that the London newspapers have hitherto allowed their reporters to enjoy, will be taken from them?—I think it is very probable that they will seek to show that they require that accommodation which they now have, exclusively for their own use as a means of resisting any proposal to curtail it; and that they will, as a step towards that, order their representatives to do no work for other papers. In fact, I have been informed that one of the papers already has determined upon that course. Now if the other papers follow the example, certainly the provincial press, and especially the Irish press, which labours under exceptional difficulties, will be in a very bad way.

Mr. E. D. Gray,
M.P.

14 July 1876.

way. The exceptional difficulty which we labour under is this, that telegraphing across channel is very much slower, and more uncertain than telegraphing over land.

2475. I was going to ask that point: that is one of the difficulties under which the Irish press labours more than any of the Scotch or English provincial newspapers?—Yes, and it is a very serious difficulty.

2476. That will perhaps, to some extent, account also for the difficulty that you have in getting the Press Association reports as early as we get them in the provinces?—It will, to a certain extent, account for it.

2477. Your opinion is that there is an increasing demand for Parliamentary reports in Ireland?—I am quite certain of it.

2478. And therefore an increasing interest in Parliamentary proceedings?—No doubt, owing to the great importance of the Irish matters which are brought under the attention of the House.

2479. We have this fact in evidence that the London newspapers of the largest circulation give the smallest Parliamentary reports?—That is quite true.

2480. Then we may infer from your answer, that while there is an increasing interest in Parliamentary proceedings in Ireland, there is a decreasing interest in England?—Quite so; every Irishman is a politician.

2481. Dr. Lyon Playfair.] The honourable Member for Newcastle asked you whether certain provincial papers were not active in commanding the services of the reporters of the London papers; would not the same energetic papers be more active in commanding their own staff, if they had a staff, and in producing efficient reports for their own newspapers?—No doubt; but I scarcely think that "activity" is the correct word to use with regard to their having secured these advantages. They were fortunate enough at the time to make those arrangements. If any other paper desired to make arrangements now, it would be impossible.

2482. But newspapers that are energetic could have much more efficient reports if they had their own staff, and they knew what they wanted?—No doubt.

2483. Now take to-night, the subject of discussion in the House being Intermediate Education in Ireland; that is a question which is likely to interest the whole Irish people, and it would be just that the Irish papers should have a commanding influence in reporting it?—I think so; that they should, at least, have reasonable facilities.

2484. And at the present moment they have not?—At the present moment they have not; I am quite uncertain whether of that debate, if it continues at any length, we shall have ten columns or two in the "Freeman." It does not depend upon me; it depends upon chance.

2485. Lord Francis Hervey.] I do not think you have told the Committee how many seats you think would be required for the Irish press?—That is a matter that I have thought over a good deal. I do not think there are more than three Irish newspapers at the utmost which would be entitled by their position, and the amount of their circulation, to claim representation in the gallery. Then with regard to accommodation of these papers, to do the work thoroughly effectively with their own staff a paper would require, no doubt, two seats; it would require, at any rate, one in front and one behind. I can see, seeing the limited nature of the accommodation, that there is a great difficulty about that; and in view of the fact that even Members themselves have not got seats on a crowded night, I think that some modified arrangement is the only one practicable; and what I have been thinking might fairly satisfy the provincial press, or at any rate improve their present position, would be to give to the Press Association and to the "Central News," that is to say, to the two Press Associations, additional accommodation, which would enable them to a considerable extent to make up for the deficiencies which I have just mentioned, and then to give to these leading Scotch and Irish papers (I put the Scotch and Irish papers in a totally different category from the English provincial papers for the reasons that I have stated), one seat in, or one admission to, the gallery each; they would then be in this position, that the representative of each of these leading papers would be always on the spot, and would be able to give directions to the reporters of the Press Associations, speech by speech, what amount to report, and would be able to supervise them. I think that is about

about the only thing that we could hope for at present. I would very much prefer, if we could have accommodation for a staff of our own, and would be quite prepared to go to the expense necessary for that purpose if it could be given; but I do see great difficulties in accommodating all the papers that would require room for a special staff. I think that a considerable improvement might be made in the way I have suggested.

2486. To meet the wishes of the three Irish papers which you think might require a separate staff of their own to report in the gallery, you would have three front seats and three back seats?—Yes, to do the work efficiently; but I think if they had each got a seat, and if the general representatives of the entire press, that is to say, the Press Association, got a considerable amount of additional accommodation, so that they could really do the work, the provincial papers, though not able to work perfectly, could do a great deal better than at present. I see nothing else for it.

2487. It has been put to us by two of the witnesses who have had practical experience, that it is impossible to report from the back seats at all; that the summary work, and so on, might be done from there, but not the actual work of reporting?—Quite so. What I would propose as the only modification that I consider practicable would be to give for reporting perhaps a considerable extension of front seat accommodation to the Press Association and to the "Central News," and to give admission to the gallery to the representatives of the leading Scotch and Irish papers.

2488. To the back seats of the gallery?—To the back seats of the gallery, if nothing better could be done; they could write their summaries and supervise the whole work that was done from them. I also think that some condition ought to be put upon the London papers if they are to be allowed to retain the large amount of advantage which they at present enjoy; that they should not restrict their reporters in the way which I understand is about being proposed; that the reporters should be permitted to do other work, if they could do it, after having discharged their duties to the London press; because if that exclusion is practised it will come to be a very serious matter.

2489. Mr. Barclay.] Would such an arrangement be practicable?—The accommodation is given merely as a favour, and is given for the general advantage of the public. Of course it would continue, as at present, to be given year by year. I do think, therefore, that such an arrangement would be perfectly practicable. No paper has a right to claim that accommodation to the exclusion of others.

2490. If the reporter has two masters it might be difficult, in fact, impossible, for him to please both?—He only has one master at present, in the sense that no person can remove him from his seat in the gallery except the conductor of the London paper which employs him. The provincial papers, if they are not pleased with his services, can simply discontinue employing him; it is only in that sense that the provincial paper is at all his master. I think it would be better that the Serjeant at Arms or Mr. Speaker should intimate to the London papers that if they adopt any steps which would have the effect of crippling the provincial press the arrangements will require revision; and I think that that intimation would be quite sufficient to induce them to continue simply as they have been doing.

2491. Are you for adopting this principle in regard to the giving of front seats in the gallery, that the House of Commons should not deal with it as a favour to the newspapers, but should take into consideration what the newspapers do in the way of reporting Parliamentary proceedings?—I think that the suggestion of seeing that the papers which have this accommodation should discharge their duties to the public, by giving fairly full reports, is an admirable one, and I thoroughly concur with it, and I think it is a most fair condition.

2492. Does it come to this, that you would not give any newspaper whatever a seat in the gallery, unless it actually gave a special independent report of a certain minimum length by its own reporters?—It is very hard to lay down a hard and fast line, but my view would certainly come very much to that.

2493. In your own case, by referring to past years, would you be able to say what would be the minimum space that you would be prepared to give in your newspaper to Parliamentary proceedings, if you got a special seat in the gallery?—That is to say, a minimum average I suppose you mean?

0.121.   A A 4   2494. Over

Mr. E. D. Gray,
M.P.

15 July 1878.

2494. Over the whole Session?—I would have no hesitation in saying that we would report three columns a day.

2495. Have you any difficulty in dealing with reporters just now whom you get to supplement your Press Association Reports?—I know nothing about them, and I never complain when they break down, because I cannot get at them, and I know that I must take what I can get.

2496. The reporter rather has a command over you than you a command over the reporter?—Yes, quite so; we are very glad to get anything sometimes. If there has been a long debate the night before, or a considerable amount of special work done by the reporters (which is very remunerative work) they may say, "We are very tired to-night and want to go home." We are very much more the servants of the reporters than they are ours; and in fact, I never dream of looking after them; I simply take what I can get, and leave the matter so.

2497. It comes to this, that the present arrangement gives a certain number of reporters who have seats in the gallery for London newspapers, a quasi monopoly of the business of reporting for the provincial newspapers?—And a most lucrative monopoly.

2498. What did you mean by saying that the "Glasgow Herald" was represented in the gallery of the House; is this gentleman who occupies the box an official of the "Glasgow Herald," or is he simply very much in the position which the reporters occupy who report for you?—It is not easy to get at the exact arrangements which may exist between two newspapers with which you have no connection; but the "Globe," of course, is published in the evening, and does not require the services of a gentleman after, perhaps, half-past four or five o'clock. This gentleman occupies the seat, as I am informed, all night, and I would regard him as being the representative of the "Glasgow Herald," and doing some work for the "Globe;" I would regard it as a reversal of the ordinary arrangement.

2499. Does not this gentleman make also a summary for the "Globe" the next day?—Whether he does or not I do not know, but it does not require a person to be in the gallery to do that.

2500. Except occasionally, when the House sits until three or four in the morning, and then it would be necessary, would it not?—It might; it certainly would not require a special seat to do it, because most of the London papers cease reporting very much before that time.

2501. But I have seen sometimes a special report in the "Globe" of a late sitting of the House which did not appear in any other paper?—That might be very occasionally; certainly on such exceptional occasions there would be no difficulty for the representative of such a paper to obtain accommodation in some of the seats which would not be occupied by some of the other papers, owing to their work being finished.

2502. I presume you have got a representative in some form or another in the Reporters' Gallery?—Yes.

2503. Does not that representative occupy very much the same position in regard to you that this gentleman you speak of occupies in regard to the "Glasgow Herald"?—No, because he does not sit and report.

2504. Do I rightly understand that this gentleman who acts for the "Glasgow Herald" writes detailed reports for that newspaper?—I believe he does; I do not know whether in detail or not, but occupying a box, I presume he does. I do not see why he should not.

2505. He might be a summary writer, but he could scarcely give a detailed report himself, unless there were several besides?—He could only do a portion of it.

2506. Do I rightly understand you to say that the "Glasgow Herald" has several reporters who occupy this box at night?—No; I think they have only one; and then they supplement their own report in the same way that we and the "Scotsman" and every other paper do.

2507. Colonel Arbuthnot.] I think you said that a co-operation of three or four newspapers would be impossible or undesirable, on account of the identity of the reports; but you also said that you had not an insuperable objection to taking your Parliamentary report from an official report; will you state why identical reports would not be objectionable if they were taken from an official report,

report, and yet would be objectionable if taken from any other?—There is a vast difference between the two. The official report which alone, I say, would answer for the press at all, would be a verbatim report, which would be, say, 20 or 25 columns. From that every paper could take that portion which suited its own requirements. A joint report would be only, perhaps, two columns long, and it might suit a Dublin paper and not a Cork paper; it might suit a Liberal paper, and not a Conservative paper. I may mention, in that connection, that it was suggested that joint reports might be used for papers in various localities; well, for general matters, matters of Imperial interest, duplicated reports, if not used by two papers published in the same town, are quite as good as independent reports, and do no injury to the paper; but for other Parliamentary matters they are no good at all, because you want a report of interest in the locality.

2508. You would not accept an official condensed report?—No.

2509. You would do the condensing through your own employés?—Yes. We would not, under any circumstances, accept an official condensed report. You are, of course, aware that political feeling runs higher in Ireland than in England; and an official condensed report, no matter how impartially done, would be regarded with profound suspicion in Ireland; and, in fact, even if the " Freeman's Journal " were willing to accept it, I am quite certain that it could not take it.

2510. You know the Reporters' Gallery well?—Yes.

2511. Have you looked at it with a view to forming an opinion as to the the raising of the back seats?—No, but I have been informed that it would be a certain amount of convenience.

2512. But have you obtained statements from people qualified to give an opinion, that if those seats were raised two or three feet they would be very nearly as good for reporting from as the front seats?—No; the only opinion which I have obtained was from some of the gentlemen who worked for us, and from our manager in the gallery, who says that the back seats would do fairly well for summary work; and I think he intimated that they would do better if they were raised.

2513. Sir Alexander Gordon.] You stated just now when you were speaking of the gentleman who acts as your agent in the gallery, that he does not sit and report?—Not for us.

2514. But he reports for others?—He reports for others, I think.

2515. I understood you to mean that he did not sit and report at all?—No, he reports, I think, for others; that is to say, for the paper with which he is primarily connected.

2516. We have it in evidence that the "Globe" newspaper has six reporters in the gallery, and that the Central News has seven?—Yes.

2517. You seem to be very conversant with the arrangements and the duties of the gallery; is it your opinion that the "Globe," which only reports, I think, for an hour, can employ six reporters, when the Central News, which reports all night, has only seven?—It is my opinion that if the " Globe" has six reporters, either the "Globe " is wasting its money in a most extravagant way, or those gentlemen do other work.

2518. Or does it not also happen that the privilege of a reporter's seat carries with it a pecuniary advantage other than the service rendered to the paper to which the seat was given?—Quite so. These gentlemen could do the entire work for the "Glasgow Herald." I do not myself know the facts, but I have no doubt that if the " Globe " has six men they do the "Glasgow Herald's" work.

2519. Therefore giving the seat to the "Globe" is making them a present of a pecuniary advantage?—Yes.

2520. They get paid for whatever work they do for the "Glasgow Herald," or whatever paper it may be?—I cannot say what arrangement exists; whether the conductors of the "Globe " are paid or not, I could not say, but that there is some arrangement between them I have not the slightest doubt.

2521. These gentlemen evidently do not do it for nothing?—Certainly not.

2522. And therefore the money is paid either to them or to those who employ them?—Yes.

2523. You

0.12).   B 3

Mr. E. D. Gray,
M.P.

14 July 1878.

2523. You made use of the expression, "the two press associations," but we have had evidence that there are three ; do you know anything of the Central Press?—No, I do not think the Central Press does any real work. I do not think that any important part of the press is interested in the Central Press. In fact I do not know what the Central Press does ; I was under the impression that it had disappeared long ago.

2524. *Chairman.*] I wish to ask you again, whether you are quite accurate in your statement as to the summary writer of the "Morning Advertiser:" the witness who was examined before you has asked to be re-examined, in order to state it as the summary writer of the "Morning Advertiser" is a reporter of that paper, and not of the "Manchester Guardian;" it probably is a personal question, and the statement might do mischief to the individual in question unless it be corrected, if it be inaccurate ?—I can only speak from my information. He may be an employé of that paper: I did not say that he was not ; but I said that he practically represented the "Manchester Guardian" in the gallery, and, subject of course to the correction of the last witness, I adhere to that statement.

2525. I think the Committee understood you to say that you were able at the present time to make use of reporters for other London newspapers to obtain a report for the "Freeman's Journal?—Except the "Times." The "Times," I understand, has a standing rule, that their reporters shall not report for other newspapers. I do not know that they prohibit them from generally dealing with them ; in fact, I have reason to believe that they do not ; but actual reporting work for other papers is, I believe, prohibited by the "Times."

2526. So that you have not been able to avail yourselves of the services of gentlemen on the staff of the "Times" to obtain work for the "Freeman's Journal"?—Not to obtain reporting ; I draw a distinction between reporting and merely representing in other capacities. I will not enlarge, but I may say that on one occasion we had a gentleman who belonged to the "Times," and who did some exceptionally good reporting work for us ; so good, that I believe attention was called to it, and he discontinued doing that class of work for us.

2527. I have had a letter from Mr. Robinson, the manager of the "Daily News," and I should like to ask you whether his views, which I will read to you, are correct, in your judgment. He says, "While confessing the inability of the penny press to give long debates, I feel still more that we could give none at all if we had not the reporting in our own hands. This alone enables us to get to press in time as it is." With your knowledge of the press (and I know you have been connected with it for a great many years), do you confirm the view which Mr. Robinson expresses in this letter?—No doubt an official report would subject the London papers to greater difficulties than it would a paper such as the "Freeman's Journal," because the London papers go to press so very much earlier, and they have now such admirable facilities for getting their work done. A reporter does a very short amount late at night, goes up to the office, perhaps, at once with it, and delivers it, and no time whatever is lost. The getting out of the official report would lose a great deal of time for them, and although I do not know that it would be to the extent which Mr. Robinson says, it would be a great disadvantage to them probably.

2528. It would stand in the way of giving a fair and accurate account of the proceedings in Parliament to the public ?—I do not think that many of them do anything like that at present ; but undoubtedly it would cripple them to some extent.

Mr. Thomas Senior Townend, re-called ; and further Examined.

Mr. T. S. Townend.

2529. *Chairman.*] Are you anxious to make any statement to the Committee on the subject of the summary writers of the "Morning Advertiser" and the "Manchester Guardian"?—I wish to state that the last witness has certainly shown no correct knowledge of the facts. The "Manchester Guardian" arranges, as I described, for a special report ; and it is perfectly true that the summary writer of the "Morning Advertiser," who is paid by the "Morning Advertiser," who does the "Morning Advertiser's" ordinary work, who owes his first allegiance to that paper, who writes a longer summary for the "Morning Advertiser" verdict" than appears in any other paper but the "Times," does give us some assistance; but he is not the only gentleman; and were I to enter into details, I could show that a vast amount of work is done by others as well as by this particular member of the staff. I am desirous of correcting that statement, because the witness made it a point that provincial papers send boxes belonging to London papers surreptitiously. I do not think that is a fair statement, certainly it is not the case in regard to the "Manchester Guardian," nor is it in regard to the "Glasgow Herald"—so far as my knowledge goes, which is pretty intimate—and the "Globe."

2530. Mr. Cowen.] Any arrangement of that kind is done with the assumed knowledge of the newspaper proprietors?—Certainly; I know it is so in the case of the assistance that is rendered to us by any reporter on the "Morning Advertiser."

2531. What I wish to convey is, that there is no attempt to deceive any one in the arrangement that is made?—Not in the slightest degree. In fact, were the London papers to restrict the reporters to writing for their own papers exclusively, they would have to double or treble their salaries all round.

2532. We had it in evidence, I think, at the beginning of the inquiry, that the money which the reporters got from provincial papers went in mitigation, to some extent, of the salaries of the reporters for the London press, and that, therefore, the editor of the "Morning Advertiser" is quite conscious that this gentleman does your work?—He is perfectly aware that he gives us some assistance.

2533. Mr. Mitchell Henry.] I would ask you, did you hear the word "surreptitiously" employed by the last witness?—I think it was employed by a Member of the Committee in asking a question of the witness. I will withdraw the word if it is objected to.

2534. Any reference that the word could have to the evidence given was as I take it as regards the House, and not as regards the newspapers; that the seat in the gallery was given by the House for the summary writer of a particular newspaper, but that that seat is not employed for that purpose, but is employed for reporting for provincial papers. That I understood to be the evidence of Mr. Gray?—If that is so then the evidence is incorrect.

2535. In what way is that evidence incorrect?—Because the gentleman occupying the seat occupies it the whole night for the "Morning Advertiser," and writes their summary the whole of the night. If you examine the paper you will find that it is a genuine summary, and a very long summary.

2536. The "Manchester Guardian" has supplied to it a Parliamentary letter as well as a report: is that letter written by the summary writer that you have spoken of?—I am afraid I cannot give you information upon that point. I should not feel justified in doing so unless the Committee deemed it necessary for the purposes of the inquiry.

2537. Chairman.] I think I understand you to admit that the summary writer of the "Morning Advertiser" does some of the work for the "Manchester Guardian"?—Yes, some of the work, as in the case of other reporters; but the box is not used for the "Manchester Guardian" in any special way.

2538. I wish to ask you whether the summary writer of the "Morning Advertiser" is employed in Parliamentary reporting, in its ordinary sense, for the "Manchester Guardian," or in summary letter writing?—Do you mean by summary writing, a news summary of the Parliamentary proceedings?

2539. Yes?—He is sometimes employed to give us assistance in both respects, but only very partially in regard to the news summary. The "Morning Advertiser" changes its summary writer. We cannot keep up our arrangement to rely upon any one man for any particular work.

2540. There would not be continuity, you mean?—I think we have had nothing whatever from the "Morning Advertiser's" summary writer for the last six weeks.

2541. Mr. Mitchell Henry.] Does the "Morning Advertiser" change its summary writer?—Occasionally. They have one man who is supposed to do the duty, but he has been in failing health for a long time.

Mr. F. S. Townsend

16 July 1878.

Friday, 19th July 1878.

Colonel Arbuthnot.
Mr. Cowen.
Viscount Crichton.
Mr. Dunbar.
Sir Alexander Gordon.
Mr. Hall.
Mr. Mitchell Henry.

Lord Francis Harvey.
Sir Henry T. Holland.
Mr. Hutchinson.
Mr. Mills.
Mr. William Henry Smith.
Mr. Walter.
Sir Henry Drummond Wolff.

THE RIGHT HONOURABLE WILLIAM HENRY SMITH, IN THE CHAIR.

Mr. *John Taylor*, called in ; and Examined.

Mr. John Taylor.

19 July 1878.

2542. *Chairman.*] I THINK you are one of the officers of the Office of Works? —I am Surveyor for the London district.

2543. Are you acquainted with the structural arrangements of the Reporters' Gallery, and of that part of the House immediately adjacent to the gallery?— Yes.

2544. Are you of opinion that that accommodation can be increased or improved without trenching upon the seats allotted to Members of the House? —I have made a plan showing how the number of reporters' seats might be increased if the arrangements for the reliefs can be managed by the reporters themselves.

2545. Is it possible to increase the space which would be appropriated to reporters by going further backward in any way, or by raising the existing seat in any way?—At present the reporters, as I understand, report exclusively from the front seat. There are two seats, the seat behind being too narrow for the purpose. There would be no difficulty in recessing the second seat underneath the Ladies' Gallery, so as to give sufficient depth for that seat to be reported from also, in the same way as the front row.

2546. Then the effect of that would be, that reporters waiting to take their turn in the front seats would have to remain out of the gallery?—That would be so, I am afraid.

2547. That would increase the accommodation for actual reporting, but would exclude those who are waiting to take their turn in front?—Yes.

2548. Is there no other way in which increased accommodation could be given to the Reporters' Gallery, without trenching upon the gallery allotted to Members?—I know of no other way.

2549. You cannot carry the seats back in any other way, or raise them up, you think?—Only the few inches I have spoken of in recessing the second row.

2550. Do you propose to raise the existing back seat at all?—No.

2551. But to leave it on precisely the same level as now?—The present level.

2552. But by recessing, you mean putting the seats for the reporters under the canopy, that is to say, under the Ladies' Gallery, some few inches ; that is your proposal?—That is so.

2553. Mr. *Walter.*] Have you explained that plan which you have in your hand to any of the reporters, to know whether it would meet their views?—No, it has only been finished within the last half-hour.

2554. They would not be able to see the Members in the House from that back seat, would they?—I think, from about the middle of the House, they would.

2555. *Chairman.*]

2555. *Chairman.*] The canopy over their head would be about as high as the canopy over the Speaker's head, would it not?—Scarcely so high, and it would be perfectly flat.

2556. *Mr. Walter.*] This plan of yours involves also cutting into the wall?—Yes.

2557. To what depth?—Just over a foot.

2558. Have you ever considered the possibility of raising the back seats some three or four feet against the side of this wall (*pointing to the plan*) without cutting into the wall at all?—That would be impossible, for this reason, that if you do not cut into the wall there is not sufficient depth.

2559. Sir *Alexander Gordon.*] Would it be possible to lower the existing gallery a few feet, and then to put a gallery directly over it?—That would interfere very materially with the panelling of the House all round.

2560. With nothing else but the panelling?—I have not looked at the building with a view to such an alteration.

2561. Did you ever consider the possibility of altering the arrangements of the House so as to give additional accommodation to reporters as well as Members by something in the way I have roughly indicated on that plan (*handing a sheet of paper to the Witness*), doing away with the Upper Gallery altogether, and extending the Reporters' Gallery on both sides to the same extent, and bringing all the seats of Members within one sort of amphitheatre?—I have considered that.

2562. May I ask what conclusion you have arrived at?—It would involve the shoring up of the roof, the complete removal of the side walls, and the introduction of columns, or heavy piers.

2563. But could not the area be spanned by a single roof?—It would take the bearing away from the main walls. At present the walls on which the roof rests are the walls of the House, and not the walls of the lobby.

2564. But with a new roof entirely, could it not support a new roof entirely upon the walls, extending the gallery in the way I have suggested?—I have no doubt that a new roof could be supported.

2565. Therefore, that plan is feasible as far as architectural construction is concerned?—Yes; but very expensive, I may add.

2566. But by that means you would then get additional reporters' accommodation on both sides of the present Reporters' Gallery?—Yes, but the accommodation would not be good, I think, because the gallery would intervene between the reporters and the Members.

2567. Mr. *Dunbar.*] You propose to put reporters in the back row under the Ladies' Gallery?—Yes, recessing them partially under the Ladies' Gallery.

2568. How would they hear there?—They would only be a foot further back than the second row is now.

2569. Would there not be the projection overhead interfering with their hearing?—Not to impede the sound of the voice from the House; it would not be deep enough for that.

2570. Would there be any place where the men could stop while waiting for their turn?—They would have to come from the room behind; there would be no space inside the House.

2571. Have you examined those rooms?—Yes.

2572. Is there sufficient accommodation there?—I do not think there is not nearly sufficient accommodation.

2573. There are a good many messengers and people about, are there not?—I have no knowledge of the arrangements in regard to messengers.

2574. Did you examine any of the arrangements, urinals, and those things?—I have not examined the urinals specially with reference to this inquiry, but I know the accommodation they have.

2575. Mr. *Mitchell Henry.*] If this arrangement that you suggest was made with regard to the back seats, that would prevent, would it not, the reporter who is about to come on duty from hearing the tale end of the portion of the debate which the previous reporter had taken?—That would be so.

2576. I understand that that is an essential thing in reporting, that the reporter

Mr. *John Taylor.*

19 July 1878.

reporter who is to succeed shall be present for a moment or two during the completion of the previous turn?—Yes, I should think it necessary.

2577. Then with respect to raising the seats, it would be impossible, in your opinion, to raise the back seat at all?—It is impossible.

2578. And if it were possible to raise it, would it not be open to this objection, that the reporters would be disturbed by the talking in the Ladies' Gallery, and that the privacy of the ladies would be interfered with by the fact of the reporters being immediately underneath them, and therefore able to hear everything that was said?—I think that would be so.

2579. Mr. *Cowen.*] The objection to your plan that would present itself to the reporters is, that they could not hear so well where you propose to put them to do their work; that would be the first objection; you have not tried it yourself, I suppose?—I have been in the seats with a view of seeing how far I could see into the House, but I have not tried it as regards the sound.

2580. Another inconvenience would be that the accommodation behind would be destroyed by the seat being carried so far back?—The passage would be kept the same width as it is now, but the seats would be recessed under the wall; that would give an additional width to the desk.

2581. But, as Mr. Mitchell Henry has mentioned, it is obviously necessary for a reporter who succeeds another to know what was said a few minutes before; and there would be no provision made by your plan for these relays to hear what was going on?—I have failed altogether in finding a way to accomplish that.

2582. Mr. *Mills.*] I understand you to say that, in your opinion, it would be impossible to raise the back seats?—I have said that it would be impossible without raising the sill of the Ladies' Gallery, which I think would be fatal to the Ladies' Gallery.

2583. The structural difficulty is that it would interfere with the present arrangement of the Ladies' Gallery?—Yes.

2584. Colonel *Arbuthnot.*] May I ask why it would be necessary to raise any part of the Ladies' Gallery if the back seats are simply raised without deepening them at all?—There would not be sufficient depth to sit in them; they say they are too narrow now.

2585. But I understand that the complaint as regards narrowness is not of the seat, but of the desk on which the reporter's book is placed?—That is so; but the width of the seat is reduced to a minimum, and they can then only get so many inches of board, leaving a sufficient passage to get through between the seats.

2586. But if the back seats were raised, and the desk were made broader, would it not be possible for the reporters to pass backwards and forwards; in the event of their being raised three feet, for instance, would not that very fact of their being raised three feet and the desk widened enable the reporters to pass; although I quite admit that if the desks were widened in their present position it would interfere with free passage?—It would not be practicable, for this reason, that if you were to raise the seats three feet you would require six steps to get down from them to the present level of the passage; where are those steps to be put? there is not space for them.

2587. Could not that be arranged at the two ends?—It would be impossible for the reporters to pass each other to get to the ends.

2588. How do they get backwards and forwards now?—By raising the flap and going in direct.

2589. Mr. *Hall.*] I am told that the real objection to the back seats is the continual passing to and fro of reporters and messengers; is that so?—A reporter would be better able to answer that question than I can. I have no knowledge of that, but I should think it very likely.

Mr. *Henry Dunphy*, called in; and Examined.

Mr. *H. Dunphy.*

2590. *Chairman.*] You are connected with the "Morning Post"?—I am.

2591. Have you acted as reporter?—Some years ago I acted as reporter; I write now a summary.

2592. You

2592. You are the summary writer for the " Morning Post " in the gallery?   Mr. E. Dwyer.
—Yes.

2593. You occupy one of these front seats in the gallery?—Yes.   19 July 1878.

2594. Evidence has been given to the Committee as to the insufficiency of the accommodation in the gallery; are you acquainted with the facilities for hearing in the back seats?—I am.

2595. Would it be possible for a reporter to report with general accuracy an ordinary speaker from the back seats of the gallery?—Most certainly not.

2596. Why could not reporters report there; is it due to the passing to and fro of persons between them and the front seat, or to difficulty of hearing the speaker, or to the difficulty of seeing him?—It is due to all those causes; chiefly to the defective construction of the House itself; from the back seats you cannot see many Members and cannot hear them. It would be perfectly impossible to report from them; it would be impossible to summarise a debate from the back seats in a satisfactory manner.

2597. Is it a fact that there is a good deal of summary writing or reporting in the back seats?—I cannot say that. I do not think it is possible; it is tried, I have no doubt.

2598. But you think not successfully tried?—Not successfully tried, certainly.

2599. Gentlemen who are taking notes from the back seats are, in your opinion, taking notes with an unsatisfactory result?—Under difficulties; they can neither see the speaker nor hear him occasionally.

2600. Have you any suggestion to offer to the Committee with a view to the improvement of the accommodation for reporters?—I think it is extremely difficult to deal with the gallery as it is. It is nothing more, as you know, than a narrow slip cut off from that end of the House; there is only room for about 15 gentlemen in the front, and even that room is extremely bad; it is very much cribbed and confined, and very inconvenient to those who are obliged to pass many hours there; in fact the facilities are of the very worst description in every way. I should like, if the Committee will allow me, to refer to the evidence which a gentleman, I think from Scotland, gave; he seemed to think that a number of country newspapers might be represented, and these newspapers would have corps: I think he mentioned six or seven, or eight; now there is no accommodation whatever for these corps in the gallery, either waiting to come on or present.

2601. At the present time you mean?—At the present time. Then the raising of the back seat would bring the heads of those who sat on the back seat nearly on a level with the Ladies' Gallery; which would be obviously inconvenient, I think. Besides, there is no room to make a staircase to the proper seats; in fact, two people cannot now pass; you are obliged to lift this little shelf and retire into the seat in order to allow another person to pass.

2602. Would that objection be overcome if the seats were recessed, as was suggested by an officer from the Office of Works?—So far as the Ladies' Gallery is concerned it would; but I think it would be extremely difficult to hear in those recesses; they would be extremely hot, and they would take away from the very limited accommodation behind. There are two or three little rooms that are more like dress than apartments, behind the gallery, where the temperature is very high in summer, and where a great number of persons have to be in attendance; there are now telegraph agencies, there are special wires, there are telephones, there are all sorts of things in these three little rooms, and the demands on the space are constantly increasing.

2603. Are the Committee to understand that, so far as the existing gallery is concerned, you see little opportunity for improvement?—There is none unless you take some of the seats right and left from the Members' Gallery.

2604. I am speaking now of the existing Reporters' Gallery?—Every inch of that is absorbed.

2605. And, in your opinion the proposed recessing of the back seat would not afford satisfactory accommodation to the reporters who would use it?—That is my opinion.

2606. Mr. Cowen.] Your opinion is, that the accommodation at present is bad, and that the proposed changes would make it worse?—Quite so.

0.121.   B B 4   2607. That

2607. That the small amount of space which is already afforded to reporters, and the traffic and the talking together, would put the reporters into a worse position than they are in now if these changes were made?—Yes.

2608. I asked a question, at the beginning of this inquiry, about these back rooms, and I was told (I think by some gentleman connected with reporting) that these back rooms were not so much used now as they used to be, because the reporters write out their copies in a committee room?—There is one committee-room so used; after many years' struggle a committee-room was obtained; first a portion of a committee-room was given; then, by degrees, the whole of the committee-room was given; and that certainly is a great relief to the corps.

2609. Could not another committee-room be given, and all the writing out behind the gallery be stopped?—Quite so.

2610. Would that be any advantage?—I think it would; in fact, the rooms behind are only fit for messengers, and not for business purposes; there is no repose, no quietude about them, no silence.

2611. I think that any man who has visited them will be quite of your opinion, that it is a very unsuitable place for any man to condense a speech in, both by reason of the atmosphere, and by reason of the size of the place; that is your own view, at any rate?—Yes.

2612. The object of the Committee is to have a suggestion from some practical men as to what improvement could be made here, always recollecting the size of the House, and the circumstances; and I take it that your opinion is that the only change that could be made would be by taking in on each side of the Reporters' Gallery some portion of the gallery now appropriated to Members?—I do not see any other way; and even then it would be unsatisfactory, because a person who might have a seat there on one side of the House would always have the Minister's back to him.

2613. Sir *Henry T. Holland.*] If the gallery were enlarged, and the provincial press admitted, it would then become absolutely necessary to have another committee-room for copying, would it not?—Certainly.

2614. Because that would increase very much the number of the persons in the rooms behind the Reporters' Gallery?—I should estimate that admitting seven journals and their corps, and the necessary messengers and telegraphic agencies in connexion with them, would add a hundred persons to the *personnel* of the gallery.

2615. What is the difficulty in taking a summary from the back seat; of course it is not so convenient as taking it from the front seat; but what is the difficulty of taking a summary from there?—The difficulty of hearing. As it is now, there is great difficulty of hearing in the front seats, especially Ministers when answering questions.

2616. The back seats are used now by those who are waiting to relieve the reporters in front?—That is so; but there are no desks; it is nothing but a little ledge; there is no convenience whatever for writing a summary, nothing to put the pens, paper, or envelopes upon.

2617. Mr. *Mitchell Henry.*] If the back seats are not used for reporting, and are not used for summary writing, what are they used for; are they used for the sketching and painting work?—No, I do not know that they are. I do not think any one sketches there; I have not seen any one doing so.

2618. What use is made of them?—They are used by leader writers, and also used by gentlemen who are waiting for their turns. In fact there is nothing but a little ledge in front; not a desk, but only a ledge of a few inches.

2619. Mr. *Dunbar.*] I suppose a man ought to be in the gallery a minute or two before he goes on duty as a reporter?—Certainly, to hear the argument.

2620. It would be a great inconvenience to have to come out of the room at the moment and jump into the box?—Yes.

2621. Sir *Alexander Gordon.*] Are you aware that papers such as the "Scotsman," the "Leeds Mercury," and leading papers in the country, write their summaries from the reports which they receive from reporters in London?—I am not aware of that fact, but I presume they do.

2622. But

Mr. H. Dunphy

19 July 1878.

2632. But being summary writer of the "Morning Post," has it ever occurred to you to know how the "Scotsman" writes its summary?—It has no interest to me whatever.

2623. Has it never occurred to your mind how they obtain their summaries?—I was not aware that the "Scotsman" had a summary till you were good enough to tell me so. I never saw the paper more than once in my life, and then accidentally.

2624. They have a summary very much the same as the "Morning Post," I imagine; and they make the summary after they have received the speeches by telegraph. If you were to adopt that plan for the "Morning Post," should you find any difficulty in preparing a summary of the speeches?—Yes, you never would get the same trouble colouring that you would get from a summary written by some one seeing the proceedings of the House; and you would have to wait for many hours till the report was put into type, and then you would have to see the corrected proof.

2625. Your summaries are not dry, matter-of-fact summaries; they are "coloured" according to circumstance, I understand you to say?—The expression was perhaps rather an inaccurate one; I did not mean coloured in the sense which you seem to understand; I meant that the summaries would be a truer representation of what passed if the proceedings were written by a person who had them under his eye.

2626. You said that there was no convenience for writing in the back seats; could not that convenience be added to them?—No, for this reason, that there is nothing now but a little ledge of about eight or ten inches, and the papers would fall off it.

2627. Is there no room to add a wider ledge?—No, because as it is now, two persons cannot pass; the space between this knifeboard ledge, and the back of the seat where the reporters sit, is so narrow that two persons cannot pass as it is.

2628. Are there no means of increasing the desk towards the front?—No, none whatever.

2629. Sir *Henry Drummond Wolff*.] Is there any difficulty in hearing in the back bench of the gallery from any talking in the Ladies' Gallery?—There is occasionally.

2630. I suppose what you meant by "colouring" is that you sometimes bring little incidents into your summary which would not be put into the actual report of the speech?—No; what I meant was that it is impossible for a man to write a summary from reports as well as he could write it if he were present in the House.

2631. Mr. *Mills*.] You do not know who exactly occupy these back seats; sometimes they are occupied by what are called leader-writers, sometimes by the reporters waiting for their turn?—Quite so.

2632. But I suppose it would not be any part of your business to inquire how those seats are allotted; to whom, or in what proportion?—None whatever.

Mr. *Thomas Curson Hansard*, re-called; and further Examined.

Mr.
T. C. Hansard.

2633. *Chairman.*] I do not propose to ask you any further questions, but if you wish to make any statement to the Committee, the Committee will bear you?—No; I think in my first evidence I gave all the information I wished to convey. I shall be happy to answer any questions the Committee may desire to put to me.

2634. Sir *Alexander Gordon*.] I should like to ask, with reference to the Paper (Appendix, No. 4) which you have given in, is that prepared from any doubt as to the feasibility of carrying out either of the first two proposals which you have laid before the Committee?—No.

2635. Mr. *Hall*.] This Paper (Appendix, No. 4) only supposes a continuation of the present system of collating from the newspapers, I apprehend?—No, it contemplates the addition of the points there named, to be especially reported, in addition to the four points which are already arranged for with the Chancellor of the Exchequer. These are additional and special points.

C c 2636. What

2636. What I mean is, that excluding these special points which have nothing to do with the ordinary second reading debates, you would obtain your reports of debates on second reading by collating newspaper reports ?—Yes.

2637. That you propose to continue ?—Yes.

2638. Would it be possible, without going into the great expenditure shown in these other Papers, for you to have your own independent reporter in the gallery, from whose reports you could collate, as well as from the newspaper reports ?—I do not think it would be possible for one reporter; it must be a staff.

2639. As large a staff as you have made provision for here ?—No, probably not so large, but still a considerable staff. I do not think that there is any half-way house between the present arrangement of reports partly special, partly by collation, and complete reports.

2640. It is only special as far as regards these points ; never as regards the second reading of Bills ?—You may take it so.

2641. Lord *Francis Harvey.*] How are you enabled to fulfil your present engagement to report fully the debates on Private Bills " by Order," in Committees of Supply and Ways and Means, and in Committees on Public Bills, either on Wednesdays or during morning sittings, or generally before six o'clock in the evening, seeing that your reporter is not entitled to a seat on the front bench until that hour of six o'clock ?—I have made an arrangement with one gentleman to manage my reporting staff, and he is able to manage that matter for me; in fact, it is upon sufferance. I may say that we have never found any difficulty in getting a seat for a reporter.

2642. Still you say it is on sufferance ?—It is on sufferance.

2643. And that is not a state of things which is entirely satisfactory to yourself ?—Certainly not.

2644. Mr. *Mitchell Henry.*] In your evidence you expressed the opinion that Members of both Houses of Parliament should be supplied with the reports of the proceedings in Parliament, speeches, and so on, just in the same way as they are now provided with blue books ?—Yes.

2645. If that is your opinion, what would be the additional cost which would require to be added to your third estimate to provide a copy of Hansard, if it came out weekly, to each Member of Parliament ?—I have thought over the matter well, and the first thing that struck me was that in addition to the Peers and Members, the Public Offices also would be entitled to the same gratis supply, and taking into account the Peers, the Members of the House of Commons, and the Public Offices, I come to the conclusion that the private subscription list would be entirely destroyed, and therefore the cost of supplying these gratis copies would be very considerably larger. I think, than I should like to name as an addition. Still it is a matter of public policy, and I am of the same opinion notwithstanding the cost.

APPENDIX.

LIST OF APPENDIX.

APPENDIX.

Appendix, No. 1.

PAPER handed in by Captain *Gosset.*

NAME of PAPER.	Tickets Issued.	Number of Seats in Gallery.
Central News - - - - - - - -	7	1
Press Association - - - - - - -	10	1
Globe and - - - - - - - -	6	1
Hansard (after six o'clock) - - - - -	4	1
Morning Post - - - - - - - -	11	2
Standard (Morning and Evening) - - -	17	2
Morning Advertiser - - - - - - -	15	2
Daily Telegraph - - - - - - -	12	2
Times - - - - - - - -	16	5
Daily News - - - - - - -	10	2
Pall Mall and - - - - - - -	6	1
Daily Chronicle (after six o'clock) - - -	7	1
Echo - - - - - - - -	2	1
Sun and Central Press - - - - -	3	1
Reuter's Telegram - - - - - -	1	Back seat.
Weekly Newspapers:		
News of the World - - - - -	1	One day only.
Westminster Gazette - - - -	1	- ditto.
The Economist - - - - - -	1	- ditto.
Truth - - - - - - -	1	- ditto.
Weekly Messenger - - - - -	1	- ditto.
Illustrated London News - - - -	1	- ditto.

R. A. Gosset,
Serjeant at Arms.

PAPER handed in by Mr. *T. C. Howard.*

PARLIAMENTARY REPORTING.

Scheme No. 1.—T. C. Hansard.

SUFFICIENT STAFF of REPORTERS for LORDS and COMMONS, Directorate, and Management.

THE proofs of speeches of each day's debate up to (10 o'clock, p.m.), to be laid on table of Revising Room at House of Commons by (5 o'clock, p.m.) of the following afternoon.

Proofs of speeches from (10 p.m.) to (15 o'clock, a.), to be laid on table by (6 o'clock, p.m.) of the following evening.

Proofs of speeches to (5 o'clock, a.m.), to be laid on table by (6 o'clock, p.m.), same evening.

Proofs of speeches after (5 o'clock, a.m.) to be reserved to the next morning; but if the prorogation of the sitting be not much beyond 2 a.m., probably the proofs to be produced (5 p.m.) that evening.

These proofs of speeches to lie on table of Revising Room (irrespective of the above hours) until (10 o'clock, p.m.) of the subsequent day; thus giving to Members two sittings of the House for revision; the table to be cleared peremptorily at that hour.

The speeches of Ministers to be sent to their offices.

The speeches of Members who may have made their revision before the prescribed hour (10 o'clock), to be placed in a box, which will be cleared at specified hours.

The revised proofs being thus gathered into the printing office, the revised debate to be published complete, either—

1. On the third day after the debate (Saturday and Sunday not counting):—

Day of Debate.	Day for Revision.	Day for Publication.
Monday	Tuesday, Wednesday	Thursday (at 5 o'clock).
Tuesday	Wednesday, Thursday	Friday (ditto).
Wednesday	Thursday, Friday	Saturday (ditto).
Thursday	Friday, Saturday, Monday	Tuesday (ditto).
Friday	Saturday, Monday, Tuesday	Wednesday (ditto).

2. Or bi-weekly, viz:—

Day of Debate.	Day for Revision.	Day for Publication.
Monday	Tuesday, Wednesday	} Saturday, 8 p.m.
Tuesday	Wednesday, Thursday	
Wednesday	Thursday, Friday	
Thursday	Friday, Saturday, Monday	} Wednesday, 8 p.m.
Friday	Saturday, Monday, Tuesday	

One copy to be delivered gratis, at the residence of each Peer and Member, either with the Parliamentary Papers, Votes, &c., and by the same agency; or, by Special delivery, to the Government Offices; and to the Stationery Office, for distribution to the Colonies.

These Numbers to be on sale to the Public while in stock at ½ d. per sheet.

Members may have the privilege, on the payment of a small fixed sum, to direct the publisher to forward a copy of this publication to any of the Public Institutions within his constituency.

A limited number of copies to be retained at the Debates Office, at the Sale Offices for Parliamentary Proceedings, the Stationery Office (and any others), for sale to the public.

Special sales in large number of particular debates to be printed and supplied, on previous notice, at the rate of 1½ d. per sheet.

Extra copies for the supply of public sales to be kept in stock, if it be found desirable.

I estimate the cost of production of a complete report of the Debates in both Houses of Parliament, according to the above Scheme, and for an ordinary Session—

	£	s.	d.
Expense of Publishing and Delivery - -	15,787	-	-
	800	-	-
£	16,577	-	-

Nightwork and amelioration.

Thos. C. Hansard.

Appendix, No. 3.

PAPER handed in by Mr. *T. C. Hansard.*

PARLIAMENTARY REPORTING.

SCHEME No. 2.—T. C. HANSARD.

SUFFICIENT STAFF of REPORTERS for LORDS and COMMONS, Directorate, and Management.

A FULL Report of each Day's Debate, up to 3 o'clock a.m., unrevised by Members, to be published in Royal quarto, 2,000 copies.

Five hundred copies to be delivered at the House for use of Peers and Members at 4 o'clock the following afternoon.

One copy to be delivered gratis at the residence of each Peer and Member, either with the Parliamentary Papers, Votes, &c., and by the same agency, or by special delivery, and to the Government Offices.

These numbers to be on sale to the public while in stock at 1 d. per sheet.

Members may have the privilege, on payment of a small fixed sum, to direct the publisher to forward a copy of this publication to any of the public institutions within his constituency.

A limited number of copies to be retained at the Debates Office, at the Sale Offices for Parliamentary Proceedings, the Stationery Office (and any others), for sale to the public.

Special sales in large number of particular Debates to be printed and supplied, on previous notice, at the rate of 1 d. per sheet.

Extra copies for the supply of public sales to be kept in stock if it be found desirable.

Copies of this unrevised edition, to be placed in a Revising-room within the House, to remain on the Table   days for each speaker's revision; at the expiration of that term, a revised Library edition of 2,000 copies to be printed in the present form of Hansard; one copy to be delivered to each Member in weekly parts or boarded volumes.

ESTIMATE of COST of producing UNREVISED EDITION, 2,000 Copies, namely:

Editing.	Stitching.
Reporting.	Publishing.
Printing.	Delivering, &c.
Paper.	

Extra for night work, if required.

LIBRARY EDITION:

Remaking-up, and corrections.	Wrappers.
Press work.	Binding.
Paper.	Delivery, &c.

I estimate the cost of production of a complete Report of the Debates in both Houses of Parliament, according to the above scheme, and for an ordinary Session:

	£.
First Unrevised Edition - - - - -	16,076
Second Library Edition - - - - -	4,464
TOTAL of both Editions - - £.	20,540

Nightwork and acceleration.

Thos. C. Hansard.

Appendix, No. 4.

LETTER from Mr. T. C. Hansard to the Chairman of the Committee.

Scheme No. 2.

Sir,   4, Paper-buildings, Temple, 11 July 1878.

HAVING been present when Mr. Speaker gave his Evidence before your Committee, I find his opinion to be that "Hansard," with an extension of the existing arrangement, together with weekly publication, would meet all the requirements of Parliament.

I beg, therefore, to hand in to you a proposal founded upon that suggestion.

I propose, in addition to the four points already provided for, to report more fully—

    1. Questions and Answers.

    2. The Proceedings on Public Bills when brought up on Report.

    3. The Consideration of Public Bills as amended in Committee.

    4. To commence reporting the late Debates at 11.30 instead of 12.30, as provided for at present.

    5. And I further propose to give fuller reports of the Wednesday's sittings.

As regards publication, I propose that the Debates of each week shall be published, after being submitted for a sufficient number of days for the revision of Members, in a complete and revised form a fortnight after the expiration of each week.

The extension of the existing arrangement, with a weekly publication at the interval named, may be effected at an increase of 8,000 l. upon the present subvention.

                                     I have, &c.

The Right Hon. the Chairman of the Select   (signed)   Thos. C. Hansard.
    Committee on Parliamentary Reporting.

PAPERS handed in by Mr. T. C. Hansard.

ABSTRACT of sent Copy and Speeches sent out and returned, for Sessions 1869, 1870, and 1871.

	Lords.				Commons.		
Session.	First Copy.	Speeches sent out.	Returned.	Session.	First Copy.	Speeches sent out.	Returned.
1869	12	740	454	1869	98	2,472	1,44?
1870	8	779	542	1870	154	3,118	1,7?5
1871	17	706	37?	1871	236	3,90?	1,3?5
Total . . .	37	5,349	1,37?	Total . . .	4?9	9,?4?	4,57?4

ABSTRACT of sent Copy and Speeches sent out and returned, for Session 1872.

LORDS.

Date.	Sent Copy.	Speeches sent out.	Returned.	Date.	Sent Copy.	Speeches sent out.	Returned.	Date.	Sent Copy.	Speeches sent out.	Returned.
6 Feb. .	1	6	3	23 April .	—	7	4	28 June .	1	8	1
9 „ .	—	3	1	24 „ .	—	17	4	29 „ .	1	8	1
13 „ .	—	4	5	27 „ .	—	1	—	1 July .	—	16	4
15 „ .	—	8	1	29 „ .	—	7	8	2 „ .	—	7	4
16 „ .	—	2	—	30 „ .	—	10	9	3 „ .	—	10	4
19 „ .	—	10						4 „ .	—	8	2
22 „ .	—	5	5	3 May .	—	5	1	5 „ .	—	16	5
23 „ .	1	10	7	4 „ .	—	7	10	8 „ .	—	2	8
26 „ .	1	11	9	7 „ .	—	16	10	10 „ .	—	7	9
30 „ .	1	7	4	10 „ .	—	24	12	11 „ .	—	6	4
1 March .	—	8	4	11 „ .	2	10	4	15 „ .	—	10	6
2 „ .	—	4	3	13 „ .	2	31	11	16 „ .	—	10	6
4 „ .	—	3	—	14 „ .	—	8	8	19 „ .	—	10	6
6 „ .	—	5	2	20 „ .	—	10	4	20 „ .	—	10	4
9 „ .	—	12	10	21 „ .	—	16	7	23 „ .	1	37	11
11 „ .	—	8	1					26 „ .	—	18	4
12 „ .	—	1	1	1 June .	1	16	10	27 „ .	—	10	6
16 „ .	—	6	3	3 „ .	—	15	9	29 „ .	—	7	3
26 „ .	1	15	9	7 „ .	—	15	5	30 „ .	—	5	3
18 „ .	1	6	4	10 „ .	—	8	3				
19 „ .	—	2	2	11 „ .	—	12	4	1 Aug. .	—	7	7
				12 „ .	1	19	8	6 „ .	—	14	8
9 April .	—	6	4	13 „ .	—	17	6	8 „ .	—	15	6
12 „ .	—	10	4	17 „ .	—	10	4	9 „ .	1	33	4
16 „ .	—	14	6	18 „ .	—	11	6	11 „ .	—	6	4
17 „ .	—	13	—	21 „ .	1	16	6	12 „ .	1	3	1
18 „ .	1	17	10	22 „ .	—	7	4				
19 „ .	—	13	6	23 „ .	—	21	4	Total .	19	830	3?5
22 „ .	—	14	6	24 „ .	—	16	6				

Abstract of *** Copy and Speeches *** out and returned, for Session 1878—*continued.*

COMMONS.

Date.	Sent Copy.	Speeches sent out.	Re- turned.	Date.	Sent Copy.	Speeches sent out.	Re- turned.	Date.	Sent Copy.	Speeches sent out.	Re- turned.
4 Feb	9	4	4	16 April	—	11	20	21 June	—	41	21
	—	26	27	2	69	15		—	42	10
	—	51	19	20	51	16		1	4	4
	—	16	10	21	14	9		1	65	16
	—	17	11	22	70	10	23	9	29	10
	9	66	15	23	19	11	26	1	34	18
	—	19	19	26	66	25	29		21	19
	4	21	13	27	22	14	30	—	17	9
	—	64	10	28	65	12	July			
	2	65	24	30	39	65	2	1	63	77
	—	31	24					—	63	27
	—	17	18	8 May	1	66	80		—	94	22
	4	10	13	4	1	66	10		—	16	6
	—	77	73	6	9	21	14		1	66	69
	—	60	17	6	62	32		4	20	70
1 March	9	29	10	7	66	16		—	31	91
	9	26	13	9	64	64		—	36	16
	3	16	11	11	37	21		1	39	7
	1	64	70	12	60	21		1	60	21
	—	20	24	13	76	66		1	16	26
	4	16	16	14	66	20		1	26	16
10	1	19	16	16	66	27		2	66	9
11	1	66	24	16	64	11		—	66	26
12	1	66	24	17	60	11		2	46	65
17	9	47	73	31	60	17		1	64	17
	9	66	51		66	19		1	66	16
	1	47	66	3 June	9	66	16		1	44	91
	9	46	16	6	9	9	9		1	46	19
				6	62	17		3	67	21
6 April	1	61	91	7	66	26	2 Aug			
6	1	67	26	9	9	6		1	60	16
7	1	10	66	10	17	9		—	61	19
8	1	67	66	11	66	91		—	63	16
9	1	66	31	14	66	21		9	66	69
10	1	67	16	16	61	66		1	66	20
13	1	66	66	16	14	9		1	66	13
14	1	66	66	17	66	21				
16	—	44	76	18	66	91	Total	166	4,966	2,963

SUMMARY.

Session 1878.

	Sent Copy.	Speeches sent out.	Returned.
Lords	19	669	609
Commons	166	4,965	2,661
Total	160	5,097	2,926

Appendix, No. 6.

PAPER handed in by Mr. Cooper.

STATEMENT showing the Length of the PARLIAMENTARY REPORTS in the "SCOTSMAN," from the First of June till the Date of Mr. Cooper's Examination, as compared with those in the "TIMES" and other leading LONDON and PROVINCIAL PAPERS.

Date	Times	Standard	Daily News	Daily Telegraph	Scotsman	Glasgow Herald	Leeds Mercury
	Cols.	Cols.	Cols.	Cols.	Cols.	Cols.	Cols.
1 June	5¼	3¼	3	3½	3	3½	3¼
3 „	10½	4½	5½	4¼	4¼	4¼	4
5 „	7¼	3½	3	3¼	7	4¼	3¼
7 „	3½	4½	5¼	3½	4¼	3¼	3½
8 „	3¼	3¼	3½	3	3½	3	3¼
14 „	5½	4½	3	3	4½	3½	3¼
13 „	7½	3	3½	3½	3½	3½	3
19 „	3	4	4	3½	3	5½	3½
19 „	6½	3	3½	3½	36	33½	3½
20 „	4	3	3½	—3	4½	3½	3½
21 „	3½	3½	3	—½	33½	3½	3½
22 „	3	4½	3½	3½	3½	3½	3
25 „	10½	3½	4½	3	5	3½	3½
26 „	5½	3½	3½	—½	3½	3	3½
27 „	4	3½	3½	—½	3½	3	4½
28 „	11½	7½	3½	3½	4½	3½	3½
29 „	4½	3½	3½	—½	3½	3½	3½
2 July	11½	4½	3½	3½	3½	4½	3
3 „	5½	3½	3½	3	33½	4½	3½
4 „	4½	3½	3½	—½	7½	3	3½
5 „	10½	3½	4½	3½	3	3½	3½
6 „	6½	4½	3½	3½	3½	3	3½
Total	134	66	60	33½	104½	77	54½

INDEX

ANALYSIS OF INDEX.

LIST of the PRINCIPAL HEADINGS in the following INDEX, with the Pages at which they may be found.

INDEX.

C.

CANADA:

Subsidy given in Canada for an official report of the debates; time allowed to Members to make verbal corrections, *Hansard* 287-290——The "Dominion Hansard" is under the management of a Select Standing Committee, *ib.* 288——Belief that since the "Dominion Hansard" was established there has been no independent reporting for the newspapers, *ib.* 301, 302.

Information in detail relative to the system of reporting the proceedings of Parliament in Canada; change of practice from time to time, the object sought being to obtain, not an official or verbatim report, but as near an approximation as possible to the "Hansard" of this country, *Sir J. Rose* 1955-1957. 1962-1963. 1968, 1969——Official authorities then of special reports of the debates upon confederation, *ib.* 1957. 1968, 1969. 1983——Arrangement adopted in 1874 for procuring by contract 2,500 copies of reports, similar to "Hansard," at a cost of from 2,500 *l.* to 3,000 *l.* a year; distribution of them to Members of both Houses, to the press, &c.; *ib.* 1957. 1984.

Practice in Canada as to correction of their speeches by Members, &c.; supervision exercised by a joint Committee of both Houses, *Sir J. Rose* 1957. 2090-2095——Several objections in Canada to an official or verbatim report, *ib.* 1957——Difficulty felt in Canada upon the score of privilege and libel in connexion with an official report, this not applying in the case of a publication like "Hansard," *ib.* 1957. 2015-2017. 2045-2060.

Arrangement between the chief Canadian newspapers for a common system of reporting; satisfaction given thereby, *Sir J. Rose* 1957. 1969-1971. 1985-1987. 2007. 2048-2051——Belief that in the provincial legislatures there is no official report, *ib.* 1980, 1981——Use made by the local press in Canada of the reports in the "Toronto Globe," and other leading newspapers rather than of the reports in the "Dominion Hansard"; limited delay, however, in the publication of the latter, *ib.* 1985-1987. 2011-2013. 2024-2025.

Shorter reports given in the "Dominion Hansard" than in the English "Hansard," *Sir J. Rose* 1955-2000——Late hours for which the House sometimes sits in Canada; practice of the press in bringing their reports down to the latest moment, *ib.* 2001-2006. 2040, 2041——Responsibility of the contractor to Parliament for the accuracy of the semi-official report, *ib.* 2008, 2009——Arrangements for the accommodation of the reporters, *ib.* 2010.

Explanation as to the speeches being reported sometimes in the first person and sometimes in the third, *Sir J. Rose* 2018. 2035——Necessity of a quorum of the House in Canada, *ib.* 2019-2023——Great public interest in the proceedings in Parliament, these being promptly telegraphed to distant towns, *ib.* 2018. 2035——Much larger Parliamentary reports in the press in Canada than in the United States, *ib.* 2042-2044.

Semi-official character of the "Dominion Hansard"; advantage if the responsibility rested with a private gentleman of enterprise, as in this country, *Sir J. Rose* 2058-2060. 2072, 2073——Practice in Canada as to semi-official reporting the speeches in English or in French, there being an edition in each language, *ib.* 2066-2068——Efficiency of the reports now supplied through the Canadian press, a record in the nature of "Hansard" being at the same time very useful, *ib.* 2069-2073.

"*Central News.*" Supply by the "Central News" of two kinds of Parliamentary reports for provincial newspapers, one report being of a general character, and the other consisting mainly of speeches of local members reported expressly for the local papers, *Saunders* 1210——Improved accommodation required in the Reporters' Gallery by the "Central News," the reports made from the seat in the back row being much complained of, but not those made from the front seat, *ib.* 1110. 1110-1112. 1123, 1124. 1126. 1240-1242. 1299. 1300.

Varying length of the ordinary reports; discretion exercised in the matter by the reporters, *Saunders* 1111-1118. 1130-1133. 1362-1365——Very moderate cost of the ordinary reports provided through the "Central News," *ib.* 1129-1131——Difficulty as to hearing in the seat at the end of the gallery occupied by the "Central News," *ib.* 1196-1199——Particulars as to the number and class of newspapers supplied by the "Central News," some of them being Scotch papers, *ib.* 1215-1219.

See also Irish Newspapers. "*Leeds Mercury.*" *Provincial Newspapers.* *Scotch Newspapers.*

"*Central Press.*" Impression that the "Central Press" does not now do any real reporting work, *Urry* 1563.

Circulation of Newspapers. Conclusion as to the circulation being a good test of the claim of any paper to a seat in the Reporters' Gallery, *Cowper* 1684, 1685. 1812.

Colonies.

Report, 1878—continued.

Colonies. Adoption of the name of "Hansard" in the official reports of debates in the several colonies, *Hansard* 314, 315.—*See also Canada.*

Committee-Room Reporters. Absence of any complaint to witness as to the accommodation in the room in which the reporters write out their reports, *Gossel* 84, 85.

Concessions if a second committee-room were placed at the disposal of the reporters admitted to the gallery, *Denzley* 808-811.

Condensed Reports. Opinion that change is required in the shape of compression rather than expansion of Parliamentary reports, and that a good reporter should condense at the time, *Ross* 540-542, 633-645.——Advantage of the system in former years when the assistance of the exercises was reported accurately, but few shorthand reporters having been employed, *ib.* 611, 613.

Suggestion as to the extent to which compression of speeches for publication should be carried; that is, in comparison with the memories now given in the newspapers, *Ross* 640-651, 745-751, 798-803.——Sufficiency of properly condensed reports in the "Times" and other papers, without any necessity arising for an official publication, *ib.* 798-803, 812, 813.——Condensed rather than full reports which witness would give if he were entrusted with discretionary powers in carrying out an official plan, *ib.* 818-833.

Statement on the question of a reporter reading out his notes to several others, so that they might produce a full report or a condensed report; less difficulty in condensing from short notes than from full notes, *Lowell* 985-994.

Expediency of a verbatim report being the basis of an official report, and of any condensation being carried out subsequently, *Salter* 1853-1857.

Constituencies. Limited advantage of full official reports in reference to the information to be given to country constituents, *Ross* 814-821.——Opportunity of any Member for sending his speech in full to "Hansard," *ib.* 814-851, 852.

Cooper, Charles Alfred. (Analysis of his Evidence.)—Is assistant editor of the "Scotsman;" has also had experience as a Parliamentary reporter, 1428-1431.——Practice of obtaining full reports for the "Scotsman" by employing for the purpose reporters engaged on the staff of the London press; great inconvenience of that arrangement, 1432, 1433.——Application made on the part of the "Scotsman" for admission to the gallery; objection raised that, if one provincial paper were admitted others would make the same claim, 1434.

Belief that not more than eight or ten papers would apply for admission (if there were room), on account of the expense involved, 1435, 1451, 1452, 1550-1553.——Suggestion that no paper be admitted which did not keep a staff of its own, and did not give independent reports; proposed exercise of this check through the Serjeant-at-Arms, 1438-1439, 1443, 1453, 1459.——Contemplated prohibition of reporters for the "Scotsman" from reporting for other papers, though reporters for the London press are not now prohibited from reporting for the "Scotsman," 1440-1441, 1467-1474, 1554-1557.

Usefulness, for several reasons, of an official report, so far as the "Scotsman" is concerned; conclusion, moreover, that it could not be published or received in time to be available, 1445-1451, 1454-1456, 1462, 1508-1515, 1579-1576.——Dissent from Mr. Saunders' evidence as to the shortness of the time in which an official report would be ready for the use of newspapers and of members, 1445-1451.——Explanation as to the "Scotsman" not using the reports of the Press Association; objection more especially that these reports are identical with those furnished to other newspapers, and are, moreover, insufficient and unsuitable for the purposes of the "Scotsman," 1431-1453, 1459-1461, 1537-1544.

Unfairness of an official report as a work of reference; exceedingly limited demand on the part of the public, 1456-1458, 1407, 1814, 1815.——Private character of the arrangement under which reporters for the London papers report also for the "Scotsman;" liability of the latter reports to be stopped at any moment, 1463-1466, 1845.

Concurrence in the suggestion that the summary writers might be put on the back seats of the gallery, 1475.——Improved accommodation by raising the back seats three or four feet, *ib.*——Increased space to be provided by extending the gallery at each end, so as to take in a portion of the Members' Gallery, 1476, 1477.

Contemplated right of selection in the Speaker as to the papers to be admitted to the gallery; that is, on certain rules and conditions, 1478-1481.——Claim of Scotland and Ireland to have their own representatives in the gallery; statement hereon as to the exceedingly imperfect and scanty reports of Scotch and Irish questions under the present system, 1478, 1483-1487, 1490-1494, 1516-1593, 1568-1572, 1599-1603, 1844-1849, 1853.——Decided objection to all the provincial papers being dependent for their reports on two or three news agencies; undue monopoly thereby, 1481, 1824-1826, 1829.

Much greater advantage attached to expenditure for improving the accommodation available for reporters than to the expenditure necessary for an official report; large annual outlay in the latter case, 1495, 1604-1611, 1676.——Less necessity for an

Report, 1878—continued.

Cooper, Charles Alfred. (Analysis of his Evidence)—continued.

official report if full reports were provided for the provincial papers by their own staff, 1490, 1491, 1492, 1503——Probable employment of six or eight reporters by the "Scotsman," if it had a seat in the gallery, 1497-1499.

Grounds for the conclusion that an increased interest is felt by the people of Scotland in Parliamentary debates, 1500-1508, 1516-1526, 1645-1650——Increased facilities required by the "Scotsman" for meeting the demand for full reports, 1506——More full reports now given in the "Scotsman" than in any but two of the London papers; also than in any other Scotch paper, 1506, 1517, 1518, 1566-1571, 1579——Increasing circulation of the "Scotsman," owing very much to its Parliamentary reports, 1500, 1501, 1584——Limit to the number of papers applying for seats in the gallery, as each such paper should have a special wire and a staff of six or eight reporters, 1529-1535, 1550-1653.

Decided improvement in the reports for Scotland if there were a direct representation of Scotch papers in the gallery, 1538——Want of full reports, to be selected in each case by the "Scotsman," but not of identically full reports, 1546-1549, 1572-1583——Facilities of telegraphic communication adverted to as favouring the demand of Scotch papers for independent reports, 1558, 1559.

Increasing extent of the reports given in Scotland, while some London papers have been curtailing their reports; claim, on this score, to increased facilities in the former case, 1560-1564——Better materials for an official record, such as "Hansard," if the provincial papers would give independent reports, 1571, 1583, 1584——Very large circulation of the "Scotsman;" this should entitle it to increased facilities in Parliamentary reporting, 1564, 1565, 1611.

Further statement as to the impracticability of the "Scotsman" getting the graphic and press reports required through the Press Association, or otherwise than through a staff of its own, 1577-1583, 1611-1648, 1637——Doubt as to the expediency of stipulating that each paper having a seat in the gallery should devote a certain space to its reports, 1584-1587——Large proportion of the provincial papers for which the reports of the news agencies would still suffice, 1588-1592, 1613-1615.

Exception further taken to the system whereby the Parliamentary reporters for the London press supply reports also to provincial papers by private arrangement, 1593-1598——Further statement as to the comparative usefulness of an official report; that is, more for purposes of reference, 1604-1611, 1618, 1650-1652, 1644, 1656, 1664, 1665, 1668-1672.

Evidence in further disapproval of identical reports, whether under an official system or through news agencies, 1514-1630——Denial that there would be anything in the nature of a monopoly or of special legislation by permitting certain conditions for admitting provincial papers to the Reporters' Gallery, 1617-1592——Protest by the Scotch papers against being excluded from a position in which they have a right to be put, 1633-1636.

Facility with which the "Scotsman" prepares a summary of the Parliamentary report without having a summary writer in the gallery, 1638-1641——Use by the "Scotsman" of two special wires between their office in Fleet-street and the Edinburgh office, 1642, 1643——Expediency of a good report of the speeches generally, rather than of the speeches merely of the local Members, 1646-1648.

Approval of England, Ireland, and Scotland being represented in the gallery in proportion to their Members, 1653——Expectation that room could be provided in the House for a gradually increasing number of papers in course of time, 1657-1659——Objection to the Scotch papers, or to particular districts, joining in order to have a common or identical report, 1661-1665, 1666, 1667.

Belief that an official report would not have any beneficial influence upon newspaper reports; the former would be harmless if needless, 1661, 1662, 1665——Demand of the public for full reports of the speeches of many Members besides local Members, 1671, 1672.

Fallacy of the assumption that the "Times" incurs an exceedingly heavy annual loss through its Parliamentary reports, 1673, 1674——Opinion that there should be some record of the debates for the use of Members, and that some public money may well be devoted to this purpose, 1675, 1676.

Correction of Reports. Difficulty of witness as to stating the precise extent to which speeches are corrected by Members; refusal on his part to allow any unfair correction, *Hansard* 191, 199, 200, 304-307, 370-373——Limited revision contemplated on the part of Members in connection with a system of full official reports, ib. 346-373——Desire also of Members of the House of Lords and of the House of Commons to get the greatest amount of accuracy possible, ib. 450-452.

Great suspicion with which the public would regard official reports if Members were allowed to revise their speeches, *Rass* 646, 662, 663——Explanation as to the extent to which

Report, 1878—*continued*.

Correction of Reports—continued.

which correction of speeches should be allowed in connection with official reports *Saunders* 1787–1793. 1811.

Limited extent to which correction of official reports should be allowed, *Right Hon. The Speaker* 1742.

Slight extent to which, as a rule, questions and answers in Select Committees are corrected by the Members and the witnesses; instances of Committees in which no opportunity has been allowed for correction, *Salter* 1856–1860—— Circumstances of no opportunity for correction being allowed in report of the proceedings of a Committee in a Private Bill in either House, *ib.* 1887–1890—— Great importance of facilities for Members' corrections if there were an official report, *ib.* 1893.

Facilities for reporting evidence given before Select Committees, there being no inaccuracies of any moment, *Lord Eversley* 1954, 1955.

Arrangements proposed on the score of revision, under Mr. Hansard's scheme, App. 906.

See also " *Hansard's Debates*," 2.

Country Newspapers. See *Provincial Newspapers*.

D.

" *Daily Chronicle*." Necessity, in the case of the " Daily Chronicle," of, when, after six o'clock, the seat occupied in the reporters' gallery by the " Echo" so to that hour, *Good* 15, 16—— Access recently allowed to the " Daily Chronicle" in consequence of a vacancy through the discontinuance of the " Hour," *ib.* 147, 148.

Representation by witness, who is proprietor of the " Daily Chronicle," as to the extreme inconvenience consequent upon his not having a seat for a reporter in the front row of the gallery till six o'clock, *Lloyd* 1018–1028. 1070—— Large and increasing circulation of the " Daily Chronicle," it being now a national instead of a local paper, *ib.* 1072–1034. 1071–1077—— The paper has been in existence more than twenty years, but has given Parliamentary reports only within the last eighteen months, *ib.* 1077, 1078.

Occupation by an evening paper up to six o'clock of the seat in the gallery then allocated to the " Chronicle," *Lloyd* 1049, 1050—— Desire of witness for two front seats, though he could make shift with one by having the summary writer in the back row, *ib.* 1031. 1035–1048.

Varying space devoted in witness' paper to Parliamentary reports, according to the demands of its readers and the importance of the subject; very condensed reports at times on Scotch and Irish questions, *Lloyd* 1046–1057. 1072–1075. 1082–1084. 1098–1101. 1106, 1107—— Prohibition of the " Daily Chronicle" reporters from reporting for provincial papers, *ib.* 1060–1065.

Employment on an average of six reporters for the " Chronicle," who occupy the seat in turns from six o'clock till the House closes; extra-staff employed when occasion requires, *Lloyd* 1065–1070. 1087–1090—— Question considered as to witness' paper having any stronger claim to accommodation in the Reporters' Gallery than provincial, or Scotch, or Irish papers, which give Parliamentary reports at equal length, *ib.* 1079–1086. 1091. 1098–1101—— Interest taken by the public in the reports, the accommodation allotted to the " Chronicle" not sufficing to provide adequate reports, *ib.* 1091–1098.

Dunphy, Henry. (*Analysis of his Evidence.*)—Experience of witness some years ago as reporter for the " Morning Post," in the House of Commons; he is now summary writer for the paper, and occupies a front seat in the gallery, 2590–2593—— Great difficulty, or rather impossibility, of reporting, or of summary writing in the back seats of the gallery, 2594–2599. 2615, 2618. 2616–2619—— Extending deficiency of the accommodation generally for reporters; there is no room whatever for any large increase of reporting staff, 2600–2607. 2618–2614.

Objections to using the back seats in the gallery; impracticability of rendering these seats fit for reporting, 2601–2618. 2616–2619—— Objections also to the proposal for resuming the seats in the back rows under the ladies' gallery, 2601–2607. 2619, 2620.

Increase of accommodation by taking some seats right and left from the Members' gallery, 2620, 2621—— Convenience if a second Committee-room were allotted to the reporters, 2608–2611—— Numerous staff involved in the admittance of seven or eight provincial papers to the gallery, 2614.

Modes of occupation of the persons now occupying the back seats, 2617, 2618. 2621, 2627—— Statement as to the necessity of a summary writer hearing the speeches in order to do his work efficiently, 2621–2625. 1630.

E.

Electric and Magnetic Telegraph Company. Representation of the provincial papers in the reporters' gallery formerly by the company, which had one seat, and employed two or three reporters, *Gowell* 79.

Eversley, The Right Hon. Viscount. (Analysis of his Evidence.)—Sufficient accommodation in the reporters' gallery to meet the demands of the press during the time that witness was Speaker, 1905-1907. 1914. 1937——Opinion that an official or verbatim report would be an inconvenience and disadvantage to the House, and is not required by Parliament or by Members as a record, 1908-1911. 1916. 1917. 1930——Very full and accurate character of the reports in the press; belief as to these giving every satisfaction to the public, 1910. 1913-1915. 1918. 1972-1919.

Faithful record by means of "Hansard's Debates," due time being allowed to Members for the correction of their speeches, 1917-1919. 1620. 1631. 1940-1945.——Approval of the steps recently taken for securing through "Hansard" a sufficient report of the proceedings in Committee and on Private Bills, 1919. 1920. 1631. 1633——Contemplated withdrawal of official or other reporters when strangers are excluded, 1921. 1924——Approval of arrangements whereby "Hansard" might appear once a week; that is, by way of a history or record, and not in competition with the daily papers, 1931-1634. 1960-1653.

Difficulty in meeting any demand by the provincial press for accommodation in the reporters' gallery, 1931-1937. 1946-1949——Misfortune if an official report interfered with independent newspaper reports; salutary competition at present, 1938. 1939. 1951. 1953——Facilities for reporting evidence given before Select Committees, there being no inaccuracies of any moment, 1954. 1955.

F.

Factories Bill. Sufficiency of the condensed report in the "Times" in the matter of the Factories Bill, *Reed* 739-741.

Foreign Countries. Belief that in respect of an official report of Parliamentary proceedings the Imperial Parliament is behind all the other Legislatures of Europe, *Howard* 499——Doubt as to the amount of unofficial reports in newspapers in those countries in which there are official reports; independent as well as official reports in the German empire, *ib.* 495-508. —— *See also American Congress. France. Germany.*

France. Long period for which there has been an official publication of debates in France; particulars as to the mode of publication, *Howard* 439. 440. 469-473——Less satisfactory reports in the newspapers in France, where there are official reports, than in the English papers, *ib.* 497. 498.

Excellent facilities for reporting in the French Assembly, owing chiefly to the speeches being delivered from the tribune, *Salter* 1816-1820. 1877. 1878. 1931——Information relative to the staff engaged on the official report at Versailles; comparatively small staff of newspaper reporters, the papers using largely the official report, *ib.* 1811-1816.

Arrangements at Versailles for the revision and correction of the reports of their speeches by Members; extent to which correction is carried, and check exercised, *Salter* 1817-1838——Belief as to there being a large circulation of the "Journal Officiel," *ib.* 1845-1847——Explanation as to the time within which the official report is published in extenso, *ib.* 1864-1872.

"Freeman's Journal." Considerable length at which Parliamentary debates are reported in witness' newspaper, the "Freeman's Journal," *Gray* 2400-2402. 2408——Supply of reports for the "Freeman" through the Press Association, and through reporters for the London newspapers, *ib.* 2403-2415.

Strong complaint as to the utterly unsatisfactory character of the arrangements by which Parliamentary reports are supplied to the "Freeman's Journal," it being quite impossible to obtain good reports, *Gray* 2408-2415——Instances of the difficulty experienced in the case of the debate on the Sunday Closing Bill, *ib.* 2415. 2458. 2459.

Explanation in connection with letter from the manager of the "Freeman's Journal" to the Speaker in April last, submitting claims to a direct representation in the reporters' gallery, *Gray* 2421-2424 —— Circumstances of the paper having been represented in the gallery in 1843, *ib.* 2432. 2433.

Further particulars as to the arrangement by which reports are now provided for witness' paper; recourse had not only to the Press Association, but to individual reporters for London papers, in order to obtain proper reports on Irish questions, *Gray* 2446-2448. 2458-2460. 2495-2497. 2513-2515.

Germany. Existence of independent newspaper reports in the German Empire concurrently with an official report, *Hansard*, 506.

Very good facilities for reporting at Berlin; official character of the report, opportunities being allowed for correction, *Salter* 1837-1844. 1879 —— Belief as to the beneficial effect upon the quality of Members' speeches in Germany, through there being an official report, ib. 1894, 1896.

"Globe." Use after six o'clock by Mr. Hansard of the seat occupied up to that hour by the "Globe," *Grant* 17-19. 34-36. 116, 117.

Limited extent to which the seat appropriated to the "Globe" is used for the purpose of that paper, the staff who occupy it being engaged, by some private arrangement, after five or six o'clock in reporting for the "Glasgow Herald," *Gray* 2415-2427. 2461-2464. 2496-2906. 2516-2672.

There is no attempted concealment of the fact that the reporters of the "Globe" are paid also by the "Glasgow Herald" for reports, *Tennant* 2549-2631.

Grant, Ralph Allen. (Analysis of his Evidence.)—Control exercised by witness, as Serjeant-at-Arms, over the arrangements for Parliamentary reporting in the House of Commons; he has no control over the reports, 1, 2. 110-112 —— Plan submitted showing the accommodation appropriated in the reporters' gallery, there being nineteen front seats and a row of back seats, 3-8. 29, 30 —— Uselessness of the back seats for reporting purposes, these being occupied by the reliefs for the front row, by leader writers, and by reporters for London weekly papers one day in the week, 8, 29. 61-83. 104-109.

Appropriation of fifteen seats in the front row to the London daily press, of three to the Press Associations, and of one to Mr. Hansard, 8 —— Supply of reports for the provincial press, and the Scotch and Irish papers through the three Press Associations, 134 daily papers being thus represented; reference herein to the date of establishment of each association, 9, 10. 24-27. 68, 69. 91-103. 144-148. 149-157 —— Orders given by witness for admission to the gallery on the application of the editors at the beginning of the Session, 11, 12.

Bare sufficiency of the existing accommodation, 13, 14 —— Scarcity in the case of the "Daily Chronicle" of using after six o'clock the seat occupied by the "Echo" up to that hour, 15, 16 —— Provision of a seat for Mr. Hansard, by order of the Speaker, since the beginning of the present Session, the seat of the "Globe" being thus used after six o'clock, 17-19. 34-36. 116, 117 —— Absence of complaint to witness on the part of the provincial press, though applications have been made for seats in the gallery, 18. 30-33. 56-68. 70-72.

Appropriation of two seats to each of the London daily papers, one for the reporter and one for the summary writer, the "Times" alone having three seats, 20-23 —— Obstacle to any enlargement of the gallery, or the provision of any more front seats, 18. 67. —— Practice as to the admission of London and provincial reporters to the lobby by witness; admission also of strangers on an order from witness, 37-39. 60-64.

Information as to the frequent change of reporters during the evening, and as to the number employed by each paper and Press Association, 40-55 —— Long standing rule as to the admission, exclusively, of London papers to the gallery; impracticability of accommodating the provincial press, 59. 65-67. 129. 151 —— Belief as to some of the reporters for the London papers supplying also provincial papers; witness is not cognisant of any restriction to the contrary, 73-80. 109, 110. 136-138.

Absence of any complaint to witness as to the accommodation in the room in which the reporters write out their reports, 81, 83 —— Facilities of the press generally in the matter of telegraphic communication with the House, 86-90 —— Long period for which the London press had seats in the gallery before the Press Associations applied, the latter being obliged to have seats at the side instead of in the centre, 111-113.

Room within for another Press Association, are for a Scotch or Irish paper; explanation, moreover, that in the event of a vacancy the seat would be given in preference to a London paper, 119-134. 139-143. 149-157 —— Access recently allowed to the "Daily Chronicle" in consequence of a vacancy through the discontinuance of the "Echo," 147, 148.

Gray, Edmund Dwyer (Member of the House). (Analysis of his Evidence.)—Considerable length at which Parliamentary debates are reported in certain newspapers, the "Freeman's Journal," 2400-2402. 2408 —— Supply of reports for the "Freeman" through the Press Association and through reporters for the London newspapers, 2403-2405 —— Entire change in the system of reporting for the Irish papers since the introduction of the Government telegraph system, 2406, 2407.

Report, 1878—continued.

Gray, Edmund Dwyer. (Analysis of his Evidence)—continued.

Strong complaint as to the utterly unsatisfactory character of the arrangements by which Parliamentary reports are supplied to the "Freeman's Journal," it being quite impossible to obtain good reports, 2408–2415——Great dissatisfaction of Irish Members on account of the very imperfect way in which they are reported in the "Freeman's Journal" and other Irish papers, whilst they are still worse reported in the English press, 2408, 2411, 2412.

Contrast discussion in the House of Irish questions of vital importance, which demand a full and fair report, 2412, 2413——Willingness of the Press Association to do the best it can, witness submitting, however, that a special and efficient report is wanted upon Irish questions, and that such report cannot now be obtained, and is not given in the English press, 2414–2420. 2459——Instance of the difficulty experienced by the "Freeman's Journal" in the case of the debate on the Sunday Closing Bill, 2414, 2458, 2459.

Explanations in connection with letter from the manager of the "Freeman's Journal" to the Speaker in April last, submitting claim to a direct representation in the reporters' gallery, 2421–2424——Frequent applications previously made to the Serjeant-at-Arms, but without success, 2421, 2424.

Complaint as to the great unfairness of the present arrangements as regards the London press, several seats being allotted to London newspapers, which seats are not required nor used for reporting purposes for such paper, 2425–2431——Limited extent to which the seat appropriated to the "Globe" is used for the purposes of that paper, the staff who occupy it being engaged, by some private arrangement, after five or six o'clock in reporting for the "Glasgow Herald," 2425–2427, 2461–2464, 2495–2508, 2516–2571——Statement, also, as to the seat allotted to the summary writer of the "Morning Advertiser" being practically used by representatives of the "Manchester Guardian," 2437, 2482, 2483, 2488, 2584.

Several of the London papers having seats for summary writers, whereas each paper hardly gives any summary; unfairness in these seats being retained to the exclusion of other papers, 2428, 2429, 2465–2472, 2488–2490, 2495–2497——Practical, though indirect, admittance of two or three provincial papers under the present system, 2430, 2431, 2436, 2461–2464, 2481, 2482, 2497——Circumstance of the "Freeman's Journal" having been represented in the gallery in 1843; 2477, 2483.

Increased and increasing demand in Ireland for Parliamentary reports, 2434, 2435, 2437–2480——Decided objection to a joint report for Irish papers by the same reporting staff, 2437–2440, 2450, 2451, 2507——Belief that not more than two or three Irish papers could establish a claim to independent representation in the gallery, 2430, 2451, 2465, 2466.

Approval of an official report if promptly and efficiently done; the difficulty as to summarising is not insuperable, 2440–2446, 2507——Particulars as to the arrangement by which reports are now provided for witness' paper; recourse had not only to the Press Association but to individual reporters for London papers in order to obtain proper reports on Irish questions, 2446–2448, 2455–2460, 2495–2497, 2513–2516——Uselessness, for the Irish press, of the semi-official reports in "Hansard," 2452–2454.

Stringent rule of the "Times" that its staff shall not report for other papers, 2455, 2473–2476, 2506——Great inconvenience to Irish papers if, as is probable, other London newspapers besides the "Times" prohibited their reporters from doing work for the provincial press, 2455–2474——Explanation that there is nothing understood in the arrangement by which the London press reporters are paid by Irish and other papers for special reports; the system is, however, altogether wrong, 2457, 2489–2472, 2481, 2482, 2495–2497.

Exceptional difficulty in the case of reports for the Irish press through the slowness of the telegraphing across the Channel, 2474–2476——Expediency of Irish papers having reasonable facilities for fully reporting the debates on all important Irish questions, 2483, 2484.

Suggestion that, in view of the difficulties of increased accommodation, the Press Association be given a considerable increase of front seats, and the leading Irish and Scotch papers be allowed access to the back seats, so that their representatives might give instructions on the spot as to the length and character of the reports required from the association, 2485–2488——One front and one back seat should, if possible, be given to each of the leading Irish papers; this does not appear practicable at present, 2485, 2486.

Inexpediency of the London papers being allowed to prohibit their staff in the gallery from reporting for other papers, 2488–2490——Entire concurrence in the suggestion that papers should only be allowed access to the gallery on condition that they gave fairly full reports, 2491–2494——Necessity of Irish papers making their own arrangements for an official report, 2507–2509.

Belief

Report, 1878—continued.

Gray, Edward Dwyer. (Analysis of his Evidence)—continued.

Belief that the back seats in the gallery would do fairly well for summary work, especially if ruled, 2510-2512.——Impression that the Central Press dare not now do any real reporting work, 2513.——Enhanced difficulties of the London papers in using an official report, as they go to press at a very early hour, 2517, 2518.

Gurney, Messrs. Duty of the firm to take notes of all evidence before Committees of the two Houses, and of any proceedings at the Bar, Saltar 1813-1815. 1887.——Dispatch and economy by the practice of Messrs. Gurney, whereby clerks transcribe the short-hand writers' notes; subsequent comparison of the transcript with the original short-hand, *ib.* 1810-1863. 1901-1904.

H.

Hansard, Thomas Curson. (Analysis of his Evidence.)—Origination of Hansard's Parliamentary Debates by witness' father in 1806, the work having been carried on by witness since 1834, without any recognition from Government till the present year, 158-160. 248-251.——Particulars as to the compilation of "Hansard," the system of collating from newspapers, the practice as to revision and correction, &c., &c., 160 *et seq.*

Information in connection with recent arrangements with Government for special reports on certain points; financial condition involved, 179-188. 282. 353. 374.

Explanations with reference to the publication in the United States of the "Congressional Globe," and subsequently of the "Congressional Record," the latter being distributed gratis to the extent of 14,000 copies, 123-131. 164-168. 181-186.——Objections to the publication daily of a verbatim report of speeches, and nothing else; opinion that it would not sell, 190. 231-238. 263-268. 273-276.——Long period for which there has been an official publication of debates in France; particulars as to the mode of publication, 239, 240. 269-273.

Arrangement made with witness by Government, in 1855, in regard to the supply of copies of the debates for the public offices; small pecuniary gain derived from the Government supply, 242-245.——Complaints by Members as to the inaccuracy of the reports in the newspapers; general satisfaction with witness' reports, 246-251.——Exceedingly imperfect reports of the proceedings on Wednesday, this being the great blot of the present system, 254-262. 276-280. 345-347.

Practice of the daily newspapers to report very fully the speeches of Ministers and ex-Ministers, whilst the speeches of ordinary Members are greatly abbreviated, 259-262.——Steps taken by witness with a view to a fair report of Wednesday's speeches in "Hansard," 278-280.——Verbatim report in "Hansard" of the debate on the Women's Disabilities Bill, private arrangement made with him in the matter, 280. 398-401.

Subsidy given in Canada for an official report of the debates in the "Dominion Hansard"; from allowed to Members to make verbal corrections, 187-190.——Belief that in New Zealand there is no payment by Government, and that the publication of the debates is a private speculation, 290-293.——Efficiency of witness' arrangements for reporting part of the debates in the House of Commons, whilst for the rest of the debates, and especially on Wednesday, improved arrangements are greatly needed, 194-196. 275-282.

Conclusion that official reports have become a public necessity, 197-199. 363. 366.——Inexpediency of any interference with private reports, if official reports be established; strong moral claim of witness to consideration in any change that may be made, 300. 301, 303.

Instances of verbatim reports made expressly for Members, 308-310.——Preference for full and accurate reports, as compared with verbatim reports, 311, 312.——Long period for which "Hansard" has been quoted in the House almost as an official publication, 313-321.——Superior reports for some years in the "Mirror of Parliament," which, however, ceased to exist many years ago, 311. 351-354.

Further evidence in detail relative to "Hansard," together with explanations and suggestions on various points, 354 *et seq.* 487 *et seq.*——Explanation that the answers of Ministers to Members' questions are not reported for "Hansard" by witness' staff, but are obtained by him from the London papers; belief as to accuracy being secured in this respect, 381-384.——Instances of Members wishing to be reported verbatim, 403.

Payment of 56,000 *l.* a year by the American Congress for an inferior publication of their proceedings, 408-410.——Opinion that "Hansard" should be supplied to Members entirely at the cost of the public, 412-416.——Expediency, if there be official reports, of what is unnecessary in a speech, as well as what is necessary, being reported, 417-421.

Suggestion that if there be official reports, seats should be provided for the reporters in the body of the House; practice to this effect in the United States, France, Italy, &c.,

Report, 1878—continued.

Hansard, Thomas Curson. (Analysis of his Evidence)—continued.

422, 423, 426–437——Doubt as to the expediency of attempting to deliver to Members, at four o'clock in the day, a report of the speeches down to the termination of the previous day's sitting, 424, 425, 428–431——Instances of Bills having been reported in the two papers as having passed a stage without discussion, when there has been discussion, 432.

Obstacle to newspapers being furnished with reports by a staff of official reporters in the debate in going on, 443–447——Desire alike of Members of the House of Lords, and of the House of Commons, to get the greatest amount of accuracy possible, 450–452.

Explanation as to witness not having applied for seats in the gallery for a staff of reporters, 453–455——Printing of the "Debates" from type, stereo-plates not being used; objections to stereotyping for the purpose, 456–462.

Requirement of full and accurate reports, nearly verbatim, by a limited number of the public, 463——Requirement of a staff of some sixteen or eighteen reporters for a system of official reports, 464——Estimate of nine volumes of "Hansard" as sufficient for containing full and accurate reports of the debates of the Session, 465–468.

Suggested power, if there be official reports, of reporting in a more concentrated form those debates which take place late at night, where there is much repetition of argument, 480, 481——Tendency of verbatim reports to raise the public opinion of the House of Commons; instances to this effect, 482–484.

Conviction of witness that the public expenditure necessary for full official reports would be money wisely spent, and that the cost would be small as compared with the benefit derived, 487–491, 494——Provision in the United States for the official publication of speeches which have not been made, 492, 493.

Doubt as to the amount of unofficial report in newspapers in those countries in which there are official reports; independent as well as official reports in the German Empire, 495–506——Less satisfactory reports in the newspapers in France, where there are official reports, than in the English papers, 497, 498——Excellent reports still given by some of the London daily papers, but not by all, 507–509.

[Second Examination.] Explanation that witness proposes to continue the present system of collating newspaper reports, in order to obtain reports of debates on second reading, 1834–1837——Independent staff of reporters necessary for supplying reports if witness were to collate from their reports as well as from the newspapers, 1838–1840.

Unsatisfactory arrangement by which witness obtains a seat for a reporter in the front row before six o'clock, 1841–1843——Increased charge if witness were to supply weekly copies of "Hansard," not only to Members of both Houses of Parliament, but to the public offices; expediency of such supply, 1844, 1845.

HANSARD'S DEBATES:

1. *Origin and Management of "Hansard's Parliamentary Debates" :*

Commencement of the publication of "Hansard's Parliamentary Debates" by witness' father in 1804, the work having been carried on since that time without any official recognition till the present year, *Hansard* 158–160, 241–245——Management of the work by witness since 1834, when, upon his father's death, he became proprietor, *ib.* 160.

2. *Particulars as to the Compilation of the Work, the System of collating Newspaper Reports, and the practice as to Revision and Correction :*

Practice as to collating the reports of the Members' speeches and putting them into type, the proofs being sent to the speakers for correction; particulars herein as to the number of speeches in the House of Lords, and in the House of Commons, sent out for revision, and as to the number returned corrected, *Hansard* 167–177, 201–205, 335–337
——Large

Report, 1878—continued.

Hansard's Debates—continued.

2. *Particulars as to the Compilation of the Work, &c.—continued.*

——Large number of speeches not returned, the speakers being satisfied with the proof reports, *Hansard* 170. 379, 380.

Important improvement in the revision and collation by witness' staff of revisers, irrespectively of the staff now specially employed in reporting fully on the four subjects embraced in the arrangement, under which he is paid 1,000l.; *Hansard* 187-189.

Care taken not to put into a speech any matter not supported by authority, or any words not spoken, unless with a view to grammatical accuracy, *Hansard* 190. 301-303 ——Acceptance of some speeches by witness from Members on their own authority, ib. 194-198.

Shortened period which now elapses between the date of the speech and the date of its final revision, and its publication by witness, *Hansard* 213-217. 277 ——Much shorter time after the end of the Session in which Members will in future receive the last of the publication, ib. 218, 219.

Practice of witness as to sometimes cancelling collated reports of speeches in favour of more accurate reports; he never suppresses a report, *Hansard* 338-344 ——Careful verification by the revisers before the shorthand writers' notes are put into type, ib. 345. 346 ——Circumstances under which some speeches are reported in the first person, and some in the third, ib. 347-351.

Further explanation of the practice of revising and collating the speeches for "Hansard," *Hansard* 437-441 ——In no instance has any pressure been brought to bear with a view to the omission of a debate, ib. 448, 449.

Large excess of the "reports in "Hansard" over and above the length of those given in the London daily papers, *Hansard* 469-476 ——Province of witness to report debates fully, though much repetition and surplusage may be involved, ib. 477-479. 483, 488 —— In no instance has a speech been supplied to "Hansard" before it was made in the House, ib. 491, 492.

Proposed continuance of the present system of collating newspaper reports in order to obtain reports of debates on second reading, *Hansard* 1634-1637.

Abstract (submitted by Mr. Hansard) of sent copy and speeches sent out and returned for Sessions 1869, 1870, and 1871, in the Lords and Commons respectively, *App.* 210.

Further abstracts of sent copy and speeches sent out and returned for the Session of 1874, in the Lords and in the Commons, *App.* 210, 211.

3. *Reporting Staff :*

Various sources from which the debates have been compiled; special occasions only upon which reporters have been employed by witness in the reporters' gallery, *Hansard* 160-167 ——Employment of 10 reporters in the gallery in reporting exclusively the four kinds of debate neglected more or less by the daily papers, ib. 206-208 —— Large staff of reporters which he would require in order to report the whole proceedings in Parliament fully, ib. 338, 339. 1638-1640 ——Staff of four reporters employed by witness, who report for him exclusively; assistance largely derived from other reporters on any special occasion, ib. 376-378. 380. 440, 441.

4. *Seat recently placed at Mr. Hansard's disposal in the Reporters' Gallery :*

Provision of a seat for Mr. Hansard, by order of the Speaker, since the beginning of the present Session, the seat of the "Globe" being then used after six o'clock, *Comm.* 17-19. 34-38. 116, 117.

Explanation as to witness not having applied for seats in the gallery for a staff of reporters, the limited size of the "Debates" not justifying the expense, *Hansard* 453-465.

Instructions were given by witness to the Serjeant-at-Arms to provide a seat for Mr. Hansard's representative, *Right Hon. The Speaker* 1798.

Private arrangement by which witness obtains, on sufferance, a seat for a reporter in the frame now before six o'clock; this is not satisfactory, *Hansard* 1641-1643.

5. *Financial Arrangement with Government ; Price charged for the Debates to Members and to Public Offices :*

Arrangement made with witness by Government in 1855, whereby he supplied 100 copies of the Debates for the public offices at the same price as to private Members; 114 copies are now supplied to Government, *Hansard* 241-244 ——Reduction in price as a condition of the supply to Government; actual pecuniary gain of only 40 l. a year derived by witness, ib. 244, 245 ——Increased price for an increased number of volumes unless Government were to give a larger subvention, ib. 338-341.

Condition as to the volumes of "Hansard" for the Session being purchased collectively, *Hansard* 404. 405 ——Statement on the question of Members getting "Hansard"

Report, 1878—continued.

HANSARD'S DEBATES—continued.

6. *Financial Arrangement with Government; Price charged, &c.—continued.*

at a reduced cost in consideration of the subsidy of 1,000 L a year, paid to writers by Government; opinion that they should be supplied to Members entirely at the cost of the public, *Hansard* 416-418. 6644. 6645——Estimate of nine volumes of "Hansard" as sufficient for containing full and accurate reports of the debates of the Session, ib. 436-458.

6. *Character and Reputation of the Work; eminent Testimony to its Value:*

Great satisfaction given to Members, with few exceptions, by the report of speeches in "Hansard's Debates," *Hansard* 191, 192——Complaints by Members as to the inaccuracy of the reports in the newspapers, whilst very general satisfaction has been expressed with writers' reports, though he has had no reporter in the gallery, ib. 248-251.

Quotation of "Hansard" in the House almost as an official publication long before full reports were given by the newspapers, the authority of the work having, in fact, always rested upon the confidence placed in those who conduct it, *Hansard* 313-311 ——Testimony paid to the work in the Colonies, where the name of "Hansard" is adopted in the official reports of debates; this was also the case for some time in Prussia, id. 314, 325.

Reference to "Hansard," as a most valuable publication and as fulfilling the purpose of an official record; advantage if it were published weekly, *Right Hon. The Speaker*, 1748-1762. 1769. 1778. 1799-1802——Recommended continuance of "Hansard" in the interest of the public, ib. 1769——Advantage in "Hansard" being a unabridged report, rather than an official report, ib. 1770-1772. 1803, 1804. 1810, 1811.

Less objection to the discretion exercised as to the length at which any speech is reported in "Hansard" than to its being an actual official report, *Right Hon. The Speaker* 1775-1777. 1795-1797.

Faithful record by means of "Hansard's Debates," due time being allowed to Members for the correction of their speeches, *Lord Barnley* 1917-1919. 1940-1945. 1490, 1491.

Value attached to "Hansard" as a faithful record of proceedings; fuller record desirable as regards proceedings in Committee and on Private Bills, *Sir J. Raw* 1587.

7. *Recent Arrangement with Government for Special Reports on certain Points, and for supplying the Debates at a Maximum Price, irrespectively of the Number of Volumes:*

Particulars relative to the arrangement entered into between witness and Government in December 1877, whereby he undertook, for the sum of 1,000 L, to provide special reports on four points very imperfectly given in the newspapers, *Hansard* 179-184. 150——Undertaking, also, in consideration of a further sum of 1,000 L, to supply the whole debates at the price of five guineas, without any increase when there are more than four volumes, ib. 160-184. 253.

Explanation as to a supplementary estimate for the foregoing sum of 3,000 L not having been taken in the present Session; vote taken for this amount in the Stationery Estimate for 1878-79; *Hansard* 184, 185. 374.

Opinion that the recent arrangement with Mr. Hansard will meet the deficiency hitherto as regards a historical record, whilst the newspaper reports fairly meet the wants of the general public, *Lovell* 1007, 1008. 1011-1016.

Reference to the recent arrangement with Mr. Hansard as calculated to supply the deficiency of reports with respect to private Bills, proceedings in Committee, &c., *Right Hon. The Speaker* 1691. 1723-1724.

Approval of the steps recently taken for securing through "Hansard" a sufficient report of the proceedings in Committee and on Private Bills, *Lord Barnley* 1919, 1920. 1931, 1933.

8. *Suggestions for a Weekly Publication; increased Cost involved:*

Obstacles to a prompt or daily publication of "Hansard" on account of the necessity of allowing time for correction of speeches, *Right Hon. The Speaker* 1758-1761 ——Sufficiency of the reports generally if there were a weekly publication of "Hansard," concurrently with a fair representation of the debates, Irish, and provincial press in the reporters' gallery, ib. 1778.

Approval of arrangements whereby "Hansard" might appear once a week; that is, by way of a history or record, and not in competition with the daily papers, *Lord Barnley* 1951-1954. 1950-1953.

Enhanced cost if witness were to supply weekly copies of "Hansard" not only to Members

Report, 1878—continued.

HANSARD'S DEBATES—continued.

3. *Suggestions for a Weekly Publication; increased Cost involved*—continued.

Members of both Houses of Parliament, but to the public offices; expediency of such supply as a matter of public policy, *Hansard* 1844, 1845.

Letter from Mr. Hansard, dated 11th July 1878, submitting a proposal, founded on the suggestion by The Speaker, for an extension of the existing arrangement with a weekly publication; estimates that this may be effected at an increase of 2,000 *l.* upon the present subvention, *App.* 209.

2. *Papers submitted by Mr. Hansard explanatory of Schemes for Complete Reports; Estimated Cost:*

Paper explanatory of scheme for the production of a complete report of the debates in both Houses of Parliament; estimate of 16,577 *l.* as the total cost for an ordinary Session, *App.* 206, 207.

Further scheme submitted by Mr. Hansard, the total cost being estimated at 20,540 *l.*, *App.* 208.

See also Answers of Ministers.   Correction of Reports.   Libraries and Institutions. Official Report. 4.   Wednesday (Report of Proceedings).   Women's Disabilities Bill.

Henry, Mitchell (Member of the House). Failure of a motion by Mr. Mitchell Henry, in 1878, for a Select Committee on Parliamentary Reporting, *Hansard* 178.

Highways Bill. Defence of the great compression in the "Times" of a recent discussion which lasted for several hours upon the Highways Bill, *East* 725–730. 317–891.

House of Lords. Change of duties by the same reporters between the Lords and the Commons, *East* 513. 549——Much worse accommodation for the reporters in the House of Lords than in the House of Commons, *Q.* 761–763.

I

Identical or Joint Reports. Evidence in disapproval of identical reports, whether under an official system or through news agencies, *Casper* 1451–1453. 1450–1480. 1514–1528. 1811–1830——Objection to the Scotch papers, or to particular districts, joining in order to have a common or identical report, *ib.* 1561–1563. 1666, 1667.

Disapproval of an identical report for the "Leeds Mercury" and other provincial papers, *Reid* 2131–2133. 2207–2209——Opinion that not more than two provincial papers could conveniently combine in order to have identical reports, *ib.* 2164–2167.

Obstacles to a satisfactory combination between two or three papers; preference for the existing facilities through the Press Association, *Jaffray* 2145–2148. 2178–2181——Comment upon the objection of some papers to identical reports, *ib.* 2189, 2190.

Objection by country papers in the same district to combine, so as to have an identical report; less difficulty of joint arrangements between two papers at a distance from each other, *Tweeford* 1326. 1337.

Strong objection to a system of identical or joint reports for Irish newspapers, *Gray* 2437–2440. 2450, 2451. 2507.

Irish Newspapers. Supply of reports by the "Central News" and by the Press Association to all, or nearly all, the Irish papers, *Saunders* 1381–1387.

Offer made by witness on several occasions, but not accepted, to find a seat in the gallery for the Irish press and another for the Scotch press, *Right Hon. The Speaker* 1694–1697——Good ground for the claim made by Irish newspapers, as well as by Scotch, for increased facilities for reporting, *ib.* 1710–1717. 1726, 1727.

Entire change in the system of reporting for the Irish papers since the introduction of the Government telegraph system, *Gray* 2406, 2407——Great dissatisfaction of Irish Members on account of the very imperfect way in which they are reported in the "Freeman's Journal," and other Irish papers, whilst they are still worse reported in the English press, *ib.* 2408. 2411. 2413.

Constant discussion in the House of Irish questions of vital importance, which demanded a full and fair report, *Gray* 2412, 2413——Willingness of the Press Association to do the best it can, witness admitting, however, that a special and efficient report is wanted upon Irish questions, and that such report cannot now be obtained and is not given in the English press, *ib.* 2414–2416. 2460.

Increased and increasing demand in Ireland for Parliamentary reports, *Gray* 2434, 2435. 2477–2480——Decided objection to a joint report for Irish papers by the same *reporting*

Irish Newspapers—continued.

reporting staff, *Gray* 2431-2440. 2450, 2451. 2507——Belief that not more than two or three Irish papers could establish a claim to independent representation in the gallery, *ib.* 2439. 2451. 2483. 2496.

Unfairness for the Irish press of semi-official reports in " Hansard," *Gray* 2452-2454——Great inconvenience to Irish papers if (as is probable) other London newspapers besides the " Times," prohibited their reporters from doing work for the provincial press, *ib.* 2455. 2474——Expediency of Irish papers having reasonable facilities for fully reporting the debates on all important Irish questions, *ib.* 2483, 2484.

Suggestion that, in view of the difficulties of increased accommodation, the News Association be given a considerable increase of front seats, and the leading Irish and Scotch papers be allowed access to the back seats, so that their representatives might give instructions on the spot as to the length and character of the reports required from the Association, *Gray* 2485-2488.

One front and one back seat should, if possible, be given to each of the leading Irish papers ; this does not appear practicable at present, *Gray* 2434, 2486——Necessity of Irish papers making their own summaries of an official report, *ib.* 2507-2509.

See also " Freeman's Journal." Reporters' Gallery.

J.

Jeffray, John. (Analysis of his Evidence.)——Long experience of witness in connection with the " Birmingham Daily Post," of which he is one of the proprietors, 2219-2221 ——Supply of Parliamentary reports to the paper entirely through the agency of the Press Association; special orders given to the Association as to the kind of reports required, such orders being unsatisfactorily complied with, 2220-2224. 2227, 2228. 2231. 2247. 2265-2287——Probability of the " Birmingham Daily Post " employing reporters of its own if there were accommodation available in the gallery, though hitherto no difficulty has been experienced in getting the special reports required, 2225-2218.

Belief that nothing would be gained in rapidity of transmission, if witness' paper had its own staff of reporters ; illustration of the exceeding promptness with which reports are now supplied, 2229-2231. 2260-2269——Slight effect of the reports upon the circulation; public interest, however, taken in the reports on special occasions, 2232. 2253-2256——Important provincial papers represented in the management of the Press Association, 2234——Conclusion as to the provincial press generally being able to obtain such reports as they may require through the medium of the Association, 2234, 2236-2247. 2248. 2252. 2276, 2277. 2286-2290. 2302.

Still more complete reports furnished by the Press Association but for the defective accommodation at its disposal in the reporters' gallery; claim of the Association to better facilities in this respect, 2238. 2249. 2250. 2257-2259. 2268. 2290——Entire uselessness of official reports to the provincial press and to newspapers generally, 2237-2241. 2254-2256——Suggestion that seats in the gallery (if available) be offered to provincial papers on the condition that real and *bonâ fide* use is made by them, and that independent reports are given in each case, 2243. 2249. 2250. 2270-2271. 2291-2298. 2301-2307.

Objection to the provision of a special wire as a condition of access to the gallery ; statement hereto as to the " Birmingham Daily Post " not requiring a private wire, 2243. 2284. 2301. 1303——Calculation that sixteen or seventeen papers would apply for accommodation in the gallery if it were available, 2244. 2273-2275. 2301——Obstacle to a satisfactory combination between two or three papers ; preference for the existing facilities through the Press Association, 2245-2248. 2278-2281.

Other sources of supply of reports to country newspapers than through the Press Association or Central News, 2251——Expediency of the London press having full facilities for giving summaries of the debates ; doubt as to front seats in the reporters' gallery being necessary for this purpose, 2269. 1308.

Comment upon the objection of some papers to identical reports, 2277. 2285. 2289. 2290——Three classes of reports given by the Press Association ; facility, moreover, in obtaining full reports of the speeches of local members, 2282-2288.

Joint Reports. See Identical or Joint Reports.

L

Late Sittings. Prolonged sittings of the House after midnight in the last two Sessions, the speeches, as reported, having doubtless been greatly compressed ; belief, however, that in the " Times " all really important information was chronicled, *Rose* 685-694. 840, 851.

" Leeds

Report, 1878—*continued.*

"*Leeds Mercury.*" Insufficiency, in the case of the "Leeds Mercury," of the reports supplied by the "Central News," or Press Association; practice of obtaining the ordinary report in the paper from reporters employed also by the London press, *Reid* 2078–2083. 2100–2103. 2117. 9140. 9140—Very full reports given in the "Leeds Mercury"; much fuller, in fact, than in some of the London papers having reporters in the Gallery, ib. 2079. 2115. 2130. 9176, 9177—Belief that longer reports are published in the "Mercury" than in any other provincial paper, ib. 2079—Delay in the transmission of telegraphic messages from the Home to the London office of the "Leeds Mercury," so that coin are now used, ib. 2092. 2094. 9147. 9158.

Statement showing the heavy cost incurred by the "Leeds Mercury" for Parliamentary reports, including special reports and the cost of telegraphing; reduction of cost to some extent through being associated in the matter with smaller paper, *Reid* 2095–2099. 2111–2114. 2134–2136—The cost of the report is about 7*l.* a year, the cost of telegraphing being at least 40*l.* a year, ib. 2096—Several reasons which make it essential for the "Leeds Mercury" to employ its own reporters, instead of depending upon any of the news associations, or upon the partial services of the reporters for the London press, ib. 2100–2104. 2117–2115. 9118.

Expediency of full and prompt reports in the paper in order to keep up its reputation, the expense being fully justified thereby, through the circulation is not materially affected, *Reid* 2105–2110. 2116. 2210–2211—Much earlier period of the day at which the Leeds public obtain Parliamentary news through the "Leeds Mercury," than through the London papers, ib. 2120–2128.

Satisfaction of women if one seat in the Gallery were allotted to his paper, *Reid* 2129. 2130—There are about 400 columns of Parliamentary reports telegraphed every Session, ib. 2132—The average length of the reports during the present Session has been four columns a day; fifteen columns have been given, all telegraphed, ib. 9177—Grounds for concluding that the Press Association could not supply the prompt reports required by the "Leeds Mercury," ib. 2178–2189.

Further explanation of the arrangement whereby reports are supplied to the "Leeds Mercury" by reporters for the London press, through on special occasions it is necessary to obtain the services of the "Central News" and Press Association, *Reid* 2400–2204—Impracticability of the paper obtaining the required reports sufficiently promptly from the Press Association; this difficulty would equally apply to an official report, ib. 2117. 2118.

Lewis, Sir George Cornewall (the late). Value attached by the late Sir George Lewis to the reports in the "Times" as ample for all purposes, *Ross* 813.

Libraries and Institutions. Demand for complete sets of "Hansard's Debates" for libraries and institutions, *Hansard* 406, 407. 418.

Lloyd, Edward. (Analysis of his Evidence.)—Representation by witness, who is proprietor of the "Daily Chronicle," as to the existence encouragement upon his not having a seat for a reporter in the front row of the Gallery till six o'clock, 1018–1046. 1070—Large and increasing circulation of the "Daily Chronicle," it being now a national journal of a local paper, 1017–1034. 1071–1073—Occupation by an evening paper up to six o'clock of the seat in the Gallery then allotted to the "Chronicle," 1049, 1050.

Desire of witness for two front seats, though he could make shift with one by having the summary writer in the back row, 1031. 1035–1045—Varying space devoted in witness' paper to Parliamentary reports, according to the demands of its readers and the importance of the subject; very condensed reports at times on Scotch and Irish questions, 1046–1057. 1070–1075. 1081–1084. 1098–1101. 1106, 1107—Objection to the London papers combining in order to have a joint report, each paper wishing to act for itself, 1058, 1059. 1106–1107.

Prohibition of the "Daily Chronicle" reporters from reporting for provincial papers, 1060–1065—Inconvenience if the summary writer had to sit in the Speaker's Gallery, 1066—Employment on an average of six reporters for the "Chronicle," who occupy the seat in turns from six o'clock till the House closes; extra staff employed when occasion requires, 1068–1070. 1087–1090.

Question considered as to allowing any paper having any stronger claim to accommodation in the Reporters' Gallery than provincial or Scotch or Irish papers which give Parliamentary reports at equal length, 1072–1088. 1091. 1096–1101—Interest taken by the public in the reports, the accommodation allotted to the "Chronicle" not sufficing to provide adequate reports, 1091–1098.

Lobby of the House. Practice as to the admission of London and provincial reporters to the Lobby by witness; admission also of strangers on an order from witness, *Gosset* 37–40. 60–64.

Report, 1878—continued.

Local Members. Special reports made of the speeches of certain Members by one of the Press Associations for the local papers; none made of those reports by witness' revisers, *Howard* 209-211.

Explanation that speeches of certain Members are reported more or less fully at the request of the local newspapers, the Members themselves having no voice in the matter, so far as the Press Association is concerned, *Lowell* 871-875, 984, 1006, 1009, 1010, 1017 — Full length at which certain Members are reported for the press of the localities which they represent in Parliament, *ib.* 871-875, 984.

Large increase in the demand for special reports of speeches of local Members, although the cost is considerable, *Saunders* 1110, 1116-1114, 1152, 1153, 1168, 1166, 1207, 1208 — Importance of an official report of speeches of local Members, *ib.* 1341-1347, 1416, 1417.

Expediency of a good report of the speeches generally, rather than of the speeches merely of the local Members, *Cooper* 1646-1652.

London Newspapers. Appropriation of two seats in the Reporters' Gallery to each of the London daily papers, one for the reporter, and one for the summary writer, the "Times" alone having three seats, *Gosset* 10-13 — Long-standing rule as to the admission, exclusively, of London papers to the Gallery; impracticability of accommodating the provincial press, *ib.* 59, 65-69, 159, 161.

Non-objection to London papers combining to employ a press association to report for them, several of the daily papers not giving full reports, *Rose* 561-563.

Question whether the London papers might not have a press association of their own; necessity of such arrangement if they were deprived of some of their seats in the Gallery, *Lowell* 940-945, 951-953 — Monopoly now enjoyed by the London papers, *Townsend* 2312.

Complaint as to the great unfairness of the present arrangements as regards the London press, several seats being allotted to London newspapers, which seats are not required nor used for reporting purposes for such papers, *Gray* 2425-2431.

Paper submitted by Captain Gosset showing the number of seats occupied by the staff of each London paper, and the number of tickets in each case, *App.* 205.

See also "Daily Chronicle."   "Globe."   "Morning Advertiser."   *Provincial Newspapers*, 2.   "Standard."   *Summary Writers.*   "Times."

Lowell, John. (Analysis of his Evidence.)—Has been Manager of the Press Association since its establishment in 1869; 864, 865 — Origin of the Association in the transfer of the telegraphs to Government; miscellaneous as well as Parliamentary news supplied by it to the provincial press, 866-869 — Reference to the Central Press and Central News Associations as being trading concerns, whilst the Press Association is simply a co-operation body not working for profit, 870, 871.

Total of 131 newspaper proprietors, members of the Press Association, a committee of nine being appointed every year; supply also by the Association of 101 newspapers and ninety-nine exchanges and news-rooms, not members, 872, 876, 877 — Particulars as to the arrangements for the supply of Parliamentary reports at greater or less length to different classes of provincial papers; supplemental and full reports sent to the larger papers, and to the Scotch and Irish papers, 872, 878, 882, 883 — Full length at which certain Members are reported for the Press of the localities which they represent in Parliament, 871-875, 984.

Large increase in the quantity of Parliamentary news supplied to the country press since the supply was provided by the telegraph companies; increase also in the number of papers taking full reports, though the demand would now appear to have reached its maximum, 877-889 — Somewhat similar reports supplied by the "Central News" and "Central Press," as by the Press Association, 889, 985, 904.

Opinion that an official report or historical record of the proceedings in Parliament is very desirable in the interests of Members, but would be of little use to the newspapers, there not being much public demand for complete reports, 886, 887, 890, 896, 915-920 — Conclusion that the demand of the public for Parliamentary information is now sufficiently met, 890-894, 915-917.

Statement as to the very inconvenient character of the accommodation provided in the Gallery of the House for the Press Association, 891, 901, 995-1000 — Sufficient facilities (if there were better accommodation) for supplying the wants of the country press, without any employment of special reporters by the latter, 901-914 — Considerable proportion of the provincial papers which do not require Parliamentary reports, 921-923.

Large extension of the system of special news, as a means of supplementing the information conveyed by the several Press associations, 924-929 — Exception taken to the view that newspapers having special news should have some preference as regards access

Report, 1878—continued

Lowell, John. (Analysis of his Evidence)—continued.

to the Reporters' Gallery, 930-935 · Expediency of full facilities to provincial newspapers, if admitted to the Strangers' Gallery, 936-939. 954-957.

Question whether the London papers might not have a Press Association of their own ; necessity of such arrangement if they were deprived of some of their seats in the Gallery, 940-945. 951-953——Means of increasing the accommodation for reporters by placing the summary writers in the back seats ; inconvenience, however, of the latter, 946-950. 958-963.

Exclusive employment of ten reporters by the Press Association, assistance being required also from several others, 957——Shortening of the "turns" in the evening advances, 959. 960——The Association does not supply private individuals, 961-968——Supply of special as well as ordinary reports by the Association, 968. 969-977——Supply of reports by the Association to the "Scotsman" and other leading Scotch papers ; special reports obtained by the "Scotsman" from reporters for the London press, 969-977——Practice of the Association to send off reports promptly, down to the latest sitting of the House, 978-983.

Statement as to the question of a reporter reading out his notes to several others, so that they might produce a full report or a condensed report ; and difficulty in condensing from short notes than from full notes, 985-995——Conclusion as to its not being feasible to frame an official report and a newspaper report from the same machinery or staff, 1001-1005.

Explanation that speeches of certain Members are reported more or less fully at the request of the local newspapers, the Members themselves having no voice in the matter, so far as the Press Association is concerned, 1006. 1009. 1016. 1017——Opinion that the recent arrangement with Mr. Hansard will meet the deficiency hitherto as regards a historical record, whilst the newspaper reports fairly meet the wants of the general public, 1007. 1008. 1011-1016.

M.

"Manchester Guardian." Supply of the "Manchester Guardian," with reports partly by the Press Association, and partly by gentlemen who have seats as reporters for the London Press ; special reports supplied by the latter, Thwaites 2315. 2335——Important difference between the circumstances of the "Birmingham Daily Post," and of the "Manchester Guardian," so that prompt transmission of reports by means of special wire is very essential in the latter case, but not in the former, ib. 2316-2319. 2312-2354.

Early hour at which the "Guardian" goes to press ; that is on account of its widespread and distant circulation, Thwaites 2317, 2318. 2342-2354——Insufficiency of a good summary, without any report of the speeches, for the "Guardian," ib. 2334——Sufficiency of one seat in the Gallery for the requirements of the "Guardian," ib. 2357.

See also "Morning Advertiser."

Members' Gallery. Increased space to be provided by extending the Reporters' Gallery at each end, so as to take in a portion of the Members' Gallery, Saunders 1902, 1903. 1265-1270 ; Casper 1476, 1477 ; Reid 2086. 2168. 11691 Thwaites 2311, 2323. 2353 ; Dunphy 2603.2612.

Proposal for appropriating to the reporters the seats between the Reporters' Gallery and the door leading into the Members' Gallery, Right Hon. The Speaker 1703, 1704. 1747. 1791. 1809——inconvenience to Members by the proposed alteration ; loss thereby of twenty-two seats in the Gallery out of 124, ib. 1791. 1809.

Plan submitted by the Speaker, showing the proposed new seats for reporters by appropriating some of the seats of the Members' Gallery, App. 217.

Members' Reports of Speeches. Very few Members who furnish reports of their speeches to the papers, Saunders 1152.

Ministers' and Ex-Ministers' Speeches. Very full report given generally in the newspapers of the speeches of Ministers and Ex-Ministers, Hansard 359-361——Rule of reporting Ministers and ex-Ministers at length in the "Times," Rose 708-715——Concurrence in the view that on important occasions the leading utterances of the day should be fully reported, belief that this is done by the "Times," ib. 848.

Report, 1878—continued.

"*Mirror of Parliament.*" Superior reports for some years in the "Mirror of Parliament," which, however, ceased to exist many years ago, *Hansard* 318. 351-354.

"*Morning Advertiser.*" Good summary given by the "Morning Advertiser," *Townsend* 1308.

Statement as to the man allocated to the summary writer of the "Morning Advertiser" being practically used by representatives of the "Manchester Guardian," *Grey* 2467, 2498, 2465, 2466, 2624 —— Impression that the summary in the "Morning Advertiser" is not to be compared to that of the "Times," "Standard," or "Morning Post," *ib.* 2466, 2467.

Explanation of the arrangement under which the summary writer of the "Morning Advertiser" reports for the "Manchester Guardian" and occasionally supplies a summary for the latter paper, *Townsend* 2529-1541 —— Long and genuine summary written for the "Morning Advertiser" by the gentleman who does work also for the "Manchester Guardian," *ib.* 2529, 2634, 2636 —— Longer summary in the "Morning Advertiser" than in any other paper except the "Times," *ib.* 1529.

N.

New Zealand. Belief that in New Zealand there is no payment by Government, and that the publication of the debates is a private speculation, *Hansard* 290-293.

NEWSPAPER REPORTS:

Representation of 134 daily papers in the provinces and in Scotland and Ireland by the three Press Associations having seats in the Reporters' Gallery, *Grant* 9, 10, 68, 69, 91, 92, 100-103, 149-157.

Practice of the daily newspapers to report very fully the speeches of Ministers and ex-Ministers, whilst the speeches of ordinary Members are greatly abbreviated, *Hansard* 259-262 —— Instances of Bills having been reported in the newspapers as having passed a stage without discussion, when these had been a discussion; illustration in the case of the Municipal Franchise Bill, *ib.* 496 —— Excellent reports still given by some of the London daily papers, but not by all, *ib.* 507-509.

Belief that Parliamentary reports are less read than formerly, and that it is not to the interest of newspapers to give full reports, *Ross* 679-681 —— Incomplete but not unfair character of the newspaper reports, *ib.* 682 —— Necessity of going to press at a much earlier hour than in former years, *ib.* 583, 684 —— Sufficient supply of reports by the press for meeting the demands of the public, *Lowell* 690-694, 915-917.

Several advantages of the present system of reports through the newspapers; serious misfortune if the press were driven off the field by the competition of an official report, *Right Hon. The Speaker*, 1687, 1690, 1719-1721 —— Deficiency of the present reports with respect to Private Bills, proceedings in Committees, and proceedings after midnight, *ib.* 1691 —— Incompleteness also of the existing reports on subjects of local interest, including Scotch and Irish questions, *ib.* 1691-1693.

Sufficiency of the reports generally if there were a weekly publication of "Hansard," and if the Scotch, Irish, and provincial press could be fairly represented in the gallery, *Right Hon. The Speaker* 1778.

Very full and accurate character of the reports in the press; belief as to these giving every satisfaction to the public, *Lord Eversley* 1910, 1913-1915, 1918, 1923-1929 —— Misfortune if an official report interfered with independent newspaper reports; salutary competition at present, *ib.* 1938, 1929, 1932, 1983.

Great evil if an official report interfered with the present reports in the press; belief as to the accuracy and sufficiency of these in reference to the general public, *Sir J. Ross* 1962, 1966, 1967, 1970, 1973.

See also Canada. "*Central News.*" "*Hansard's Debates.*" Irish Newspapers. London Newspapers. Official Report, &c. Political Bias. Press Association. Provincial Newspapers. "*Times*" Wednesday (*Reports of Proceedings*).

Nova Scotia. Doubt as to their being any full official reports in Nova Scotia, *Sir J. Ross* 1982.

Report, 1878—*continued.*

O.

OFFICIAL REPORT:

1. *Views of Mr. Hansard and Mr. Saunders as to the Expediency of an Official Parliamentary Report; estimated Cost.*
2. *Objection to an Official Report.*
3. *Question of Verbatim Reports, or of Full Reports.*
4. *Question of Interference with Private or Newspaper Reports.*
5. *Obstacles to the use of an Official Report by the Press.*
6. *Time required for Publication.*
7. *Staff of Reporters required; suggestions as to their Accommodation in the House.*

1. *Views of Mr. Hansard and Mr. Saunders as to the Expediency of an Official Parliamentary Report; estimated Cost:*

Conclusion that official reports have become a public necessity, Hansard 197–199, 364, 366——Estimate of slow rotation of "Hansard" as sufficient for continuing full and accurate reports, ib. 485–498——Conviction of witness that the public expenditure necessary for full official reports would be money easily spent, and that the cost would be small as compared with the benefit derived, ib. 491–492, 494.

Papers submitted by Mr. Hansard explanatory of schemes for a complete official report, the cost of each scheme being estimated at 16,777 *l.* and 20,540 *l.* respectively, *App.* 406–408.

Opinion that a complete official report, if published immediately, would obtain an extensive circulation, and would supersede the special reports now made of the speeches of local members, *Saunders* 1133–1138, 1164, 1165, 1333, 1334, 1079, 1973——Estimate of 350 *l.* a week as the cost of preparing and printing an official report, exclusive of the paper; about 100 *l.* a week might be recouped by sale to provincial newspapers, ib. 1143–1145, 1168–1171, 1190–1194, 1175–1178, 1956.

Great length to which a verbatim report would extend; contemplated mile at a penny a day, *Saunders* 1176–1178, 1314, 1305, 1325–1332——Limited receipts to be derived from an issue of official reports on special subjects, in a separate form, ib. 1874, 1875.

Further reference to the probable cost of an official report; contemplated payment by newspapers supplied with each report, *Saunders* 1303–1309——Several queries whence there would probably be a demand for copies of an official report, ib. 1333, 1334—— Great length of official reports which might be supplied for one penny a day, this covering the cost of paper and printing, ib. 1398–1403.

Extent of public demand for an official report further adverted to, *Saunders* 1409–1418——Varying size of the official publication according to the extent of the speeches, ib. 1497.

2. *Objections to an Official Report:*

Several grounds upon which witness objects to full official reports of the debates in Parliament, *Ross* 618–619, 601–603——Very limited extent to which a full official report could be read by the public; few persons who read the debates in extenso in the "Times," ib. 619, 638, 639, 591–595, 617–619——Comparatively small number of members or speakers who would be affected by the scheme for an official report, ib. 619, 632–635.

Witness repeats that an official system of reports is inexpedient, the reports in the "Times" being, in fact, fuller than is required, *Ross* 784, 785——Small number of Members who speak very frequently, or at much length, ib. 616, 617, 618.

Usefulness of an official report as a work of reference; exceedingly limited demand on the part of the public, *Casper* 1456–1458, 1507, 1814, 1815——Much greater advantage attached to expenditure for improving the accommodation available for reporters, than to the expenditure necessary for an official report; large annual outlay in the latter case, ib. 1495, 1604–1611, 1678.

Further statement as to the comparative uselessness of an official report; that is, save for purposes of reference, *Casper* 1604–1611, 1818, 1650–1654, 1655, 1656, 1664, 1665, 1668–1670——Opinion that there should, however, be some record of the debates for the use of Members, and that same public money may well be devoted to this purpose, ib. 1678, 1679.

Several objections urged against an official report of Parliamentary proceedings; very limited extent to which a verbatim report would be read, especially if delayed for the purpose of correction by Members, *Right Hon. The Speaker* 1677–1628, 1744——Less important objection on the score of expense than on other grounds, ib. 1680, 1681, 1761, 1763.

Difficulty apprehended in regard to official reports being protected by privilege, *Right Hon. The Speaker* 1681–1684——Inconvenience likely to arise from differences between the reported speech and the corrected speech, ib. 1685–1688——Advantage of an official report as a historical record for purposes of reference, ib. 1718.

OFFICIAL REPORT—continued.

3. Objections to an Official Report—continued.

Further considerations as to the difficulty on the score of privilege in connection with an official report, *Right Hon. The Speaker* 1730-1736, 1763 — Inexpediency of a forced circulation of official reports by their being published at a very low price at the public expense, *ib.* 1743-1746.

Opinion that an official or verbatim report would be an inconvenience and disadvantage to the House, and is not required by Parliament or by Members as a record, *Lord Emerley* 1908-1912, 1916, 1917, 1930.

4. Question of Verbatim Reports, or of Full Reports:

Objections to the publication daily of a verbatim report of speeches and nothing else; opinion that it would do no mil, *Hansard* 230, 231-238, 263-268, 273-276 — Instances of members wishing to be reported verbatim, *ib.* 308-310, 403 — Preference for full and accurate reports as compared with verbatim reports, *ib.* 311, 319, 363 — Expediency, if there be official reports, of what is unnecessary a speech as well as what is necessary being reported, *ib.* 417-421.

Suggested power, if there be official reports, of reporting in a more concentrated form those debates which take place late at night, when there is much repetition of argument, *Hansard* 480, 481 — Tendency of verbatim reports to raise the public opinion of the House of Commons; instances to this effect, *ib.* 482-484.

Effect of verbatim official reports in leading to a multiplication of speeches and to more frequent adjournments, *Bass* 518, 536-538 — Decided preference further expressed for full rather than verbatim report, *ib.* 599-603.

Conclusion as to verbatim reports not being required in the case of great constitutional and political questions; all the arguments and opinions of each speaker should be given, and undue repetition being avoided, *Ross* 610-614, 847-851 — Excessively voluminous publication if there were a verbatim official report, *ib.* 630, 649, 650.

The report should be almost verbatim, *Saunders* 1310, 1311, 1315 — Impression that long reports are not valued very much by the public, an official report being useful chiefly for historical purposes and for reference, *ib.* 1381, 1382.

Tendency of a verbatim report to affect prejudicially the quantity of speeches and to lengthen debates, *Right Hon. The Speaker* 1741, 1759-1762.

Suggestion that a verbatim report in the basis of an official report, and that any condensation should take place subsequently, *Sadler* 1853-1857 — Frequent use of intemperate expressions in the heat of debate, which are much better not reported verbatim, *Lord Emerley* 1911 — Decided objection on several grounds to an official verbatim report in this country, *Sir J. Ross* 1962, 1966.

5. Question of Interference with Private or Newspaper Reports:

Inexpediency of any interference with private reports, if official reports be established; strong moral claim of witness to consideration in any changes that may be made, *Hansard* 303, 321, 323.

Belief that an official report would not have any beneficial influence upon newspaper reports; the former would be harmless if needless, *Couper* 1862, 1864, 1886 — Disadvantage of an official report if it prejudicially affected the system of reports in the press, *Right Hon. The Speaker* 1692, 1719-1721; *Lord Emerley* 1936, 1939, 1951, 1963; *Sir J. Ross* 1962, 1966, 1967.

Improbability of an official report interfering with the newspaper reports; prospect rather of the former becoming obsolete, *Right Hon. The Speaker* 1719-1722.

6. Obstacles to the use of an Official Report by the Press:

Difficulties in the way of newspapers being furnished with reports by a staff of official reporters as the debate is going on, *Hansard* 443-447.

Opinion that an official report or historical record of the proceedings in Parliament is very desirable in the interests of Members, but would be of little use to the newspapers, there not being much public demand for complete reports, *Lovell* 886, 887, 891, 892, 915-920 — Conclusion as to its not being feasible to frame an official report and a newspaper report from the same machinery or staff, *ib.* 1001-1004.

Doubt as to an official report having any effect as regards the ordinary or condensed reports published by the newspapers, *Saunders* 1134, 1135, 1139-1149, 1164, 1165, 1381, 1399-1399 — Uselessness for several reasons of an official report as far as the "Scotsman" is concerned; conclusion moreover that it could not be published or rendered in time to be available, *Couper* 1445-1451, 1454-1456, 1468, 1506-1515, 1570-1576.

Grounds for considering that an official verbatim report would not enable the leading newspapers to dispense with reporters and with independent reports, *Reid* 2213-2215 — Entire uselessness of official reports to the provincial press and to newspapers generally,

OFFICIAL REPORT—continued.

5. *Obstacles to the use of an Official Report by the Press*—continued.

generally, *Jeffrey* 1237-1242, 1251-1256——Objection of the press to take official reports gratuitously, *ib.* 1242.

Objection of the press to the use of official reports as involving delay, and as being identical, *Townend* 2316-2318——Immense difficulty as regards the summarising of an official report in time for press, *ib.* 2329-2331.

Approved of an official report if promptly and efficiently done; the difficulty as to summarising is not insuperable, *Grey* 2440-2445, 2507——Enhanced difficulties of the London papers in using an official report as they go to press at a very early hour, *ib.* 2537, 2562.

6. *Time required for Publication;*

Probable time in which a full report of the speeches up to twelve o'clock at night might be printed and laid upon the Table of the House, *Hansard* 360-364——Doubts as to the expediency of attempting to deliver to Members at four o'clock in the day a report of the speeches down to the termination of the previous day's sitting, *ib.* 424, 425, 428-434.

Practicability of arrangements by which official reports might be in the hands of Ministers next day; by the public generally they would never be read, *Ross* 614-619——Great promptitude with which speeches could be officially reported and published, *Saunders* 1134, 1137, 1138, 1167, 1172-1175, 1194, 1195.

Further statement as to the very short time within which official reports might be in the hands of Members and of the provincial press, *Saunders* 1246-1253, 1857, 1958, 1988, 1303, 1376-1388——Illustration of the mode in which short-hand might be printed every twenty minutes to the House during the course of a debate, *ib.* 1478.

Dissent from Mr. Saunders' evidence as to the shortness of the time in which an official report would be ready for the use of newspapers and of Members, *Cowper* 1448-1451——Suggestion as to the time within which an official report might be published; dispatch feasible so far as shorthand writing and printing are concerned, *Salter* 1851, 1861-1863.

7. *Staff of Reporters required; Suggestions as to their Accommodation in the House;*

Suggestion that if there be official reports seats should be provided for the reporters in the body of the House; practice to that effect in the United States, France, Italy, &c., *Hansard* 401, 415, 418-427——Requirement of a staff of some sixteen or eighteen reporters for a system of official reports, *ib.* 484.

Considerable staff necessary for the purpose of an official verbatim report of the debates, *Ross* 557——Inexpediency of the reporters being placed in front of the chair, in connection with a system of official reports, *ib.* 591, 592.

Estimate of strong twenty reporters as necessary for official reporting, *Saunders* 1283, 1284, 1321, 1302——Suggestion that official reporters be on the floor of the House, *ib.* 1284, 1285, 1336, 1336——Contemplated control over official reporters as being officers of the House, *ib.* 1404, 1405.

Suggestion, that besides room for two reporters at the table of the House, certain accommodation be allotted to them for the purpose of writing out their notes, and that everything up to completion for press be done within the building, *Saunders* 1418-1428.

Want of room for the accommodation of official reporters on the floor of the House, *Right Hon. The Speaker* 1793, 1794.

Evidence to the effect that if it be decided to have an official report in this country the House would probably accommodate the official reporters at or near the table of the House, *Salter* 1848-1851, 1873-1876, 1896-1900——Sufficiency of two seats in a good position, *ib.* 1849——Varying time for which each official reporter should sit, accordingly as the transcript is required more or less promptly, *ib.* 1885, 1886.

Contemplated withdrawal of official or other reporters when strangers are excluded, *Lord Eversley* 1921, 1922.

See also American Congress. Canada. Correction of Reports. France. Germany. "Hansard's Debates."

P.

Pneumatic Tubes. Great improvement if there were increased facilities of communication by means of pneumatic tubes; that is, for the convenience of special-wire newspapers, *Reid* 2157-2161.

Political Bias. Belief that there is little, if any, ground for complaint on the score of political partisanship in the reporting by the press, *Ross* 702-707 —— Entire absence of political bias in the reporting by the "Central News," *Saunders* 1151.

Press Association:

Origin of the association in the transfer of the telegraphs to Government; miscellaneous as well as Parliamentary news supplied by it to the provincial press, *Lowell* 866-869 —— Large increase in the quantity of Parliamentary news supplied to the country press since the time when the supply was provided by the telegraph companies; increase also in the number of papers taking full reports, though the demand would now appear to have reached its maximum, *ib.* 877-883.

Reference to the Central Press and Central News Associations as being trading concerns, whilst the Press Association is simply a co-operative body and working for profit, *Lowell* 870, 871 —— Total of 171 newspaper proprietors, members of the association, a committee of management being appointed every year; supply also by the association of 101 newspapers and thirty-nine exchanges and news-rooms, not members, *ib.* 872, 876, 877.

Particulars as to the arrangements for the supply of Parliamentary reports of greater or less length to different classes of provincial papers; supplementary and full reports sent to the larger papers, and to the Scotch and Irish papers, *Lowell* 872, 873, 886, 889 —— Sufficient facilities (if there were better accommodation) for supplying the wants of the country press, without any employment of special reporters by the latter, *ib.* 909-914.

Statement as to the very inconvenient character of the accommodation provided in the gallery of the House for the Press Association, *Lowell* 891, 909, 998-1000 —— Exclusive employment of ten reporters by the association, assistance being received also from several others, *ib.* 998 —— The association does not supply private individuals, *ib.* 961-963 —— Supply of special as well as ordinary reports by the association, *ib.* 965, 969-977 —— Practice of the association to send off reports promptly during the latest sitting of the House, *ib.* 978-983.

Grounds for the complaint that neither as regards the reports themselves, nor as regards prompt despatch of the reports, can the "Leeds Mercury" depend upon the Press Association, *Reid* 2078-2080. 2100-2103. 2178-2182. 2218 —— The smaller newspapers, as being the most numerous, have the largest representation in the management, *ib.* 2101 —— Exception taken to the view that unpartial reports are more likely to be obtained from the Press Association than if the leading papers had independent reports, *ib.* 2183-2190.

Important provincial papers represented in the management of the Press Association, *Jeffrey* 2934 —— Conclusion as to the provincial press generally being able to obtain such reports as they may require through the medium of the association, *ib.* 2934, 2935, 2947, 2948, 2936, 2976, 2977, 2986-2990. 2300 —— Supply by the association of whatever its individual members require, *ib.* 2935, 2948-2952.

Still more complete reports furnished by the association but for the defective accommodation at its disposal in the reporters' gallery; claim of the association to better facilities in this respect, *Jeffrey* 2935, 2949, 2950, 2957-2959, 2968. 2999 —— Three classes of reports given by the association; facility, moreover, in obtaining full reports of the speeches of local members, *ib.* 2982-2988.

See also Irish Newspapers.   "Leeds Mercury."   "Manchester Guardian."
Provincial Newspapers.   Scotch Newspapers.   "Scotsman."

Provincial Newspapers:

1. *Supply of Parliamentary Reports for the Provincial Press mainly through the News Association.*
2. *Supply also through Reporters for some of the London Newspapers.*
3. *Difficulty as to the direct Admission of Provincial Papers to the Reporters' Gallery; Claim on their part.*
4. *Conditions subject to which Applications might be granted.*
5. *Small Number of Newspapers likely to Apply.*
6. *Demand in the Provinces for Parliamentary Reports.*

1. *Supply*

PROVINCIAL NEWSPAPERS—continued.

1. *Supply of Parliamentary Reports for the Provincial Press mainly through the News Associations:*

Explanation of the system of supply of reports for the provincial press and the Scotch and Irish papers through the three Press Associations, 134 daily papers being thus represented; reference hereon to the date of establishment of each association, Garnet, 9, 10. 14-27. 68, 69. 91-103. 144-14 & 149-157.

Ample opportunity of the country newspapers (for whom there is no accommodation in the reporters' gallery) to obtain reports from the three Press Associations, Reid 514, 515. 571-476——Somewhat similar reports supplied by the "Central News" and "Central Press" as by the Press Association, Lovell 884. 885. 904——Very long reports, in some provincial papers, supplied by the "Central News" or Press Association, Saunders 1369-1397.

2. *Supply, also, through Reporters for some of the London Newspapers:*

Belief as to some of the reporters for the London papers supplying also provincial papers; witness is not cognisant of any restriction to the contrary, Garnet 73-80. 101, 102. 126-138.

Conclusion as to the reporters for the London papers not neglecting their duties through reporting also for the provincial press, Reid 625-701——Supply of the provincial press with reports, not only by the "Central News" and two other associations, but by reporters for the London papers, who are paid separately for this work, Saunders 1313-1314. 1366-1370.

Exceptions taken to the system whereby the Parliamentary reporters for the London press supply reports also to provincial papers by private arrangement, Casper 1593-1598——Other sources of supply of reports to country newspapers than through the Press Association or "Central News," Jaffray 1251.

Practical, though indirect, admittance of two or three provincial papers under the present system, Gray 2430, 2431. 2436. 2461-2464. 2481, 2484. 2497——Explanation that there is nothing underhand in the arrangement by which the London press reporters are paid by Irish and other papers for special reports; the system is, however, altogether wrong, ib. 2457. 2469-2472. 2481, 2484. 2495-2497.——Inexpediency of the London papers being allowed to prohibit their staff in the gallery from reporting for other papers, ib. 2488-2490.

Inaccuracy of any statement implying that provincial papers used, surreptitiously, seats in the gallery belonging to London papers, Townend 1659-1653.

3. *Difficulty as to the direct Admission of Provincial Papers to the Reporters' Gallery; Claim on their part:*

Absence of complaint to witness on the part of the provincial press, though applications have been made for seats in the gallery, Garnet 18. 30-33. 56-58. 70-73——Impracticability of admitting the provincial papers, Reid 758.

Hardship upon the provincial press in being entirely excluded from the gallery, Saunders 1100, 1201——Claim on the part of the provincial press to at least twelve front seats, ib. 1259-1204. 1296-1299——Expediency of facilities for special reports as well as for historical reports for the country press, ib. 1170-1283.

Decided objection to all the provincial papers being dependent for their reports on two or three news agencies; undue monopoly thereby, Casper 1481. 1524-1598. 1614-1629——Less necessary for an official report if full reports were provided for the provincial papers by their own staff, ib. 1494, 1496. 1561, 1563——Better materials for an official record, such as "Hansard," if the provincial papers could give independent reports, ib. 1561, 1563, 1654——Expectation that room could be provided in the House for the gradually increasing number of papers in course of time, ib. 1637-1659.

Dissatisfaction of the provincial press with the arrangement for the supply of reports through the news associations; inability, however, of witness to allot seats to representatives of local newspapers, Right Hon. The Speaker 1694. 1698-1700——Difficulty in providing that the press generally (out of London) be represented by a distinct arrangement; expediency, however, of the provincial press being accommodated as far as possible, ib. 1701-1706.

Considerable difficulty in meeting any demand by the provincial press for accommodation in the reporters' gallery, Lord Barnley 1935-1937. 1946-1949.

Claim of the provincial press, as well as of the London press, to seats in the gallery, Reid 2169, 2163——Admission as to the "Central News" and Press Association having a prior claim to individual provincial papers to seats in the gallery, ib. 2170-2175.

Claim of provincial papers to seats in the reporters' gallery if additional accommodation can be provided, Townend 2311, 2312——Statement as to the news associations not meeting the requirements of many of the leading provincial papers; illustration in the case of the Manchester papers, ib. 2311. 2316, 2317.

PROVINCIAL NEWSPAPERS—continued.

2. Difficulty as to the direct Admission of Provincial Papers, &c.—continued.

Proposition, as an alternative measure, that the news associations be allowed increased accommodation, and that the leading Irish and Scotch papers be admitted to the back seats, whence their representatives could give instructions as to the precise reports required, *Grey* 2485-2498.

Numerous staff involved in the admittance of seven or eight provincial papers to the gallery, *Dunphy* 2614.

3. Conditions subject to which Applications might be granted:

Suggestion that no paper be admitted which did not keep a staff of its own and did not give independent reports; proposed exercise of this check through the Serjeant-at-Arms, *Cowper* 1436-1439. 1443. 1488, 1489——Contemplated right of selection in the Speaker as to the papers to be admitted to the gallery; that is, on certain rules and conditions, *ib.* 1476-1481——Doubt as to the expediency of stipulating that each paper having a seat in the gallery should devote a certain space to its reports, *ib.* 1484-1487——Denial that there would be anything in the nature of a monopoly or of special legislation by prescribing certain conditions for admitting provincial papers to the reporters' gallery, *ib.* 1617-1633.

Great difficulty apprehended unless careful limitations and conditions be laid down in connection with applications from the local press for available seats, *Right Hon. The Speaker* 1701, 1702. 1708, 1709. 1747. 1773. 1774. 1807, 1808.

Expediency of accommodation being provided in the gallery for those provincial papers which are prepared to publish independent reports and have special wires, *Reid* 2076. 2077. 2084-2099——Objection to a condition that a certain number of reporters should be employed by any paper putting in a claim for a seat; preference for a condition as to the reports being of a certain length, *ib.* 2151-2158.

Suggestion that seats in the gallery (if available) be offered to provincial papers on the condition that real and bonâ fide use is made of them, and that independent reports are given to them, *Jeffrey* 2743. 2749, 2750. 2750-2752. 2791-2798. 2801-2807——Concurrence in the foregoing view, *Grey* 2491-2494.

Objection to a condition that papers claiming a seat should undertake to devote a certain minimum space to the reports. *Toward* 2356-2363——Similar conditions desirable in terms both for provincial and London newspapers, *ib.* 2370-2377. 2383, 2384.

4. Small Number of Newspapers likely to Apply:

Probability of eight or ten provincial papers wishing to keep a staff of reporters if they had accommodation in the gallery, *Saunders* 1534-1536——Prospect of some provincial papers employing reporters of their own, if there were room for them, by way of supplementing reports from the news associations, *ib.* 1406-1408.

Belief that not more than eight or ten papers would apply for admission (if there were room), on account of the expense involved, *Cowper* 1438. 1481, 1482. 1550-1552——Limit to the number of papers applying for seats in the gallery, as each such paper should have a special wire and a staff of six or eight reporters, *ib.* 1590-1595. 1550-1565.

Calculation that on condition of giving independent reports, and having special wires, not more than ten papers would apply, the cost involved being considerable, *Reid* 2084-2099. 2137-2145. 2151-2158. 2174. 2199——Very large circulation of the ten papers which would probably apply for seats if available, *ib.* 2174——The estimate of ten such papers includes Scotland and Ireland, *ib.* 2199.

Calculation that sixteen or seventeen papers would apply for accommodation in the gallery, if it were available, *Jeffrey* 2744. 2773-2775. 2801——Grounds for the conclusion that not more than ten or twelve provincial new papers (including Scotland and Ireland) would apply for seats; that is, on account of the great expense of staff and special wires, *Toward* 2313, 2314. 2320, 2321. 2338-2341. 2364-2369. 2387-2389.

5. Demand in the Provinces for Parliamentary Reports:

Considerable proportion of the provincial papers which do not require Parliamentary reports for their readers, *Lovell* 901-903——Increased interest of the provincial public in Parliamentary reports, this feeling hardly applying to the London public, *Saunders* 1110. 1115-1124. 1127, 1128. 1133, 1134. 1165, 1166. 1207-1212. 1341-1347.

Large proportion of the provincial papers for which the reports of the news agencies would in any case suffice, *Cowper* 1588-1597. 1613-1615——Belief that there is an increasing desire in the provinces for extended Parliamentary reports, *Toward* 2390-2392.

See also "*Birmingham Daily Post.*"   "*Central News.*"   *Identical or Joint Reports.*   *Irish Newspapers.*   "*Leeds Mercury.*"   *Local Members.*   "*Manchester Guardian.*"   *Press Association.*   *Reporters' Gallery.*   *Scotch Newspapers.*   "*Scotsman.*"   *Publication*

Report, 1878—continued.

Public, The. Conclusion that the demand of the public for Parliamentary information is now sufficiently met, *Ismall* 890-891. 915-917——Statement as to there being an increased demand in the provinces for full reports of the speeches of the local Members; doubt as to the wisdom of long newspaper reports otherwise, *Saunders* 1110. 1115-1124. 1165, 1166. 1341-1347. 1416, 1417——Demand of the public for full reports of the speeches of many Members besides local Members, *Gaspey* 1671, 1672.

See also *Irish Newspapers*. *Official Report*. *Scotch Newspapers*. *" Times."*

Publication and Delivery (Official Report). See *Official Report, &.*

R.

Re-appointment of Committee. Recommended re-appointment of the Committee at the commencement of the next Session, *Rep.* iii.

Reid, T. Wemyss. (Analysis of his Evidence.)—Former experience of witness in the Reporters' Gallery, whilst for the last eight years he has had charge of the Parliamentary reports in the "Leeds Mercury," 2074, 2075——Expediency of accommodation being provided in the gallery for those provincial papers which are prepared to publish independent reports, 2076, 2077——Insufficiency, in the case of the "Leeds Mercury," of the reports supplied by the "Central News" or Press Association; practice of obtaining the ordinary reports in the paper from reporters employed also by the London papers, 2078-2083. 2100-2103. 2117. 2149. 2150.

Very full reports given in the "Leeds Mercury;" much fuller, in fact, than in some of the London papers having reporters in the gallery, 2079. 2113. 2130. 2176, 2177——Approval of those provincial papers only being accommodated in the gallery which would give independent reports, and have special wires; estimate of out there being ten such papers, the cost involved being considerable, 2084-2090. 2137-2148. 2151-2158. 2174-2175——Contemplated enlargement of the gallery as suggested by the Speaker, 2118-2120. 2168, 2169.

Delay in the transmission of telegraphic messages from the House to the London office of the "Leeds Mercury," so that cuts are now used, 2092, 2094. 2157, 2158——Statement showing the heavy cost incurred by the "Leeds Mercury" for Parliamentary reports, including special reports and the cost of telegraphing; reduction of cost to some extent through being associated in the matter with another paper, 2095-2099. 2111-2114. 2134-2136——Several reasons which make it convenient for the "Leeds Mercury" to employ its own reporters, instead of depending upon any of the News Associations, or upon the partial services of the reporters for the London press, 2100-2104. 2117-2119. 2118.

Expediency of full and prompt reports in the paper in order to keep up its reputation, the expense being fully justified thereby, though the circulation is not materially affected, 2105-2110. 2116. 2110-2112——Much earlier period of the day at which the Leeds public obtain Parliamentary news through the "Leeds Mercury" than through the London papers, 2120-2128——Satisfaction of witness if out met in the gallery were allotted to his paper, 2129, 2130.

Objection to an identical report for the "Leeds Mercury" and other provincial papers, 2131-2133. 2147-2150——Inexpediency of a hard-and-fast rule that a paper must have a special wire in order to obtain a seat in the gallery, 2143-2146——Objection to a condition that a certain number of reporters should be employed by any paper putting in a claim for a seat; preference for a condition as to the reports being of a certain length, 2151-2158.

Great improvement if there were increased facilities of communication by means of pneumatic tubes; that is, for the convenience of special wire newspapers, 2157-2161——Claim of the provincial press, as well as of the London press, to seats in the gallery, 2162, 2163——Opinion that not more than two provincial papers could conveniently combine in order to have identical reports, 2164-2167.

Admission as to the "Central News" and Press Association having a prior claim to individual provincial papers to seats in the gallery, 2170-2173——Very large circulation of the two papers which would probably apply for seats, if available, 2174——Grounds for concluding that the Press Association could not supply the precise reports required by the "Leeds Mercury," 2178-2181——Exception taken to the view that impartial reports are more likely to be obtained from the Press Association than if the leading papers had independent reports, 2163-2190.

Advantage to the accessory writers for the London papers having seats in the gallery; they might all be in the back row, 2191-2198——Further explanation of the arrangement whereby reports are supplied to the "Leeds Mercury" by reporters for the London press, though on special occasions it is necessary to obtain the services of the "Central News"

a. 171.   2 2 2   *News"*

Report, 1878—continued.

Redd. T. Wemyss. (Analysis of his Evidence.)—*continued.*

News and Press Association, 2200-2304——Very defective accommodation in the back seats of the gallery even if they were raised, 2204, 2206.

Grounds for concluding that an official verbatim report would not enable the leading newspapers to dispense with reporters and with independent reports, 2213-2216——Impracticability of the "Leeds Mercury" obtaining the required reports sufficiently promptly from the Press Association; this difficulty would equally apply to an official report, 2217, 2218.

Reporters. Information as to the frequent change of reporters during the evening, and as to the number employed by each paper and Press Association, *Grant* 40-55; *App.* 245.

Great pressure of time in recent years, the "turns" being now very short, so that there is increased difficulty in accurately reporting or condensing, *Ross* 543-548. 562. 569-571——Requirement of about four reporters each for a quarter of an hour to report a speech one hour long, *ib.* 582——A quarter of an hour's shorthand would take about three-quarters of an hour to write out fully, *ib.* 583——Gradual shortening of the "turns" toward the close of an important debate, *ib.* 588.

Varying time taken by different reporters in writing out their shorthand notes for press, *Ross* 604-609——Responsibility of each reporter for writing out in full his own shorthand notes; important distinction between mere shorthand writing and good reporting, *ib.* 625-632——Discretion exercised by the reporters as to reporting speakers more or less fully, Ministers and ex-Ministers being as a rule reported at length, *ib.* 707-715——Varying practice as to reporting the actual language of the speaker, *ib.* 757-760.

Shortening of the "turns" as the evening advances, *Lovell* 959, 960.

Discretion now exercised by the reporters as to the length of the reports; absence of discretion in official reporters, *Right Hon. The Speaker* 1739, 1740.

Advantage in a paper having its own reporting staff so that it may adapt the report to the requirements of each particular day, *Townend* 2368.

See also London Newspapers. Official Report, 7. *Provincial Newspapers. Reporters' Gallery.*

REPORTERS' GALLERY:

     1. *Jurisdiction and Control in regard to Admission, &c.*
     2. *Extent and Character of the present Accommodation generally.*
     3. *Front Seats; how occupied, and Alterations suggested.*
     4. *Back Seats; inferiority of the Accommodation therein, and Improvements suggested.*
     5. *Accommodation for the Press Association and "Central News."*
     6. *Difficulties in the way of an increased Number of Seats; Enlargement suggested by Absorption from the Members' Gallery.*
     7. *Suggested Conditions of Admission to the Gallery; difficulty felt by the Speaker in the Matter.*

1. *Jurisdiction and Control in regard to Admission, &c.:*

Control exercised by witness, as Serjeant-at-Arms, over the arrangements for Parliamentary reporting in the House of Commons; he has no control over the reports, *Gosset* 1, 2. 110-114——Orders given by witness for admission to the gallery on the application of the editors at the beginning of the Session, *ib.* 11, 12.

Jurisdiction of witness, rather than of the Serjeant-at-Arms, with respect to the Reporters' Gallery, *Right Hon. The Speaker* 1730, 1731. 1798.

2. *Extent and Character of the present Accommodation generally:*

Plan submitted showing the accommodation appropriated in the Reporters' Gallery, there being nineteen front seats and a row of back seats, *Gosset* 3-8. *sp.* 30.——Bare sufficiency of the existing accommodation, *ib.* 13, 14——Room neither for another Press Association, nor for a Scotch or Irish paper; explanation moreover that in the event of a vacancy, the seat would be given in preference to a London paper, *ib.* 129-134. 139-143. 149-157.

Very good accommodation for the reporters as compared with that which existed when witness first entered the gallery fifty-eight years ago, *Ross* 512, 513. 528-531. 563-568. 764.

Inability of witness to meet the applications made from time to time for seats in the Reporters' Gallery for representatives of the local press, *Right Hon. The Speaker* 1694——Sufficient accommodation in the Reporters' Gallery to meet the demands of the press during the time that witness was Speaker, *Lord Sherbrook* 1905-1907. 1914. 1937.

Exceeding deficiency of the accommodation generally for reporters; there is no room whatever for any material increase of staff, *Dunphy* 2600-2607. 2811-2814.

Name

REPORTERS' GALLERY—continued.

2. *Extent and Character of the present Accommodation generally—continued.*

Name of each paper having seats in the gallery, number of tickets of admission in each case, and number of seats, *App.* 776.

8. *Front Seats ; how occupied, and Alterations suggested :*

Appropriation of fifteen seats in the front row to the London daily press, of three to the Press Association, and of one to Mr. Hansard, *Const* 5——Occupation of the front row in the gallery by reporters, the "*Times*" staff being the largest, and comprising fifteen altogether, *Reid* 502, 503.

Want of a front seat for ordinary reports and of another front seat for special reports of local Members' speeches, the back seats being used by summary writers, *Saunders* 1337-1340. 1348-1361——Occupation of front seats in the gallery by persons who are not really reporters ; room for provincial reporters by putting the former in back seats, *ib.* 1294, 1295, 1313-1318.

Expediency of the front seats being all occupied by reporters, the summary writers being removed to the back seats, *Right Hon. The Speaker* 1705-1708——Necessity of reporters having front seats in order to efficiently report ; belief that they would not be content with back seats, even if improved by being raised, *ib.* 1716, 1729. 1767-1770.

4. *Back Seats ; inferiority of the Accommodation therein, and Improvements suggested :*

Unfitness of the back seats for reporting purposes, three being occupied by the relish for the front row, by lender writers, and by reporters for London weekly papers one day in the week, *Const* 8. sq. 81-83. 104-109.

Occupation of the seats behind the front row by other than reporters ; these seats are to some extent suitable for reporting, *Reid* 524-527 ——Limited interference with the reporters in the front gallery through talking going on in the row behind, *ib.* 751-755 ——

Very defective accommodation in the back seats of the gallery, even if they were raised, *Reid* 1804, 1806——Improved accommodation by raising the back seats three or four feet, *Cooper* 1475——Belief that the back seats in the gallery would do fairly well for summary work, especially if raised, *Grey* 2510-2512.

Explanations in connection with plan for raising partially under the Ladies' Gallery the second row of seats in the Reporters' Gallery, thus increasing the number of seats for reporters ; important difficulty, however, through there being no accommodation for the reporters exiting for their turns, *Taylor* 2542-2567. 2567-2670. 2572-2581—— Serious obstacles to raising the back seats, with a view to rendering them fit for reporters ; this arrangement is, in fact, impracticable, *ib.* 2548-2650. 2552. 2577, 2578. 2580-2589.

Objection to raising the back seats ; impracticability of rendering them fit for reporting, *Dunphy* 2601, 2618. 2648-2650 ——Objections to the proposal for raising the seats in the back row under the Ladies' Gallery, *B.* 2601-2607. 2619, 2620 ——The back row is, in fact, a mere lounge, and there are no desks, *ib.* 2616. 2618. 2616-2618 —— Modes of occupying of the persons now occupying the back seats, *ib.* 2617, 2618. 2631, 2632.

5. *Accommodation for the Press Association and "Central News."*

Long period for which the London press had seats in the gallery before the News Association applied, the latter being obliged to have seats at the side instead of at the centre, *Const* 180-182.

Claim of the Press Association to increased facilities and improved accommodation, *Lewis* 891, 902. 998-1000 ; *Jeffery* 2236. 2249, 2250. 2257-2259. 2268. 2299.

Very defective accommodation at the disposal of the "Central News," *Saunders* 1110. 1180-1149. 1115, 1116. 1196-1199. 1240-1242. 1299, 1300——Large proportion of the population of the United Kingdom which are provincial papers, whereas the reporters for these papers have but three front seats in the worst part of the gallery, 1346-1361.

6. *Difficulties in the Way of an increased Number of Seats ; Enlargement suggested by Abstraction from the Members' Gallery.*

Obstacle to any enlargement of the gallery, or the provision of any more front seats, *Const* sib. 67——Inability of witness to suggest any improvement in the accommodation for reporters, *Rose* 589, 590.

Suggestion that the seats in the front of the two galleries adjoining the Reporters'

Report, 1878—continued.

REPORTERS' GALLERY—continued.

6. *Difficulties in the Way of an increased Number of Seats, &c.—continued.*

Gallery too far a certain distance thrown into the latter, Saunders 1807, 1873. 1865-1870; Cooper 1476, 1477.

Increased number of seats available by appropriating to the reporters the space between the Reporters' Gallery and the door leading into the Members' Gallery; inferiority, however, of these seats as compared with those now in use, Right Hon. The Speaker 1703, 1704, 1747 —— Failure hitherto of proposals for improving the existing accommodation by structural alterations, ib. 1805, 1806 —— An addition of eight feet and six inch seats would be gained by the proposed alterations, ib. 1809.

Contemplated enlargement of the gallery as suggested by the Speaker, Reid 2088, 2168, 2169 —— Increased and improved accommodation in the Reporters' Gallery by extending it on each side, and by raising the back seats, Townend 2370, 2371.

Structural objections to a plan for doing away with the upper gallery, and for extending the Reporters' Gallery on both sides to the same extent; heavy expenses involved, Taylor 2559-2566 —— Increase of accommodation by taking some seats right and left from the Members' Gallery, ib. 2603, 2611.

Plan submitted by the Speaker, showing the Reporters' Gallery and the proposed new seats suggested to be taken from the Members' Gallery, App. 212.

7. *Suggested Conditions of Admission to the Gallery; Difficulty felt by The Speaker in the Matter.*

Inexpediency of a hard and fast rule, that a paper must have a special wire in order to obtain a seat in the gallery, Lowell 930-9351 Reid 2143-2145 —— Different conditions suggested in connection with the admission of provincial papers to the gallery, Cooper 1436-1439. 1443. 1478-1481. 1584-1587. 1697-1633; Reid 2076, 2077. 2084-2099. 2151-2156.

Suggestion that seats (if available) be offered to provincial papers on condition that application is made of them, and that independent reports are given in each case, Jeffrey 2143. 2149, 2150. 2370-2371. 2191-2198. 2301-2307 —— Objection to the provision of a special wire as a condition of access to the gallery; unknown, however, as to the "Birmingham Daily Post" not requiring a private wire, ib. 2143. 2164, 2301, 2302.

Opinion that in the selection of papers for seats in the gallery, those should have preference which had special wires and London offices, and which maintained a certain staff of reporters, Townend 2314, 2315. 2370-2378 —— Way in which further applications for seats should be dealt with if the reasonable demands of the provincial press at the present time were satisfied; expediency of similar conditions in future in the case of both London and provincial papers, ib. 2370-2377. 2383, 2384.

Entire concurrence in the suggestion that papers should only be allowed access to the gallery on condition that they gave fairly full reports, Gray 2491-2494.

Considerable difficulty to be felt by witness if it rested with him to select the papers for seats in the gallery; expediency of careful limitations and conditions being applied, Right Hon. The Speaker 1701, 1702. 1708, 1709. 1747. 1773. 1774. 1779-1786. 1807 —— Explanation that in the event of a vacancy not being at witness' disposal he would decide the applications for it on their merits, without limiting the matter to the metropolitan press, ib. 1710, 1711.

See also "Birmingham Daily Post."   "Central News."   "Daily Chronicle." "Freeman's Journal."   "Globe."   Irish Newspapers.   "Leeds Mercury." London Newspapers.   Provincial Newspapers.   Reporters.   Scotch Newspapers.   "Scotsman."   Summary Writers.   "Times."

Raw, Sir John, Bart., K.C. M.G. (Analysis of his Evidence)—Information in detail relative to the system of reporting the proceedings of Parliament in Canada; change of practice from time to time, the object sought being to obtain, not an official or verbatim report, but as near an approximation as possible to the "Hansard" of this country, 1956, 1957. 1961-1965. 1968, 1969 —— Official authorization of special reports of the debates upon consideration, 1967, 1968. 1968, 1969. 1983 —— Arrangement adopted in 1874 for procuring by contract, 2,600 copies of reports, similar to "Hansard," at a cost of from 2,500 l. to 3,000 l. a year; distribution of these to Members of both Houses, to the press, &c., 1957, 1984.

Practice in Canada as to correction of their speeches as Members; supervision exercised by a Joint Committee of both Houses; 1957. 2030-2035 —— Several objections in Canada to an official or verbatim report, 1957 —— Difficulty felt in Canada upon the score of privilege and libel in connection with an official report; this not applying in the case of a publication like "Hansard," 1957. 2015-2017. 2055-2060 —— Arrangement between the chief Canadian newspapers for a common system of reporting; satisfaction given thereby, 1957. 1969-1971. 1988-1987. 2007. 2048-2051.

Particulars relative to the system of reporting in the United States, there being an official

Report, 1878—continued.

Row, Sir John, Bart., K.C.M.G. (Analysis of his Evidence)—continued

official verbatim report of the proceedings in Congress, through the "Congressional Record," for which there is a very large appropriation annually, 1955-1960 —— Numerous copies of the "Congressional Record" supplied to Members for local distribution among their constituencies, &c., 1961. 1956-1958. 2006 —— Several reasons for an official report in the United States which do not apply in England, 1962. 1974-1979.

Decided objection of witness, on several grounds, to an official verbatim report in this country, 1962. 1966 —— Great evil of an official report interfered with the present reports in the press; belief as to the accuracy and sufficiency of these in reference to the general public, 1962. 1966, 1967. 1972, 1973 —— Value attached to "Hansard" as a faithful record of proceedings; fuller record desirable as regards proceedings in Committee and on Private Bills, 1967.

Comparative unimportance of the press of Washington, there being no adequate publication of the proceedings in Congress except through the "Congressional Record," 1974-1979. 1988-1990. 2014 —— Belief that in the Provincial Legislatures in Canada there is no official report, 1980, 1981 —— Doubt as to these being any full official reports in Nova Scotia, 1982 —— Use made by the local press in Canada of the reports in the "Toronto Globe" and other leading newspapers, rather than of the reports in the Dominion "Hansard"; limited delay, however, in the publication of the latter, 1985-1987. 2011-2013. 2024-2029.

Shorter reports given in the Dominion "Hansard" than in the English "Hansard," 1993-2000 —— Late hours for which the House sometimes sits in Canada; practice of the press in bringing their reports down to the latest moment, 2001-2006. 2040, 2041 —— Responsibility of the contractor to Parliament for the accuracy of the semi-official report, 2008, 2009 —— Arrangements for the accommodation of the reporters, 2010 —— Explanation as to the speeches being reported sometimes in the first person and sometimes in the third, 2016. 2055.

Necessity of a quorum of the House in Canada, 2019-2023 —— Great public interest in Canada in the proceedings in Parliament, these being promptly telegraphed to distant towns, 2040-2042. 2069-2071 —— Much longer Parliamentary reports in the press in Canada than in the United States, 2042-2044 —— Semi-official character of the Dominion "Hansard"; advantage of the responsibility rested with a private gentleman of enterprise, as in this country, 2046-2060. 2071, 2073.

Brief space occupied by Parliamentary reports in the States as compared with England or Canada, 2061-2064 —— Practice in Canada as to semi-officially reporting the speeches in English or French, there being an edition in each language, 2066-2068 —— Efficiency of the reports now supplied through the Canadian press, a record in the nature of "Hansard" being at the same time very useful, 2069-2073.

Ross, Charles. (Analysis of his Evidence.)—Long experience of witness in charge of the reporting arrangements of the "Times" in the Gallery of the House of Commons, 510, 511 —— Very good accommodation for the reporters, as compared with that which existed when witness first entered the Gallery fifty-eight years ago, 512, 513. 518-521. 587-588. 763 —— Ample opportunity of the country newspapers (for whom there is no accommodation) to obtain reports from the three electric companies, 514, 515. 671-575.

Several grounds upon which witness objects to full official reports of the debates in Parliament, 516-519. 592-609 —— Effect of verbatim official reports in leading to a multiplication of speeches, and to more frequent adjournments, 518. 536-538 —— Very limited extent to which a full official report would be read by the public; few persons who read the debates so extensively in the "Times," 519. 538, 539. 592-595. 617-619 —— Comparatively small number of Members and of speakers who would be affected by the scheme for an official report, 519. 533-635.

Late hour in the morning down to which very full reports of the speeches appear in the "Times" of the same day; mechanical arrangement in contemplation for an extension of the time down to which reports shall be given, 520. 540 —— Nature of the superintendence exercised by witness over the "Times" reporting staff, 521. 610, 611 —— Occupation of the front row in the Gallery by reporters, the "Times" staff being the largest, and comprising fifteen altogether, 521, 523 —— Change of duties by the same reporters between the Lords and the Commons, 523. 646.

Occupation of the seats behind the front row by other than reporters; these seats are to some extent available for reporting, 524-527 —— Considerable staff necessary for the purpose of an official verbatim report of the debates, 532 —— Sacrifice made by the "Times" in reporting the debates so fully; gain to the paper if there were an official report, 532. 596-598 —— Opinion that change is required in the shape of compression, rather than of expansion of the reports, and that a good reporter should condense as the time, 540-542. 633-636 —— Great pressure of time in recent years, the "space" being now very short, so that there is increased difficulty in accurately reporting or condensing, 543-546. 562. 569-571.

Report, 1878—continued.

Ross, Charles. (Analysis of his Evidence)—continued.

Grounds for dissenting from the view that a system of verbatim official reports would be advantageous as regards the answers of Ministers to Members' questions, 549-561 ——Limited extent to which the accommodation in the Gallery for the "Times" reporters is better than that allotted to other newspapers, 575-580——Employment, as a rule, of the same number of reporters for the "Times" every night, 581.

Requirement of about four reporters, each for a quarter of an hour, to report a speech an hour long, 582——A quarter of an hour's shorthand would take about three-quarters of an hour to write out fully, 583——Occupation of nearly three columns of the "Times" by an hour's speech reported verbatim, 584-587——Gradual shortening of the "turns" towards the close of an important debate, 588.

Inability of witness to suggest any improvement in the accommodation for reporters, 589, 590——Inexpediency of the reporters being placed in front of the Chair, in connexion with a system of official reports, 591, 592——Decided preference further expressed for full rather than verbatim reports, 599-603——Varying uses taken by different reporters in writing out their shorthand notes for press, 604-609——Advantage of the system in former years when the substance of the speeches was reported accurately, but few shorthand reporters having been employed, 610, 613.

Practicability of arrangements by which official reports might be in the hands of Ministers next day; by the public generally they would never be read, 614-619—— Great suspicion with which the public would regard official reports if Members were allowed to revise their speeches, 616, 651, 653—— Belief that the great majority of the readers of the "Times" are satisfied by the summary, 619——Conclusion as to which reports not being required in the case of great constitutional and political questions; all the arguments and opinions of each speaker should be given, undue repetition being avoided, 620-624, 647-651.

Responsibility of each reporter for writing out in full his own shorthand notes; important distinction between mere shorthand writing and good reporting, 625-631—— Practice of reporting verbatim the answers of Ministers to questions, the former being necessarily short, 636-639——Suggestions as to the extent to which compression of speeches for publication should be carried; that as in connexion with the summaries now given in the newspapers, 640-651. 745-751. 798-803.

Accommodation available in the back row of the Gallery for summary writing, though the work could not be so conveniently done as in the front row, 654-660——No objection to London papers combining to employ a press association to report for them, several of the daily papers not giving full reports, 661-665.

Information relative to the Parliamentary Record published by witness, and the circumstances under which he has for some years received a Government subvention of 500 l. a year for the work, 666-676——Very few subscribers to witness' publication, 674-678.

Belief that Parliamentary reports are less read than formerly, and that it is not to the interest of newspapers to give full reports, 679-681——Incomplete but not unfair character of the newspaper reports, 581——Necessity of going to press at a much earlier hour than in former years, 632, 682——Prolonged sittings of the House after midnight in the last two Sessions, the speeches as reported having doubtless been greatly compressed; belief, however, that in the "Times" all really important information was chronicled, 685-694——Conclusion as to the reporters for the London papers not neglecting their duties through reporting also for the provincial press, 695-701.

Belief that there is little if any ground for complaint on the score of political partizanship in the reporting by the press, 702-707——Discretion exercised by the reporters as to reporting speakers more or less fully, Ministers and ex-Ministers being as a rule reported at length, 707-718——Ample length of the reports in the "Times," too ample in witness' opinion, 711. 737——Explanation of the character of the "Times" reports in particular instances of well-known Members who had never been Ministers; full reports frequently given, 716-768. 771-776.

Defence of the great compression in the "Times" of a recent discussion which lasted for several hours upon the Highways Bill, 722-738. 817-821——Sufficiency also of the condensed report in the "Times" in the matter of the Factories Bill, 739-741—— Practice of reporting "scenes" or personal disputes as being interesting to the public, 742-744——Opinion that the proceedings on Wednesdays are given at sufficient length, though the curtailment may be very great, 745-750.

Limited interference with the reporters in the front gallery through talking going on in the row behind, 751-755——Impracticability of silencing the provincial papers, 766 ——Varying practice as to reporting the actual language of the Speaker, 757-760—— Much worse accommodation for the reporters in the Lords than in the Commons, 761-769.

Report, 1878—continued.

Ross, Charles. (Analysis of his Evidence)—continued.

763 — Witness repeats that no official system of reports is inexpedient, the reports in the "Times" being fuller than is required, 764, 765.

Impression that as a rule the reports in the "Times" do not take up so much space as they did fifteen years ago, but that important debates are still reported quite as fully, 766-770 — Much fuller reports in the "Times" than in other daily papers, 771-786, 797 — Late period of the day at which important debates in former years appeared in the "Times," 780-785 — Practice at present of reporting fully down to about one in the morning, 786-789.

Probability of less full reports being given in the "Times" if there were an official report; very large annual outlay by curtailing the reports, and giving more space to advertisements, 791-795, 804-811, 854, 857-860, 563 — Sufficiency of properly condensed reports in the "Times" and other papers, without any necessity arising for an official publication, 796-803, 812, 813 — Value attached by the late Sir George Lewis to the reports in the "Times" as ample for all purposes, 813 — Limited advantage of full official reports in reference to the information to be given to country constituents, 814-821 — Opportunity of any Member for reading the speech in full in "Hansard," 814, 844, 856 — Small number of Members who speak very frequently or at much length, 816, 857, 858.

Very few complaints by Members as to the way in which their speeches are reported in the "Times," 822-827 — Condensed rather than full reports which witness would give, if he were entrusted with discretionary power in carrying out an official plan, 828-832 — Excessively voluminous publication if there were a verbatim official report, 833-849, 850 — Responsibility of witness for the selection of cases in which very full reports are given in the "Times," 834-836.

Concurrence in the view that on important occasions the leading statements of the day should be fully reported; belief that this is done by the "Times," 836-848 — Supply of "Hansard" through the "Times," 838 — Opinion that all material points are now reported, and that the reports in the "Times" are too full rather than otherwise, 851, 861, 862.

Ross's "Parliamentary Record." Information relative to the Parliamentary Record published by witness, and the circumstances under which he has for some years received a Government subvention of 400 *l.* a year for the work, all the public offices being supplied; net return of about 150 *l.* a year, the labour being considerable, Ross 666-676 — Very few subscribers to witness' publication, there being very small demand for purely Parliamentary matter, ib. 671-678.

S.

Selter, William Henry Gurney. (Analysis of his Evidence.) — Representation by witness of the firm of Messrs. Gurney, he being the shorthand writer to the House, 1811, 1814 — Duty of the firm to take notes of all evidence before Committees of the two Houses, and of any proceedings at the Bar, 1812-1813, 1887.

Excellent facilities for reporting in the French Assembly, owing chiefly to the speeches being delivered from the tribune, 1815-1800, 1877, 1878, 1891 — Information relative to the staff engaged on the official report at Versailles; comparatively small staff of newspaper reporters, the papers using largely the official report, 1841-1846 — Arrangements at Versailles for the revision and correction of the reports of their speeches by Members; extent to which correction is carried, and check exercised, 1847-1856.

Very good facilities for reporting at Berlin; official character of the report, opportunities being allowed for correction, 1857-1844, 1870 — Belief as to there being a large circulation of the "Journal Officiel" in France, 1845-1847.

Evidence to the effect that if it be decided to have an official report in this country, the House would probably accommodate the official reporters at or near the Table of the House, 1848-1861, 1873-1876, 1898-1900 — Opinion that two seats in a good position would suffice, 1849 — Suggestions as to the time within which an official report ought be published; dispatch feasible so far as shorthand writing and printing are concerned 1862, 1881-1863.

Suggestion that a verbatim report be the basis of an official report, and that any condensation should take place subsequently, 1832-1837 — Slight extent to which as a rule questions and answers before Committees are corrected by Members and the witnesses; instances of Committees in which no opportunity has been allowed for correction, 1858-1862.

Explanation as to the time within which the official report in France is published in extenso, 1864-1879 — Dispatch and economy by the process of Messrs. Gurney whereby clerks transcribe the shorthand writers' notes; subsequent comparison of the transcript

Report, 1878—continued.

Salter, William Henry Gurney. (Analysis of his Evidence)—continued.

with the original shorthand, 1880–1883. 1901–1904——Varying time for which each official reporter should sit, accordingly as the transcript is required more or less promptly, 1884, 1885.

Circumstance of no opportunity for correction being allowed as regards the proceedings of a Committee on a Private Bill in either House, 1887–1896—— Great importance of facilities for Members' corrections if there were an official report, 1893——Belief as to the beneficial effect upon the quality of Members' speeches in Germany through there being an official report, 1894, 1895.

Saunders, William. (Analysis of his Evidence.)—Management by witness of the "Central News" agency; he was formerly proprietor of the "Central Press," 1108, 1109—— Supply by the "Central News" of two kinds of Parliamentary reports for provincial newspapers, one report being of a general character, and the other containing mainly of speeches of local Members, reported expressly for the local papers, 1110——Large increase in the demand for special reports of speeches of local Members, although the cost is considerable, 1110. 1116–1124. 1131, 1132. 1165, 1166. 1207, 1208.

Improved accommodation required in the Reporters' Gallery by the "Central News," the reports made from the seat in the back row being much complained of, but not those made from the front seat, 1110. 1110–1112. 1115. 1116. 1240–1242. 1299, 1300—— Varying length of the ordinary reports; discretion exercised in the matter by the reporters, 1111–1115. 1130–1133. 1362–1365——Increased interest of the provincial public in Parliamentary reports, this feeling hardly applying to the London public, 1107, 1108. 1153, 1154. 1165, 1166. 1207–1212——Very moderate cost of the ordinary reports provided through the "Central News," 1129–1131.

Opinion that a complete official report, if published immediately, would obtain an extensive circulation, and would supersede the special reports now made of the speeches of local Members, 1133–1138. 1154, 1155. 1171–1173. 1332, 1334——Doubt as to an official report having any effect as regards the ordinary or condensed reports published by the newspapers, 1134. 1135. 1139–1142. 1154, 1155. 1361. 1390–1391——Great promptitude with which speeches could be officially reported and published, 1134. 1137. 1138. 1167. 1172–1175. 1194, 1195——Information relative to the Parliamentary sketches, or scenes in the House, published by some papers; way in which supplied, 1141, 1142. 1146–1150. 1179–1189. 1371–1378.

Estimate of 350l. a week as the cost of preparing and printing an official report, exclusive of the paper; about 100l. a week might be recouped by sale to provincial newspapers, 1143–1148. 1168–1171. 1176–1178. 1190–1193. 1356——Entire absence of political bias in the reporting by the "Central News," 1151——Very few Members who furnish reports of their speeches to the papers, 1151——Difficulty in reporters getting access to the Speaker's Gallery, 1156, 1157——Uselessness of the Strangers' Gallery for reporting purposes, 1158.

Explanation of the charges paid to the Telegraph Department by the "Central News" for transmission of reports, 1161–1164. 1323, 1324——Great length to which a verbatim report would extend; contemplated mile at 1 d. a day, 1176–1178. 1904, 1905. 1325–1331——Estimate of about twenty reporters as necessary for official reporting, 1193. 1194. 1283, 1284. 1301. 1302——Difficulty as to hearing in the seat in the gallery used by the "Central News," 1196–1199.

Hardship upon the provincial press in being entirely excluded from the gallery, 1200, 1201——Suggestion that the front seats (about six) now used by upstairs writers and superintendents be devoted to reporting, 1202. 1204–1206. 1237. 1360, 1361——Suggestion also that the seats in the front of the two galleries adjoining the Reporters' Gallery be for a certain distance thrown into the latter, 1201, 1203. 1365–1370.

Supply of the provincial press with reports not only by the "Central News" and two other associations, but by reporters for the London papers, who are paid separately for this work, 1213–1214——Particulars as to the number and class of newspapers supplied by the "Central News," some of them being Scotch papers, 1222–1229——Probability of eight or ten provincial papers wishing to keep a staff of reporters if they had accommodation in the gallery, 1234–1236.

Want of a front seat for ordinary reports and of another front seat for special reports of local Members' speeches, the back seats being used by summary writers, 1237–1242. 1337–1340. 1358–1361——Exceptional instances of long-hand reports in provincial papers until the charges for telegraphic special reports were reduced, 1343–1345—— Further statement as to the very short time within which official reports might be in the hands of Members and of the provincial press, 1246–1253. 1257, 1258. 1286. 1303, 1378–1380.

Claim on the part of the provincial press to at least twelve front seats, 1259–1264. 1296–1298——Limited receipts to be derived from an issue of official reports on special subjects, in a separate form, 1274, 1275——Expediency of facilities for special reports as well as for identical reports for the country press, 1276–1282——Suggestion that official

Report, 1878—continued.

Saunders, William. (Analysis of his Evidence)—continued.

official reporters be on the floor of the House, 1284, 1285, 1335, 1336——Explanation as to the extent to which correction of speeches should be allowed in connection with official reports, 1307-1303. 1312.

Occupation of front seats in the gallery by persons who are not really reporters; room for provincial reporters by putting the former in back seats, 1294, 1295. 1313-1320——Further reference to the probable cost of an official report; contemplated payment by newspapers supplied with such report, 1305-1309——The report should be almost verbatim, 1310, 1311. 1325.

Several quarters whence there would probably be a demand for copies of an official report, 1333, 1334——Further statement as to there being an increased demand in the provinces for full reports of the speeches of the local Members; doubt as to the wisdom of long newspaper reports otherwise, 1347-1347——Large proportion of the population of the United Kingdom which are provincial papers, whereas the reporters for these papers have but three front seats in the worst part of the gallery, 1348-1361.

Statement with further reference to the work done by some of the London press reporters for provincial papers, 1368-1370——Impression that long reports are not valued very much by the public, an official report being useful chiefly for historical purposes and for reference, 1371. 1389——Supply of reports by the " Central News," and by the Press Association to all or nearly all the Irish papers, 1384-1387——Exceptional instances of Scotch papers not taking their reports from the Press Association or " Central News," 1388.

Very long reports in some provincial papers, supplied by the " Central News," or Press Association, 1393-1397——Great length of official reports which might be supplied for 1 d. a day, this covering the cost of paper and printing, 1398-1403——Contemplated control over official reporters, as being officers of the House, 1404, 1405.

Probability of some provincial papers employing reporters of their own, if there were room for them, by way of supplementing reports from the News Associations, 1406-1408——Extent of public demand for an official report, further adverted to, 1409-1415——Importance of an official report as a means of supplying complete reports of speeches of local Members, 1416, 1417.

Suggestion that besides room for two reporters at the Table of the House, certain accommodation be allotted to them for the purpose of writing out their notes, and that everything up to completion for press be done within the building, 1418-1406——Illustration of the mode in which there might be presented every twenty minutes to the House during the course of a debate, 1406——Varying size of the official publications according to the extent of the speeches, 1477.

Scenes in the House. Practice of newspapers in reporting " Scenes," or personal discussion, as being interesting to the public, Home 742-744——Information relative to the Parliamentary sketches, or scenes in the House, published by some papers; way in which supplied, Saunders 1141, 1142. 1146-1150. 1179-1189. 1371-1376.

Scotch Newspapers. Several daily and weekly newspapers in Scotland supplied with reports by the " Central News," Saunders 1278——Exceptional instances of Scotch papers not taking their reports from the Press Association or " Central News," ib. 1388.

Claim of Scotland and Ireland to have their own representatives in the gallery; statement hereon as to the exceedingly imperfect and scanty reports of Scotch and Irish questions under the present system, Cooper 1478. 1483-1487. 1490-1494. 1510-1513. 1568-1578. 1649-1652. 1644-1649. 1653——Exceedingly curtailed reports of Scotch questions in the " Times," and other London papers, ib. 1473.

Grounds for the conclusion that an increased interest is felt by the people of Scotland in Parliamentary Debates, Cooper 1500-1506. 1516-1506. 1645-1651——Decided improvement in the reports for Scotland if there were direct representation of Scotch papers in the gallery, Q. 1596——Pacifico of telegraphic communication adverted to as favouring the demand of Scotch papers for independent reports, ib. 1658, 1659.

Increasing extent of the reports given in Scotland, whilst some London papers have been curtailing their reports; claim on this score to increased facilities in the former case, Cooper 1562-1564——Protest by the Scotch papers against being excluded from a position in which they have a right to be put, ib. 1633-1636——Approval of England, Ireland, and Scotland being represented in the gallery in proportion to their Members, Q. 1653.

Offer made by witness on several occasions, but not accepted, to find a seat for the Scotch press, Right Hon. The Speaker 1694-1697——Good ground for the desire evinced by Scotch and Irish and by provincial papers for facilities enabling them to give independent and more complete reports on local questions; expediency, moreover, of compromise in the matter, ib. 1711-1717. 1726, 1727.

Dissent from the view that Scotch and Irish papers have any stronger claim to seats in the Gallery than the leading provincial papers in England; that is, in order to obtain full and

0.191.   II 2   special

Report, 1878—continued.

Scotch Newspapers—continued.

special reports on subjects relating specially to Ireland or Scotland, *Townsend* 2324. 2379-2381. 2393-2399.

See also " *Scotsman.*"

" Scotsman." Supply of reports by the Press Association to the " Scotsman," and other leading Scotch papers; special reports obtained by the " Scotsman " from reporters for the London press, *Lavell* 969-977.

Practice of obtaining full reports for the " Scotsman," by employing for the purpose reporters engaged on the staff of the London press; great inconvenience of this arrangement, *Cooper* 1438. 1433——Applications made on the part of the " Scotsman " for admission to the Gallery; objection raised that if one provincial paper were admitted others would make the same claim, *ib.* 1434——Contemplated prohibition of reporters for the " Scotsman " from reporting for other papers, though reporters for the London press are not now prohibited from reporting for the " Scotsman," *ib.* 1440-1444. 1467-1474. 1654-1657.

Explanation as to the " Scotsman " not using the reports of the Press Association; objection more especially that these reports are identical with those furnished to other newspapers, and are moreover insufficient and unsuitable for the purposes of the " Scotsman," *Cooper* 2451-2453. 1460-1469. 1577-1594. 1614-1650——Private character of the arrangement under which reporters for the London papers report also for the " Scotsman ;" liability of the latter reports to be stopped at any moment, *ib.* 1463-1466. 1543.

Probable employment of six or eight reporters by the " Scotsman " if it had a seat in the gallery, *Cooper* 1477-1490——Increased facilities required by the paper for meeting the demand for full reports, *ib.* 1506.

More full reports now given in the " Scotsman " than in any but two of the London papers; also thus in any other Scotch paper, *Cooper* 1500. 1507, 1508. 1566-1571. 1579——Increasing circulation of the " Scotsman " owing very much to its Parliamentary reports, *ib.* 1500, 1501. 1564——Want of full reports to be selected in such case by the " Scotsman," but not of identically full reports, *ib.* 1546-1549. 1577-1583——Very large circulation of the " Scotsman ;" this should entitle it to increased facilities for Parliamentary reporting, *ib.* 1564, 1565. 1612——Belief that as regards length of reports the paper is the third in the United Kingdom, *ib.* 1570, 1571.

Further statement as to the impracticability of the " Scotsman " getting the complete and precise reports required through the Press Association, or otherwise than through a staff of its own, *Cooper* 1577-1583. 1612-1608. 1697——Use of two special wires between the office in Fleet-street and the Edinburgh office, *ib.* 1642, 1643.

Statement submitted by Mr. Cooper, showing the length of the Parliamentary reports in the " Scotsman " from the 1st of June till the 6th July 1878, as compared with those in the " Times " and other leading London and provincial papers, *App.* 914—— High daily average of the " Scotsman " for this period, it being second only to the " Times," *ib.*

Serjeant-at-Arms. See *Reporters' Gallery*, 1.

Speaker, The Right Hon. Mr. (Analysis of his Evidence.)—Several objections urged against an official report of Parliamentary proceedings; very limited extent to which a verbatim report would be read, especially if delayed for the purpose of correction by Members, 1677-1682. 1744——Less important objection on the score of expense than on other grounds, 1680, 1681. 1762, 1763——Difficulty apprehended in regard to official reports being protected by privilege, 1639-1684——Inconvenience likely to arise from difference between the reported speech and the corrected speech, 1685-1688.

Several advantages of the present system of reports through the newspapers; serious misfortune if the press were driven off the field by the competition of an official report, 1689, 1690. 1719-1721——Deficiency of the present reports with respect to private Bills, proceedings in Committee, and proceedings after midnight, 1691——Reference to the recent arrangement with Mr. Howard as calculated to supply the foregoing deficiency, 1691. 1723-1724——Incompleteness also of the existing reports on subjects of local interest, including Scotch and Irish questions, 1691-1693.

Inability of witness to meet the applications made from time to time for seats in the Reporters' Gallery for representatives of the local press, 1694——Offer made by witness on several occasions (but not accepted) to find a seat in the gallery for the Irish press, and another for the Scotch press, 1694-1697——Dissatisfaction of the provincial press with the arrangement for the supply of reports through the News Associations, 1698-1700.

Great difficulty apprehended unless careful limitations and conditions be laid down in connection with applications from the local press for available seats, 1701, 1702. 1708, 1709. 1747. 1773, 1774. 1807, 1808——Increased number of seats available by appropriating

Report, 1878—continued.

Speaker, The Right Hon. Mr. (Analysis of his Evidence)—continued.

relating to the reporters the space between the Reporters' Gallery and the door leading into the Members' Gallery; inferiority of these seats as compared with those now used, 1703, 1704. 1747——Expediency of the front seats being all occupied by reporters, the summary writers being removed to the back seats, 1705-1708.

Explanation that in the event of a vacant seat being at witness' disposal he would decide the applications for it on their merits, without limiting the matter to the metropolitan press, 1710, 1711——Good ground for the desire evinced by Scotch and Irish and by provincial papers for facilities enabling them to give independent and more complete reports on local questions; expediency moreover of competition in the matter, 1718-1717. 1726, 1727.

Advantage of an official report as a historical record for purposes of reference, 1718——Improbability of an official report interfering with the newspaper reports; prospect, rather, of the former becoming obsolete, 1719. 1720.

Necessity of reporters having front seats in order to efficiently report; belief that they would not be content with back seats, even if improved by being raised, 1718, 1719. 1787-1790——Jurisdiction and control in witness with respect to admission to the Reporters' Gallery, 1730, 1731. 1798.

Further considerations as to the difficulty on the score of privilege in connection with an official report, 1730-1738. 1753——Discretion now exercised by the reporters as to the length of the reports; absence of discretion in official reporters, 1730. 1740——Tendency of a verbatim report to effect prejudicially the quality of speeches and to lengthen debates, 1741. 1769-1768——Limited extent to which correction of official reports should be allowed, 1742.

Inexpediency of a forced circulation of official reports by their being published at a very low price at the public expense, 1743-1748——Reference to "Hansard" as a most valuable publication, and as fulfilling the purpose of an official record; advantage if it were published weekly, 1748-1752. 1769. 1778. 1799-1801——Opinion that there is at present a sufficient report of the answers of Ministers, 1754-1757.

Obstacle to a prompt or daily publication of "Hansard," on account of the necessity of allowing time for correction of speeches, 1758-1761——Recommended continuance of "Hansard," in the interest of the public, 1769——Advantage in "Hansard" being a substantial report, rather than an official report, 1770-1778. 1803, 1804. 1810, 1811.

Considerable difficulty to be felt by witness if it rested with him to select the papers for seats in the Gallery, 1773, 1774. 1779-1786. 1807——Less objection to the discretion exercised as to the length at which any speech is reported in "Hansard," than to its being an actual official report, 1776-1777. 1796. 1797——Sufficiency of the reports generally if there were a weekly publication of "Hansard," and if the Scotch, Irish, and provincial press could be fairly represented in the gallery, 1778.

Difficulty in providing that the press generally (out of London) be represented by a district arrangement; expediency however of the provincial press being accommodated as far as possible, 1781-1786——Inconvenience to Members by appropriating portion of the Members' Gallery to reporters, 1791. 1809.

Want of room for the accommodation of official reporters on the floor of the House, 1793, 1794——Failure hitherto of proposals for improving the existing accommodation by structural alterations, 1805, 1806.

Explanation that an addition of eight front and six back seats would be gained by the suggested use of portion of the Members' Gallery for reporters; reduction thereby of the Members' seats by twenty-two out of a total of 124 in the gallery, 1809.

Speaker's Gallery. Difficulty to reporters getting access to the Speaker's Gallery, Saunders 1166, 1167.

Special Wires. Large extension of the system of special wires as a means of supplementing the information conveyed by the several Press Associations, Lovell 924-929——Exception taken to the view that newspapers having special wires should be entitled to a preference as regards access to the Reporters' Gallery, Lovell 930-936; Ridd 1143-1145; Jeffrey 1242-1254. 1302, 1303——Approval of a condition that a newspaper admitted to the gallery should have a special wire, Townsend 2324, 2325. 2370-2378.

Stereo-plates. Printing of "Hansard's Debates" from type, stereo-plates not being used; objections to stereotyping for the purpose, Hansard 450-462.

Strangers' Gallery. Expediency of full facilities to provincial newspapers, if admitted to the Strangers' Gallery, Lovell 936-939. 964-967——Usefulness of the Strangers' Gallery for reporting purposes, Saunders 1158.

Report, 1878—continued.

Summary Writers. Accommodation available in the back row of the Reporters' Gallery for summary writing, though the work could not be so conveniently done as in the front row, Reid 664—660——Means of increasing the accommodation for reporters by placing the summary writers in the back seats; inconvenience, however, of the latter, Lord 948-950. 956-958——Inconvenience if summary writers had to sit in the Speaker's Gallery, Lloyd 1066.

Suggestion that the front seats (about six) now used by summary writers and superintendents be devoted to reporting, Saunders 1902. 1904—1146. 1437. 1360, 1361——Concurrence in the suggestion that the summary writers might be put in the back seats of the gallery, Caper 1475.——Facility with which the "Scotsman" prepares a summary of the Parliamentary report, without having a summary writer in the gallery, ib. 1698-1691.

Advantage in the summary writers for the London papers having seats in the gallery; they might all be in the back row, Reid 2191-2198——Expediency of the London press having full facilities for giving summaries of the debates; doubt as to front seats in the Reporters' Gallery being necessary for this purpose, Jaffray 3189. 3308——Importance of good accommodation for the summary writers of the "Times," and some other papers; sufficiency of less favourable seats for other summary writers, Toward 2311. 2333. 2385. 2386——Excellent summary given by the "Times," whilst the "Morning Post," "Standard," and "Morning Advertiser" also give good summaries, ib. 2386.

Several London papers having seats for summary writers, whereas such papers hardly give any summary; unfairness in these seats being retained to the exclusion of other papers, Gray 2418, 2419. 2455-2471. 2488-2490. 2493-2497.

Impracticability of efficient summary writing in the back seats, Dunphy 2541-2549. 2616, 2616. 1816-1819——Statement as to the necessity of a summary writer hearing the speeches in order to do his work efficiently, ib. 1811-1615. 1630.

See also "Morning Advertiser."

T.

Taylor, John. (Analysis of his Evidence.)—Explanation in connection with plan for reopening partially under the Ladies' Gallery the second row of seats in the Reporters' Gallery; important difficulty through there being no accommodation for the reporters waiting for their turn, 2542-2557. 2567-2578. 2577-2581.

Serious obstacles to raising the back seats with a view to rendering them fit for reporters; this arrangement is in fact impracticable, 2548-2550. 2558. 2577. 2578. 2580-2589——Structural objections to a plan for doing away with the Upper Gallery, and for extending the Reporters' Gallery on both sides to the same extent; heavy expense involved, 2559-2566.

Telegraphic Arrangements. Facilities of the press generally in the matter of telegraphic communication with the House, Genet 88-90.

Explanation of the charges paid to the Telegraph Department by the "Central News" for transmission of reports, Saunders 1181-1184. 1323. 1324——Few instances of lengthened reports in provincial papers until the charges for telegraphic special reports were reduced, ib. 1243-1244.

Exceptional difficulty in the case of reports for the Irish press through the slowness of the telegraphing across the Channel, Gray 2474-2478.

"Times":

Late hours in the morning down to which very full reports of the speeches appear in the "Times" of the same day; mechanical arrangement in contemplation for an extension of the time down to which reports shall be given, Ross 810. 840——Nature of the superintendence exercised by writers over the reporting staff, ib. 581. 610, 611——Sacrifices made by the "Times" in reporting the debates so fully; gain to the paper if there were an official report, ib. 619. 691-698.

Limited extent to which the accommodation in the Reporters' Gallery for the "Times" reporters is better than that allotted to other newspapers, Ross 876-880——Employment as a rule of the same number of reporters every night, ib. 581——Occupation of nearly three columns by an hour's speech reported verbatim, ib. 585-557——Belief that the great majority of the readers of the "Times" are satisfied by the summary, ib. 619.

Dissent from the conclusion that the compression of 1,000 columns of speech, as delivered after midnight, into twenty columns in the "Times," excluded important matter, Ross 688-694. 850, 851——Ample length of the reports; too ample in witness' opinion, ib. 711. 727-756——Explanation of the character of the "Times" reports in particular instances of well-known Members who had never been Ministers; full reports frequently given, ib. 716-726. 771-778.

Impression that as a rule reports in the "Times" do not take up so much space as they did

" *TIMES* "—continued.

did fifteen years ago, but that important debates are still reported quite as fully, *Rem* 766-770——Much fuller reports in the " Times " than in other daily papers, ib. 770-786, 797——Late period of the day at which lengthened debates in former years appeared, ib. 782-784——Practice at present of reporting fully down to about one in the morning, ib. 785-789.

Probability of less full reports being given if there were an official report; very large annual saving by curtailing the reports, and giving more space to advertisements, *Rem* 791-795, 804-811, 854, 857-860, 863——Very few complaints by Members as to the way in which their speeches are reported, ib. 822-827——Responsibility of witness for the selection of cases in which very full reports are given, ib. 834-836——Opinion that all material points are now reported, and that the reports in the " Times " are too full rather than otherwise, ib. 851, 861, 864.

Fallacy of the assumption that the " Times " incurs an exceedingly heavy annual loss through its Parliamentary reports, *Casper* 1673, 1674.

Stringent rule of the " Times " that its staff shall not report for other papers, *Gray* 1455 1473, 1515, 2528.

See also Lewis, Sir George Cornewall (*the late*).

Timmral, Thomas Senior. (Analysis of his Evidence.)—Experience of witness for about ten years as London manager of the " Manchester Guardian," 1309, 1310——Claim of provincial papers to seats in the Reporters' Gallery, if additional accommodation can be provided, 1311, 1312——Monopoly now enjoyed by the London papers, 1311——Statement as to the more restrictions not meeting the requirements of many of the leading provincial papers; illustration in the case of the Manchester papers, 1312, 1316, 1317.

Grounds for the conclusion that not more than ten or twelve provincial papers (including Scotland and Ireland) would apply for seats; that is, on account of the great expense of staff and of special wires, 1313, 1314, 1320, 1321, 1338-1341, 1367-1369, 1367-1369——Supply of the " Manchester Guardian," with reports partly by the Press Association and partly by gentlemen who have seats as reporters for the London press; special reports supplied by the latter, 1315, 1335.

Important difference between the circumstances of the " Birmingham Daily Post " and of the " Manchester Guardian," so that prompt transmission of reports by means of special wire is very essential in the latter case but not in the former, 1316-1319, 1342-1354——Early hour at which the " Guardian " goes to press; that is, on account of its widespread and distant circulation, 1317, 1318, 1342-1354.

Increased and improved accommodation in the Reporters' Gallery by extending it on each side, and by raising the back seats, 1332, 1333——Importance of good accommodation for the summary writers of the " Times," and some other papers; sufficiency of less favourable seats for other summary writers, 1331, 1333, 1385, 1386.

Dissent from the view that Scotch and Irish papers have any stronger claim to accommodation in the gallery than the leading provincial papers in England; that is, in order to obtain full and special reports on subjects relating especially to Ireland or Scotland, 1373, 1379-1381, 1393-1399——Opinion that in the selection of papers for seats in the gallery, there should have preference which had special wires and London offices, and which maintained a certain staff of reporters, 1394, 1395, 1370-1378.

Objection of the press to the case of official reports, as involving delay, and as being introduced, 1316-1326——Advantage to a paper having its own reporting staff, so that it may adapt the report to the requirements of each particular day, 1328.

Impracticability of condensing official verbatim reports for prompt publication in the provincial press, 1329-1331——Insufficiency of a good summary, without any report of the speeches, for the " Manchester Guardian," 1334——Objection by country papers to the same district to combine, so as to have an identical report; less difficulty of joint arrangements between two papers at a distance from each other, 1336, 1337.

Sufficiency of one seat in the gallery for the requirements of the " Manchester Guardian," 1357——Objection to a condition that papers claiming a seat should undertake to devote a certain minimum space to the reports, 1358-1363.

Way in which further applications for seats should be dealt with, if the reasonable demands of the provincial press at the present time were satisfied; expediency of similar conditions in future in the case of both London and provincial papers, 1370-1377, 1383, 1384——Belief that there is an increasing desire in the provinces for extended Parliamentary reports, 1390-1392.

Explanation of the arrangement under which the summary writer of the " Morning Advertiser " reports for the " Manchester Guardian," and occasionally supplies a summary for the latter paper, 1539-1541——Inaccuracy of any statement implying that provincial papers need, surreptitiously, seats in the gallery belonging to London papers, 1539-1534——Long and genuine summary written for the " Morning Advertiser " by the gentleman who does work also for the " Manchester Guardian," 1534, 1535.

www.ingramcontent.com/pod-product-compliance
Lightning Source LLC
Chambersburg PA
CBHW020848270326
41928CB00006B/596